Developmental Follow-up

Developmental Follow-up

CONCEPTS, DOMAINS, AND METHODS

Edited by

Sarah L. Friedman
Human Learning and Behavior Branch
National Institute of Child Health and Human Development
Bethesda, Maryland

H. Carl Haywood
Department of Psychology and Human Development
Vanderbilt University
Nashville, Tennessee

and

Graduate School of Education and Psychology
Touro College
New York, New York

Academic Press
San Diego   New York   Boston   London   Sydney   Tokyo   Toronto

Copyright © 1994 by ACADEMIC PRESS, INC.
All Rights Reserved.
No part of this publication may be reproduced or transmitted in any form or by any
means, electronic or mechanical, including photocopy, recording, or any information
storage and retrieval system, without permission in writing from the publisher.

Academic Press, Inc.
A Division of Harcourt Brace & Company
525 B Street, Suite 1900, San Diego, California 92101-4495

United Kingdom Edition published by
Academic Press Limited
24-28 Oval Road, London NW1 7DX

Library of Congress Cataloging-in-Publication Data

Developmental follow-up / concepts, domains, and methods / edited by
  Sarah L. Friedman, H. Carl Haywood.
      p.   cm.
    Includes bibliographical references and index.
    ISBN 0-12-267855-9. -- ISBN 0-12-267856-7 (paper)
    1. Child development--Longitudinal studies.   I. Friedman, Sarah
  L.   II. Haywood, H. Carl [date]
  HQ767.9.O49   1994
  305.23'1--dc20   94-4843
                                                                  CIP

PRINTED IN THE UNITED STATES OF AMERICA
94   95   96   97   98   99   EB   9   8   7   6   5   4   3   2   1

Contents

Developmental Theory, Prediction, and the Developmental Equation in Follow-up Research

Frances Degen Horowitz

Ecological Perspectives on Longitudinal Follow-up Studies

Arnold Sameroff

Section II EXAMPLES OF DOMAINS FOR FOLLOW-UP RESEARCH

Developmental Research in Behavioral Teratology: Effects of Prenatal Alcohol Exposure on Child Development

Heather Carmichael Olson, Ann Pytkowicz Streissguth, Fred L. Bookstein, Helen M. Barr, and Paul D. Sampson

Health Surveillance and the Development of Children

Jack P. Shonkoff

Early Cognitive Development and the Contribution of Peer Interaction: A Piagetian View

Hermina Sinclair

Expanding the Boundaries of Evaluation: Strategies for Refining and Evaluating Ill-Defined Interventions

Debra J. Rog

Developmental Psychopathology of Multiplex Developmental Disorder

Donald J. Cohen, Kenneth E. Towbin, Linda Mayes, and Fred Volkmar

Section III   SOURCES OF DATA: PERSONS AND INSTRUMENTS

Assessing Child Psychopathology in Developmental Follow-up Studies

Craig Edelbrock

Section IV   EXPERIMENTAL DESIGN AND DATA ANALYSIS

Section V   RESEARCH AT THE CUTTING EDGE

Child Care and Child Development: The NICHD Study of Early Child Care

The NICHD Early Child Care Network

Contributors

Numbers in parentheses indicate the pages on which the authors' contributions begin.

Helen Barr (67), Department of Psychiatry and Behavioral Sciences, University of Washington, Seattle, Washington 98115

John E. Bates (197), Department of Psychology, Indiana University, Bloomington, Indiana 47405

Fred Bookstein (67), Center for Human Growth and Development, University of Michigan, Ann Arbor, Michigan 48109

Robert H. Bradley (235), Center for Research on Teaching and Learning, University of Arkansas at Little Rock, Little Rock, Arkansas 72204

Stephen L. Buka (331), Department of Maternal and Child Health, Harvard School of Public Health, Boston, Massachusetts 02115 and Center for the Study of Human Development, Brown University, Providence, Rhode Island 02912

Bettye M. Caldwell (235), Department of Pediatrics, University of Arkansas for Medical Sciences, Little Rock, Arkansas 72204

Heather Carmichael Olson (67), Department of Psychiatry and Behavioral Sciences, University of Washington, Seattle, Washington 98115

Donald Cohen (155), Child Study Center, Yale University School of Medicine, New Haven, Connecticut 06520

Carl J. Dunst (277), Allegheny-Singer Research Institute, Early Childhood Intervention Program, Pittsburgh, Pennsylvania 15212

Craig Edelbrock (183), Department of Human Development and Family Studies, Pennsylvania State University, University Park, Pennsylvania 16802

Sarah L. Friedman (3), Human Learning and Behavior Branch, National Institute of Child Health and Human Development, National Institutes of Health, Bethesda, Maryland 20852

H. Carl Haywood (3), Department of Psychology and Human Development, Vanderbilt University, Nashville, Tennessee 37203 and Graduate School of Education and Psychology, Touro College, New York, New York 10010

Frances Degen Horowitz (27), Graduate School and University Center, City University of New York, New York, New York 10036

Helena Chmura Kraemer (259), Department of Psychiatry and Behavioral Sciences, Stanford University, Stanford, California 94305

Lewis P. Lipsitt (331), Department of Psychology Child Study Center, Brown University, Providence, Rhode Island 02912

Karen Livesey (3), Department of Psychology, University of Maryland, College Park, Maryland 20742

Linda Mayes (155), Child Study Center, Yale University School of Medicine, New Haven, Connecticut 06520

NICHD Early Child Care Network (377), National Institute of Child Health and Human Development, Bethesda, Maryland 20892

Ann Pytkowicz Streissguth (67), Department of Psychiatry and Behavioral Science, University of Washington, Seattle, Washington 98102

Debra J. Rog (139), Institute for Public Policy Studies, Vanderbilt University, Washington, D.C. 20009

Arnold J. Sameroff (45), Center for Human Growth and Development, University of Michigan, Ann Arbor, Michigan 48109

Paul D. Sampson (67), Department of Statistics, University of Washington, Seattle, Washington 98102

Keith G. Scott (351), Linda Ray Intervention Center, University of Miami, Miami, Florida 33136

Kimberly H. Shaw (351), Department of Pediatrics, Division of Adolescent Medicine, University of Miami School of Medicine, Miami, Florida 33101

Jack P. Shonkoff (113), Department of Pediatrics, University of Massachusetts Medical School, Worcester, Massachusetts 01655

Linda S. Siegel (217), Department of Applied Psychology, Ontario Institute for studies in Education, Toronto, Ontario, Canada M5S 1V6

Hermina Sinclair (129), Department of Psychology, Geneva University, 1227 Corouge, Geneva, Switzerland

Judith D. Singer (315), Graduate School of Education, Harvard University, Cambridge, Massachusetts 02138

Kenneth E. Towbin (155), Department of Psychiatry, Children's Hospital Medical Center, Washington, D.C. 20010

Carol M. Trivette (277), Center for Family Studies, Western Carolina Center, Morganton, North Carolina 28655

Jennifer C. Urbano (351), Department of Psychology, Vanderbilt University, Nashville, Tennessee 37203

Fred Volkmar (155), Child Study Center, Yale University School of Medicine, New Haven, Connecticut 06520

John B. Willett (315), Graduate School of Education, Gutman Library, Harvard University, Cambridge, Massachusetts 02138

Foreword

The developmental sciences and professions—including, notably, developmental psychology, developmental neuroscience, pediatrics, child psychiatry, and epidemiology—are concerned both with the "normal" course of human development, that is, how children grow and elaborate from conception to independence, and with the effects of a large number of events on the course of development. In this latter category one can list relatively benign events such as variations in the language that mothers use with their infants and young children, as well as threatening events such as environmental toxins, nervous system injuries, premature birth, deprivation of psychological supports, and chronic illness. Assessment of the effects of all these variables, and many others, on the subsequent development of children depends on the scientist's ability to account for a host of influencing variables, including the quality of the rearing environment, the unpredictable events that intervene in development, the measurement characteristics of the instruments used for assessment, and an almost infinite number of possible variations in the influencing events themselves (e.g., timing, intensity, frequency, and co-occurrence with other influencing events). Developmental scientists have recognized for a long time that "longitudinal" studies, that is, those in which the same participants are studied over a long time period, yield the potentially richest data. In spite of that recognition, developmental science is bedeviled with research strategies and assessment instruments that do not match across disciplines, investigators within disciplines, and time within long studies. The editors of this book have tried to introduce some order into the field of developmental follow-up research by assembling this collection of papers by distinguished investigators in the developmental sciences, addressing some aspect of the methodological problems of developmental follow-up research. This collection is intended to represent state-of-the-art thinking about developmental follow-up research, designing follow-up studies, selecting variables and instruments for criterion assessment, and analyzing developmental data.

Since its establishment in 1963, the National Institute of Child Health and Human Development (NICHD) has funded both field-initiated research and solicited research. The NICHD has also organized conferences with the purpose of assisting developmental scientists to design and test the methods they use to assess the progress of human development; to use sophisticated research designs and innovative statistical techniques aimed at enabling them to take account of the myriad variables that jointly influence human development; and to identify the best available methods for assessing the outcomes of developmental processes as well as the effects of developmental treatments and the effects of environmental events.

The NICHD supports longitudinal follow-up research conducted by demographers, sociologists, psychologists, and physicians. Such research includes studies of topics such as (a) effects of changing economic and social conditions on the demographic characteristics of the population, (b) demographic and psychological conditions that influence migration, (c) demographic influences on marriage, fertility, and employment, (d) family variables and their relation to the labor market, (e) adolescent pregnancy loss and reproductive health, (f) physical growth of infants and children, (g) prenatal and perinatal conditions associated with low birth weight, (h) effects of low birthweight on developmental outcome, (i) sequela of antisocial and violent behavior associated with mental retardation, (j) detailed classification of persons with dyslexia, (k) demographic, economic, and psychological characteristics of poverty and their effects on the psychological well-being of children, and (l) effects of maternal employment, child care, and after-school care on the growth, health, cognitive, linguistic, social, and emotional development of infants and children. Many of the longitudinal studies that NICHD has supported over the years have been focused on the many interrelated aspects of the development of children and families and have contributed to the concepts and methods reported in this volume.

Longitudinal research is expensive in both time and money. It is often true that not all the data that have been collected are actually used by the investigators who gathered them. Demographers and sociologists recognize that fact, and many place their data sets in the public domain, making their observations available for others to study so as to answer research questions that the original investigators either did not get to or did not even think about. Consequently, many of the longitudinal research projects supported by NICHD are designed to use existing data sets. Either because their data sets are generally small or because of a tradition that places high value on primary investigations, psychologists are less likely than are demographers and sociologists to invite others to use data from their studies, or to accept invitations when these are offered. Even though some important psychological data sets can be obtained for secondary analysis (e.g., the Fels Institute longitudinal studies, the Early Training Project of Gray and Klaus, and the earlier Harvard and Berkeley longitudinal studies; for an inventory, see Verdonick & Sherrod, 1984), NICHD has rarely been asked to support such analyses. Perhaps for the same reason, this volume, which is edited by psychologists, does not include discussion of issues pertaining to secondary data analysis of longitudinal data sets.

Leading developmental psychologists have come to appreciate the value of secondary data analyses (e.g., Barrat, 1991; Baydar & Brooks-Gunn, 1991; Belsky & Eggebeen, 1991; Chase-Landsdale *et al.*, 1991). In particular, we have seen increasing interest in the analysis of the data set of The National Longitudinal Survey of Labor Market Experience of Youth (NLSY). The NLSY is a longitudinal survey of youth who were first interviewed in 1979. Initial interviews were completed with about 12,500 young men and women 14 to 21 years old. The research participants have been interviewed annually. As of 1986, approximately 5500 women between the ages of 21 and 29 remained in the sample. The 1986, 1988, 1990, and 1992 waves of the National Longitudinal Survey of Work Experience of Youth included the administration of an extensive set of assessments to the children of the female participants. These assessments encompass cognitive, socio-emotional, and physiological aspects of the children's development as well as information of the quality of the home environment. The recognition of the research opportunities provided by secondary analyses of large data sets has led NICHD to the establishment of a consortium of investigators, including leaders from demography, sociology, economics, pediatrics, and developmental psychology, to work together to answer questions about children's well-being. The investigators are expected to bring the same research questions to different large data sets and investigate how these different data sets, some of which are longitudinal, shed light on our understanding of families and children.

The creation of the children's assessment component of the NLSY was, in large part, the result of an NICHD staff initiative. NICHD foresight and initiative also led to the creation of the NICHD Study of Early Child Care (Johnson, 1991), a multi-site study described in this volume. It was clear to me and the NICHD staff that the effects of child care on child development depend on the interaction of many demographic, cultural, economic, familial, parental, and child factors. We knew that a limited study or a cross-sectional study would not answer the major questions that are posed by parents, educators, health care workers, and public policy makers. Therefore, NICHD invested in a large comprehensive study of family environments, child care experiences, and the many facets of children's developmental outcomes. The detailed descriptions of children's environments and the evaluation of the growth, health, cognitive, linguistic, social, and emotional development of the children will make the data from this study extremely valuable for future investigation of child development. I hope that developmental psychologists currently not involved with the study will make extensive use of the data set, once the original investigators release it for public use.

Possibly because it is so obvious, investigators do not dwell on a point that has important funding consequences: When the research questions pertain to interactions among multiple biological and/or environmental variables in relation to developmental outcomes, small studies cannot provide scientifically valid answers. This fact has led NICHD to invest sizeable resources in large studies that promise to provide important information pertaining to the health of children. In addition to the studies mentioned above, NICHD, in collaboration with other funding sources, is supporting a large follow-up study of very low birthweight infants (610 new infants per year over the duration of a long-term neonatal network study) and another study of 4000 infants of substance-abusing mothers. Because of the cost of such large, longitudinal studies, it is clear that funding agencies, in conjunction with the scientific community, need to carefully weigh the merits and limitations of big, versus small, science and arrive at a balanced allocation of resources that is scientifically and fiscally responsible.

The chapters in this book, individually and collectively, provide scientist-readers, whether novices or veterans, with the most up-to-date knowledge available about developmental follow-up strategies. The major strength of this volume is that it combines historical, theoretical, and methodological considerations. The editors' conviction that the choice of research strategies must be guided by the researchers' conceptual model and by their research goals is made obvious by the selection of contributors and the organization of the volume. The specific scientific domains that are represented in the book range from basic to applied, with greater emphasis on the importance of using follow-up methods when investigating public health and social problems (behavioral teratology, psychiatric problems, homelessness, and nonmaternal care). The proposed research methods represent contributions not only from developmental psychology but from other methodological perspectives that promise to enrich psychological research on child development, including psychiatry, epidemiology, and actuarial data analysis, and their application to novel research contexts.

Today's behavioral scientists are asking questions about development that are of great long-range interest for our society, whether it be assessing intermediate and long-term outcomes of survivors of neonatal intensive care units, results of early infant or childhood interventions, consequences of prenatal exposure to drugs, postnatal child abuse and neglect, or, as in the final chapter, the long-term effects of early infant day-care experience. It is my belief that the information in this book will improve the capability of these developmental investigators, increase the confidence of society in the validity of the results, and help provide critically needed guidance for solving the major problems that developmental research addresses.

Duane Alexander
Director, National Institute of Child Health and Human Development

REFERENCES

Barrat, M. S. (1991). School-age offspring of adolescent mothers: Environments and outcomes. *Family Relations, 40,* 442–227.

Baydar, N., & Brooks-Gunn, J. (1991). Effects of maternal employment and child care arrangements on preschoolers' cognitive and behavioral outcomes: Evidence from the children of the National Longitudinal Survey of Youth. *Developmental Psychology, 27,* 932–945.

Belsky, J., & Eggebeen, D. J. (1991). Early and extensive maternal employment and young children's socioemotional development: Children of the National Longitudinal Survey of Youth. *Journal of Marriage and the Family, 53,* 1083–1099.

Chase-Lansdale, P. L., Mott, F. L., Brooks-Gunn, J., & Phillips, D. A. (1991). Children of the National Longitudinal Survey of Youth: A unique research opportunity. *Developmental Psychology, 27,* 919–931.

Johnson, D. (1991). Psychology in Washington: What science needs is more bureaucrats. *Psychological Science, 2,* 1–2.

Verdonick, F., & Sherrod, L. R. (1984). *An inventory of longitudinal research on childhood and adolescence.* New York: Social Science Research Council.

THEORETICAL PERSPECTIVES

From the Past to the Future of Developmental Follow-up Research

Sarah L. Friedman
H. Carl Haywood
Karen Livesey

INTRODUCTION

The history of developmental follow-up research is long and rich, and one may wonder what more can be said or written about the topic. Skepticism may be replaced by curiosity about what can yet be learned if one thinks of longitudinal follow-up methodology as a vessel into which each generation of scientists pours its novel ideas, its concerns about the human condition at that particular time, and the methodological and technological advances of the day.

In this chapter we place this volume in a historical context by presenting the characteristics of developmental follow-up research from the early 1920s to the late 1980s, and by describing themes and issues that are raised in the other chapters of this future-oriented volume. To present the characteristics of past research, we summarize data from studies initiated over seven decades. Based on the trends thus identified, we characterize as "early" studies those initiated before the 1950s, and those started in the 1950s or later as "later" studies.

3

Overall, there has been a sharp increase from the early to the later period in the number of follow-up studies initiated. There was a tendency for early studies to focus on persons who were not at any known risk and follow these subjects across their life spans rather than over any conceptually selected, limited age period. The domains of interest, primarily dependent variables, have not changed much over the years, except that the interest in health and growth that characterized the early studies has declined markedly in the later period. Early investigators often assessed general constructs within domains such as cognition and personality, whereas in later studies, there has been an interest in specific aspects within a domain, reflecting a more or less standard trend toward differentiation in science, and in processes as distinguished from outcomes of development, reflecting perhaps the most encouraging trend in the developmental sciences.

In this chapter we also present an overview of and commentary on the chapters in this volume, thereby providing readers with a window on the future of follow-up research. The authors of this volume elaborate on conceptual frameworks and propose new emphases and new methods pertaining to issues of design, measurement, and analysis in follow-up research. For example, a theme that appears repeatedly is that of the need to study in depth (and not just discuss) transactional processes between persons and their environments and to understand development in the context of individual differences and variations in the physical and social contexts of development. The importance of evaluating the interplay among biological, psychological, and environmental variables adds a new emphasis to this theme and may very well be at the heart of the longitudinal research of the next decade. The question of whether follow-up research ought to be designed for hypothesis testing only, or also for description, or for exploring new ideas, relates to the broader question of whether developmental psychology should be trying to mimic the physical and biological sciences. This question is addressed in several of the chapters, along with discussions of the advantages of different methods of data collection (e.g., self-report questionnaires vs. direct observations) and of different sources of information (e.g., parents, children, teachers). Developmental epidemiology, a novel approach for design and analysis of developmental research is introduced as are methods of analysis borrowed from actuarial research. Therefore, in addition to providing some information about past research, this volume focuses on new directions for the next wave of developmental follow-up studies.

PLACING DEVELOPMENTAL FOLLOW-UP STUDIES IN HISTORICAL CONTEXT

Much of our knowledge about development comes from cross-sectional studies, in which different individuals are studied at different times during their development. For example, in a study of the development of problem solving, one would use problem-solving tasks with a group of 4-year-old children, with another group of 5-year-olds, and with still another group of 6-year-olds. Conclusions would then be drawn about developmental changes in problem solving. The assumption underlying such studies is that individuals who are similar along specific dimensions are interchangeable, and that the children of a younger cohort will have the characteristics of those in an older cohort when they reach the same age, thereby legitimizing the use of such cross-sectional study designs for the purpose of drawing conclusions about development. Although such studies can and do yield rich information about children's cognitive processes (e.g., problem solving, attention, memory) at a given age, or about such accomplishments at different ages, the developmental results of such research are less precise than are results of research in which information is collected from the very same individuals over time. This is the case because the age differences that are found in cross-sectional research may be due not only to developmental changes, but also to many undocumented differences among the specific individuals who constitute the cross-sectional samples at different ages. Consequently, predictions from early to later ages or developmental trends that are found must be qualified by the possibility that the results might have been markedly different had the study relied on a longitudinal methodology.

Some developmental questions require follow-up studies that involve repeated assessment of the same individuals over time. Such studies include, for example, those focusing on the effects of early life conditions on later developmental outcomes, studies of change from before to after an experimental intervention, or studies of the effects of practice on learning—all of which are almost inconceivable within a cross-sectional framework. In spite of these obvious cases, investigators do sometimes evaluate the effects of intervention without repeated assessment of the same individuals (Campbell & Stanley, 1963, see reference to the "one shot case study"). Studies of psychological or behavioral processes (e.g., habituation) are by definition studies that require repeated data from the same individuals and cannot be investigated with a cross-sectional design.

Longitudinal data have been collected at the national level for more than 300 years (Menard, 1991) and follow-up research on psychological and physical development has been conducted since the early 1920s. Many books, chapters, and research articles have been written describing the specific studies. An inventory of longitudinal studies in social sciences has been published and it includes references based on each of the studies (Young, Savola, & Phelps, 1991). Several other publications have appeared that have focused (directly or indirectly) on methods, their implementation, analyses of results, and other general issues (e.g., Mednick, Harway, & Finello, 1984; Campbell, 1988; McCall & Applebaum, 1991; Magnusson, Bergman, Rudinger, & Torestad, 1991; Menard, 1991). This literature allows social scientists to ask questions about historical and developmental changes in the use of longitudinal research methods for psychological research about the development of children. It is reasonable to expect that the changes that have occurred in the field of child development in terms of conceptual emphasis, interest in specific special populations, and technological and methodological sophistication would be reflected in the longitudinal follow-up research that has been undertaken.

Kagan (1964) wrote an article on longitudinal research on psychological development in the United States in which he summarized 10 longitudinal projects. Our review of the longitudinal literature is based in 169 studies from two inventories that we reviewed: Verdonick and Sherrod's (1984) inventory of longitudinal research on childhood and adolescence, and Young, Savola, and Phelps's (1991) inventory of longitudinal studies in the social sciences. These two inventories were initiated by the Social Science Research Council and were published to stimulate further analyses of existing databases. Our review also refers to studies that were not yet found in the inventories and that represent a cross between survey research and research in developmental psychology, and epidemiological research and research in developmental psychology. The studies that were surveyed do not include all possible longitudinal follow-up studies. A search of the PSYCHLIT data bank revealed that during the period between January 1974 and December 1992, 5340 longitudinal studies of children (infants, preschool age, school age, or adolescents) were initiated. The survey we conducted of these inventories suggests that the studies we examined are more or less representative of the longitudinal research that was carried out during the periods surveyed. Therefore, we present information on various aspects of the studies surveyed with the assumption that if we had surveyed more studies we would have found similar information and reached similar conclusions.

Ideally, we would go into the literature to find descriptive papers for each of the studies that we surveyed. When attempting to do so, however, it was discovered that for many of the studies, a single source describing the overall plan could not be found. Some of the published descriptions appeared many years after the studies themselves were initiated, and after many specific findings had been disseminated in the scientific literature. For example, the longitudinal study undertaken by the Institute of Child Welfare at the University of Minnesota, initiated in 1925, was described in 1963 (Anderson, 1963). The Berkeley Growth Study that was started in 1928 was described as a whole in a publication that appeared in 1941 (Jones & Bayley, 1941). The Fels Research Institute longitudinal study, started in 1929, was described in full in 1962 (Kagan & Moss, 1962). The Harvard Growth Study, started in 1930, was described as a whole in 1959 (Stuart & Reed, 1959).

In surveying the inventories, we tabulated the several categories of information for each study. The information recorded included the study's duration, the age periods investigated, characteristics of the sample (e.g., size, representativeness), research instruments, and domains of follow-up. Examination of the data revealed that studies initiated before the 1950s and those that were initiated later appeared to be distinguishable along many of the characteristics examined.

FOLLOW-UP CHILD DEVELOPMENT RESEARCH FROM THE EARLY 1920s TO THE LATE 1980s

Number of Studies and Their Duration

One striking finding of our review is that the number of the surveyed follow-up studies has grown enormously over the years. In the 1920s, only seven longitudinal follow-up studies of children were started. In the 1930s, five were started. Only two were initiated in the 1940s. The great increase in the volume of such studies began with the 1950s, when 15 new studies were begun. Thirty-eight surveyed studies were initiated in the 1960s, 81 in the 1970s, and 21 in the 1980s (the last study reported in the inventory was initiated in 1988).

Of these studies, 43.8% are still ongoing. A larger percentage (78.6%) of studies initiated in the 1920s through the 1940s than of those initiated later (40.6%) have not been terminated to date. This difference reflects the earlier investigators' interest in a life span perspective on development. Their commitment to this approach is further emphasized by the fact that their studies were initiated during the depression years when research funds were less available than in later years. The length of each terminated study was calculated and it was found that of the early studies that were terminated, the average length was 42 years, and of the later studies, the average length was 9.3 years: A striking difference in developmental perspective.

Characteristics of the Samples

Size   Studies in the 1920s through the 1940s tended to have more subjects than did studies in the period starting in the early 1950s. The mean sample size for the early studies was 7328, with a standard deviation of 2312 and a range of 61 to 87,508. For the later studies, the mean sample size was 4117, with a standard deviation of 30,633 and a range of 3 to 377,015. This trend is surprising in the context of the technological changes occurring over the period of our survey. One would think that with the introduction of and the rapid increase in the use of computers, investigators would be seduced into collecting more and more data. The change in the average sample size could be due to a combination of scientific and financial realities. We will see that the later studies focused on more constructs in each domain of investigation and that they are also richer in their use of more time-intensive and expensive data collection methods (observations and tasks). Given constant resources, the more intensive the methods of investigation, the smaller the number of subjects that can be studied. Therefore, we speculated that the decrease in the average number of subjects results from historical trends in scientific interest and the availability of resources in terms of constant dollars (i.e., dollars adjusted for inflation). We sought support for our hypothesis by examining correlations between the sample size of the studies and either the number of constructs investigated for the reliance on time-intensive methods of data collection. The correlations were close to zero. With no information about the cost of the studies, we could not test the possibility that the availability of funding was associated with the historical trend in the area of sample size.

Type and Representativeness   In the 1920s through the 1940s, 10 of the 14 studies reviewed (71.4%) followed up only those children who were believed to be free of risk or of any special status. Of the remaining studies (28.6%), one was of exceptionally gifted children, one was of children at risk for involvement with the law, one study was of twins, and two studies assessed at-risk children and a control group of normally developing children. In the 1950s through the 1980s, 58 out of 155 (37.4%) studies were of children who could be classified as at risk or who had some special status such as mental retardation, being in foster care, or being classified as hyperactive. This increased interest in special populations reflects a general trend in the scientific literature about child development.

Apart from eight studies described in the inventories we surveyed and a small number of more recent studies that were not mentioned in these inventories, the samples examined in the studies we surveyed were samples of convenience. In most of the studies, there was no attempt to get a representative sample, either regionally, nationally, or within a subgroup of special subjects (e.g., children at biological risk). This reality is changing as the fields of demography, sociology, and psychology converge. Sociologists have recently become interested in adding psychological measures to their surveys of large and demographically well-defined samples (e.g., Baker & Mott, 1989; Zaslow, Coiro, & Moore, 1993). Educational researchers are also moving in the direction of using representative samples (e.g., Ingels, Abraham, Karr, Spencer, & Frankel, 1990; McLaughlin & Talbert, 1992), and developmental psychologists are adopting epidemiological methods to study biomedical and social risks for developmental outcome (see Buka & Lipsitt, this volume; Scott, Shaw, & Urbano, this volume). At the same time, developmental psychologists who are interested in variations within the "normal" course of development are beginning to preplan the scientific criteria for subject inclusion and to define carefully the representativeness of the samples in their child development research (e.g., Friedman, 1990; the NICHD Early Child Care Network, 1993; The NICHD Early Child Care Network, this volume).

Age Brackets   The ages at which the children were assessed were classified into five categories: infancy (0–2 years of age), preschool (3–5), school

(6–10), adolescence (11–18), and adult (19 years and older). Table I shows the distribution of the number and percentage of studies that had assessments in the different age categories. In the last 15 years, there has been a great increase in the interest of developmental psychologists in the area of infant development. A similar trend has taken place over the last 10 years or so in the area of adolescent development. Yet, Table I does not reflect the same trends. If anything, the trends seems to be reversed. Table I does not, however, reveal the fact that whereas none of the early studies focused exclusively on infancy or adolescence, six of the later studies focused only on infancy and twelve later studies focused only on adolescence. This exclusive focusing on specific periods of development suggests that the trends shown in Table I are somewhat misleading. We did not have access to information about the number of constructs studied per assessment in each age period and therefore we could not evaluate the possibility that the growth of interest in research on the periods of infancy and adolescence was expressed by the number of constructs studied.

Age Spans Table II shows that all the studies started between the 1920s and the end of the 1940s followed up the children across developmental periods rather than within one developmental period (by "developmental period" we refer to infancy, preschool age, grade school age, or adolescence). Of the later studies (1950s–1980s), 131 (84.52%) followed the children beyond a specific developmental period. Eight of the early studies (57.14%) followed the children from infancy through a later age, whereas 59 (38.06%) of the studies initiated in the 1950s through the 1980s followed the infants from infancy through some later period.

Number of Assessments per Age Bracket The increase in the number of studies focusing on relatively more limited age periods was associated with

Table I Number of Studies per Decade with Assessments within Each Age Period

Age periods	1920	1930	1940	Early total	1950	1960	1970	1980	Late total
Infancy	6	1	1	8	8	12	37	8	65
	85.7%	20.0%	50.0%	57.1%	53.0%	31.6%	45.7%	38.1%	41.9%
Preschool	5	2	1	8	5	20	46	10	81
	71.4%	40.0%	50.0%	57.1%	33.3%	52.6%	56.8%	47.6%	52.3%
School	4	3	1	8	10	24	54	10	98
	57.1%	60.0%	50.0%	57.1%	66.7%	63.2%	66.7%	47.6%	63.2%
Adolescence	6	5	2	13	12	29	46	13	100
	85.7%	100.0%	100.0%	92.9%	73.3%	76.3%	56.8%	61.9%	64.5%
Adult	7	5	2	14	11	21	12	0	44
	100.0%	100.0%	100.0%	100%	73.3%	55.3%	14.38%	0%	28.4%

Table II   Number of Studies with Assessments within One Period or Ranging over Assessment Periods

Age ranges	Decades								
	1920	1930	1940	Early total	1950	1960	1970	1980	Late total
Infancy only	0	0	0	0	0	1	4	1	6
Preschool only	0	0	0	0	0	0	2	0	2
School only	0	0	0	0	0	0	3	1	4
Adolescence only	0	0	0	0	0	0	6	6	12
Infancy—later	6	1	1	8	8	11	33	7	59
Preschool—later	1	1	0	2	2	9	16	3	30
School—later	0	1	0	1	2	10	9	3	24
Adolescence—later	0	2	1	3	3	7	8	0	18
Infancy—adult	6	1	1	8	6	1	1	0	8

greater depth of investigation. It is quite possible that this association results from the fact that for many psychological constructs, measurement instruments are applicable only to a limited age range. For example, whereas instruments for assessing general intelligence were developed for wide age ranges, instruments for assessing constructs such as attachment or temperament were designed for very limited age ranges. In a later section, we survey the domains and constructs that have been investigated; however, our sources did not allow us to determine the relationship between specific age ranges and the constructs that were assessed, so we could not evaluate the possible association between the age range studied and the availability of instruments appropriate for specific age ranges.

For studies that provided such information, we counted the number of assessments per age period and found that the percentage of studies with frequent assessments within age periods increased dramatically in the 1950s and beyond. For example, 100% of the early studies with assessments in the infancy periods (and for which we have data about the number of assessments) included two or fewer assessments ($M = 1.60$ assessments, $SD = .49$), whereas only 52.30% of the later studies with assessments in infancy included two or fewer assessments ($M = 3.48$ assessments, $SD = 3.92$). Of the early studies in which adolescents were examined (and for which we have data about the number of assessments), 77.78% included two or fewer assessments ($M = 2.56$ assessments, $SD = 2.27$), whereas 64.58% of the later studies had two or fewer assessments ($M = 2.42$ assessments, $SD = 1.78$). Table III provides details.

Table III   Number of Studies with Two or Fewer versus More Than Two Assessments within Infancy and Adolescence

				Decades					
Period	1920	1930	1940	Early total	1950	1960	1970	1980	Late total
Infancy									
Two or fewer	3	1	1	5	5	7	20	1	33
More than 2	1	0	0	1	3	4	17	5	29
Total	4	1	1	6	8	11	37	6	62
No. missing[a]	3	0	0	3	0	1	0	2	3
Adolescence									
Two or fewer	2	3	2	7	10	17	27	8	62
More than 2	1	1	0	2	2	10	18	4	34
Total	3	4	2	9	12	27	45	12	96
No. missing[a]	3	1	0	4	0	2	1	1	4

[a] Some of the studies did not provide specific information about the number of assessments within age ranges.

Research Instruments

The research instruments used were classified into nine types: interviews, questionnaires, published instruments (e.g., intelligence tests), ratings, records (primarily school records but also police records), health exams, observations, sociometric evaluations, and behavioral tasks (such as Piagetian tasks or laboratory learning tasks). The number of studies within a decade in which each of these methods was used is presented in Table IV. The table shows that most of the methods were used across the seven decades surveyed.

Published instruments and questionnaires retained their appeal as instruments of choice, the appeal of observational methods has increased, and that of interviews and the use of official records has declined. Sociometric evaluations were introduced in the 1950s but their use declined soon after. Experimental tasks, also introduced into the surveyed longitudinal studies in the 1950s, were used through the 1970s when their use peaked.

This information is relevant to the ongoing debate about the relative merits of information collected from informants versus information collected through direct observation or testing (see Bates, this volume). The increase in observational protocols and experimental tasks suggests that more and more investigators favor methods that do not rely on an informant's memory and judgment.

The decrease in the use of health data is probably a result of the fact that more and more psychologists in the United States have come to assume

Table IV   Number and Percentage of Studies Using Different Types of Measures

Measures	1920	1930	1940	Early total	1950	1960	1970	1980	Late total
Interview	4	4	2	10	11	20	42	10	83
	57.0%	80.0%	100.0%	71.4%	77.3%	52.6%	51.9%	46.7%	53.5%
Observation	1	2	0	3	6	11	36	8	61
	14.2%	40.0%	0	21.4%	40.0%	28.9%	44.4%	38.1%	39.4%
Published	7	5	2	14	14	27	66	15	122
	100%	100%	100%	100%	93.3%	71.1%	81.5%	71.4%	78.7%
Questionnaire	3	2	0	5	12	17	43	13	85
	42.8%	40.0%	0	35.7%	80.0%	44.7%	53.1%	61.5%	54.8%
Ratings	1	1	0	2	5	8	17	2	32
	14.2%	20.0%	0	14.3%	33.3%	21.1%	21.0%	9.5%	20.6%
Records	2	3	1	6	8	11	14	2	35
	28.5%	60.0%	50.0%	42.9%	53.0%	28.9%	17.3%	9.5%	22.6%
Sociometric	0	0	0	0	3	2	4	2	11
	0	0	0	0	20.0%	5.3%	4.9%	9.5%	7.1%
Tasks	0	0	0	0	2	6	25	0	33
	0	0	0	0	13.0%	15.8%	30.9%	0	21.3%
Health Exams	6	3	1	10	5	7	14	2	28
	85.0%	60.0%	50.0%	71.4%	33.3%	18.4%	17.3%	9.5%	18.1%

good health as a standard and decide to focus on psychological variables only. More of them have left the realm of health to pediatric investigators. The wisdom of that trend is questioned in this volume in the chapter by Shonkoff, who predicts a systematic relationship between the health status of individuals and their psychological status.

Domains of Follow-up

The survey of the 169 studies on which this review is based yielded information about nine domains of assessment. We classified the domains as follows: characteristics of the environment, cognition and related constructs, social and related constructs, personality, health and related constructs, career, deviant behavior/development, marriage, and miscellaneous. We found that the average number of domains studied over the early period was 5.07 out of the nine domains, and the comparable number for the later period was 3.94. Table V shows the number of early and late studies assessing the nine domains and permits readers to infer historical trends in studies of child development. Table VI shows information pertaining to the mean number of constructs per domain that were studied in the same set of studies. Across domains, the average number of different constructs investigated in the earlier studies was 11.86, as compared with an average of 10.61 in the

Table V Number and Percentage of Studies Assessing Each Domain

Domains	Early studies	Late studies
Environment	10	128
	(71.4%)	(82.6%)
Cognition	13	135
	(92.9%)	(87.1%)
Social	9	112
	(64.3%)	(72.3%)
Personality	11	98
	(78.6%)	(63.2%)
Health	13	61
	(92.9%)	(39.4%)
Career	6	23
	(42.9%)	(14.8%)
Deviant Behavior	2	28
	(14.3%)	(18.1%)
Marriage	4	9
	(28.6%)	(5.8%)
Miscellaneous	3	16
	(21.4%)	(10.3%)

Table VI Mean Number of Constructs Assessed in Each Domain

Domains	Early studies	Late studies
Environment	2.30	3.45
	$(SD = 1.00)$	$(SD = 2.44)$
Cognition	2.15	3.28
	$(SD = 1.29)$	$(SD = 2.49)$
Social	1.44	2.30
	$(SD = 0.83)$	$(SD = 1.43)$
Personality	1.64	2.62
	$(SD = 0.77)$	$(SD = 2.01)$
Health	4.77	2.20
	$(SD = 3.79)$	$(SD = 1.18)$
Career	1.67	1.57
	$(SD = 1.11)$	$(SD = 0.88)$
Deviant Behavior	2.0	1.46
	$(SD = 1.0)$	$(SD = 0.68)$
Marriage	1.0	1.11
	$(SD = 0.0)$	$(SD = 0.31)$
Miscellaneous	1.33	1.44
	$(SD = 0.47)$	$(SD = 0.50)$

later studies. Information about the domains assessed and the constructs subsumed under each domain follows.

Characteristics of the Environment   These included demographic variables, assessments of the home environment, psychological characterstics of the family (e.g., stress and supports, maternal anxiety, maternal depression, parent personality, locus of control, and child rearing styles), marital relationship, parent–child relationship, peer relationship, and the school environment (because some of these constructs could have been considered social outcomes, the studies were examined to determine when these variables were actually used to assess the environment rather than social outcome).

In the early studies, the mean number of constructs by which environmental variables were assessed was 2.30, and in the later studies the mean was 3.45. Perhaps the most noteworthy point to make is that psychologists' interest in the environment is at least as old as the history of longitudinal research about child development. The difference in the number of specific aspects of the environment that were measured reflects the growing interest on the part of psychologists in the environment as an influencer of child development and reflects their increasing awareness of the complexity of environmental variables. This interest has culminated in the last decade in theoretical models proposed by Bronfenbrenner and Crouter (1983), by Sameroff and Chandler (1975), and by Horowitz (1987). Also see the chapters by Horowitz and by Sameroff in this volume.

Cognition and Related Constructs   First, the number of constructs used to assess the domain was tabulated. Then, to determine what types of constructs were assessed, the cognitive constructs were classified into three groups: general, specfiic, and related. The general cognitive constructs included developmental level (e.g., Bayley scores) and IQ. Specific constructs included attention, memory, problem solving, and planning. Related constructs included perception, exploration, imagination, social cognition, creativity, field dependence, and school achievement (including reading and math).

The cognitive domain was evaluated by an average of 2.15 constructs in the early years and an average of 3.36 in the later years. In the early years, there was a greater tendency to use measures of overall cognitive functioning: 92.31% of the early studies used some global measures of intelligence. Only 68.89% of the later studies relied on such measures; however, when the number of measures of specific cognitive constructs was tabulated, it became apparent that in the early years no such measures were used, whereas in the later decades these variables were coded by 20.74% of the studies. In 46.15% of the early studies and 67.4% of the late studies, the constructs classified as "related" were assessed.

Social and Related Constructs   These include parent–child interactions and relationship, peer interaction and relationship, as well as other aspects of social behavior. We first tabulated the number of all constructs used to assess the social domain, and then we tabulated the number of certain types of constructs assessed. These constructs included peer, mother–child, parent–child, school, maladjustment, and attachment. Table VII contains the number of early and late studies in which these specific constructs were assessed.

In studies in which the social domain was assessed, the number of different aspects investigated increased from 1.44 in the early years to 2.30 in the later years, a difference that reflects a historical trend in all studies of child development. None of the early studies included assessments of peer interactions, mother–child interactions, maladjusted social behavior or attachment, whereas in the later studies these specific constructs were more likely to be examined. Of the studies in which the social domain was assessed, more of the early studies (44.44%) than later studies (11.61%) examined social behavior in relation to the school context.

Personality The number of personality constructs assessed was tabulated first, then the constructs were categorized as general or specific. The general constructs in this category included global data from published tests of personality and temperament. The specific constructs included coping behavior, delay of gratification, ego development, self-esteem, locus of control, sex roles, extraversion, impulsivity, leadership, self-concept, self-control, and self-awareness. The mean number of different aspects of personality assessed was 1.64 in the early studies and 2.54 in the later studies.

As with the cognitive variables, general constructs were used more in the early studies (90.91%) than in the later studies (43.88%). Conversely, specific constructs were used by more of the later studies (71.43%) than the earlier studies (27.27%).

Table VII Number and Percentage of Early and Late Studies That Focused on Specific Social Constructs

Social constructs	Early studies	Late studies
Peer	0	26
	(0%)	(23.2%)
Mother–child	0	13
	(0%)	(11.5%)
Parent–child	1	14
	(11.1%)	(12.5%)
School	4	13
	(44.4%)	(11.6%)
Maladjustment	0	35
	(0%)	(31.25%)
Attachment	1	13
	(11.1%)	(11.6%)

Health and Related Constructs This category includes both physical health and neurological integrity. Included in this category were variables such as anthropometric measurements, blood levels of various substances, diet, cardiovascular status, cholesterol levels, dental status, injuries, sleep patterns, and neurologic status.

The earlier studies were more likely than were later studies to include these health-related constructs and to include more types of variables to assess the domain. Of the early studies, 92.9% included assessment of health and related variables, whereas only 39.4% of the late studies included this domain. Not only were the early studies more likely to include the health domain, they were also characterized by greater complexity: an average of 4.77 specific health-related constructs as opposed to 2.20 specific constructs in the later studies. This clearly indicates that the early investigators were more interested in the health and related domains than were the investigators of the late studies.

Career-Related Variables These variables included job satisfaction, career plans, and professional attainment. Fully 42.86% of early studies, but only 14.8% of later studies, focused on the career domain. This difference is probably due to the fact that more of the early studies followed the subjects to adulthood.

Delinquent and Criminal Behavior and Substance Use There was little difference between early and late studies in which deviant behavior was assessed: 14.29% of early studies and 18.06% of late studies. The mean number of constructs was 2.00 for the early studies and 1.46 for the later studies, suggesting both a relatively low level of interest in this domain and a relatively uncomplicated view of it.

Marital Outcome Variables These include marital history and satisfaction. Examination of this domain revealed a substantial difference, with 28.57% of early and 5.81% of late studies including some assessment of the marital domain. The mean number of marital outcome constructs for the early studies was 1.00 and for the later studies 1.11. The decline in the percentage of studies using marital variables may be related to the fact that more of the early studies followed the subjects into adulthood.

Miscellaneous Twenty-one percent (21.43%) of early and 10.32% of late studies included assessment of miscellaneous domains such as life satisfaction and attitudes toward school.

Data Analyses

Longitudinal follow-up research is primarily justified in terms of its ability to allow investigators (a) to test hypotheses about relations between conditions imposed or observed at one time and outcomes assessed at subsequent times, and (b) to describe patterns of growth over the years along dimensions of particular interest. Even before the advent of high-speed computing and elaborate prepackaged statistical analyses (starting in the 1950s and becoming popular in the 1970s; see Castellan, 1991), analyses were carried out along these two lines of investigation. At the same time, the data from longitudinal follow-up research were also used for the purpose of answering questions that are not developmental in nature.

The inventories we surveyed referred to a limited number of representative publications (Verdonick & Sherrod, 1984, cited two references per study; Young, Savola, and Phelps, 1991, usually cited four but sometimes fewer) from each of the studies surveyed. This did not allow us to estimate either the productivity of the studies or the type of analyses conducted. To do that, one would need to have access to all the publications based on all the studies surveyed—a task we did not undertake.

Taking the Leap from the Past to the Future

This survey of historical trends in longitudinal studies initiated over seven decades is meant as background for the presentation of strategies for future longitudinal research. We have presented historical trends pertaining to variables that are easy to quantify, and have speculated on the reasons for the trends that we observed. We organized the survey around the number of studies carried out as well as their duration, sample size, type of samples and their representativeness, age bracket studied, number of assessments, research instruments, and content domains of investigation. Some of our findings surprised us in that they seemed counterintuitive. Although our somewhat primitive survey revealed some interesting and useful observations, there were important questions that could not be answered on the basis of this survey. For example, we could not tell anything about the conceptual models, if any, that guided the investigators who conducted the studies. Also, the information in the inventories did not tell us how frequently the data were treated in ways that took advantage of their longitudinal follow-up nature.

Although the survey did not reveal the conceptual orientations of past studies, we try in the next part of the chapter to suggest conceptual orientation as a dimension of prime importance in present and future studies.

A BLUEPRINT FOR FUTURE RESEARCH: OVERVIEW OF THE VOLUME WITH COMMENTARY

The chapters in this volume vary in the extent to which they focus on developmental psychological theory, theory of research design, specifics of assessment and measurement, and domains of inquiry that need to be investigated in follow-up research. Yet, there are assumptions and concepts that cut across chapters that are very different in terms of their focus. The theoretical importance of evaluating the interplay among biological, psychological, and environmental variables over time is explicitly mentioned in the chapters by Horowitz and by Sameroff. The same is alluded to by Cohen, Towbin, Mayes, and Volkmar. The question as to whether follow-up research ought to be designed only for hypothesis testing, or also for description of developmental phenomena, or for the exploration of new ideas is answered directly or indirectly by chapters authored by Bates, by Horowitz, by Kraemer, and by Scott, Shaw, and Urbano. The importance of studying noncognitive aspects of development, of investigating the relationships between different aspects of development, and of focusing on processes of development in addition to summary outcomes is expressed in most of the chapters. This emphasis is not entirely novel; however, the extent to which it is emphasized represents a major advance in the focus of interest on the part of investigators who conduct follow-up research.

The editors of this volume, like many others, recognize the importance of theoretically guided research, in general, and the importance of applying such an approach to the next generation of longitudinal follow-up research. We have noted that longitudinal follow-up research has frequently been atheoretical, thereby yielding a wealth of information that is limited in its ability to elucidate the generalized principles of human development. For example, Friedman and Sigman (1992) noted that psychological research on the development of preterm babies is visibly lacking in theoretical orientation. They observed that when theories are invoked they are used for an after-the-fact explanation of results rather than as guides for research questions or study designs. To convey the importance of theoretically guided research, the editors invited contributions from Horowitz and from Sameroff.

Horowitz argues in her chapter for the advantages of using a theoretical model of human development to guide the research questions and the methods of follow-up research. She provides a theoretical framework that includes organismic, environmental, and developmental components and that has implications for research about risks and their influence on development. Sameroff, in another chapter, also advocates a complex, nonlinear model of development that takes into account the interplay of the characteristics of individuals and the features of the social organizations within which individuals' lives play out. Sameroff discusses the intricacy and regulating power of different aspects of the environment, including family and culture.

The next set of chapters contains examples of domains of human development that have been studied or that would be fruitful to study in the context of follow-up research. For the last 15 to 20 years, researchers have related biological risk factors in children to the cognitive, intellectual, and academic performance of children. Characteristically, cognitive processes have been evaluated in infancy, and school performance and intelligence later. The chapter by Charmichel Olson, Barr, Bookstein, and Streissguth about the effects of maternal consumption of alcohol during pregnancy on child development is more comprehensive than many others of the same genre and demonstrates how much could be learned through this class of studies.

Shonkoff examines the potential inclusion of health surveillance within a comprehensive strategy for developmental follow-up of children and youth from early infancy through adolescence. The proposed research can tell about the interdependence of health and development, about the developmental consequences of various types of health impairment (common childhood illness, chronic illness), and about patterns of health care use. In much research conducted recently by developmental psychologists, there is no evaluation of individual differences in the health of children who have not been identified a priori as being at medical risk or as having a medical problem. (See, however, The NICHD Study of Early Child Care, this volume, for an exception.) Shonkoff suggests that a comprehensive conceptualization of child development should integrate psychological and health issues.

Sinclair discusses the processes by which peer interaction favorably influences the cognitive development of children who engage in exploratory play in the day care context. The novelty here is in terms of studying peer interaction for the sake of understanding cognitive processes. Researchers who investigate social influences on early cognitive development have traditionally focused on mothers as the mediators of cognitive development and only a few have focused on peers. Sinclair highlights the need to turn the focus on peer interaction. By making a contribution to this volume, she indirectly suggests that research on peer interaction in the service of cognitive development could benefit from a longitudinal follow-up approach.

The chapter by Deborah Rog about expanding the boundaries of evaluation research could be subsumed in the section on experimental design and data analysis. It was placed with the section on domains of investigation to highlight homelessness as a domain of investigation that calls for longitudinal follow-up research, and also to demonstrate an important situation in which the technology of program evaluation is brought to bear on problems of human development not typically seen as their proper province.

Cohen, Towbin, Mayes, and Volkmar write about the clinical follow-up of individual cases as a method for getting insights into principles underlying developmental psychopathology. This bottom-up approach that has proven very useful as a means for providing practical and conceptual leads in the area of psychopathology is very different from the reliance on statistical variations in group data used by developmental psychologists who study normal development or the development of individuals at biological or environmental risk. It would be optimal if conceptualizations derived from the clinical method were validated by the scientific method that is described in other chapters in this volume. It seems that developmental epidemiologists and developmental psychopathologists would be best equipped to collaborate with psychiatrists on the conduct of such developmental follow-up research.

Many of the ideas presented in the chapters contained in Section II on domains are in the forefront of their areas of research. This is important because, traditionally, developmental follow-up research has been applied research. Frequently, it has borrowed well-explored concepts and well-tried-out instruments from different subdisciplines (especially, cognition, education, and intelligence testing). The domains chapters in this volume also represent an interest in expanding the scope of developmental follow-up studies. Together, they suggest a need to study the whole person, as opposed to selecting a narrow aspect of development. The argument is made, sometimes tacitly and other times explicitly, that aspects of development and processes of development are interdependent.

Information about children's development is sometimes discussed in terms of who provides it (e.g., the target child, the mother, the father, a teacher) or in terms of the method of data collection (e.g., questionnaire, interview, observation, test). Because objectivity, or at least detachment, is a central goal of scientific measurement, there are many who prefer data collected directly from the research subject through standardized tests, experimental tasks, interviews, questionnaires, or observations by trained staff. Many scientists are less trusting of data collected from informants such as parents or teachers. The authors in Section III present detailed information about some methods of data collection, discuss the merits of different strategic approaches, and identify problems and gains associated with the use of multiple methods to study the same constructs in the same subjects.

Parents' reports are the most widely used source of data about children's social development. Investigators use them because they expect parents to be experts about their children. Bates tells us that this is the case despite the fact that these reports can be shown to be only partially objective. At the same time, he has data to show that mothers' reports converge with observers' ratings and that the subjective component of maternal reports does not outweigh the objective ones. Moreover, his research shows that mothers' reports of their children's different characteristics are differentiated both within and across ages. Edelbrock sensitizes us to the fact that different informants (e.g., parents, teachers, children) do not agree when rating children's psychopathology. He tells us that it is not clear which informants should be used to obtain specific types of information or how to reconcile or aggregate data from the different informants. He also alerts us to the fact that different informants are not equally available or accurate across development. For example, teachers are generally unavailable before age 5 or 6, but they can provide useful information during the grade school years but not for later years.

Whereas Bates focuses on the assessment of children's social development and Edelbrock focuses on the assessment of child psychopathology,

Siegel describes instruments for assessing mostly intellective development from infancy through age 12. She suggests that global scores are not particularly useful and that, consequently, specific functions should be assessed and analyzed. Caldwell and Bradley describe in their chapter their method of assessing the physical and social environment of infants and young children. The method developed by these authors is one of the more sophisticated ones for describing developmentally relevant characteristics of children's home environments. At present, the scientific field of developmental psychology is limited in the number of methods available for environmental assessment. Also, apart from methods for describing mothers' child-rearing practices and attitudes as contexts for development, most available methods are not detailed or carefully constructed (Friedman & Wachs, in press). Friedman and Sigman (1992) noted that despite the fact that many longitudinal research papers about the development of preterm babies give credit to Sameroff and Chandler's (1975) transactional model, which emphasizes the important role of environments in shaping the development of children, these papers provide limited scientific information about contexts of development and their effects on children's development. As the chapters by Horowitz and by Sameroff indicate, the next wave of longitudinal follow-up studies will undoubtedly need to assess the environment with the same care with which they have traditionally assessed psychological outcome. The NICHD Study of Early Child Care, described in the last chapter of the volume, takes important steps in this direction.

Developmental/psychological follow-up research is aimed at finding relationships between early and late psychological characteristics or between early environments or events and later psychological outcome. The designs and analyses of such studies depend on the specific aims of the study: "The purpose demands the strategy" (Haywood, 1970a, p. 4, 1970b; Heal, 1970). Studies can be observational or exploratory, or they may be aimed at testing hypotheses based on theory or on empirical findings from other studies. As we have learned from our survey, follow-up studies tend to enroll many subjects and to evaluate them along multiple dimensions over several—sometimes many—years. Therefore, issues of sampling, the definitions of the constructs under investigation, and the choice of measures are particularly important. The type and complexity of the analyses should depend on the research questions, the number of subjects, and the type and number of measures for each construct that is being studied. The chapters in Section IV of this volume address these issues in detail.

Kraemer specifies the conditions under which a large-scale longitudinal follow-up study is justified and spells out the many considerations that need to be taken into account when carrying out such a study. She finds no justification for large-scale follow-up studies that are not planned to test a predetermined set of hypotheses. On statistical grounds, she recommends limiting the number of measures for studying a given construct. She favors simple statistical analyses as opposed to complex ones, because studies that are well planned in advance should not require statistical acrobatics at the time of data analysis. Kraemer discusses at length the merits and pitfalls of the multisite method aimed at increasing the representativeness of the sample and/or its size. Multisite studies are prevalent in biomedical research and have recently been adopted by psychologists (e.g., The Infant Health and Development Program, 1990; The NICHD Study of Early Child Care, this volume). Kraemer reviews many of the principles of behavior science that every advanced student of psychology ought to know and that many seasoned investigators do not follow, primarily for pragmatic reasons, but also sometimes because of conceptual considerations (e.g., see Bates, this volume, for his views on the importance of exploratory research).

These are not easy or simple issues. It is attractive to believe that developmental theory is so good and at such an advanced state that one can foresee potential discoveries and engage in very straightforward hypothesis testing. Several authors in this book call for relatively greater emphasis on theory building as well as on theory-driven follow-up research, suggesting that developmental theory may not be at such an ideal stage. Developmental research is replete with examples of the virtue of casting a wide net, that is, of building into research designs some opportunity to capture events that could not be precisely anticipated. One such example is the work of the Consortium for Longitudinal Studies (Lazar & Darlington, 1978), a group of investigators who pooled data from 12 longitudinal studies to derive inferences about the long-term effects of preschool education on the subsequent development of children from poverty-level families. This group discovered effects that none of the studies had identified, at least in such strong form, individually. Individual investigators had focused on relatively microscopic variables such as IQ, personality characteristics, and scores on standardized school achievement tests. Subsequent analyses of the combined data sets revealed positive effects on such molar variables as frequency of retention in grade and probability of placement in special education classes. Susan Gray (e.g., Gray, Ramsey, and Klaus, 1982), an extraordinarily gifted designer of developmental follow-up research, was able to discover, years after her experimental treatment on preschool children, that preschool education experience was related to the rate of returning to school by teenage girls who had had babies (almost 8 to 1 in favor of the preschool education group), although there was no relation to the number who became pregnant. Among classical follow-up studies, that of Skodak and Skeels (Skeels, 1966) is impressive in its conceptual use of unforeseen variables. Thus, flexibility and openness to discovery may be as important as precise advance specification of dependent variables.

Dunst and Trivette describe the use of two methods that have been used independently in developmental research. The first method is Hierarchical Linear Modeling for estimating intraindividual differences in growth rate.

The second is a Risk Opportunity Framework for classifying and investigating the influences of environmental factors that function as either impediments or enhancers of developmental competence. Although the description of these strategies is not new, the combination of the two as part of the same research program is. Such a program is aimed at achieving an understanding of behavioral change and of the environmental factors that impede or promote optimal psychological development. The chapter also describes possible extensions of these approaches and how these may contribute to the improved understanding of the sequelae of developmental problems.

Singer and Willet remind us that one way to study child development is to ask how long it takes before certain events occur and how the waiting times are associated with environmental or experiential factors. Although such a method makes eminent sense, it is not frequently used in longitudinal follow-up studies, especially because data are collected at prespecified ages. Studies in which "waiting times" are used as the dependent variables should incorporate relatively new analysis techniques—the methods of survival analysis.

Because developmental psychologists have traditionally conducted studies comparing group means and correlating early events with later outcome, they have not been in a position to uncover the conditions that cause developmental problems that occur in a small percentage of children. Two chapters, one by Buka and Lipsitt and the other by Scott and his colleagues, explain that by borrowing methods from the field of epidemiology, investigators will be able to answer questions that they could not answer—and perhaps not even ask—using their traditional methods. The developmental epidemiology that they describe offers a novel and promising direction for developmental follow-up research.

It is clear that the field of developmental follow-up research is not stagnant. To the contrary, it is bursting with ideas of how to conceptualize, design, and implement studies that trace the development of children over time and look for the multiple influences that shape this development. The last section of the volume is devoted to the description of an ongoing and exemplary longitudinal, multisite follow-up study. The NICHD Early Child Care Network reports on its comprehensive study of the developmental processes and the effects associated with variations in environmental contexts. Investigators assess with great care the different environments in which infants and toddlers develop. They have positioned themselves to test a priori hypotheses about the relationship between physical and social characteristics of environments (home and child care) and developmental processes and outcomes for the approximately 1300 children who still participate in the study. The study is at the forefront of developmental follow-up research in terms of its conceptualization of issues pertaining to child care and child development, its conceptually guided study design, its measurement program, and its plans for data analyses.

CONCLUSION

Many longitudinal studies have been conducted in which aspects of the development of children have been studied repeatedly as the children matured. Some of the studies have been undertaken in order to study normal development. Other studies tracked the development of children who were at some biological or environmental risk or compared it with the development of children who were free of such risks. For example, investigators have studied the development of low birthweight children, the development of children of mothers with a psychiatric diagnosis as compared with the development of children of well mothers, or the development of children who vary in terms of their child care histories. In other studies, children who received some planned intervention have been compared with children of similar backgrounds who were not exposed to the same medical, nutritional, or educational intervention. The children enrolled in these studies most frequently were those to whom the investigators could have ready access. Their recruitment did not follow a structured plan. Choices of the aspects of development that have been monitored in many of the studies frequently seem to have been based on access to instruments of evaluation, rather than on theoretical or methodological considerations. For example, the decision to use intelligence tests has not been based necessarily on theoretically guided hypotheses that certain adverse biological or environmental conditions are likely to affect intellectual functioning; nor has it necessarily been based on hypotheses about the effects of specific interventions on specific aspects of intellective performance. (In fact, intelligence tests were designed to provide a predictor variable rather than a criterion variable, so it is rather strange that IQ has been used so often in developmental research to show the effects of some planned intervention.) Sources of data (e.g., observations of behavior, test performance, parental reports, teachers' reports) have also been frequently determined by the availability of instruments or resources rather than by methodological considerations.

The scientific body of knowledge that has grown out of the type of studies described here is rich, informative, and interesting. Yet, at this time in the history of developmental follow-up research investigators are ready for more conceptually inspired and methodologically guided follow-up studies. In this chapter we have set the stage for the presentation of facts and ideas about past, current, and future follow-up developmental research.

REFERENCES

Anderson, J. E. (1963). *Experience and behavior in early childhood and the adjustment of the same persons as adults.* Minneapolis: Institute of Child Development.
Baker, P. C., & Mott, F. L. (1989). *NLSY child handbook: A guide and resource document for*

the *National Longitudinal Survey of Youth 1986 Child Data*. Columbus, OH: Center for Human Resource Research.

Bronfenbrenner, U., & Crouter, A. C. (1983). The evolution of environment models in developmental research. In P. H. Mussen (Ed.), *Handbook of child psychology*. New York: Wiley.

Campbell, D. T., & Stanley, J. C. (1963). *Experimental and quasi-experimental design for research*. Chicago: Rand McNally.

Campbell, R. T. (1988). *Integrating conceptualization, design, and analysis in panel studies of the life course*. In K. W. Schaie, R. T. Campbell, W. Meredith, & S. C. Rawlings (Eds.), *Methodological issues in aging research*. New York: Springer.

Castellan, N. J. (1991). Computers and computing in psychology. Twenty years of progress and still a bright future. *Behavior Research Methods, Instruments and Computers, 23*, 106–108.

Friedman, S. L. (1990). NICHD infant child-care network: The national study of young children's lives. *Zero to Three, 10*, 21–23.

Friedman, S. L., & Sigman, M. D. (1992). Past, present and future directions in research on the development of low-birthweight children. In S. L. Friedman & M. D. Sigman (Eds.), *The psychological development of low birthweight children*. Norwood, NJ: Ablex.

Freidman, S. L., & Wachs, T. D. (Eds.). (In press). *Measurement of the environment across the life span*. Washington, D.C.: American Psychological Association.

Gray, S. W., Ramsey, B. K., & Klaus, R. A. (1982). *From 3 to 20: The early training project*. Baltimore: University Park Press.

Haywood, H. C. (1970a). Symposium: The purpose demands the strategy. *American Journal of Mental Deficiency, 75*, 4.

Haywood, H. C. (1970b). Mental retardation as an extension of the developmental laboratory. *American Journal of Mental Deficiency, 75*, 5–9.

Heal, L. W. (1970). Research strategies and research goals in the scientific study of the mentally subnormal. *American Journal of Mental Deficiency, 75*, 10–15.

Horowitz, F. D. (1987). *Exploring developmental theories: Toward a structural/behavioral model of development*. Hillsdale, NJ: Lawrence Erlbaum.

Infant Health and Development Program. (1990). Enhancing the outcomes of low birth-weight, premature infants: A multisite, randomized trial. *The Journal of the American Medical Association, 263*, 3035–3042.

Ingels, S. J., Abraham, S. Y., Karr, R., Spencer, B. D., & Frankel, M. R. (1990). *User manual. National Educational Longitudinal Study of 1988*. Data Series DR-NELS: 88-88-1.2. U.S. Department of Education. Office of Educational Research and Improvement.

Jones, H. E., & Bayley, N. (1941). The Berkeley Growth Study. *Child Development, 12*, 167–173.

Kagan, J. (1964). American longitudinal research on psychological development. *Child Development, 35*, 1–32.

Kagan, J., & Moss, H. A. (1962). *Birth to maturity: A study of psychological development*. New York: Wiley.

Lazar, I., & Darlington, R. (1978). *Lasting effects after preschool: A report of the Consortium for Longitudinal Studies* (HEW Grant 90 c-1311). Washington, DC: U.S. Government Printing Office.

Magnusson, D., Bergman, L. R., Rudinger, G., & Torestad, B. (Eds.). (1991). *Problems and methods in longitudinal research: Stability and change*. New York: Cambridge University Press.

McCall, R. B., & Appelbaum, M. I. (1991). Some issues of conducting secondary analyses. *Developmental Psychology, 27*, 911–917.

McLaughlin, M. D., & Talbert, J. E. (1992). *Summary description of CRC core database: Integrating field and national survey research*. Report about cooperative agreement between Stanford University and the U.S. Department of Education (#OERI-G0087C235).

Mednick, S. A., Harway, M., & Finello K. M. (Eds.). (1984). *Handbook of longitudinal research*. New York: Praeger.

Menard, S. (1991). *Longitudinal research.* Newbury Park, CA: Sage.

The NICHD Early Child Care Network. (1993). *The National Institute of Child Health and Human Development (NICHD) Study of Early Child Care: A comprehensive longitudinal study of young children's lives.* ERIC Document #ED353087.

Sameroff, A., & Chandler, M. (1975). Reproductive risk and the continuum of caretaking causality. In F. D. Horowitz, M. Hetherington, S. Scarr-Salapatek, & G. Siegel (Eds.), *Review of child development research.* (Vol. 4, pp. 187–244). Chicago: University of Chicago Press.

Skeels, H. M. (1966). Adult status of children with contrasting early life experiences. *Monographs of the Society for Research in Child Development, 31* (3, Whole No. 105).

Stuart, H. C., & Reed, R. B. (1959). Description of project. Paper no. 1., *Pediatrics, 24,* 875–885.

Verdonik, F., & Sherrod, L. R. (1984). *An inventory of longitudinal research on childhood and adolescence.* New York: Social Science Research Council.

Young, C. H., Savola, K. L., & Phelps, E. (1991). *Inventory of longitudinal studies in the social sciences.* Newbury Park, CA: Sage.

Zaslow, M., Coiro, M. J., & Moore, K. (1993). *Methodological work within the jobs—Child and family subgroup study.* Paper presented at the American Statistical Association Meetings. Fort Lauderdale, FL, January 1993.

Developmental Theory, Prediction, and the Developmental Equation in Follow-up Research

Frances Degen Horowitz

INTRODUCTION

In the last 50 years we have seen considerable growth in our knowledge of human behavioral development, especially with respect to childhood. Yet, the broad outlines of the basic theories of development have, until the last few years, undergone little change. In discussing Gottlieb's recent theoretical proposal about experience serving as a canalizing agent in development (Gottlieb, 1991), Cairns began his commentary with the following observation: "The idea of development is as subtle as it is singular . . . . Gottlieb believes—correctly, I fear—that the revolutionary implications of the developmental perspective have been blurred by weak metaphors and trivialized by vague statements of 'interaction' and 'organization'" (Cairns, 1991 p. 23).

Indeed, the currently fashionable buzz words in the area of developmental theory discourse include such terms as interaction, organization, transaction, system, dynamic, and dynamical. The weakness of these terms as metaphors is not inherent in their meaning but rather in the fact that they often serve as euphemisms for the notion that development and behavior are complexly governed. The recognition of how fully complex our conceptualization of development needs to be is a welcome advance in thinking. This is especially true with respect to how we think about predicting developmental outcome. It has particular relevance for the theoretical perspective chosen to guide developmental follow-up research.

Early in the 1970s, developmental theories began to be classified and discussed in terms of whether they were organismic or mechanistic in orientation (Overton, 1984; Overton & Reese, 1973). Organismic and mechanistic were considered two different "world views" involving what were thought to be contradictory sets of assumptions. Piagetian theorizing and the cognitively oriented theories were classified as organismic; behaviorism was mechanistic. Freudian theory and social learning theory, with labels involving some variant of "dynamic," did not fit so easily into this dichotomy, but that was not enough to disturb the categorical approach.

Developmental theory discourse is, however, changing. A significant stirring among the heretofore polarized positions can be detected. A growing sophistication in the posing of research questions and in research methodology has provided reason to challenge the simpler theoretical distinctions (Konner, 1989). Advances in biology and the neurosciences are seen as having relevance for developmental behavioral research and the genotype/ phenotype distinctions are increasingly regarded as too simplistic (Oyama, 1985; Plomin, 1986, 1989). In recent years, the literature gives ample evidence that theoretical models involving multiple sets of assumptions have become much more attractive for thinking about development (Horowitz, 1980, 1987, 1989; Konner, 1989; van Geert, 1987, 1988).

Applying these theoretical advances to how we think about developmental prediction and developmental follow-up requires that we think in terms of what van Geert (1988) calls the "grammar" of developmental theories. The grammar of developmental theory refers to how the constituents of a theory are put together to tell the story of development. In this chapter, I discuss the range of components that need to be considered for a developmental theory grammar, as well as a set of propositions regarding behavioral development. I then apply the perspective that results in a theoretical approach to developmental follow-up research.

COMPONENTS OF DEVELOPMENTAL THEORY

Organization of Development: Sequences and Stages

The documentation of the regular sequencing of early motor development, along with descriptions of regular sequences in early mental development in children, are among the earliest observations in the field of child development (Baldwin, 1906; Gesell, 1925, 1928, 1933; Preyer, 1909a, 1909b). The notion of sequence is not equivalent to the notion of stage, though stages usually imply sequence. The concept of stage in developmental theory has typically been defined as a period in development bounded by ages in which there is a defining set of behaviors and characteristics. Gesell used the term "stage" as synonymous with an age period but did not further formalize the concept. Piagetian and Freudian theory are heavily invested in the idea of stage as the basic organization of the developmental sequence (Freud, 1905, 1917; Piaget, 1926, 1952), providing detailed descriptions of behaviors occurring in each stage. Behaviorism used the concept of stage only in the most colloquial sense.

The concepts of both sequence and stage have traditionally been accompanied with the surplus meaning of "fixed" and organismically based. The view adopted is that there is a sequence of events in a developmental course within a particular developmental domain, such as motor development, cognitive development, or language development. This sequence has a further organization in which there is a "chunking" of parts of the sequence into stages—the sensorimotor stage, the preoperational stage, the oral stage, and the anal stage. Children are described as going through these stages in a fixed sequence. The fixedness is often considered inherent in the nature of the organism.

Stage also has an extensive colloquial utility. Negativism is referred to as a stage. Adolescence is broadly considered a stage in development. A life span perspective of development makes reference to middle adulthood and aging as stages in life recalling Shakespeare's poetic representation of the stages of human ages. Stage thus becomes not so much a scientific concept as a shorthand heuristic for parsing development across time.

The evidence for sequences and stages is variable. There is strong documentation for sequence in embryological and motor development, and for many aspects of physical and physiological development (Tanner, 1970; Eichorn, 1970; Carmichael, 1954). The evidence as to whether or not there are clear discrete stages that mark off sections of the well-documented sequences is more negative than positive. The notion of stage applied to these domains remains still more of a colloquial than a scientific concept.

Although some general sequences have been verified in the areas of language and cognitive development, there is not strong support for Piaget's theory of stage as it relates to sensorimotor and cognitive development (Gelman & Baillargeon, 1983; Harris, 1983). In the area of language development, the current consensus rests more on evidence for the existence of a general developmental sequence in language acquisition skills (Rice, 1989) than on agreement about a stage organization per se.

The Freudian analysis of development is heavily invested in stage concepts with respect to social, emotional, and personality development. Freud's use of the notion of stage involved the operation of mechanisms and variables at different points in developmental time. His developmental theory can be thought of as among the more sophisticated of the stage theories. The stages Freud described are considered by many practicing Freudians to be clinically useful. Although their descriptive labels (oral, anal, oedipal, etc.) permeate the western world's thinking and actions in areas as diverse as everyday language, art, and literature, there has not been extensive objective verification that they exist or function as Freud described them.

The notion that there are sequences in behavioral development, especially in the early period of development, is widely accepted. It is not clear, however, whether some aspects of the sequences are conditioned by cultural and environmental task demands (Feldman, 1980). The evidence for the existence of stages in behavioral development is not strong, though, as has been noted, the concept of stage has widespread colloquial utility. There is also an aspect of this discussion of sequences and stages that is beginning to be scientifically and intellectually old-fashioned. The fact is that the developmental theory landscape has become more complex in the last several years. There are several efforts to advance developmental theory in the form of a number of important qualifications and considerations that have been introduced into the discourse.

The qualifications contributing to this complexity are several. First, there is the matter of the growing attention to the fact of some degree of interdependence among the domains of development. This is especially the case with respect to language and cognition and to emotion and cognition (Haviland & Kramer, 1991; Rice, 1989; Sternberg & Lubart, 1991). Second, there is no longer any reason to believe that sequences and stages (to the extent they exist) involve an automatic unfolding of events across time, independent of context. The social context is stressed by those who talk in terms of transactional systems (Sameroff, 1983), as well as by those who find Vygotsky's theory an important reference (Rogoff, 1982, 1990). Finally, discussions of development that are influenced by dynamical systems theory address the question of sequence and stage by focusing on multiple parameters affecting resource constraints that interact across more than one developmental domain (Fogel, 1990; Thelen, 1989; van Geert, 1991). We appear now to have embarked on an era of theory development that is rapidly making the old dichotomies obsolete.

Nature of the Organism

Any discussion of development requires recognition of the obvious fact that the human organism's development is influenced by genes, by physiological structure, and by biological function. Even as strong an advocate of environmental influence and the importance of experience as John B. Watson gave credit to the role of genes and structure in behavioral development (Watson, 1930; Horowitz, 1992). Additionally, the development of behavior in the human organism needs to be seen in an evolutionary context. This is a point of view shared by most developmentalists and psychologists, representing widely disparate intellectual traditions (e.g., Skinner, 1974; Hinde, 1983; Scarr-Salapatek, 1976).

At birth, the human organism's genetic, physiological, and biological characteristics reflect not only its evolutionary history, but also hereditary familial contributions, as well as environmental influences that affect the organism's development during the prenatal period. Environmental context and experience appear to be important even to genetic expression (Gottlieb, 1991; Oyama, 1985). There is also a growing appreciation for the complexity of gene–environment relationships across the life span (McCartney, Harris, & Bernieri, 1990; Loehlen, Horn, & Willerman, 1989).

In most instances, it is no longer reasonable to talk about genetic contributions to development independent of environment. Nor is there support for equating genetic with organismic influences. Organismic influences on the development of behavior can reflect genetic elements but be independent of genes. Modifications of organismic function and structure can occur as the result of infection or accident, or from the behavior of the individual in areas related to nutrition, smoking, alcohol, and drug ingestion. Exposure to injurious or beneficial environmental agents also affects organismic function and structure.

There are as yet many unanswered questions concerning the role that the nature of the organism plays in behavioral development given that the organism at any point in time reflects the cumulative effects of both genetic and environmental influences. It is likely that organismic contributions, summarized as individual differences, will be found in almost all developmental areas and across much if not all of the life span (Horowitz, 1987, 1989). Thus, some individuals will have greater or less susceptibility to the influence of environmental variables at a particular moment in developmental time. The level of susceptibility may or may not be stable across the life span. From this point of view, the success or failure of an environmental intervention will be determined by the nature of the intervention *and* by the response to the intervention as it is conditioned by organismically based individual differences.

Environment as Partner/Intervention

There is no development in the absence of environmental context. Yet, environment can be analyzed for its contextual role in development at a number of different levels ranging from the influence of an individual stimulus to the influence of the highly complex organization of environment in the form of culture (Bronfenbrenner, 1979; Bronfenbrenner & Crouter, 1983; Horowitz, 1987; Rogoff, 1990). Environment is also, as has been noted, a context for the expression and operation of genes (Gottlieb, 1991; Kuo, 1967; Oyama, 1985, 1989).

Our knowledge of how environment operates differentially at different levels to influence development exists in only the most general way. We do not know how to specify the functional units of environmental variables. Nor can we pinpoint, in many cases, how organism–environment interactions function. Yet, all the evidence we have about the general influence of environment leads us to the basic proposition that environmental variables are powerful and pervasive as partners in development.

Environmental variables appear to operate whether or not they are deliberately manipulated. For example, it is clear that environmental input is necessary for the normal development of language. For most normal children, language will develop in the absence of specific, consciously pursued, environmental manipulations, as long as there is some threshold of normal environmental experience. On the other hand, there are some children, especially those who have handicaps or disabilities, whose language development will be aided or made possible only by deliberate environmental interventions (Rice, 1989).

The notion of environmental determinism in developmental theory has been most often associated with the behaviorists. The conceptualization of environmental determinism in this tradition has made use of a broad definition of environment at many levels for theoretical purposes. Empirically, however, studies of environmental influence have been much more limited. The tests of the effects of environment on behavior have employed highly controlled environmental settings and/or quite specific conditions of reinforcement. Thus, behavior is described in terms of particular stimulus–response relationships and the stimulus conditions are, for the most part, quite proximal in nature. As a result, the environmentalist position has been seen from a relatively constricted focus.

Consideration of environmental influence need not be so limited. In many ways, the current interest in social context as conceptualized in a Vygotskian perspective is as much a position on environmentalism and environmental determinism as a Watsonian or Skinnerian point of view. Such a proposition requires acceptance of the notion that environment as social context gets defined in terms of a very complex set of variables involving both proximal and distal influences. Thus, social context can include family, neighborhood and school configurations, attitudes, socioeconomic conditions, cultural values, cultural patterns, the historical period, and national and transgenerational historical consciousness.

How the environment operates, whether it is defined by its proximal features of stimuli and responses or by its more complex characteristics as social context, remains an empirical question. It is possible to take the point of view that at the simple or complex level a certain amount of the functional aspects of environmental influence will ultimately be understood as the operation of principles that govern learning and learning opportunities (Horowitz, 1968, 1969, 1984, 1987, 1992). That is, learning and learning opportunities will define much of what is discussed as the effect of the environment.

Evidence for incorporating this point of view is already available. For example, Fischer's theory of cognitive development, focusing on "the control and construction of hierarchies of skills," gives explicit recognition to the role of operant learning in cognitive development (Fischer, 1980). The same is true in Hinde's discussion of the ethology of mother–infant attachment (Hinde, 1983). Also, van Geert's dynamical systems model of the growth of language and cognition provides for the contribution of the environmental variables external to the organism, including a motivational/energizing role for reinforcement (van Geert, 1991).

Continuities and Discontinuities: If, Then, Unless

It might be said of the behaviorists in relation to behavioral development that they were short on the description of the phenomena of development (i.e., what happens and when it happens) and long on principles or processes of behavioral acquisition. Gesell and the Piagetians, on the other hand, can be thought of as being long on the description of the phenomena of development and short on the principles that account for development. In this regard the Freudians are theoretically but not empirically long on both.

Questions regarding continuity and discontinuity in development are most often posed in terms of the stability or instability of measures of phenomena, such as attachment category or intelligence or temperament. Does the child's attachment category remain the same from one time to another? Is intelligence stable across age? Is an extremely shy child at the age of 2 also an extremely shy child at the age of 7? Attempts to answer such questions are fraught with difficulties.

The very nature of development is that the behavioral indices of phenomena, such as attachment, intelligence, and temperament, will change with age. When a securely attached 10-month-old turns out not to be observed to be securely attached at 4, when above-average intelligence at 3 is not found at 7, and when a shy 2-year-old is not a shy 7-year-old, several explanations are possible. One is that the measures that define the concept are different at the comparison ages and instabilities can therefore be attributed to measurement changes. Another possible explanation is that there are inherent developmental discontinuities across ages. This may be based on the notion that the developmental course involves a sequence of stages in development and that there is no necessary continuity in development from one stage to another.

Another approach is to suggest that the questions about continuity and discontinuity in development need a different focus. Instead of looking for continuity in terms of measures of a characteristic over two points in time, perhaps one needs to ask what processes have occurred that will account for continuities and what processes account for discontinuities.

Developmental theories that are not well stocked with process mechanisms to account for development and for the observations of continuity and discontinuity in development are weak theories. Similarly, developmental theories with a strong focus on the principles or processes of development but without concern for what develops are also weak developmental theories. Weak developmental theories are not necessarily unproductive for the field, nor are strong developmental theories necessarily fruitful. Piagetian theory is a weak theory on the process side but it stimulated important research that resulted in significant increases in descriptions of the phenomena of child development. Behaviorism is weak as a developmental theory but research in this tradition has been highly productive with respect to principles of learning. Freudian theory is a strong developmental theory but its empirical verification as an account of development is lacking. It can be considered as productive for developmental research with respect to some general parameters about the dynamic nature of development and for its focus on the influence of affective variables on development.

It is important to focus on processes in trying to understand the conditions that account for continuity and discontinuity in development because such focus brings one directly to the nature of laws in science. A scientific law typically takes the form of an "if, then" statement. An "if, then" form is fully applicable to the laws governing behavioral development, behavioral functioning, and developmental outcome at any given developmental time across the life span. The general form of an "if, then" law makes reference to outcomes that pertain "on average" and implies variation around some central tendency. Also implied is the further qualification of "if, then. . . unless."[1] "If, then. . . unless" is a form for stating a law pertaining to a general relationship that then gets qualified by the operation of particular variables: If a child is born with normal sensory abilities, then normal sensory development will occur, unless the level of sensory stimulation in the environment falls below a certain threshold; or, unless an infection or accident intervenes to destroy or modify significantly one of the sensory systems.

The "if, then . . . unless" statements are, in essence, equations that specify the givens in the form of relationships of variables and the weighting of variables within the relationships. "If, then . . . unless" statements can become extremely complex. Further, they will take up different sets of variables and weigh them differently at different times in developmental time. For example:

1. If the auditory system is intact and the level of normal informal language learning opportunities is at or above a minimum threshold, then normal language development will occur in the first 2 years of life, unless the auditory system is adversely affected by infection or accident.

[1] I am grateful to the participants in the discussion group at a meeting of the directors of the MacArthur Health Research Networks, who provided the stimulation that led to some of the ideas expressed in this section of the chapter.

2. If normal language development is occurring in the first 2 years of life, then the observed individual differences in rate of development will be a function of the child's receptivity to language learning opportunities *and* the degree to which the environment makes such opportunities available above a certain minimum threshold level *and* the degree to which the child's receptivity *and* the environmentally created opportunities are compatible, unless accident or infection or drastically unstable environmental conditions intervene.

These kinds of statements are obvious from the point of view of their content, but they also illustrate a basic point concerning continuities and discontinuities in development. Whether or not a continuity or discontinuity will be observed is a function of the degree to which the processes involved result in the same or a different relative outcome. The question is not whether there is or is not continuity in the level of language development. The question is whether the conditions or processes that account for language development are constituted with the same variables operating in the same relative relationships across time. Further, across longer periods of time, as new variables become relevant, stability or continuity will be found *if* the equation adjusts to produce continuity. If the equation is not adjusted, then the expectation should be for discontinuity.

The issue of continuity and discontinuity over developmental time is thus a function of the comparability of the equations that account for the processes at different periods. The equations can become as complex as the conditions require. They can be devised to include not only the child and his or her immediate surround but wider and wider circles of relevant social contexts as well.

Some aspects of behavioral development are more susceptible to variations in social context than others. The Structural/Behavioral model of development (Horowitz, 1987) makes the distinction between Universal behaviors and non-Universal behaviors. Universal behaviors, as the name implies, develop in all normal individuals in all normal environments and with little intentional teaching, although learning opportunities may be involved in their acquisition. Non-Universal behaviors are much more heavily dependent on learning opportunities and often on direct instruction. It follows, then, that continuities in the Universal behaviors will be a function of organismic stabilities, given relative environmental stabilities, whereas continuities and discontinuities in the non-Universal behaviors will be determined by both organismic and environmental stabilities and instabilities.

The relationship between organism and environment across development is governed by potentially different equations at different periods in development. Figure 1 presents the Structural/Behavioral model that depicts the theoretical possibilities of organism–environment transactions. As values on the organismic dimension change, comparable balancing changes will be required on the environmental dimension and vice versa in order for stability or continuity to occur. It must be stressed that this is a theoretical model and that in some instances there is now no known environmental compensation that can result in optimal development for some organismically based conditions.

The phenylketonuria story is the most dramatic example of changes in developmental outcome as a function of environmental compensation (in the form of nutritional intervention) for an organismically based difficulty (Berman, Waisman, & Graham, 1966). There are also instances involving organismically normal children who are being reared in environments judged not to be developmentally facilitative. In this instance, where an environmental intervention is attempted, the goal is to affect developmental outcome by providing a more developmentally facilitative environment than the children would otherwise experience. Such intervention research has produced mixed results. In some instances early dramatic improvements were not always sustained (Garber, 1988; Garber & Heber, 1977). Critics of such intervention efforts have attributed the findings to an inherent discontinuity in develop-

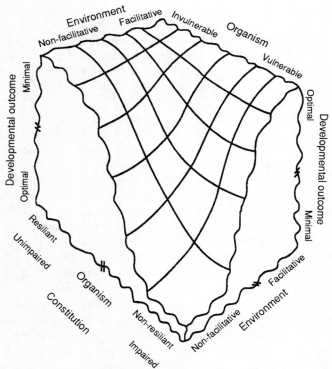

Figure 1   The Structural/Behavioral model as adapted from Horowitz, 1987.

ment or to ultimate genetic determination (Jensen, 1989; Garber & Hodge, 1989). The issues raised here have direct relevance to how developmental theory and expectations about development find their way into developmental follow-up research.

PRINCIPLES OF DEVELOPMENTAL DYNAMICS

It is certainly clear that the dichotomy of theoretical world views of behavioral development into organismic and mechanistic are no longer warranted. Not only has our knowledge base about development and its complexity taken us beyond that but more sophisticated formulations of developmental theory have changed the nature of the discourse. What follows here is an attempt to extract from the literature a set of principles about the dynamics of behavioral development that can serve to stimulate and guide research of both a basic and an applied nature.

Principle 1.

All behavior begins as potential and no behavior is predetermined or automatically unfolds into the repertoire during development.

This principle has its basis in the ideas of Kuo (1967), Schneirla (1957, 1966), and Gottlieb (1991).

Principle 2.

Individual behavioral potentials and the actualization of behavioral capability are influenced by proximal and distal heredity, by biological and social context, by opportunities to learn, and by capacity and resource regulators that reflect constraints in biological and social systems.

This principle has its basis in the ideas of those just cited as well as Oyama (1985, 1989), Plomin (1986, 1989), Seligman (1970; Seligman & Hager, 1972), Horowitz (1987), von Bertalanffy, (1968, 1975), Skinner (1974), Thelen (1989), and van Geert (1991).

Principle 3.

Behavioral development will follow the path of least adjustment of organism and environment unless deliberate interventions occur.

Principle 4.

There is a universal human behavioral repertoire that is acquired by all normal human organisms in minimally normal environments.

Principle 5.

The human organism has the potential to acquire behaviors in addition to the universal behaviors and the acquisition of these behaviors is determined entirely by opportunities to learn the behaviors.

Principle 3 follows from the ideas presented by Horowitz (1987), and principles 4 and 5 are elaborated on in this work.

There are several issues related to behavioral development on which these principles are silent but which are subsumed by the principles. One of these involves the question of existence of sequences and stages in behavioral development. In discussing stages in the context of the Structural/Behavioral model, a suggestion was made that a stage might be defined as a period of time during which there is stability in the nature and form of the equation affecting behavioral acquisition (Horowitz, 1987). Support for this idea can be found in the work of van Geert (1991). Working from a dynamical systems approach, van Geert has presented a compelling, quantitatively based model for cognitive and language development and tested it against data. Stages are seen in van Geert's model as resulting when there are large changes in the relationships and functions of what he describes as the *resource* and *control* variables operating in a system. These resource and control variables serve to shape the development of behavior within a period of time and thus give an *empirical* basis for a stage concept. When the resource and control variables change, a new set of dynamics (processes) come into play—a new stage has arrived. The model appears to account for data on cognitive and language development: It remains to be seen whether or not it generalizes to other developmental domains.

Another issue not addressed by the five principles is the relationship between domains of development. We can suppose that there is much more developmental interrelatedness than currently thought. Cognitive and language development have been studied for their interactions and these systems do appear to interact to some degree. If one broadens language development to consider the development of communicative skills, then it is likely that development in the emotional/affective system will be shown to be very relevant to communicative development and much affected by social context and culture.

The principles of developmental dynamics listed here are by no means a complete set of principles, nor could one assert that they will remain unchanged as we learn more about development. Nevertheless, they can serve, along with the perspective adopted in the preceding discussion, as a basis from which to consider the relevance of developmental theory to developmental follow-up research.

PREDICTING DEVELOPMENTAL OUTCOMES IN FOLLOW-UP RESEARCH

The understanding of human behavioral development rests on our having a good account of the general course of behavioral development as well as the individual course. It is the latter, embodying as it does the entire area of individual differences as well as the question of continuity and discontinuity in development, that is most involved in the issue of whether or not we can predict individual developmental outcome.

If one takes the position that the level of development of most behavioral characteristics of interest is fixed by organismic characteristics, then the question of predicting individual developmental outcome becomes one of trying to obtain the earliest reliable measure of the behavior for the purposes of projecting to the future. This model has some utility in physical growth. Adult height can be predicted with very good accuracy from nine years of age on by using a metric involving chronological age, bone age, and present height (Tanner, 1970)—unless, of course, there are occurrences of accident or illness or serious malnutrition that intervene.

The early efforts to devise a test of infant intelligence were fueled by a belief that IQ was a fixed characteristic of the organism and that an early infant measure of it would predict adult IQ (Bayley, 1933). The results did not permit the conclusion that the early infant measure of intelligence was predictive of later intelligence.

The quest has recently been revived in the form of studies of infant visual novelty preference and its ability to predict later intelligence (Fagan, 1984; Fagan & McGrath, 1981; Fagan & Singer, 1983; McCall, 1989, 1990; Rose, Feldman, Wallace, & McCarton, 1989; Rose & Feldman, 1990). The results appear now to be more successful. Claims for stability or continuity of intelligence as a function of organismic characteristics are again being made. As with the early effort, however, one must question the model on which the basic proposition for continuity is based. The problem with all these efforts is not in the findings of moderate, typically significant relationships between an early measure of behavior and later intelligence but in the rather simple model of development that is implied by the interpretations.

It is time to relinquish the simple models of prediction and adopt ones that attempt to approximate the complexity of human behavioral development. A review of recent literature on longitudinal and follow-up studies is encouraging in this regard. Continuities and discontinuities in intelligence are being discussed in terms of models involving multiple variables following different paths. For instance, in one major longitudinal study, contextual risk factors affecting IQ outcomes were found to be moderated by maternal teaching style and by child attentional behavior (Barocas et al., 1991). In another study, maternal teaching styles were found to influence IQ through relationships that appeared to strengthen the acquisition of efficient self-regulatory behaviors (Mischel, Shoda, & Rodriguez, 1989). In still another study, the distinction was made between contemporary or "near-in" predictors of adaptation in middle childhood and earlier predictors to assess the incremental contribution to prediction from different sources (Sroufe, Egeland, & Kreutzer, 1990).

Of interest is not only that more complex models are appearing in the literature, but that the way in which significant relationships are being discussed is being qualified. These qualifications lead to the position that there is no reason to talk about a significant correlation of .36 or .40 as indicative of a prediction. Rather, such findings should be discussed in terms of *how much of the variance* is being accounted for by the correlation. The goal is to account for as much of the variance as possible, to tell the developmental story as fully as possible.

A measure at one time and a measure at a later time, if yielding a significant correlation, account for a particular amount of the variance. That is the beginning, not the end, of the story. The question is what else, between those occasions in time and contemporaneously with the outcome measure, can be added to the equation to account for more of the outcome variance. The addition of these intervening and contemporaneous events will, in some cases, increase the finding of continuity; in some instances, the result will be a finding of discontinuity or what Belsky and his colleagues have recently discussed in terms of "lawful discontinuity" (Belsky, Fish, & Isabella, 1991). The emphasis here should be on "lawful." With enough knowledge, one ought to be able to *predict* continuities and discontinuities.

The Structural/Behavioral model shown in Figure 1 and the developmental dynamics principles previously listed can be used to specify when to expect continuities in developmental outcome and when to expect discontinuities. A constant relationship between organism and environment such that both organismic characteristics and the nature or adequacy of the environment for facilitating development stay the same should produce continuities. Shifts in one dimension, *if* compensated for directly in the other dimension, should also result in continuities. Shifts in one dimension not compensated for by a comparable shift in the other dimensions should produce discontinuities.

Continuities and discontinuities occurring "naturally," that is, without deliberate interventions on either the organismic or environmental dimensions are the result of development following the path of least resistance. Theoretically, interventions can alter that path, creating either continuities or discontinuities as a result. Practically, the ability of deliberate interventions to alter the path is limited by our knowledge and ability with respect to manipulating environmental and or organismic variables. Interventions that are not deliberate can occur that produce the shifts in organismic and/or environmental variables. All of these combinations and the outcomes that ensue exemplify what has been described as the "if, then . . . unless" form that must ultimately guide how we think about development, how we think about interventions, and how we think about the results from longitudinal and follow-up research.

Accounting for the grammar of development will continue to require models that approximate the complexity of development. There is no reason to expect that developmental outcome will be accounted for by anything less than an understanding of the variables and their relationships and how they constitute themselves into the equations describing development and developmental processes over time. The kind of complex models that must now inform developmental research will require the questions to be phrased in terms of how much of the variance in the outcome we can account for and what more we need to know to increase the amount of variance we can account for—especially with respect to the events that occur between two occasions of measurement. From this point of view, it follows that lawful development will only be understood in terms of the conditions that produce continuities and the conditions that produce discontinuities.

REFERENCES

Baldwin, J. M. (1906). *Mental development in the child and the race.* New York: Macmillan.

Barocas, R., Seifer, R., Sameroff, A. J., Andrews, T. A., Croft, R. T., & Ostrow, E. (1991). Social and interpersonal determinants of developmental risk. *Developmental Psychology, 27,* 479–488.

Bayley, N. (1933). Mental growth during the first three years. *Genetic Psychology Monographs, 14,* 1–92.

Belsky, J., Fish, M., & Isabella, R. (1991). Continuity and discontinuity in infant negative and positive emotionality: Family antecedents and attachment consequences. *Developmental Psychology, 27,* 421–431.

Berman, P. W., Waisman, H. A., & Graham, F. K. (1966). Intelligence in treated phenylketonuria children—A developmental study. *Child Development, 37,* 731–747.

Bronfenbrenner, U. (1979). *The ecology of human development: Experiments by nature and design.* Cambridge, MA: Harvard University Press.

Bronfenbrenner, U., & Crouter, A. C. (1983). The evolution of environmental models in developmental research. In P. H. Mussen (Ed.), *Handbook of child psychology* (4th ed., Vol. 1). W. Kessen (Ed.), *History, theory and methods* (pp. 357–414). New York: Wiley.

Cairns, R. B. (1991). Multiple metaphors for a singular idea. *Developmental Psychology, 27,* 23–26.

Carmichael, L. (1954). The onset and early development of behavior. In L. Carmichael (Ed.), *Manual of child psychology* (pp. 60–185). New York: Wiley.

Eichorn, D. (1970). Physiological development. In P. H. Mussen (Ed.), *Carmichael's manual of child psychology* (Vol. 1, pp. 157–283). New York: Wiley.

Fagan, J. (1984). The relationship of novelty preferences during infancy to later intelligence and later recognition memory. *Intelligence, 8,* 339–346.

Fagan, J., & McGrath, S. K. (1981). Infant recognition memory and later intelligence. *Intelligence, 5,* 121–130.

Fagan, J., & Singer, L. (1983). Infant recognition memory as a measure of intelligence. In L. Lipsitt & C. Rovee-Collier (Eds.), *Advances in infancy research* (Vol. 2, pp. 31–78). Norwood, NJ: Ablex.

Feldman, D. H. (1980). *Beyond universals in cognitive development.* New York: Ablex.

Fischer, K. W. (1980). A theory of cognitive development: The control and construction of hierarchies of skills. *Psychological Review, 87,* 477–531.

Fogel, A. (1990). The process of developmental change in infant communicative action: Using dynamic systems theory to study individual ontogenies. In J. Colombo & J. Fagen (Eds.), *Individual differences in infancy: Reliability, stability, prediction* (pp. 341–358). Hillsdale, NJ: Lawrence Erlbaum.

Freud, S. (1905). Three essays on the theory of sexuality. In J. Strachey (Ed.), *The standard edition of the complete psychological works* (Vol. 17). London, UK: Hogarth Press.

Freud, S. (1917). Introductory lectures on psychoanalysis. *The standard edition of the complete psychological works of Sigmund Freud* (Vols. 15, 16). London, UK: Hogarth Press.

Garber, H. L. (1988). *The Milwaukee Project*. Washington, DC: American Association on Mental Retardation.

Garber, H. L., & Heber, R. (1977). The Milwaukee Project: Indications of the effectiveness of early intervention in preventing mental retardation. In P. Mittler (Ed.), *Research to practice in mental retardation: Care and intervention* (Vol. 1). Baltimore: University Park Press.

Garber, H. L., & Hodge, J. D. (1989). Reply: Risk for deceleration in rate of mental development. *Developmental Review, 9*, 259–300.

Gelman, R., & Baillargeon, R. (1983). A review of some Piagetian concepts. In P. H. Mussen (Ed.), *Handbook of child psychology* (Vol. 3). J. H. Flavell & E. M. Markman (Eds.), *Cognitive development* (pp. 167–230). New York: Wiley.

Gesell, A. (1925). *The mental growth of the preschool child.* New York: Macmillan.

Gesell, A. (1928). *Infancy and Human Growth.* New York: Macmillan.

Gesell, A. L. (1933). Maturation and the patterning of behavior. In C. Murchinson (Ed.), *A handbook of child psychology.* Worcester, MA: Clark University Press.

Gottlieb, G. (1991). Experiential canalization of behavioral development: Theory. *Developmental Psychology, 27*, 4–13.

Harris, P. L. (1983). Infant cognition. In P. H. Mussen (Ed.), M. M. Haith & J. J. Campos (Vol. Eds.), *Handbook of child psychology: Vol. 2. Infancy psychobiology* (pp. 689–782). New York: Wiley.

Haviland, J. M., & Kramer, D. A. (1991). Affect-Cognition relationships in adolescent diaries: The case of Anne Frank. *Human Development, 34*, 143–159.

Hinde, R. A. (1983). Ethnology and child development. In P. H. Mussen (Ed.), M. M. Haith & J. J. Campos (Vol. Eds.), *Handbook of child psychology: Vol. 2. Infancy & developmental psychobiology* (pp. 27–93). New York: Wiley.

Horowitz, F. D. (1968). Infant learning and development—Retrospect and prospect. *Merrill-Palmer Quarterly, 14*, 101–120.

Horowitz, F. D. (1969). Learning, developmental research, and individual differences. In L. P. Lipsitt & H. W. Reese (Eds.), *Advances in child development and behavior* (Vol. 4, pp. 84–126). New York: Academic Press.

Horowitz, F. D. (1980). Intervention and its effects on early development: What model of development is appropriate? In R. Turner & H. W. Reese (Eds.), *Life-span developmental psychology: Intervention* (pp. 235–248). New York: Academic Press.

Horowitz, F. D. (1984). The psychobiology of parent–offspring relations in high-risk situations. In L. P. Lipsitt & C. Rovee-Collier (Eds.), *Advances in infancy research* (Vol. 3, pp. 1–22). Norwood, NJ: Ablex.

Horowitz, F. D. (1987). *Exploring developmental theories: Toward a structural/behavioral model of development.* Hillsdale, NJ: Lawrence Erlbaum.

Horowitz, F. D. (1989). Using developmental theory to guide the search for the effects of biological risk factors on the development of children. *Journal of Clinical Nutrition, 50*, 589–597.

Horowitz, F. D. (1992). John B. Watson's legacy: Learning and environment. *Developmental Psychology, 28*, 360–367.

Jensen, A. R. (1989). Raising IQ without increasing g: A review of "The Milwaukee Project: Preventing mental retardation in children at risk." *Developmental Review, 9*, 234–258.

Konner, M. J. (1989). Spheres and modes of inquiry: Integrative challenges in child development research. In P. R. Zelazo & R. G. Barr (Eds.), *Challenges to developmental paradigms: Implications for theory assessment and treatment* (pp. 227–258). Hillsdale, NJ: Lawrence Erlbaum.

Kuo, Z. Y. (1967). *The dynamics of behavioral development.* New York: Random House.

Loehlen, J. C., Horn, J. W., & Willerman, L. (1989). Modeling IQ change: Evidence from the Texas Adoption Project. *Child Development, 60,* 993–1004.

McCall, R. B. (1989). Issues in predicting later IQ from infant habituation rate and recognition memory performance. *Human Development, 32,* 177–186.

McCall, R. B. (1990). Infancy research: Individual differences. *Merrill-Palmer Quarterly, 36,* 141–157.

McCartney, K., Harris, M. J., & Bernieri, F. (1990). Growing up and growing apart: A developmental meta-analysis of twin studies. *Psychological Bulletin, 107,* 226–237.

Mischel, W., Shoda, Y., & Rodriguez, M. L. (1989). Delay of gratification in children. *Science, 224,* 933–938.

Overton, W. F. (1984). World views and their influence on psychological theory and research: Kuhn-Lakatos-Laudan. In H. W. Reese (Ed.), *Advances in child development and behavior* (Vol. 18, pp. 191–226). New York: Academic Press.

Overton, W. F., & Reese, H. W. (1973). Models of development: Methodological implications. In J. R. Nesselwade & H. W. Reese (Eds.), *Life-span developmental psychology: Methodological issues* (pp. 65–86). New York: Academic Press.

Oyama, S. (1985). *The ontogeny of information.* Cambridge, UK: Cambridge University Press.

Oyama, S. (1989). Ontogeny and the central dogma: Do we need a concept of genetic programming in order to have an evolutionary perspective? In M. R. Gunnar & E. Thelen (Eds.), *Systems and development. The Minnesota symposia on child psychology* (Vol. 22). Hillsdale, NJ: Lawrence Erlbaum

Piaget, J. (1926). *The language and thought of the child.* New York: Harcourt, Brace.

Piaget, J. (1952). *The origins of intelligence in children.* New York: International Universities Press.

Plomin, R. (1986). *Development, genetics and psychology.* Hillsdale, NJ: Lawrence Erlbaum.

Plomin, R. (1989). Environment and genes: Determinants of behavior. *American Psychologist, 44,* 105–111.

Preyer, W. (1909a). *The mind of the child: Part II. The development of the intellect.* New York: Appleton (Published originally in German, 1881–1882).

Preyer, W. (1909b). *The mind of the child: Part I. The senses and the will.* New York: Appleton (published originally in German 1881–1882).

Rice, M. L. (1989). Children's language acquisition. *American Psychologist, 44,* 149–156.

Rogoff, B. (1982). Integrating context and cognitive development. In M. E. Lamb & A. L. Brown (Eds.), *Advances in developmental psychology* (Vol. 2, pp. 125–170). Hillsdale, NJ: Lawrence Erlbaum.

Rogoff, B. (1990). *Apprenticeship in Thinking.* New York: Oxford University Press.

Rose, S. A., & Feldman, J. F. (1990). Infant cognition: Individual differences and developmental continuities. In J. Colombo & J. Fagen (Eds.), *Individual differences in infancy* (pp. 229–245). Hillsdale, NJ: Lawrence Erlbaum.

Rose, S. A., Feldman, J. F., Wallace, J. F., & McCarton, C. (1989). Infant visual attention: Relation to birth status and developmental outcome during the first 5 years. *Developmental Psychology, 25,* 560–576.

Sameroff, A. J. (1983). Developmental systems: Contexts and evolution. In P. H. Mussen (Ed.), W. Kessen (Vol. Ed.), *Handbook of child psychology: Vol 1. History, theory and methods* (pp. 273–294). New York: Wiley.

Scarr-Salapatek, S. (1976). An evolutionary perspective on infant intelligence. In M. Lewis (Ed.), *Origins of intelligence: Infancy and early childhood* (165–197). New York: Plenum.

Schneirla, T. C. (1957). The concept of development in comparative psychology. In D. B. Harris (Ed.), *The concept of development* (pp. 78–108). Minneapolis, MN: University of Minnesota Press.

Schneirla, T. C. (1966). Behavioral development and comparative psychology. *The Quarterly Review of Biology, 41,* 283–302.

Seligman, M. E. P. (1970). On the generality of the laws of learning. *Psychological Review, 77,* 406–418.

Seligman, M. E. P., & Hagar, J. L. (1972). *Biological Boundaries of Learning.* Englewood Cliffs, NJ: Prentice Hall.

Skinner, B. F. (1974). *About behaviorism.* New York: Alfred A. Knopf.

Sternberg, R. J., & Lubart, T. I. (1991). An investment theory of creativity and its development. *Human Development, 34,* 1–31.

Sroufe, L. A., Egeland, B., & Kreutzer, T. (1990). The fate of early experience following developmental change: Longitudinal approaches in childhood. *Child Development, 61,* 1363–1373.

Tanner, J. M. (1970). Physical growth. In P. H. Mussen (Ed.), *Carmichael's manual of child psychology* (Vol. 1, pp. 77–156). New York: Wiley.

Thelen, E. (1989). Self-organization in developmental processes: Can systems approaches work? In M. R. Gunner & E. Thelen (Eds.), *Systems and development. Minnesota symposia on child psychology* (Vol. 22, pp. 77–117). Hillsdale, NJ: Lawrence Erlbaum.

van Geert, P. (1987). The structure of developmental theories. *Human Development, 30,* 160–177.

van Geert, P. (1988). Graph-theoretical representation of the structure of developmental models. *Human Development, 31,* 107–135.

van Geert, P. (1991). A dynamic systems model of cognitive and language growth. *Psychological Review, 98,* 3–53.

von Bertalanffy, L. (1968). *General system theory* (rev. ed.). New York: George Braziller.

von Bertalanffy, L. (1975). *Perspectives on general system theory.* New York: George Braziller.

Watson, J. B. (1930). *Behaviorism.* New York: W. W. Norton (1970 Norton Library edition).

Ecological Perspectives on Longitudinal Follow-up Studies

Arnold Sameroff

INTRODUCTION

The idea that "the child is the father of the man" has a strong tradition in behavioral science. Such a linear model justified a search for biological or behavioral indicators in childhood that foreshadowed later emotional or cognitive disturbances. However, longitudinal studies of child development have provided a number of surprises and have offered little support for such views. Research findings have led to the following conclusions:

1. Individual differences in cognitive competence can be explained largely by differences in social environment.
2. Social contexts have substantial continuity, which may explain continuities of functioning within individuals that appear to be constitutional.
3. Theories of human development need to integrate biological, psychological, and environmental factors to make successful predictions about human development.

What are the data that have forced us to move from a singular focus on individual differences in children as the major determiners of developmental outcomes to a concern with differences in their life experiences? Retrospective data from epidemiological research was suggestive that children with a variety of disorders, from mental retardation to schizophrenia, had significantly greater rates of birth complications than children who did not have these disorders (Pasamanick & Knobloch, 1961). The effects of birth complications on later behavior was explained by a linear causal model connecting the early condition of the child with later developmental outcomes. Experience was thought to play only a minor role in producing mental illness or retardation.

To test this hypothesis generated in studies using retrospective data, a large number of prospective studies were conducted in which infants with birth complications were followed longitudinally to observe their outcomes. Surprisingly, the vast majority of children with birth complications grew up to show no evidence of their poor biological origins (Sameroff & Chandler, 1975; Sameroff, 1986). What was even more surprising was that social conditions were much better predictors of outcome for these children than either their early biological status, as measured by birth and pregnancy complications, or their psychological status, as measured by developmental scales (Broman, Nichols, & Kennedy, 1975).

In a study of the development of several hundred infants in the Louisville Twin Study, R. S. Wilson (1985) reported the correlation between biological factors, social factors, and the children's developmental status from birth to 6 years of age. In Figure 1, correlations are shown between two physical factors, birthweight and gestational age; two environmental factors, mother's education and family socioeconomic status (SES); and child mental test scores at 6, 12, 18, 24, 36, and 72 months of age. Although the two social factors are uncorrelated with developmental quotients during the first year of life, they become more potent predictors of intelligence than the two biological factors during the second year.

Strong evidence that social disadvantage was a more powerful predictor of developmental problems than biological condition led to the establishment of intervention programs that proposed to modify the early environment of lower SES children with a major goal of increasing their intellectual performance. These early intervention programs were based on traditional models of child development in which children who were identified as doing poorly early in life were expected to continue to do poorly. An early childhood education movement, as exemplified in the Headstart program, was proposed to improve the learning and social competence of children during the preschool years with the expectation that these improvements would be maintained into later life. Indeed, developmental scores went up for those children in early intervention programs. Unfortunately, follow-up research of such children has found that the major positive changes in their behavior

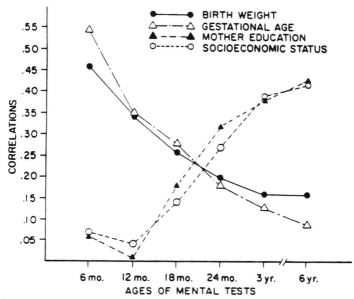

Figure 1   Relation of biological and social factors to mental test scores from 6 months to 6 years of age (Wilson, 1985).

that resulted from their preschool experience began to disappear as soon as they entered their regular elementary school system and only moderate gains were maintained into adolescence (Zigler & Trickett, 1978); although on the positive side, there were reduced rates of school failure and need for special education (Lazar, Darlington, Murray, Royce, & Snipper, 1982; Schweinhart & Weikart, 1980).

In the two research areas we have discussed, early characteristics of the child have been overpowered by factors in the later environmental context of development. Where family and cultural variables have fostered development, children with severe perinatal complications have been indistinguishable from children without complications. Where social context variables have hindered development, children from the best preschool intervention programs have developed social and cognitive deficits when supportive social programs ended. When predictions on how children will turn out are based on their early behavior, these predictions are generally wrong. When such predictions are based on their continuing life circumstances, the predictions are generally better. In this domain, an understanding of environments may have greater developmental importance than an understanding of the child at any single point in time.

ROCHESTER LONGITUDINAL STUDY

In the Rochester Longitudinal Study (RLS) my colleagues and I also found social class to be associated with developmental risk (Sameroff, Seifer, & Zax, 1982). The RLS is a study of the development of several hundred children from birth through early adolescence assessing environmental factors as well as the cognitive and social competence of the children. When we compared the development of the 262 children in our sample from different SES groupings from birth to 4 years, we found results similar to those of the Louisville Twin Study (R. S. Wilson, 1985). In Figure 2, no evidence of SES differences in developmental status at 4 and 12 months is seen, but by 30 months and again at 48 months there were clear, reliable differences with children from higher SES groups performing at higher levels than children from lower SES groups.

Although SES is the best single variable for predicting children's IQ scores, we were unsatisfied by the lack of psychological content in this sociological variable. We decided to subdivide the global variable of social class to see if we could identify factors that acted as environmental risks more directly connected to the child. The factors we chose ranged from proximal variables such as the mother's interaction with the child, to intermediate variables such as the mother's mental health, to distal variables such as the financial resources of the family.

Although causal models have been sought in which singular variables uniquely determine aspects of child behavior, a series of studies in many different areas have found that, except at the extremes of biological dysfunction, it is the number rather than the nature of risk factors that are the best determinants of outcome. This was true for neurological factors in samples of infants with many perinatal problems (Parmelee & Haber, 1973), for family factors in samples of children with many psychosocial problems (Rutter,

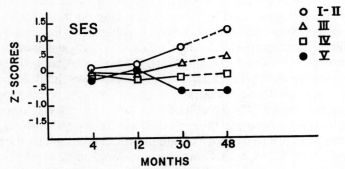

Figure 2   Mental test scores during infancy and early childhood for 215 children in different SES groups (Sameroff & Zax, 1978).

1979), and for both biological and family factors in multirisk families (Greenspan, 1981).

From the 4-year assessment of the children in the RLS, we chose a set of 10 environmental variables that are correlates of SES but not equivalents (Sameroff, Seifer, Barocas, Zax, & Greenspan, 1987). We then tested whether poor cognitive development in our preschool children was a function of low SES or the compounding of environmental risk factors found in low-SES groups.

The 10 environmental risk variables, presented in Table I, were (1) a history of maternal mental illness, with more than one psychiatric contact, (2) high maternal anxiety, (3) a parental perspectives score derived from a combination of measures that reflected rigidity in the attitudes, beliefs, and values that mothers had in regard to their child's development, (4) few positive maternal interactions with the child observed during infancy, (5) minimal maternal education, (6) head of household in unskilled occupation, (7) disadvantaged minority status, (8) reduced family support, (9) stressful life events, and (10) large family size.

When these risk factors were related to the child's 4-year verbal intelligence, major differences were found between those children with few risks and those with many. Children with no environmental risks scored more than 30 points higher than children with eight or nine risk factors, as can be seen in Figure 3. On average, each risk factor reduced the child's IQ score by 4 points.

These data support the view that IQ scores for 4-year-old children are multiply determined by variables in the social context, but the possibility exists that poverty may still be an overriding variable. To test for this possibility, two additional analyses were completed. The first analysis was to determine if there were consistencies in the distribution of risk factors, that is,

Table I   Summary of Family and Social Risk Variables

Risk variables	Low risk	High risk
Chronicity of mental illness	0–1 contact	More than 1 contact
Maternal anxiety	75% least	25% most
Parental perspectives	75% highest	25% lowest
Spontaneous interaction	75% most	25% least
Education	High school	No high school
Occupation	Skilled	Semi- or unskilled
Minority status	White	Nonwhite
Family support	Father present	Father absent
Stressful life events	75% fewest	25% most
Family size	1–3 children	4 or more children

Note. From Sameroff, Seifer, Barocas, Zax, and Greenspan (1987).

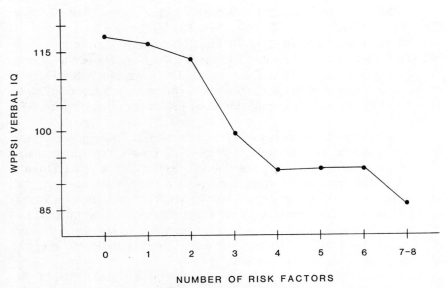

Figure 3   Relation between environmental multiple risk scores and children's IQ scores at 4 years (*n* = 215; Sameroff, Seifer, Barocas, Zax, & Greenspan, 1987).

were the same factors always present. The second analysis was to determine if the relation between more risk factors and lower intelligence could be found in high-SES as well as low-SES families.

For the first type of analysis, data from families having a moderate score of 3, 4, or 5 risk factors were cluster analyzed. The families fell into five clusters with different sets of high-risk conditions that are listed in Table II.

Different combinations of factors appear in each cluster. Cluster 2 has no overlapping variables with clusters 3, 4, or 5. Minority status is a risk variable in clusters 3, 4, and 5, but does not appear in clusters 1 or 2. Despite these differences in the specific risks among families, the mean IQs were not different for children in the five clusters, ranging from 92.8 to 97.7. Thus, it seems that it was not any single variable but the combination of multiple variables that reduced the child's intellectual performance. In every family situation a unique set of risk or protective factors was related to child outcome.

For the second analysis, the sample was split into high and low SES groups and the effect of increased number of risks was examined within each social class group. The effects of the multiple risk score were as clear within SES groups as well as for the population at large. The more risk factors, the worse the child outcomes for both high- and low-SES families, as seen in Figure 4.

These analyses of the RLS data were attempts to elaborate environmental risk factors by reducing global measures such as SES to component social

Table II   Cluster Analysis of Families With
Moderate Multiple-Risk Scores

Cluster	Risk variables
Cluster 1	Mental health
	Family support
	Mother education
	Maternal anxiety
Cluster 2	Mother–infant interaction
	Mental health
	Maternal anxiety
Cluster 3	Family support
	Minority status
Cluster 4	Mother education
	Minority status
	Occupation
Cluster 5	Parental perspectives
	Minority status
	Mother education

Note. From Sameroff, Seifer, Barocas, Zax, and
Greenspan (1987).

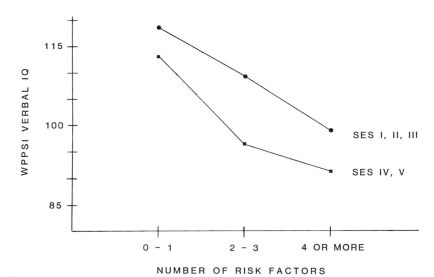

Figure 4   Relation between environmental multiple risk scores and children's 4-year IQ scores
in high (*n* = 73) and low (*n* = 142) SES groups (Sameroff, Seifer, Barocas, Zax, & Greenspan,
1987).

and behavioral variables. We were able to identify a set of risk factors that were predominantly found in lower SES groups, but also affected child outcomes in all social classes. Moreover, no single variable was determinant of outcome. Only in families with multiple risk factors was the child's competence placed in jeopardy. In the analyses of intellectual outcomes, none of the children in the low multiple-risk group had an IQ below 85, whereas 24% of the children in the high multiple-risk group did, a ratio of more than 24 to 1. Conversely, only 4% of the high risk children had IQs above 115, whereas 55% of the low risk children did, a ratio of 14 to 1.

The multiple pressures of environmental context in terms of amount of stress from the environment, the family's resources for coping with that stress, the number of children that must share those resources, and the parents' flexibility in understanding and dealing with their children all play a role in the fostering or hindrance of children's intellectual competencies.

MODELS OF DEVELOPMENT

Theories of development have varied in the emphasis they place on contributions the characteristics of the person and characteristics of the environment make to later behavior. Although this debate can be treated as merely an academic discussion, it has important ramifications for the utilization of vast amounts of social resources. From intervention efforts that cost millions of dollars to the educational system that costs billions, practitioners rationalize their efforts on the basis of scientific knowledge. One of the major flaws in such knowledge is an inadequate conceptualization of the environment. Bronfenbrenner and Crouter (1983) have traced the history of empirical investigations of the environment and have shown how theoretical limitations have limited the sophistication of research paradigms. The goal of this chapter is to expand on our understanding of the environment to lay a basis for more complex paradigms in both research and practice.

The significance of nature and nurture for development can be viewed from two perspectives: The first is whether they make a contribution at all and the second is whether these contributions are active ones or passive ones. Riegel (1978) placed models of development into four categories reflecting various combinations of passive and active persons and environments. Into the passive person–passive environment category he placed mechanistic theories that arose from the empiricist philosophy of Locke and Hume in which combinations of events that occur in the environment in the presence of observers are imprinted into their minds. This view has been the basis for learning theories in which factors such as the continuity, frequency, or recency of stimuli determine how they will be coded into the receiving mind.

In a second category, the passive person is combined with an active environment. In this category are Skinnerian approaches to behavior modification in which the conditioner actively structures the input to alter the person's behavior in particular directions, and the person is assumed to make no contribution to the outcome independent of experience.

The third category contains the concept of the active person but retains the passive environment. In this grouping fall the cognitive theories of Piaget and the linguistic views of Chomsky. Piaget sees the person as an active constructor of knowledge based on experience with the environment. The environment is a necessary part of development, but it has no active role in structuring thought or action. Similarly, Chomsky sees language development as the person's application of innate linguistic categories to linguistic experience. The organization of that experience is not a determinant of language competence.

In the fourth category are models that combine an active person and an active environment. Riegel sees these models as deriving from Marx's interpretations of the dialectical nature of development in which the actions of the individual change reality, then, in turn, the changes in reality affect the behavior of the individual. Sameroff and Chandler (1975) captured this process in their transactional model of development. In this view, developmental outcomes are not a product of the initial characteristics of the child or the context or even their combination. Outcomes are the result of the interplay between child and context across time, in which the state of one impacts on the next state of the other in a continuous dynamic process.

Arguments over appropriate theories have important implications for both research and clinical strategies. Unless one understands how development proceeds, there is little basis for attempts to alter it, either through prevention or intervention programs.

As will be seen, all development seems to follow a similar model. In this view, outcomes are never a function of the individual taken alone or the experiential context taken alone. Behavioral competencies are a product of the combination of an individual and his or her experience. To predict outcome, a singular focus on the characteristics of the individual, in this case the child, will frequently be misleading. What needs to be added is an analysis and assessment of the experiences available to the child.

Ancient theorists interpreted development as an unfolding of intrinsic characteristics that were either preformed or interacted epigenetically (Sameroff, 1983; see Figure 5). This model was countered by an environmental model of discontinuity in which each stage of development was determined by the contemporary context analogous to Reigel's (1978) passive person–active environment category. If the context remained the same, the child remained the same. If the context changed, the child changed (see Figure 6).

As interactionist position combined these two, as shown in Figure 7. Here, continuity is carried by the child but moderated by possible discontinuities in

$$C_1 \longrightarrow C_2 \longrightarrow C_3 \longrightarrow C_4$$

Figure 5   Deterministic constitutional model of development. C1 to C4 represent state of the child at successive points in time.

experience. Anastasi (1958) is credited with the important interactionist conceptual breakthrough in pointing out that development could not occur without an environment. There is no logical possibility of considering development of an individual independent of the environment. Continuity could not be explained as a characteristic of the child because each new achievement was an amalgam of characteristics of the child and his or her experience. Neither alone would be predictive of later levels of functioning. If continuities were found, it was because there was a continuity in the relation between the child and the environment, not because of continuities in either taken alone.

More recent conceptualizations of the developmental model have incorporated effects of the child on the environment posited by Rheingold (1966) and Bell (1968). These dynamic interactionist (Thomas, Chess, & Birch, 1968) or transactional (Sameroff & Chandler, 1975) models add to the independent contributions of child and environment characteristics of the environment that are conditioned by the nature of the child. Different characteristics of the child will trigger different responses from the same environment (see Figure 8).

In Figure 8 there is a continuity implied in the organization of the child's behavior by the series of arrows from C1 to C2 to C3. What is still missing from this model is a sense of continuity in the organization of the environment that would be indicated by a series of arrows from E1 to E2 to E3.

Environmental Continuity

Within the RLS, our attention has been devoted to the source of continuities and discontinuities in child performance. We have recently completed a new assessment of the sample when the children were 13 years of age

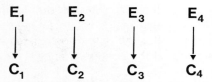

Figure 6   Deterministic environmental model of development. E1 to E4 represent experiential influences at successive points in time.

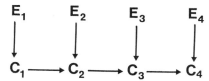

Figure 7   Interactionist model of development.

(Sameroff, Seifer, Baldwin, & Baldwin, 1989). Because of the potent effects of our multiple-risk index at 4 years, we calculated a new multiple environmental risk score for each family based on their situation 9 years later. We found the same relationship between the number of risk factors and the child's intellectual competence as can be seen in Figure 9.

The environmental risk score at 4 years explained 55% of the variance in the child's IQ. At 13 years, the environmental risk score explained 49% of the variance in the child's IQ. It should be remembered that there is no child variable in the risk index. Without looking at the child we can predict over half of the variance in his or her intelligence from preschool through adolescence.

The typical statistic reported in longitudinal research is the correlation between the children's early and later performances. We, too, found such correlations. Intelligence at 4 years correlated .72 with intelligence at 13 years. The usual interpretation of such a number is that there is a continuity of competence or incompetence in the child. Such a conclusion cannot be challenged if the only assessments in the study are of the children. In the RLS, we examined environmental as well as child factors. We were able to correlate environmental characteristics across time as well as child ones. We found that the correlation between environmental risk scores at the two ages was .76, as great or greater than any continuity within the child. Those children who had poor family and social environments at 4 still had them when they were 13 and probably would continue to have them for the foreseeable future. Whatever the child's ability for achieving high levels of competence, it was severely undermined by the continuing paucity of environmental support. Whatever the capabilities provided to the child by individual factors, it is the environment that limits the opportunities for development.

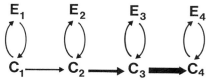

Figure 8   Reciprocal interaction model of development.

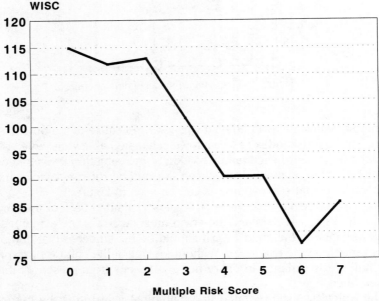

Figure 9   Mean 13-year IQs for children (n = 152) with different multiple environmental risk scores (Sameroff et al., 1988).

At 4 years, we divided the sample into high-, medium-, and low-risk groups based on the number of cumulative risks: 0 or 1 in the low-risk group, 2 or 3 in the medium-risk group, and 4 or more in the high-risk group. We then examined the distribution of IQ scores within each risk group. Of the high-risk group, 22% had IQs below 85, whereas none of the low-risk sample did. Conversely, 59% of the low-risk group had IQs above 115 but only 4% of the high-risk sample did.

After the 13-year assessment, we made the same breakdown into high-, medium-, and low-risk groups and again examined the distribution of IQs within risk groups. Again we found a preponderance of low IQ scores in the high-risk group and a preponderance of high IQ scores in the low-risk group, indicating the continuing negative effects of an unfavorable environment. But strikingly, the number of children in the high-risk group with IQs below 85 had increased from 22% to 46%, more than doubling (see Figure 10). It would appear from these data that high-risk environments operate synergystically to further worsen the intellectual standing of these children during the period from pre-school to adolescence.

As we have noted, it is impossible to study child development apart from contextual change or stability. A further dynamic ingredient of the environment is secular change. In a study completed by the House of Repre-

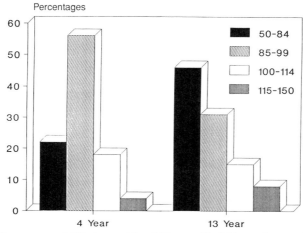

Figure 10   Percentages of 152 4-year-old and 13-year-old children whose verbal IQ scores were low (50–84), low average (85–99), high average (100–114), and high (115–150) in the high multiple-risk categories.

sentatives Ways and Means Committee reported in the *New York Times* (Passel, 1989), it was found that between the years 1973 and 1987, during which time we were doing this study, the average household income of the poorest fifth of Americans fell 12%, whereas the income of the richest fifth increased 24%. The American dream of a better future is not being realized economically, as reflected in these government figures, nor developmentally, as reflected in the data from the RLS. The poor get poorer in more than economic terms.

Regulatory Systems in Development

What kind of theory would be necessary to integrate our understanding of development? It must explain how the individual and experience work together to produce patterns of adaptive or maladaptive functioning and must relate how such past or present functioning influences the future.

The first principle to emerge in such a general theory of development is that individuals can never be removed from their contexts. Whether the goal is understanding causal connections, predicting outcomes, or intervention, it will not be achieved by removing the individual from the conditions that regulate development. There has been a great deal of attention given to the biological influences on development. What has now become necessary is the giving of equal attention to the environmental influences.

The development of each individual is constrained by interactions with regulatory systems acting at different levels of organization. The two most prominent of these are the biological and social regulatory systems. From conception to birth interactions with the biological system are most prominent. Changes in the contemporary state of the organism's embryonic phenotype triggers the genotype to provide a series of new biochemical experiences. These experiences are regulated by the turning on and off of various gene activities directed toward the production of a viable human child. These processes continue less dramatically after birth with some exceptions, for example, the initiation of adolescence and possibly senility.

The period from birth to adulthood, however, is dominated by interactions with the social system. Again, the state of the child triggers regulatory processes but now the regulators are in the social environment. Examples of such coded changes are the reactions of parents to their child's ability to walk or talk, and the changes in setting provided when the child reaches preschool or school age. These regulations change the experience of the child in tune with changes in the child's physical and behavioral development.

The result of these regulatory exchanges is the expansion of each individual's ability for biological self-regulation and the development of behavioral self-regulation. Advances in motor development permit children to control their temperatures and nutrition that initially only could be regulated by caregivers. They soon are able to dress themselves and reach into the refrigerator. Despite this burgeoning independence, each individual is never free from a relationship to an internal and external context. Should we forget this connectedness, it only takes a bout of illness or a social transgression to remind us of our constraints.

The Environtype

Just as there is a biological organization that regulates the physical outcome of each individual (the genotype), there is a social organization that regulates the way human beings fit into their society. This organization operates through family and cultural socialization patterns and has been postulated to compose an "environtype" analogous to the biological genotype (Sameroff, 1985; Sameroff & Fiese, 1990).

The environtype is composed of subsystems that not only transact with the child but also transact with each other. Although at any point in time the environtype can be conceptualized independently of the child—changes in the abilities of the developing child are major triggers for regulatory changes and in most likelihood were major contributors to the evolution of a developmental agenda that is each culture's timetable for developmental milestones.

Cultural Code

The ingredients of the cultural code are the complex of characteristics that organize a society's child-rearing system, incorporating elements of socialization and education. These processes are embedded in sets of social controls and social supports based on beliefs that differ in the amount of community consensus, ranging from mores and norms to fads and fashions. It is beyond the scope of this chapter to elucidate the full range of cultural regulatory processes that are relevant to development. As a consequence, only a few points will be highlighted to flesh out the dimensions of the cultural code.

Although the common biological characteristics of the human species have acted to produce similar developmental agendas in most cultures, there are differences in many major features that often ignore the biological status of the individual. In most cultures, formal education begins between the ages of 6 and 8 (Rogoff, 1981) when most children have reached the cognitive ability to learn from such structured experiences. On the other hand, informal education can begin at many different ages depending on the culture's attributions to the child. The Digo and Kikuyu are two East African cultures that have different beliefs about infant capacities (deVries & Sameroff, 1984). The Digo believe that infants can learn within a few months after birth and begin socialization at that time. The Kikuyu wait until the second year of life before they believe serious education is possible. Closer to home, some segments of middle-class parents have been convinced that prenatal experiences will enhance the cognitive development of their children. Such examples demonstrate the variability of human developmental contexts.

One of the major contemporary risk conditions toward which many programs are being directed is the elimination of adolescent pregnancy. Although for certain young mothers the pregnancy is the outcome of individual factors, for a large proportion it is the result of a cultural code that defines maturity, family relationships, and socialization patterns with adolescent motherhood as a normative ingredient. In such instances, to focus on the problem as one that resides wholly at the individual level would be a gross misrepresentation.

Family Code

Just as cultural codes regulate the fit between individuals and the social system, family codes organize individuals within the family system. Family codes provide a source of regulation that allows a group of individuals to form a collective unit in relation to society as a whole. As the cultural code regulates development so that an individual may fill a role in society, family codes regulate development to produce members that fulfill a role within the family and who are ultimately able to introduce new members into the shared system. Traditionally, new members are incorporated through birth and marriage, although more recently, remarriage has taken on a more frequent role in providing new family members.

The family regulates the child's development through a variety of forms that vary in their degree of explicit representation. Families have rituals that prescribe roles, stories that transmit orientations to each family member as well as to whomever will listen, shared myths that influence individual interactions, and behavioral paradigms that change individual behavior when in the presence of other family members. Reiss (1990) has contrasted the degree to which these forms regulate family behavior through explicit prescriptions: the knowledge of family rules that each member has, with the degree to which each family member's behavior is regulated by common practice, that is, the behavior of the family members when together. The most represented regulations are exemplified by family rituals and the least by family paradigms. At intermediate levels are stories and myths. Research efforts are only beginning to explore the exact nature of how these forms are transmitted behaviorally among family members and how they are represented in cognition.

Individual Code

There is good evidence that individual behavior is influenced by the family context. When operating as part of a family, the behavior of each member is altered (Parke & Tinsley, 1987), frequently without awareness of the behavioral change (Reiss, 1981). However, there is also no doubt that each individual brings his or her own contribution to family interactions. The contribution of parents is much more complexly determined than that of young children, given the multiple levels that contribute to their behavior. Although the socializing regulations embodied in the cultural and family codes have been discussed, the individualized interpretations that each parenting figure imposes on these codes has not. To a large extent, these interpretations are conditioned by each parent's past participation in his or her own family's coded interactions, but they are captured uniquely by each member of the family. These individual influences further condition each parent's response to his or her own child. The richness of both health and pathology embodied in these responses are well described in the clinical literature. In terms of early development, Fraiberg (1980) and her colleagues have provided many descriptions of the attributions that parents bring to their parenting. These "ghosts" of unresolved childhood conflicts have been shown to "do their mischief according to a historical or topical agenda, specializing in such areas as feeding, sleep, toilet-training or discipline, depending upon the vulnerabilities of the parental past" (Fraiberg, Adelson, & Shapiro, 1975, p. 420).

Parental psychopathology has long been recognized as a contributor to the poor developmental status of children. Although we acknowledge that influence, we must also be careful to note the effects of the contexts in which parental behavior is rooted: the family and cultural codes. It is important to recognize the parent as a major regulating agency of child development, but it is equally important to recognize that parental behavior is itself embedded in regulatory contexts.

An understanding of the developmental process requires an appreciation of the transactions between individuals, their biological inner workings, and their social outer workings. Continuities and discontinuities are a joint function of three systems: the genotype, the phenotype, and the environtype (see Figure 11). The genotype is the system of biological regulation and organization. The environtype is the family and cultural code that regulates the developmental opportunities available to an individual. The phenotype, or in this case the individual person, transacts through development with both the genotype and environtype to determine individual status at any point in time. To the extent that the three systems are in a state of equilibrium, continuity of performance is to be expected. To the extent that one of the systems undergoes a reorganization, then there is a corresponding reorganization of development itself.

In normal development on the biological side, reorganizations are required in response to changes such as walking or adolescence. From the environmental side, such normative transitions include the reorganizations required when beginning school and when graduating. It is in the individual that the inner and the outer workings are brought into accord, either by seeking opportunities to use capacities or fostering capacities to meet opportunities. In non-normative development, either the capacities or the opportunities are missing. The plasticity of the environtype permits compensatory regulations such as providing wheelchairs for those who cannot walk or Braille books for those who cannot see. On the other hand, this same environmental plasticity can deny education to those who are of the wrong race, or even of the wrong sex.

THE FUTURE

The appeal of models of development based solely on the study of variables in the individual stems from our purported lack of sophistication in measuring meaningful environmental variables that explain significant amounts of developmental variance. This lack of sophistication should be

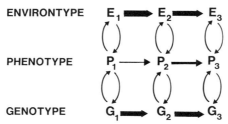

Figure 11   Transactional developmental model integrating environmental, genetic, and individual regulating systems (Sameroff, 1989).

taken as a challenge for future research rather than as an excuse for eliminating the environment as an organized contributor to our destinies.

Because of the more rapid evolution of the environtype relative to the genotype in human society, the study of human development must be characterized by greater attention to changes in the social constraints than to the biological ones. Strong evidence for this position is in a series of studies showing increases in IQ scores during the last several generations. Flynn (1984, 1987) found massive gains over the last 50 years. In one study of changes in test norms in the United States between 1932 and 1978, gains of 13.8 points were found. In another study of 14 nations over the last generation, gains of 5 to 25 points were found. What was even more surprising was that these large increases were not on IQ test subscales that would be influenced by schooling but on scales that were thought to reflect abstract problem-solving ability. There is no biological model that can explain these increases in intelligence. If we can come to understand the forces that increase the intelligence of whole societies, perhaps we can also come to understand the processes that will increase the intelligence of specific individuals within society. The research findings summarized here have identified the operation of major social factors that constrain human development. It is proposed that these environmental factors are part of an environtype that regulates human development by regulating developmental opportunities. Flynn (1987) concludes that potent, unknown environmental factors must exist to produce these results. From the perspective of establishing a research agenda for the future, the key word here is "unknown." The task of research programs directed toward understanding human development is to make these potent factors known.

In this chapter, I have described a number of developmental elaborations on the linear model that sought individual determinants for child behavior. A goal that requires simple explanations can only be achieved when experience is held constant. Ignoring for the moment the transactional axiom that experience cannot be held constant because individuals help create their experiences, one might ask what would be achieved by such predictive power? Developmentalists are not only interested in defining the determinants of human growth but also in changing the limits of human potential. If an individual's genome is a stable characteristic than the variance that must be studied is in the experiences that could be available to the individual. We must move beyond a negative definition of environmental effects as the variance that is left over after genetics and error are taken into account to a positive definition that incorporates the multiple levels of environmental organization and the multiple interactions and transactions that occur among these levels (Hoffman, 1991).

The final and most important point to be made here is that if one is interested in improving individual outcomes, then the focus should be on the most plastic part of the developmental system, that is, the part that is the most open to societal alteration and enhancement, the action of society itself. E. O. Wilson (1975), the distinguished sociobiologist, concluded that the most dynamic aspect of human evolution is the autotelic ability of human society to change itself. A focus on environmental analysis would not only lead to the understanding of the current limits of individual achievement but also of the directions society should take in amplifying achievement and the processes by which these changes could be made.

REFERENCES

Anastasi, A. (1958). Heredity, environment, and the question, "How?" *Psychological Review, 75*, 81–95.

Bell, R. Q. (1968). A reinterpretation of the direction of effects in studies of socialization. *Psychological Review, 75*, 81–95.

Broman, S. H., Nichols, P. L., & Kennedy, W. A. (1975). *Preschool IQ: Prenatal and early developmental correlates.* New York: Lawrence Erlbaum.

Bronfenbrenner U., & Crouter, A. C. (1983). The evolution of environmental models in developmental research. In P. H. Mussen (Ed.), *Handbook of child psychology* (4th ed., Vol. 1). W. Kessen (Ed.), *History, theory, and methods* (pp. 357–414). New York: Wiley.

deVries, M. W., & Sameroff, A. J. (1984). Culture and temperament: Influences on infant temperament in three East African societies. *American Journal of Orthopsychiatry, 54*, 83–96.

Flynn, J. R. (1984). The mean IQ of Americans: Massive gains 1932 to 1978. *Psychological Bulletin, 95*, 29–51.

Flynn, J. R. (1987). Massive IQ gains in 14 nations: What IQ tests really measure. *Psychological Bulletin, 101*, 171–191.

Fraiberg, S. (1980). *Clinical studies in infant mental health: The first year of life.* New York: Basic Books.

Fraiberg, S., Adelson, E., & Shapiro, V. (1975). Ghosts in the nursery: A psychoanalytic approach to the problems of impaired mother–infant relationships. *Journal of the American Academy of Child Psychiatry, 14*, 378–421.

Greenspan, S. I. (1981). *Psychopathology and adaptation in infancy and early childhood: Clinical infant reports No. 1.* Hanover, N.H: University Press of New England.

Hoffman, L. W. (1991). The influence of the family environment on personality: Accounting for sibling differences. *Psychological Bulletin, 110*(2), 187–203.

Lazar, I., Darlington, R., Murray, H., Royce, J., & Snipper, A. (1982). Lasting effects of early education: A report from the consortium for longitudinal studies. *Monographs of the Society for Research in Child Development, 47* (Serial No. 195).

Passell, P. (July 16, 1989). Forces in society and Reaganism, helped by deep hole for poor. *New York Times*, pp. 1, 20.

Parke, R. D., & Tinsley, B. J. (1987). Family interaction in infancy. In J. Osofsky (Ed.), *Handbook of infant development* (2nd ed., pp. 579–641). New York: Wiley.

Parmelee, A. H., & Haber, A. (1973). Who is the at-risk infant? *Clinical Obstetrics and Gynecology, 16*, 376–387.

Pasamanick, B., & Knobloch, H. (1961). Epidemiologic studies on the complications of pregnancy and the birth process. In G. Caplan (Ed.), *Prevention of Mental Disorders in Children.* New York: Basic Books.

Reiss, D. (1981). *The family's construction of reality.* Cambridge, MA: Harvard University Press.

Reiss, D. (1990). The represented and practicing family: Contrasting visions of family continuity.

In A. J. Sameroff & R. N. Emde (Eds.), *Relationship disturbances in early childhood: A developmental approach* (pp. 191–220). New York: Basic Books.

Rheingold, H. L. (1966). The development of social behavior in the human infant. In H. W. Stevenson (Ed.), Concept of development. *Monographs of the Society for Research in Child Development, 31,* 5(Whole No. 107).

Riegel, K. F. (1978). *Psychology, mon amour: A countertext.* Boston: Houghton Mifflin.

Rogoff, B. (1981). Schooling and the development of cognitive skills. In H. C. Triandis and A. Heron (Eds.), *Handbook of cross-cultural psychology: Developmental psychology.* (Vol. 4, pp. 233–294). Boston: Allyn & Bacon.

Rutter, M. (1979). Protective factors in children's responses to stress and disadvantage. In M. W. Kent & J. E. Rolf (Eds.), *Primary prevention of psychopathology: Vol. 3. Social competence in children.* Hanover, NH: University Press of New England.

Sameroff, A. J. (1983). Developmental systems: Contexts and evolution. In P. H. Mussen (Ed.), *Handbook of child psychology* (4th ed., Vol. 1). W. Kessen (Ed.), *History, theories, and methods* (pp. 237–294). New York: Wiley.

Sameroff, A. J. (1985). *Can development be continuous?* Paper presented at Annual Meeting of American Psychological Association, Los Angeles.

Sameroff, A. J. (1986). Environmental context of child development. *Journal of Pediatrics, 109,* 192–200.

Sameroff, A. J. (1989). Models of developmental regulations: The environtype. In D. Cicchetti (Ed.), *Development and Psychopathology* (pp 41–68). Hillsdale, NJ: Lawrence Erlbaum.

Sameroff, A. J., & Chandler, M. J. (1975). Reproductive risk and the continuum of caretaking casualty. In F. D. Horowitz, M. Hetherington, S. Scarr-Salapatek, & G. Siegel (Eds.), *Review of child development research* (Vol. 4, pp. 187–244). Chicago: University of Chicago.

Sameroff, A. J., & Fiese, B. H. (1990). Transactional regulation and early intervention. In S. J. Meisels & J. P. Shonkoff (Eds.), *Early intervention: A handbook of theory, practice and analysis* (pp. 119–191). New York: Cambridge University Press.

Sameroff, A. J., Seifer, R., Baldwin, A., & Baldwin, C. (1993). Stability of intelligence from preschool to adolescence: The influence of social and family risk factors. *Child Development, 64,* 80–97.

Sameroff, A. J., Seifer, R., Barocas, R., Zax, M., & Greenspan, S. (1987). IQ scores of 4-year-old children: Social-environmental risk factors. *Pediatrics, 79,* 343–350.

Sameroff, A. J., Seifer, R., & Zax, M. (1982). Early development of children at risk for emotional disorder. *Monographs of the Society for Research in Child Development, 47* (Serial number 199).

Schweinhart, L., & Weikart, D. (1980). Young children grow up: The effort of the Perry preschool program on youths through age 15. *Monographs of the High/Scope Educational Research Foundation,* No. 7.

Thomas, A., Chess, S., & Birch, H. (1968). *Temperament and behavior disorders in children.* New York: New York University.

Wilson, E. O. (1975). *Sociobiology: The new synthesis.* Cambridge, MA: Belnap Press.

Wilson, R. S. (1985). Risk and resilience in early mental development. *Developmental Psychology, 21,* 795–805.

Zigler, E., & Trickett, P, K. (1978). IQ, social competence, and evaluation of early childhood intervention programs. *American Psychologist, 33,* 789–799.

EXAMPLES
OF
DOMAINS
FOR
FOLLOW-UP
RESEARCH

Developmental Research in Behavioral Teratology:
Effects of Prenatal Alcohol Exposure on Child Development

Heather Carmichael Olson
Ann Pytkowicz Streissguth
Fred L. Bookstein
Helen M. Barr
Paul D. Sampson

INTRODUCTION

Behavioral teratology is an important new domain for child development research in which much can be learned about the biological bases of learning problems and psychopathology. Behavioral teratology, a new field developed over the last 15 years, examines the impact of teratogens on behavior and development (Wilson, 1977; Voorhees, 1986). A teratogen is an agent capable of producing death, congenital malformations, growth disturbances and/or behavioral deficits in the exposed embryo and fetus. Alcohol is a known and common teratogen: maternal drinking during pregnancy can cause adverse effects in offspring development. Because alcohol is a neurobehavioral teratogen, it can affect not only the formation of the body in general, but more specifically can impact the formation and function of the central nervous system, and therefore can affect behavior. In fact, prenatal exposure to alcohol is an unfortunate natural experiment in central nervous system (CNS) compromise, with effects that gradually unfold over the course of development. The study of fetal alcohol effects over the life span is an important area for longitudinal study, a research topic at the intersection of many different disciplines, and a critical focus for public policy.

In this chapter we present the hypotheses, research design, and statistical methodology of the Seattle Longitudinal Prospective Study of Alcohol and Pregnancy. The Seattle Study shows how essential longitudinal research is to a full understanding of the effects of a teratogen on how a child develops, and to the search for the biological contributions to childhood learning and behavior deficits. The chapter gives an overview of study findings on the effects of lower levels of prenatal exposure to alcohol on child development from birth to late childhood. These findings show the subtle but enduring effects of alcohol exposure before birth on child performance over the first decade of life, especially in the area of attention. The chapter ends with a brief discussion of how the Seattle Study fits into the context of other longitudinal studies of prenatal alcohol exposure, and how developmental research on the teratology of alcohol has helped to shape public policy to improve public health and for the common good.

DEVELOPMENTAL STUDY OF ALCOHOL TERATOGENESIS

Over the last two decades, experimental psychologists, epidemiologists, clinical researchers, and developmentalists have all participated in the study of prenatal alcohol effects. Research in this area was spurred two decades ago by the recognition of groups of children, born to alcoholic women, who had similarly malformed facial and other physical features, pre- and postnatal growth retardation, and signs of CNS dysfunction, including memory deficits and mental retardation (Lemoine, Harousseau, Borteyru, & Menuet, 1968; Ulleland, 1972; Jones, Smith, Ulleland, & Streissguth, 1973). This most devastating teratogenic effect of alcohol in humans was named Fetal Alcohol Syndrome (FAS) in 1973 (Jones & Smith, 1973). Fetal Alcohol Syndrome is a preventable birth defect and the leading known cause of mental retardation in the western world (Abel & Sokol, 1987). Individuals with FAS have a lifelong developmental disability resulting from prenatal exposure to alcohol, usually at the level of maternal alcoholism, and show multiple and varied manifestations of CNS dysfunction. Infants with FAS are often tremulous, have a weak suck, and show some developmental delay. Young children with FAS are often hyperactive and manifest some delay in gross motor control and some difficulty with eye–hand coordination. In research so far, the average IQ of children with FAS is in the mildly retarded range, although the IQ among children with FAS can range from the severely retarded to the normal range of intelligence (Streissguth, Clarren, & Jones, 1985; Streissguth & LaDue, 1987). Other behavioral manifestations in individuals with FAS include attentional problems, memory deficits, and poor judgment. These cognitive disabilities are often associated with behavioral management problems that become more pronounced with the onset of puberty (Streissguth et al., 1991). Studying the life histories of individuals with FAS, and those with possible fetal alcohol effects (who show a partial expression of the characteristics seen in FAS), can contribute a great deal to an understanding of the development of psychopathology, as is evident from clinical and retrospective developmental research carried out in our Seattle laboratory (Streissguth, 1992).

Over the last two decades, animal and human research has clearly shown that high levels of alcohol consumption during pregnancy can cause growth deficiencies and physical anomalies and can affect the central nervous system, with consequent learning difficulties and problems with attention, activity level, and motor skills. There are similar findings in the human and animal literature in terms of dose and type of outcomes most affected by alcohol at different stages of development (Driscoll, Streissguth, & Riley, 1990). Documentation of the etiology and mechanisms underlying alcohol effects comes from animal research, in which the genetic background, administration of the agent, rearing of the young, and assessment of behavior can be tightly controlled (Goodlett & West, 1992). Further documentation comes from neuropathological studies of the human brain (Clarren, 1986). Prenatally, alcohol crosses the placenta and may interfere with cell proliferation in the embryo, disorganize cell migration and development, and interfere with neurotransmitter production in the developing CNS (Porter, O'Connor, & Whelan, 1984; West, 1986; Clarren et al., 1990). Specific brain structures, including the hippocampus, appear to be especially sensitive to alcohol effects (West, 1986), although alcohol effects on the formation and function of the CNS actually appear to be widespread. The type of alcohol effects varies across individuals and across different outcome domains, in part because of the genetic characteristics of mother and child, other prenatal experiences, and postnatal environmental variation. The type of alcohol effects also depends on the timing, dose, and pattern of alcohol ingestion during pregnancy, in accordance with the stage of organogenesis or fetal development. Not all offspring who are exposed to alcohol in utero are affected (Clarren, 1986; Streissguth, 1986; Streissguth, Sampson, Barr, Clarren, & Martin, 1986; Streissguth, Sampson, & Barr, 1989; West, Goodlett, Bonthius, & Pierce, 1990).

To document the long-term teratogenic effects of alcohol on growth and physical development, but especially effects on behavior, longitudinal follow-up is required. Longitudinal research can examine how prenatal exposure to alcohol contributes to later learning and behavior problems, within the network of the many other influences on development. Only long-term study of the same individuals can uncover the changing manifestations of alcohol-related CNS compromise that endure across the lifespan. Longitudinal follow-up has been conducted in both animal and human studies. At high levels of exposure, not only do growth deficits and physical anomalies persist, but the behavioral effects can be lifelong. Rats exposed to large amounts of alcohol before birth have been found to show behavioral deficits as adults (Riley, 1990). In clinical study of humans diagnosed with FAS or possible fetal alcohol effects life-span difficulties in adaptive behavior, social skills, and ability to function independently have been described (Streissguth et al., 1991).

Teratogenic effects can occur across the spectrum of prenatal exposure, with larger effects from heavier doses and milder effects at lower levels of exposure. High levels of alcohol exposure before birth clearly cause problems in growth, in body formation, and, because of CNS dysfunction, in behavior. Animal studies reveal the striking fact that there are behavioral effects at alcohol exposure levels too low to produce physical malformations or growth deficiency (Driscoll et al., 1990). For child development research, then, important questions arise. Do lower levels of prenatal alcohol exposure place developing children at risk for learning and behavior problems? Can moderate to heavy drinking during pregnancy, largely within the social drinking range, have detectable consequences on child growth and development?

Figure 1 illustrates the behavioral teratogenesis of alcohol and the hypothesis that lower levels of prenatal alcohol exposure would indeed place children at risk, acting as a biological contributor to later psychopathology even at levels within the moderate to heavy range. As seen in the left-hand column of Figure 1, data from children with FAS born to alcoholic women show that these children experience major CNS deficits. Children with FAS often show a developmental pattern of problems beginning in infancy, with delayed development and sometimes failure to thrive, often progressing in childhood to hyperactivity and continued cognitive and motor delays and retardation, and the experience of "real life" problems such as academic failure. The center column of Figure 1 presents findings derived from literature on children of alcoholic women in which the children have not received a diagnosis of FAS or a label of possible fetal alcohol effects. This column shows that this group experiences fewer but still significant CNS deficits, and a childhood pattern of hyperactivity and deficits in perceptual-motor skills, attention, learning, and behavior. The right-hand column of Figure 1 shows the predicted deficits for children exposed to lower levels of prenatal alcohol. The hypothesis here, which is explored in the Seattle Study, is that moderate to heavy levels of prenatal alcohol exposure, largely within the social drinking range, would lead to smaller but meaningful CNS deficits. These deficits would place children at risk for decrements in motor and cognitive skill and increased behavioral dysfunction, and the deficits would be observable through careful laboratory assessment of a group of children who otherwise would appear clinically normal.

To examine this hypothesis about the behavioral teratology of alcohol, we have carried out the Seattle Longitudinal Prospective Study on Alcohol

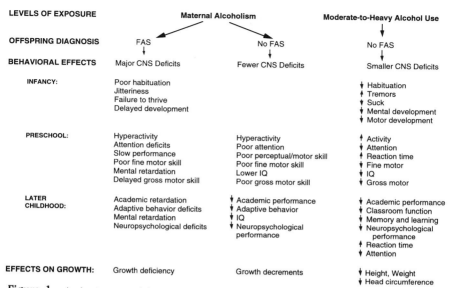

LEVELS OF EXPOSURE	Maternal Alcoholism		Moderate-to-Heavy Alcohol Use
OFFSPRING DIAGNOSIS	FAS	No FAS	No FAS
BEHAVIORAL EFFECTS	Major CNS Deficits	Fewer CNS Deficits	Smaller CNS Deficits
INFANCY:	Poor habituation Jitteriness Failure to thrive Delayed development		↕ Habituation ↕ Tremors ↕ Suck ↕ Mental development ↕ Motor development
PRESCHOOL:	Hyperactivity Attention deficits Slow performance Poor fine motor skill Mental retardation Delayed gross motor skill	Hyperactivity Poor attention Poor perceptual/motor skill Poor fine motor skill Lower IQ Poor gross motor skill	↕ Activity ↕ Attention ↕ Reaction time ↕ Fine motor ↕ IQ ↕ Gross motor
LATER CHILDHOOD:	Academic retardation Adaptive behavior deficits Mental retardation Neuropsychological deficits	↕ Academic performance ↕ Adaptive behavior ↕ IQ ↕ Neuropsychological performance	↕ Academic performance ↕ Classroom function ↕ Memory and learning ↕ Neuropsychological performance ↕ Reaction time ↕ Attention
EFFECTS ON GROWTH:	Growth deficiency	Growth decrements	↕ Height, Weight ↕ Head circumference

Figure 1   A chart summarizing information on the behavioral teratology of alcohol, based on clinical experience with affected patients and children of alcoholic mothers.

and Pregnancy. In the Seattle Study, we have examined the effects of prenatal alcohol exposure on child development, with a primary focus on lower levels of exposure as defined by moderate to heavy alcohol use within the social drinking range. Beginning in 1974, we began following a sample of about 500 children from birth through late childhood, and we now plan to follow the sample through adolescence. This developmental study of prenatal alcohol effects was the first of three federally funded prospective studies begun in the 1970s, and the only one of these first projects that is still in progress. In other laboratories, long-term studies of prenatal alcohol exposure begun more recently have so far been carried out only across infancy and early childhood, with data through, at most, the age of 8 (see, e.g., Coles et al., 1991; Day et al., 1991; Fried and Watkinson, 1990; Greene, Ernhart, Ager, et al., 1990; Russell, Czarnecki, Cowan, McPherson, & Mudar, 1991). In the Seattle Study, we have followed children into the later elementary school years, with data through the age of 11 years.

DESIGN OF THE SEATTLE LONGITUDINAL PROSPECTIVE STUDY ON ALCOHOL AND PREGNANCY

Design issues are critical in developmental research on the behavioral teratology of alcohol. The follow-up Seattle Study has a longitudinal prospective design, that is shown in Figure 2. Although the design appears complex, it can be simply stated. Prenatal alcohol exposure is the primary variable of interest and has been measured in multiple ways. Nicotine is another important prenatal exposure variable considered in the research design, and its confounding effect is dealt with by careful measurement and stratification. A large number of covariates have also been considered, given the many factors that impinge over time on the developmental process, and that affect the expression of a teratogen in child outcome. Taking a developmental viewpoint, a wide variety of developmentally appropriate physical and behavioral outcomes have been evaluated in this cohort of children. Bearing in mind the principles of behavioral teratology, potentially subtle effects on growth, dysmorphology, and behavior have all been measured via physical examination, as well as developmental and neuropsychological assessment. The children have been followed from birth through late childhood, up through 11 years of age. The study is currently continuing on through adolescence, with testing of the children at the age of 14 years. More details of the study design are available in Streissguth, Martin, Martin, and Barr (1981).

Cohort Selection

The Seattle cohort was chosen specifically to evaluate the effects of the biological risk factor of prenatal alcohol exposure. In a behavioral teratology study, the cohort must be constructed especially to study the effects of the teratogen in question. The Seattle Study started with a consecutive screening sample of 1529 women planning to deliver at either of two hospitals. These women were interviewed at the fifth month of pregnancy about their smoking, drinking, and drug use. The follow-up cohort was selected, at the time of delivery, as a subset of the screening sample. The cohort was chosen according to a set of decision rules involving maternal drinking, smoking, and other sample characteristics as needed to keep the sample balanced, with oversampling for women who were heavier drinkers. A large cohort was needed to provide adequate power, so about 500 mothers and children were chosen for the follow-up study. The level of prenatal alcohol exposure was spread across the full spectrum, from maternal abstinence to heavy maternal drinking during pregnancy. The children in the cohort were born to about 250 of the "heavier" drinkers in the screening sample (most of them heavier drinkers and moderate users of alcohol), and about 250 "light and infrequent" drinkers and abstainers.

Two of the most important confounding factors in understanding alcohol effects are socioeconomic status (SES) and smoking. Because this study began in the 1970s prior to general awareness of the adverse effects of prenatal alcohol exposure, alcohol use was reported by about 80% of the mothers in the study. There was substantial variation in drinking behavior

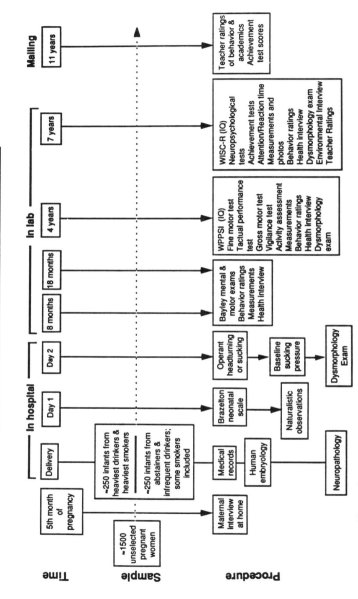

Figure 2 Study design for the Seattle Longitudinal Prospective Study on Alcohol and Pregnancy.

in all social classes and educational levels, which facilitated statistical separation of effects attributable to alcohol and to SES. However, alcohol use and smoking occur together so frequently that later statistical separation is difficult. In selecting the cohort for the Seattle Study, the sample was stratified for smoking across drinking levels, which allowed fairly effective separation of the two variables. Over one-half of the heaviest drinkers did not smoke, and almost one-third of the heaviest smokers drank infrequently or not at all. Other prenatal exposure variables, such as levels of caffeine and aspirin ingestion during pregnancy, were carefully measured and analyzed as covariates.

Selection of the follow-up cohort was based on maternal characteristics. The pregnant women comprising the sample were predominantly white, married, and middle class, and were fairly representative of the Seattle population during the mid-1970s. Using this low-risk Seattle sample allowed a focus on the effects of alcohol exposure before birth without the inherent confounds of multiple environmental risk factors that exist in a study of a high-risk sample of women. The Seattle Study involved a population-based sample. Table I presents the demographic and some drinking characteristics of the cohort.

Measurement of Alcohol Usage during Pregnancy ("Dose")

People have many drinking styles, and timing, pattern, and dose differences can influence the teratogenic effects of prenatal alcohol exposure. Therefore, alcohol exposure was assessed in several ways. The extent of maternal alcohol use was determined from self-reports with a quantity-frequency-variability interview given during the fifth month of pregnancy. Self-report is a useful method for assessing alcohol use during pregnancy, in as much as objective measures of alcohol use (such as measurement of blood levels) cannot tap use over the full course of pregnancy unless they are repeated many times. In the Seattle Study, test-retest reliability of the self-reported alcohol scores was high over a 1-week interval (.84 to .90; Streissguth, Martin, & Buffington, 1977), and steps were taken to enhance the validity of the interview measures (e.g., interviewing in private, asking about use prior to pregnancy recognition as well as during pregnancy).

To measure alcohol exposure, a summary AA score (average ounces of absolute alcohol per day) was calculated from the reported intake of all types of alcoholic beverages according to the criteria of Jessor and colleagues (Jessor, Graves, Hanson, & Jessor, 1968). An AA score of 1.0 (about 30 g absolute alcohol per day) can be thought of as roughly equivalent to an average of 14 "drinks" per week (for example two "drinks" daily or seven "drinks" on two weekend nights). As different patterns of use are not reflected in this continuous measure, several "binge" and frequency scores were

Table I Selected Characteristics of the Seattle Cohort at Enrollment in 1974–1975 ($N = 582$)

Variable				
Demographic characteristics				
Race	84%	White		
	9%	Black		
	7%	Other		
Age during pregnancy	2%	13–16 years		
	35%	17–24 years		
	57%	25–32 years		
	6%	≥33 years		
Parity	43%	Primiparous		
	57%	Multiparous		
Marital status	11%	Single		
	84%	Married		
	5%	Separated, divorced, widowed		
Education	15%	Less than high school graduation		
	30%	High school graduation		
	55%	Some college or college graduate		
Alcohol use	Mean	S.D.	Mdn.	Range
Average amount of alcohol per day prior to pregnancy recognition	0.58	1.46	0.125	0.00–25.76
Maximum "drinks" reported on any one occasion prior to pregnancy recognition	2.97	2.95	1.50	0.00–13.00

examined as well as drinking during early versus during middle stages of pregnancy. Thirteen scores reflecting frequency and pattern of alcohol use, shown in Table II, were analyzed. Information about the level of drinking in the Seattle sample is shown in Table I. The typical level of alcohol use by women in the Seattle sample fell within the realm of social drinking for the mid-1970s, and fewer than 1% of the women reported any serious problems associated with alcohol use.

Measurement of Child Outcome ("Response")

Taking a developmental perspective, child outcome was assessed in multiple and developmentally appropriate ways. Outcome measures were chosen based on the presumed effects of alcohol, derived from clinical observations and from literature on children of alcoholics, as shown in Figure 1. Measures were selected to assess effects on growth, physical anomalies, and varied

Table II Thirteen Scores Used in the Seattle Study to Assess Frequency and Pattern of Alcohol Use

Each of these scores was gathered for the period prior to pregnancy recognition and for the period during midpregnancy:
  Average ounces of absolute alcohol/day
  Binge: 5 or more drinks on any drinking occasion
  Average drinks per occasion
  Maximum drinks reported on any one occasion
  Monthly occasions of drinking
  Quantity-frequency-variability index
Ordered exposure category (ORDEXC)
  (an a priori alcohol risk score created for cohort enrollment)

dimensions of CNS function/behavior, including response speed and accuracy. Included were both subjective, clinical measures such as examiner ratings of behavior in the clinic at several ages, and objective measures such as latency and strength of the newborn sucking response and standardized intelligence test scores at age 7 years. Measures of appropriate difficulty level (to provide a suitable range of scores) and instruments capable of fine discrimination of the type and amount of deficit were used to assess the subtle effects hypothesized to result from lower levels of prenatal alcohol exposure. The primary outcome variables were derived from direct examination of the follow-up cohort on days 1 and 2 of life, at 8 and 18 months, and at 4 and 7 years of age. At ages 7 and 11, teachers were asked for ratings of classroom behavior and academic performance, and at 11 years standardized achievement test scores given by the school districts were examined. All examinations were carried out by examiners who had no knowledge of the children's exposure history (either before or after testing), their previous test performances, or the children's family background.

Measurement of Covariates

To sort out alcohol effects from the network of other influences in development, important covariates must be measured and taken into account via the research design and statistical analysis. A developmental perspective takes account of the full network of confounding influences that affect the development of children. Genetic and many prenatal factors affect children's development, as do postnatal environmental influences, such as family stress and mother–infant interaction. To the extent that these variables are associated with both the predictor and outcome variables, they can be an important source of bias. It is critical to attend to the measurement of all important covariates and, when needed, to take them into account, either in the research design itself or through statistical adjustments for their effects.

Besides alcohol, other factors potentially important in the course of pregnancy and child development, such as smoking, caffeine intake, use of other drugs, maternal diet, obstetrical history, and demographic characteristics, including parental educational level, were also assessed prenatally and examined for interaction effects or as covariates for statistical adjustment. Extensive data from medical records were obtained on the course and outcome of pregnancy for the full screening sample, and data on obstetrical medication were obtained for the follow-up cohort. Other potentially intervening variables, such as major life changes in the household, caretaking arrangements, and child accidents or illnesses, were assessed at each postnatal evaluation. For example, mother–infant interactions were assessed via examiner ratings at 8 and 18 months (Streissguth, Barr, Darby, & Ervin, 1987) and the HOME Inventory (Caldwell & Bradley, 1979) was used in a substudy at 12 months to assess the level of developmental stimulation in the home environment (Ragozin, Landesman-Dwyer, & Streissguth, 1978). Over the course of the study, more than 150 covariates were assessed. A complete list of these covariates from birth to age 7 has been discussed by Streissguth, Sampson, Barr, Clarren, and Martin (1986). Covariates used at age 11 years have been listed by Carmichael Olson, Sampson, Barr, Streissguth, and Bookstein (1992).

Sample Maintenance

Successful and intensive follow-up of the cohort over time is an essential component of a longitudinal study in order to maintain adequate sample size and protect the stratification of the sample. This is especially true in the study of alcohol teratogenesis, when the effects under investigation may be subtle and are likely to unfold over the course of development with notable individual variation. In particular, it is important to guard against selective loss of high-risk subjects whose absence could weaken results in subsequent analyses.

All scheduling and parent contacts were carried out by an outreach worker, which permitted intensive tracing and sample maintenance. Sample attrition in the present study was only 14% at the 4-year and 7-year exams. At the 7-year exam, 95% of those seen at 4 years were tested again, and when the children reached age 11 years the loss to follow-up was only 18%. There was no differential loss of high-risk subjects until the 11-year mailing to teachers (24% for high-risk subjects vs. 16% for all others), yet that did not appear to compromise findings from that phase of the study. The high rate of follow-up has been restored during the current 14-year laboratory visit. High sample maintenance has been achieved through extensive outreach activities, such as personalized birthday cards, constant tracing, bringing subjects in from out of state and, most importantly, establishing positive relationships with the subjects and viewing them as partners in achieving the goals of the study. These procedures have been explained in detail by Giunta, Barr, Gillespie, and Streissguth (1987) and by Streissguth and Giunta (1992).

USEFUL STATISTICAL METHODOLOGY IN THE DEVELOPMENTAL STUDY OF ALCOHOL TERATOGENESIS

Understanding the effects of fetal alcohol exposure on child development requires statistical methodology adequate both for assessment of the dose-response relationship between alcohol and child performance, a teratological question, and for the study of developmental phenomena. The relationship between prenatal alcohol exposure and child outcome is subtle, patterned, capable of change with age of offspring, and subject to a great deal of individual variation. Appropriate statistical methodology must be used to assess a complicated relationship between multiple and correlated measures of both alcohol exposure and child performance, none of which directly measures either the actual alcohol "dose" or the full child outcome "response." To answer developmental questions about alcohol teratogenesis, analysis in the early years of the Seattle Study was carried out using a multistep process of multiple regression and modeling techniques. More recently, during the 20-year course of this developmental follow-up project, the Seattle research group has pioneered the use of Partial Least Squares analytic techniques in behavioral teratology. These new statistical methods may be useful for other longitudinal child development studies involving large multivariate data sets.

Multiple Regression and Modeling Techniques

Traditionally, as part of our multistep analytic process, we have employed multiple regression analyses in the final analysis of each outcome in the Seattle Study. These permit statistical adjustment for the many potentially confounding variables that must be considered when examining the relationship between fetal alcohol exposure and child outcome. The process has been thoroughly described by Streissguth et al. (1986) and occurs as follows. Basic regression models are developed using alcohol and nicotine (log[mg/day + 1]) as the primary independent variables, along with a general set of potentially confounding variables, such as maternal diet during pregnancy, maternal education, and parity. For each outcome, other relevant variables are examined within this regression model, usually considered in a chronological order. Examples include drugs used during pregnancy (such as caffeine, marijuana and other illicit drugs) or the presence of high fevers in the child. Certain important confounding variables have been examined in substudies. For example, evaluation of the home environments of a subset of infants at 1 year of age using the HOME Inventory did not reveal any significant differences in the home environment associated with the levels of maternal alcohol use assessed in this study (Ragozin et al., 1978).

Partial Least Squares Methods

Multiple regression has been shown to be useful in the study of alcohol teratogenesis, and has been the basis for much of the data analysis carried out by developmentalists. In spite of its widespread use, there is a problem with multicollinearity present in multiple regression analyses when the database has highly correlated predictor variables, as is true of the multiple assessments of prenatal alcohol exposure in the Seattle Study. There is also a problem in the use of multiple regression when many correlated outcome variables are measured. To deal with these problems, the Seattle research group has been developing the application to the Seattle data of a latent variable modeling procedure, based on the Partial Least Squares (PLS) statistical methods developed by Herman Wold and his colleagues (Jöreskog & Wold, 1982). Partial Least Squares techniques are useful for investigations of dose–response effects in which high doses result in a syndrome and investigators wish to study effects that may extend downward into the normal range. These methods facilitate study of the developmental process by avoiding the multiple significance tests that are problematic when dealing with complex multivariate longitudinal data sets that involve many measures of dose and response. The PLS methodology permits detection of a basic underlying signal or pattern of association between constructs (Ketterlinus, Bookstein, Sampson, & Lamb, 1989; Sampson, Streissguth, Barr, & Bookstein, 1989). The methodology of PLS may be useful in other kinds of longitudinal research in which multiple measures of predictor and outcome variables are obtained, and in which one wishes to describe complex relationships among constructs that cannot be measured directly.

The measure of "dose" in this study, fetal exposure to alcohol, cannot be measured directly because alcohol exposure has many dimensions resulting from the many different types of maternal drinking styles. To adequately assess prenatal exposure, many alcohol consumption scores must be gathered, and in the Seattle Study 13 alcohol consumption scores were examined. Listed in Table II, these alcohol scores represent a block of variables that, when taken together, provide a multifaceted, indirect assessment of alcohol exposure or "dose" to the fetus in terms of measures of the quantity, pattern, and timing of alcohol consumption. Similarly, the outcome measures used at a particular time represent a set of indirect, correlated assessments of the "response": the child's performance in areas presumed to be sensitive to alcohol exposure before birth. Complex dose and response concepts such as these, which can only be measured indirectly, are called *latent variables* (LVs). In the process of statistical analysis using PLS, estimates of these LVs are computed using the methods of PLS, and the correlation(s) among these LVs are determined. In the study of alcohol teratogenesis, PLS methods quantify and make interpretable the complex relationship between prenatal alcohol exposure and child performance by describing it in terms of LVs. Multiple regression methods are then applied to assess whether possible intervening or confounding factors can explain (or modify) the apparent correlation between alcohol exposure and child performance expressed in terms of these LVs.

Our application of these PLS techniques is briefly outlined here, using the simplest case of our 11-year analysis, PLS techniques are discussed in more detail later in the chapter. Our aim here is to show how useful this method has been for our developmental study of prenatal alcohol exposure. Other sources, which are mentioned later, can be consulted to understand PLS more thoroughly.

To carry out a PLS analysis in the Seattle sample, an underlying dimension of net prenatal alcohol exposure was created as a weighted average of the 13 scores used to measure alcohol exposure (which are shown in Table II). This is the Alcohol latent variable (LV). Another dimension of net child performance deficit at a specific time (e.g., 11 years) was created as a weighted average of the child performance scores of interest in this analysis. This weighted average comprises the Child Performance LV at age 11 years. In combining different estimates of the same quantity that vary in precision to create each LV, as is done with alcohol and child performance, standard practice is to weight the contributions of each in proportion to its precision. This is done so that the more precise estimates are given more weight in forming the average. Thus, when creating a latent variable for child performance that is to correlate with prenatal alcohol exposure, the child performance measures are weighted in proportion to their correlation with a weighted sum of the alcohol measures. The weights are called *saliences,* and this weighting is accomplished through the use of a PLS procedure. The PLS procedure does not attempt to explain the correlations among indicators of the same block (e.g., all the alcohol scores or all the child performance scores). Instead, it determines the linear combinations of indicators in each block that are predictive of items in the opposite block. In the simplest case, this creates two LVs.

With these LVs, the pattern of correlations between gestational alcohol exposure and child school performance at a specific time can be interpreted meaningfully. In this simplest case, a single covariance and a single correlation quantify the extent of the relationship between the Alcohol LV and the 11-year Child Performance LV, and assess how well these underlying dimensions capture the empirical relationship between all the measures of prenatal alcohol exposure and child outcome. PLS also can be used when there are more than two LVs at a single point in time, and in a more complicated analysis of alcohol effects over time. The Seattle group has used PLS methods in a longitudinal analysis, to examine the relationship between fetal alcohol exposure and child outcome over the first 7 years of life in areas presumed to be affected by alcohol, such as memory and attentional skill. This more complex application of PLS techniques has been discussed in a monograph by Streissguth, Sampson, Bookstein, & Barr (1993).

Comparison of PLS and Other Statistical Methods

The coefficients of PLS are designed for use in subsequent scientific explanation, such as the exploration of a dose–response relationship. The numbers (saliences) that characterize individual alcohol dose or child outcome items, for example, represent both the role of that score in the Alcohol or Child Performance LV and the correlation of that score with the other LV. This means that the coefficient of each separate alcohol score represents both the weight of the score in the net Alcohol LV and the salience of that same score for predicting the net Child Performance LV. The same is true for the coefficient of each child outcome item. This differs from the methods of LISREL, in which the coefficient is intended to explain within-block correlations (i.e., the correlations among the alcohol scores or the correlations within the child outcome scores), as well as those correlations between blocks, but does not at the same time represent covariances explained. (As a result, the role of coefficients in LISREL is to satisfy one algebraic equation rather than the pair of algebraic equations satisfied by the coefficients in PLS.) Partial Least Squares attends only to correlations among blocks and does not model within-block factor structures. Other techniques, such as principal components analysis or factor analysis, can be used to model within-block factor structures, but do not apply to the study of a dose–response relationship.

The PLS saliences are not the same as multiple regression coefficients. Multiple regression coefficients can be interpreted only as effects *when holding other causes constant.* This is not a reasonable approach when the "other causes" are other measures of prenatal alcohol exposure. The PLS coefficients are not the same as those of canonical correlation, which represent multiple regression applied at the same time in both blocks of alcohol and child outcome scores. Canonical correlation analysis of the block of alcohol items against typical blocks of child outcome items would result in multiple "dimensions" of alcohol dose having no discriminant validity. Sampson et al. (1989) have presented more information about these issues.

Other discussions of PLS methods, such as those of Wold (Jöreskog & Wold, 1982), present PLS as a variant of structural equations modeling, concerned with equations predicting case-by-case "scores." To the Seattle research group, PLS is much more easily interpreted as a least-squares fit of two patterns of saliences directly to the cross-block correlation matrix itself. Therefore, PLS is optimizing cross-block covariance, not correlation. It is important to remember that the coefficients of the covariance-based approach, but not those of the correlation-based approach, can be used in subsequent scientific explanations. This reflects a well-known paradox of the use of multiple regression in the social sciences: The regression approach leads to numbers that serve for hypothesis testing, but not for description and explanation.

Further Information about PLS

Part of this chapter gives an overview of the findings generated by applying PLS to the Seattle data set. For more information on PLS, there are several sources. Bookstein, Sampson, Streissguth (1990) have presented the mathematical derivations and readers can contact any author for software that carries out PLS calculations using the S-Plus software system for statistical and graphical data analysis (Becker, Chambers, & Wilks, 1988). The Seattle research group has compared PLS with other statistical methods and has further discussed how PLS methods can be used to study behavioral teratology focusing on Seattle data through age 7 (Sampson et al., 1989). Ketterlinus and colleagues have discussed applications to developmental psychopathology (Ketterlinus et al., 1989). Finally, Carmichael Olson and her Seattle colleagues have presented the use of PLS methodology with the 11-year Seattle data (Carmichael Olson et al., 1992).

FINDINGS FROM THE SEATTLE LONGITUDINAL PROSPECTIVE STUDY ON ALCOHOL AND PREGNANCY

As the Seattle Longitudinal Prospective Study on Alcohol and Pregnancy has progressed over the past two decades, the research team has carefully explored the behavioral teratogenesis of alcohol according to the ideas presented in Figure 1. Over the years, the study has been guided by principles of behavioral teratology, a developmental perspective, insights from child neuropsychology, and public health issues. This section on findings and the summary section tell the story of the Seattle Study, noting that the tale is not yet finished. Throughout the discussion of the Seattle data, readers should note that there are longitudinal findings of enduring alcohol-related deficits in attention. Attention functions as a unified system for the control of mental processing (Posner & Peterson, 1990), and is a critical aspect of human development. Attentional deficits have become increasingly important in understanding the development of certain forms of psychopathology (Nuechterlein & Dawson, 1984; Mirsky, 1991). Attentional difficulties may be an important teratogenic effect of prenatal exposure to alcohol.

The results of the Seattle Study have been published in a variety of places, as indicated throughout this section. Findings presented in this chapter are the primary results of the Seattle Study on the neurobehavioral teratology of alcohol, which strongly support the hypotheses proposed in Figure 1, the chart illustrating the behavioral teratology of alcohol. Table III lists an overview of the major behavioral findings of the Seattle Study from the neonatal period through age 7 years, and gives references if the reader wishes to study the Seattle findings in detail. Tables IV and V present an example of a PLS analysis and give the 11-year findings. Papers discussing the effects of fetal alcohol exposure on growth and physical anomalies are not reviewed here, but include Hanson, Streissguth, and Smith (1978), Barr, Streissguth, Martin, and Herman (1984), Clarren et al. (1987), Graham, Hanson, Darby, Barr, and Streissguth (1989), and Sampson, Bookstein, Barr, and Streissguth (1993).

In interpreting the findings of the Seattle Study, it is important to remember three things. First, the Seattle data are correlational findings; documentation of the causal significance of prenatal alcohol exposure comes from the extensive animal literature. Findings from many different disciplines and different laboratories must be integrated to fully understand the relationship between maternal alcohol use during pregnancy and children's growth and development. Second, the children in the Seattle Study are, for the most part, normally developing children. They were not selected for known abnormalities nor do they have an unusually high rate of mental retardation. Third, statistical significance is partly a function of sample size and applies to a group of children as a whole. It is not always related to clinical significance or applicable to any individual child. Population studies of "low dose" risk factors, such as alcohol exposure before birth, do not assume that individually exposed offspring will be severely or clinically affected by these lower levels of exposure. The focus of a behavioral teratology study is to evaluate statistically whether groups of exposed offspring function differently from nonexposed groups and to look for a dose–response relationship in which lower levels of the teratogen will still have a detectable effect.

In this section, findings are organized both according to age and according to the developmentally appropriate outcome measures used to test the children. Subsections include those on neonatal, infancy, preschool, 7-year, and 11-year findings.

Neonatal Findings

Background   Neurobehavioral deficits found in the neonatal period can mean that an infant exposed to alcohol before birth is compromised prior

Table II Overview of Major Behavioral Findings of the Seattle Longitudinal Study on Alcohol and Pregnancy from Birth to Seven Years, and Key to Published References

Time and finding	Procedure	Reference for article discussing findings
Day 1		
Poorer habituation	Neonatal Behavioral Assessment Scale	Streissguth, Barr & Martin (1983)
Lowered arousal level		
More body tremors; more head-turns to left; more open-eye time; less high level body activity; more hand to face	Naturalistic observations of neonatal movement	Landesman-Dwyer et al. (1978)
Day 2		
Decreased sucking pressure (whole trial); decreased latency to suck	Sucking pressure transducer	Martin, et al. (1979)
8 months		
Decreased performance on Mental Developmental Index; decreased performance on Psychomotor Developmental Index	Bayley Scales of Infant Development (MDI and PDI)	Streissguth, Barr, Martin, & Herman (1980)

4 years

Finding	Measure	Reference
Lowered Full-scale IQ; trend toward lowered Verbal IQ; lowered Performance IQ	WPPSI (intelligence test)	Streissguth, Barr, Sampson, Darby, & Martin (1989)
More motor errors; longer latency to correct errors; more total time on the pegboard	Wisconsin Fine Motor Steadiness Battery	Barr, et al. (1990)
Decreased finger-tapping performance; More total time on Tactual Performance Test for young children	Halsted-Reitan Battery (portions); Ontario Battery (portions)	Barr, et al. (1990)
Poorer balance	Gross motor tasks	Barr, et al. (1990)
More errors of omission; more errors of commission; lower ratio of correct responses; longer reaction time (final trial); [comparable number of trials oriented to task]; [no more time in motion]	Vigilance task on microcomputer (preschool version); Motion detector	Streissguth, Martin, et al. (1984)

7 years

Finding	Measure	Reference
Lowered Full-scale IQ; lowered Verbal IQ; lowered Performance IQ	WISC-R (intelligence test)	Streissguth, Barr, & Sampson (1990)
Lowered reading scores; lowered arithmetic scores; [spelling scores not lowered]	WRAT-R (achievement test)	Streissguth, Barr, & Sampson (1990)
Longer word reading performance time; longer color naming time	Stroop (example of a neuropsychological task)	Streissguth, Bookstein, et al. (1989)
More errors of omission and commission on X and AX Tasks; longer average reaction time	Vigilance task on microcomputer (7-year version)	Streissguth, Barr, et al. (1986)

Table IV　Summary of Two-Block Partial Least Squares Analysis of 13 Alcohol Scores and 77 11-Year Child School Performance Items

Alcohol scores	Salience to Child School Performance LV
Average drinks per occasion	
Prior to pregnancy recognition	0.39
During midpregnancy	0.29
Maximum drinks reported on any occasion	
Prior to pregnancy recognition	0.38
During midpregnancy	0.33
Binge: 5 or more drinks per drinking occasion	
Prior to pregnancy recognition	0.33
During midpregnancy	0.26
Quantity-frequency-variability index	
Prior to pregnancy recognition	0.33
During midpregnancy	0.27
Ordered exposure category	0.21
Average ounces of absolute alcohol/day	
Prior to pregnancy recognition	0.18
During midpregnancy	0.18
Monthly occasions of drinking	
Prior to pregnancy recognition	0.16
During midpregnancy	0.17
% Summed squared interblock correlations explained	96%
Latent variable (LV) covariance	3.55
Latent variable (LV) correlation	0.22

Table V　Saliences for the Two-Block Partial Least Squares Analysis of Alcohol Scores and 11-Year-Child School Performance Items

Child school performance items	Salience to Alcohol LV	Child school performance items	Salience to Alcohol LV
Classroom behavior items		*Classroom behavior items (cont'd)*	
Does not do work well	.17	Does not get to work immediately	.08
Stories in illogical sequence	.16	Gets sidetracked from task	.08
Does not persist	.15	Doesn't finish tasks once started	.08
Slow to settle down	.15	Immature	.08
Not interested in reading	.14	Inhibited, needs coaxing	.08
Does not get concepts	.14	Has problem getting along	
Trouble following directions	.14	with others	.08
In constant motion	.13	Difficulty with new situations[a]	.08

(*continues*)

Table V *(Continued)*

Child school performance items	Salience to Alcohol LV	Child school performance items	Salience to Alcohol LV
Flits from one activity to another	.13	Is upset by changes in routine	.07
Distractible	.13	Has problems waiting	.07
Needs individual help	.13	Difficult to understand	.07
Reluctant about challenges	.13	Confuses application of rules	.07
Can't wait turn	.13	Requires extra help for verbal direction	.06
Trouble learning new tasks	.13	Calls out in class	.06
Trouble retaining information[a]	.12	Trouble with cooperation[a]	.05
Doesn't retain information	.12	*MIT school performance items*	
Ideas come out jumbled and incomplete	.12	Has problem learning	.16
		Can't associate sound with letter	.13
Needs repeated instruction	.12	Trouble identifying letters/numbers	.11
Concentration/persistence problems[b]	.12	Trouble forming letters and numbers	.09
Fidgety and restless[b]	.12	Won't be ready for grade until next September	.08
Violates rules and norms[b]	.11	Difficulty manipulating pencils	.05
Trouble with organization[a]	.11	Writes slowly and laboriously	.03
Needs supervision to finish	.11	*MIT teacher ratings of current academic function*	
Easily frustrated	.11	Poor decoding	.17
Has a behavior problem	.11	Poor comprehension	.16
Trouble paying attention[a]	.11	Poor arithmetic reasoning	.16
Slow to complete academic tasks	.10	Poor written expression	.15
Disorganized	.10	Problems with math processes	.13
Expresses self physically	.10	Poor handwriting	.06
Wanders aimlessly	.10	*Teacher ratings of academic performance problems[c]*	
Trouble with grammar in spoken language[a]	.10	Word recognition	.15
Restless	.09	Spelling	.14
Out of chair during worktime	.09	Arithmetic reasoning	.14
Needs reminders to listen carefully	.09	Arithmetic skill/process mastery	.13
		Reading comprehension	.12
Trouble expressing thought in words	.09	Writing sentences	.11
		Handwriting	.06
Not interested in most activities	.09	*National achievement percentile scores*	
		Lowered scores on arithmetic	.16
Uses physical violence[b]	.09	Lowered scores on total battery	.14
Loses interest before finishing	.08	Lowered scores on spelling	.12
		Lowered scores on language	.11
		Lowered scores on reading	.09

Note: LV = latent variable; MIT = Multigrade Inventory for Teachers.
[a] Items from the Pupil Rating Scale. [b] Behavior items created for the study. [c] Academic performance items created for the study. Table reprinted with permission from Carmichael Olson, Sampson, Barr, Streissguth, & Bookstein (1992).

to any influence by the postnatal environment. Information as to whether these early central nervous system (CNS) effects are transient or enduring must be determined by longitudinal assessment at later ages. Based on clinical observations of infants diagnosed with FAS, lower levels of maternal alcohol exposure were expected to have widespread, if subtle, adverse effects on neonatal behavior (see Figure 1). Therefore, in the Seattle Study, newborn behavior was comprehensively assessed. (See Figure 2 for a relatively complete list of outcome measures, and Table III for a list of findings.) Note that type and use of delivery medications was not related to maternal alcohol use in the Seattle sample.

Clinical Examination   The Brazelton Neonatal Behavioral Assessment Scale (NBAS) was used to assess newborn behavior (Brazelton, 1973). The NBAS is a standardized exam widely used by clinicians to determine newborn neurobehavioral status by observing children's reflexes, level of arousal, and, particularly, the ability of the newborns to habituate to stimuli, which is perhaps an early aspect of attentional skill. The NBAS was administered under standardized conditions to newborns in the follow-up cohort when they were between 8 and 36 hours of age (Streissguth, Barr, & Martin, 1983). Data reduction for individual Brazelton items was accomplished with a factor analysis that yielded six factors with some internal consistency. These six factors were then studied individually as outcome variables in multiple regression analyses, which permitted adjustment for potentially confounding variables such as other prenatal exposures (nicotine, caffeine), maternal nutrition, obstetrical medication, and sex and age of infant.

Two NBAS factors were significantly related to prenatal alcohol exposure: decreased habituation and low arousal. This fits with Seattle Study hypotheses. Alcohol exposure in utero was indeed expected to be associated with low arousal or frequent state changes at the low end of the arousal continuum (including infants who alternate between awake and drowsy, as well as infants who have a hard time maintaining either a good alert state or a good sleep state). Early work by Rosett and colleagues (Rosett et al., 1979) also revealed disturbed sleep states in infants exposed to alcohol before birth. The habituation finding was of particular interest in this group of infants exposed to lower levels of alcohol before birth because young infants with FAS have been observed to habituate poorly. Habituation, as assessed on the NBAS, is an indication of how quickly an infant stops responding to redundant stimuli. Infants with poor habituation do not "shut down" quickly when presented with repetitive stimuli. In the Seattle sample, increased prenatal alcohol exposure was associated in a linear fashion with poorer visual and auditory habituation, showing mild compromise of the CNS among a group of mostly healthy and normal infants. Poor habituation could have developmental repercussions for alcohol-affected infants because habituation is related to later perceptual-cognitive development and represents an important biological mechanism for protecting the organism from excessive stimulation.

Naturalistic Observations of Movement   For a subgroup of 124 children, the infants' ongoing activities prior to and during the NBAS examination were coded for 2 hours in real time by a separate team of examiners (Landesman-Dwyer, Keller, & Streissguth, 1978). Using multiple regression techniques, adjusted for relevant covariates, several behavioral variables were found to be significantly related to prenatal alcohol exposure, including increased head-turning to the left, tremulousness, hand-to-face movements, more time with eyes open, and decreased vigorous bodily activity. These are all forms of behavior that have been described as characteristic of infants at risk for poor developmental outcome, although it is not clear to what extent the levels of observed behavior in this study are comparable to those in other studies. It is interesting that prenatal alcohol exposure at the social drinking levels primarily measured in this study was not associated with increased irritability and hyperactivity, as is often reported in newborns with narcotic abstinence syndrome ("withdrawal"). In fact, the alcohol-exposed infants were less active than might be expected.

Operant Learning   Two studies were carried out on two different subsets of infants in their second day of life to determine whether alcohol exposure was related to early learning deficits (Martin, Martin, Lund, & Streissguth, 1977). One study involved an operant learning head-turning paradigm ($n = 225$), whereas the other involved an operant sucking procedure ($n = 80$). Both studies gave comparable results. The operant learning findings underline how complex it is to separate the effects of teratogens on different aspects of child behavior, even at a single stage in development. Using multiple regression, an alcohol main effect was not obtained, but an alcohol-by-nicotine interaction was statistically significant. Infants whose mothers were both drinking and smoking during early pregnancy took longer to extinguish a response once it was learned. These infants continued to perseverate and make the conditioned response even when the response was no longer reinforced, thus prolonging the extinction process. In general, note that few significant interactions were found in any phase of the Seattle Study between alcohol and other predictor variables.

Sucking Response   The sucking reflex was also assessed on a subset of 151 infants in their second day of life to determine whether neuromotor deficits were related to moderate levels of alcohol exposure before birth (Martin, Martin, Streissguth, & Lund, 1979). In this objective measure of newborn neuromotor skill, infants were presented with a non-nutritive nipple attached to a pressure transducer. A sucking response was defined as a change of at least 10 mm of mercury from a floating baseline, and the analogue signal was graphed for editing and digitized for analysis. Using multiple regression analysis with adjustment for smoking, prenatal alcohol exposure was related to poorer sucking reflex performance as assessed by less pressure on the nipple. The group of babies participating in this substudy did not contain any very heavy drinkers (only 16 women in this whole group consumed two or more drinks per day on the average).

Measurement of the strength of sucking appears to be one of the most sensitive ways to quantify the neurobehavioral effects of prenatal alcohol exposure, as significant effects were obtained with very moderate exposure levels. A weak suck has been reported clinically in children with FAS and in other newborns at risk for adverse outcome. It is interesting to note that a sucking score assessed clinically during the NBAS exam involving a 3-point rating scale was significantly correlated with the automated sucking scores, yet was not predicted by prenatal alcohol exposure (Stock, Streissguth, & Martin, 1985). In behavioral teratology research in the Seattle Study, more objective measures generally appear to be relatively more sensitive to the subtle lower level teratogenic effects of alcohol than are subjective ratings.

Infancy Findings

Background   In infancy, children with FAS make slow developmental progress. Neonatal data from the Seattle Study suggested early signs of mild CNS compromise due to lower levels of prenatal alcohol exposure. It was hypothesized that for infants prenatally exposed to lower levels of alcohol, there would be continuing signs of CNS dysfunction, with in utero exposure hindering satisfactory developmental progress (see Figure 1). See Table III for a list of findings. At the time this study was carried out, the best available measure to address this hypothesis was the clinical Bayley Scales of Infant Development (BSID), a test designed to assess the current status of an infant's development and to detect children with developmental problems. The BSID remains very widely used, but is a very general measure of development that emphasizes reaching, grasping, and orienting rather than encoding and information processing (Jacobson & Jacobson, 1991).

Infant Development   The BSID was administered to the entire available cohort at 8 and 18 months of age. At 8 months, using a multiple regression model adjusted for relevant covariates, prenatal alcohol exposure predicted both the Mental Developmental Index (MDI) and the Psychomotor Developmental Index (PDI) of the BSID (Streissguth, Barr, Martin, & Herman, 1980). These findings were statistically significant, and the mean scores of infants in different exposure categories showed a consistent though small downward shift with increasing prenatal alcohol exposure. Additional analyses indicated that these alcohol-related findings were not due to other possible differences among alcohol-exposed and nonexposed infants, such as breastfeeding, maternal separation from infant, major life changes in the household, maternal diet during pregnancy, or other prenatal exposures.

Despite the significant prenatal alcohol effects on 8-month MDI and PDI scores, the BSID administered at 18 months did not reveal effects associated with prenatal alcohol exposure. Because alcohol effects were later noted when the children reached 4 and 7 years of age, the explanation that the effects of alcohol were disappearing with increasing age of the children did not appear defensible. Instead, it appears that the BSID at 18 months was not a sufficiently sensitive outcome measure given the subtle or developmentally specific effects of alcohol on toddler outcome that may be associated with more moderate levels of drinking during pregnancy. It is possible that abilities developing at this stage in a child's life, such as language skills, are not well measured by the BSID, and in retrospect a more specific measure of language or cognitive processes might have been a better choice than a general developmental scale.

The failure to find effects at 18 months demonstrates two important points in the study of alcohol teratogenesis and underlines just how essential is ongoing longitudinal developmental research. The first point is the inconclusiveness of "failures to find effects" (null findings) along the developmental trajectory. This makes clear the danger of coming too early to the conclusion that alcohol effects attenuate with age existing only in early infancy. The second point is the importance for research in behavioral teratology of sensitive and specific outcome measures used at an appropriate stage in development. The age and stage of development at which a child is tested is critical to the detection of effects (Jacobson & Jacobson, 1991), limiting the utility of cross-sectional designs, and making cumulative longitudinal study a crucial step in the description of teratological effects. Stages of development that appear to be better times for detecting deficits are those in which new skills are emerging, rather than those in which skills are being consolidated. New and more specific infant and childhood measures, sensitive to teratogenic effects and with increased predictive validity, are now becoming available. For example, the Fagan Visual Recognition Memory paradigm (an information processing approach to infant assessment), is currently being used in the Seattle laboratory and in other laboratories studying alcohol effects as well (Jacobson & Jacobson, 1991).

Preschool Findings

Background Data from the Seattle Study indicated continuing, subtle deficits in developmentally important skills through early infancy, despite the failure to detect effects at 18 months on a general test of infant development. Clinical experience showed that preschool children diagnosed with FAS are often hyperactive and poorly coordinated, and show attentional deficits and a variety of cognitive impairments (Giunta & Streissguth, 1988). Based on this experience with FAS patients, the four domains hypothesized to show decrements associated with prenatal alcohol exposure included intelligence, fine and gross motor skills, and attention (see Figure 1). These are very active areas of development in preschool; since deficits are expected in areas where new skills are emerging, these domains were at great interest. When the children in the Seattle Study were an average of 4 years, 3 months of age, they were brought in for a comprehensive battery of psychological evaluations that focused on these four developmental arenas. The test age of 4 years, 3 months was established after pretesting as the optimal age for use of the Wechsler Preschool and Primary Scale of Intelligence (WPPSI) to avoid both baseline and ceiling effects. See Figure 2 for a list of outcome measures and Table III for a summary of findings.

Intelligence   The children's performance on the WPPSI was significantly related to prenatal alcohol exposure, as Table III indicates. IQ decrements were observed in multiple regression analyses, even after adjustment for relevant confounding factors. Among children exposed at a level of three drinks or more a day, findings indicated that IQ levels of less than 85 occurred three times more often than these lower IQ levels appeared among children exposed before birth to less than three drinks per day. [For information on all analyses in this section, see Streissguth, Barr, Sampson, Darby, and Martin (1989).]

In the study of alcohol teratogenesis, the intent of behavioral teratologists is to identify alcohol effects as one significant contributor to child outcome after adjustment for other known predictors. In this study, alcohol is not the strongest predictor of preschool intelligence. Study findings confirm what many prior studies have reported: The strongest predictors of IQ in preschool children are maternal education, mother–infant interaction, paternal education, race, and birth order. In the multiple regression models reported here, alcohol was about as strong a predictor of 4-year preschool IQ as the variable of parity, but stronger than the variable of preschool experience. Prenatal alcohol exposure was a statistically strong predictor of Performance IQ but only marginally predictive of Verbal IQ, which is generally thought to be more related to psychosocial and environmental variables.

To understand thoroughly the behavioral teratology of alcohol, it is important to establish whether the CNS effects of prenatal alcohol exposure, such as IQ decrements at age 4 years, are mediated by low birthweight. Perhaps alcohol simply leads to growth deficiency and the child's resulting low birthweight can completely explain decrements in IQ. Researchers have found an effect of very low and extremely low birthweight on later intellectual function, especially in the presence of significant ill health. Several methods were used to investigate whether the effects of prenatal alcohol exposure on preschool IQ observed in this study were mediated by birthweight decrements: birthweight, and birthweight by alcohol as a multiplicative interaction, were used in the basic regression model and two alcohol slopes fitted for low-birthweight and non-low-birthweight babies were compared. For the latter analyses, two different definitions of low birthweight were used: (a) less than 2500 grams, and (b) the lowest 10% of the Seattle cohort's birthweight distribution. These analyses indicate that lowered birthweight alone was not a marker for those alcohol-exposed children who later showed IQ decrements. This finding validates the need for long-term studies that continue beyond the neonatal period and expand beyond epidemiologic indicators, such as birthweight, which are multifactorial in origin. To evaluate the effects of agents such as alcohol, with CNS effects that do not seem to be mediated by decrements in birthweight, requires longitudinal follow-up.

Clinically, it is important to know whether infants can be recognized at birth as alcohol-affected, and whether decrements in intellectual function can be predicted from such a diagnosis. In this study, the full syndrome of FAS was identified in two children at birth and significantly lower IQs could be predicted from this diagnosis. In the Seattle Study, 10 infants were diagnosed as having possible FAE at birth on the basis of clinical examinations focusing on microcephaly, minor physical anomalies, and deficiency in growth (Hanson et al., 1978). Children with the clinical label of possible FAE were at increased risk for lower IQ compared to similarly exposed children without the newborn characteristics of possible fetal alcohol effects. Within the group of 33 infants whose mothers consumed more than three drinks per day (on the average), the 10 babies who showed characteristics of possible fetal alcohol effects as newborns had IQs that were 10.5 points lower than the mean IQ of the 23 neonates exposed at this level who had normal growth and morphology at birth. These figures derive from partial residuals in the regression models and reflect IQ decrements associated with prenatal alcohol exposure after statistically adjusting for effects of other significant predictors of child IQ. This finding should not be taken to imply that there is no effect on behavior without a diagnosis of FAS or clinical label of possible fetal alcohol effects.

Fine Motor Skills The Wisconsin Fine Motor Steadiness Battery (Matthews & Klöve, 1978) provided a comprehensive measure of the fine motor performance decrements associated with prenatal alcohol exposure in 4-year-old children. For the Fine Motor Steadiness tasks, the children used a metal stylus to trace paths on three electronic Groove Boards that emitted "beeps" when the child allowed the stylus to touch the side of the grooved maze. A Resting Steadiness Hole Board with similar characteristics was also used. Number of errors and latency to correct errors were summarized across all tasks. A Pegboard using small metal grooved pegs was also part of this battery, yielding scores on total time to complete and a total peg drop count. Two additional tasks from the Halstead Reitan Neuropsychological Battery, Finger Tapping and Grip Strength (Reitan & Davison, 1974), were adapted for 4-year-olds. The Tactual Performance Test for Young Children (TPT-YC;

Trites & Price, 1978) was also used. These are described in greater detail by Barr, Streissguth, Darby, and Sampson (1990).

In multiple regression analyses adjusting for other relevant variables, increasing levels of alcohol exposure were associated with poorer performance on both response accuracy and speed in fine motor tasks. Examiners also gave significantly lower ratings of fine motor performance using a 7-point rating scale. Better performance on all of these fine motor tasks and on the examiner ratings were significantly correlated with higher IQ. Nevertheless, adding IQ to the regression model did not substantially change the alcohol effects on the objectively measured fine motor tasks, but the association with examiner ratings did drop. Fine motor deficits associated with prenatal alcohol exposure appear to be relatively independent of IQ effects, when objectively assessed. Again, objective, quantitative, automated outcome measures seem to provide more sensitive and discriminating outcomes for use in behavioral teratology research.

Gross Motor Skill   A gross motor scale developed at the Crippled Children's Division of the University of Oregon Medical School was revised for this study and a quantifiable scoring system was developed (Barr et al., 1990). The children performed 14 tasks for control of the head, trunk, and lower extremities, and locomotion, and each task was scored for a variety of qualitative performance measures. Three gross motor summary scores were derived for balance, coordination, and distance (ability to jump or hop a distance). These summary scores were then used individually as dependent variables in multiple regression analyses. Higher prenatal alcohol exposure was significantly related to poorer balance, which is consistent with clinical reports of cerebellar signs in children with FAS (Marcus, 1987) and of cerebellar dysgenesis in neuropathology studies of alcohol teratogenesis (Clarren, 1986).

Attention and Reaction Time   Given the importance of attention as a developmental domain subject to alcohol effects, a computer-operated vigilance procedure appropriate for preschoolers was developed for this study and has been used by other researchers. Vigilance involves sustained attention on a repetitive task. Vigilance and vigilance-like tasks have been shown to discriminate the performance of normal children from those diagnosed as having brain damage and from other clinical groups, and skill on vigilance tasks is related to childhood hyperactivity (see Streissguth et al., 1984). In the Seattle Study 4-Year Vigilance Task, the young children watched a large model of a Victorian house and were instructed to press a response key whenever a kitten appeared in a window (Streissguth et al., 1984). The kitten appeared on 25 occasions during the 13-min task and the following scores were obtained: errors of omission (times the kitten appeared and the child failed to press the response key), errors of commission (times the child pressed the response key in the absence of a kitten), ratio correct (total correct responses divided by the total number of button presses), reaction time (duration in seconds after the appearance of the kitten and a response within 3 sec for a child who is oriented to the task), and the number of trials for which the child is oriented to the task. When these outcomes were analyzed individually in multiple-regression models with adjustment for appropriate covariates, there were clearly alcohol-related deficits in attention. Prenatal alcohol exposure was significantly related to almost all attentional outcomes, as shown in Table III. The higher the alcohol exposure, the less the accuracy in performance on all measures, and the slower the speed of responding as the session progressed, despite comparable orientation to the task.

School-Age Findings at Age 7 Years

Background   Building on earlier data from the study, continuing alcohol-related deficits were expected in school-aged children. Based on clinical experience with patients with FAS and the literature on children of alcoholics, domains predicted to be most affected by prenatal alcohol exposure were intelligence, achievement, neuropsychologic functioning, attention, and reaction time (see Figure 1; see Table III for a list of selected 7-year findings). When the Seattle Study children should have finished the first grade (according to the entry requirements of their individual school districts), they were brought in for another complete psychological examination. Questionnaires were also sent to their first-grade teachers to gather information about classroom behavior.

In examining these school-age findings, the multistep process using multiple regression techniques was used for some analyses, and for the first time Partial Least Squares (PLS) techniques were applied with multivariate data sets that were not as suitable for multiple regression techniques. The iterative analytic process using PLS methods, which considers all predictor and outcome variables at once, was able to address the information available in this multivariate data set in a different and productive way. Using PLS, a more complete interpretive statement could be made about the complex relationship between alcohol exposure before birth and child performance at age 7 without running the risk of multiple analyses that exceed the tolerance of the sample. The Seattle research group has found PLS techniques a useful tool in advancing an understanding of the complex dose–response relationship between prenatal alcohol exposure and child development. (See Streissguth et al. (1993) for a discussion of a recent longitudinal analysis of Seattle Study findings through age 7 years using PLS techniques.)

Intelligence   The children's performance on the Wechsler Intelligence Scale for Children-Revised (WISC-R) was significantly related to prenatal alcohol exposure in a set of multiple regression analyses adjusted for appropriate covariates. The single predictor variable used to characterize alcohol exposure in these analyses was the average amount of alcohol consumed midpregnancy (above 1 oz), and the three outcome measures were WISC-R Full-scale IQ (FSIQ), Performance IQ (PIQ), and Verbal IQ (VIQ). In analysis of 7-year IQ, a main effect of alcohol was found and, for the first time, a significant interaction was detected between environmental variables and prenatal alcohol exposure. The IQ deficits found among children exposed to more than an ounce of alcohol per day, on average, were heightened when they came from families with more children in the household, or from families in which the father was less educated. Note that because IQ is vulnerable to postnatal environmental influences, more specific measures of underlying functional deficits may better reflect teratogenic effects than an intelligence test, and patterns of performance on subtests of intelligence tests may more effectively reveal teratogenic effects than do summary scores such as FSIQ, VIQ, or PIQ. See Streissguth, Barr, and Sampson (1990) for more information.

Partial Least Squares methods were applied to the 7-year child performance data to use the available multivariate information more fully and to determine the most relevant definition or pattern of alcohol "dose" and child outcome "response" (Sampson et al., 1989). Weighted combinations of both alcohol measures and the WISC-R subtests were created as a pair of latent variables that could best summarize the entire pattern of correlations between the 13 measures of alcohol exposure (see Table I) and the 11 WISC-R subtest scores. The LVs were then adjusted for covariates. In creating these LVs, the matrix of correlations showed that Digit Span and Arithmetic were the subtests most heavily weighted, or salient, for the corresponding alcohol latent variable, whether adjusted or unadjusted for covariates.

The PLS methods describe a pattern of alcohol exposure related to a pattern of CNS dysfunction at age 7. The aspects of the Alcohol LV most highly related to child intellectual performance were measures of alcohol consumption reflecting maternal use prior to pregnancy recognition and measures reflecting a style of "massing" drinks per drinking occasion (in contrast to measures reflecting the average daily volume of alcohol consumed). The salient subtests in the 7-Year Child Performance LV tap memory, speed of cognitive performance, and abstract problem solving. The PLS LVs help us understand that bingelike drinking and drinking early in pregnancy characterized the pattern of prenatal alcohol exposure that correlated most highly with a pattern of CNS dysfunction in 7-year-olds (which was represented by poor memory and problem solving, and slow speed of performance on cognitive tasks).

Achievement and Classroom Function   At age 7 years, reading, spelling, and arithmetic achievement were measured in the laboratory with the Wide

Range Achievement Test-Revised (WRAT-R). When the WRAT-R scores were considered in multiple regression analyses, with appropriate adjustment for covariates, arithmetic achievement was strongly related to prenatal alcohol exposure, whereas reading achievement was less strongly related, and spelling achievement was not at all associated with alcohol exposure before birth (Streissguth et al., 1990).

The children's behavior at school was rated by their first-grade teachers on questionnaires, using scales created in his laboratory, as well as the Pupil Rating Scale (PRS; Myklebust, 1981). The PRS is a measure developed to screen children aged 5–14 to find those who need further assessment for learning disabilities, and includes items reflecting attentional deficits and problems in information processing. In PLS analyses of multiple teacher ratings of classroom behavior, a set of problem school behaviors was identified as associated with prenatal alcohol exposure. These behavioral items, such as "difficulty retaining information" or "lack of cooperation/impulsivity," suggested impulsivity, processing and organizational problems, as well as memory difficulties (Sampson et al., 1989).

Neuropsychological Functioning, Including Attention   The 7-year examination included a large battery of neuropsychological tests designed to assess specialized patterns of alcohol-related CNS dysfunction. Among other tasks, the children completed a vigilance task that differed from the one used at 4 years but still measured the important construct of attention. Vigilance tasks similar to the task developed in our laboratory have been widely used for assessment of children with learning disabilities or Attention Deficit Disorder, and for monitoring the efficacy of stimulant medication. In the 7-Year Vigilance Task used in the Seattle Study, there were two separate 8-min tasks, each involving the sequential presentation of 360 single letters, of which 60 were critical stimuli. In the X-task, the child was asked to push the button each time the letter X appeared; in the AX-task, the subject was asked to respond to the letter X only when it was preceded in sequence by the letter A, a cognitively more demanding sustained attention task. Each letter appeared for approximately 50 msec at intervals of 1.4 sec. Each 8-min task was divided into six epochs, with the final epoch a "distraction" condition, containing annoying auditory clicks made by the computer (Streissguth, Barr, Sampson, Parrish-Johnson, Kirchner, & Martin, 1986).

After proper statistical adjustment, multiple regression analyses revealed a significant association between alcohol exposure before birth and attentional difficulties in a group of early school-age children (see Table III). The 7-Year Vigilance Task was a sensitive measure of alcohol effects, although the division into epochs and the distraction condition were not useful task parameters. The PLS analyses further revealed the AX task as the most sensitive predictor of alcohol effects, especially in the number of "false alarms" committed by the children during the task. This might have been because of the particular setup of the Seattle Study 7-Year Vigilance Task (indeed, vigilance tasks are volatile in response to changes in task parameters). Alternatively, it might have been because alcohol exposure is related to an inability to inhibit responding, or perhaps even to more general difficulties with behavioral self-regulation. This is a rich area for research exploration because attentional difficulties and problems with behavioral self-regulation may be some of the most pervasive alcohol-related effects.

The 7-year neuropsychological battery yielded a large number of outcome variables, many of which were correlated. A PLS modeling of the relationship between alcohol exposure and individual scores from the children's battery revealed an alcohol latent variable (LV) similar to that generated in PLS analyses of 7-year IQ and achievement. The 7-Year Child Performance LV, composed of the neuropsychological findings, revealed a pattern of alcohol-related effects in child outcome that included deficits in spatial memory and integration, verbal memory and integration, flexible problem solving, and perceptual motor function. Verbal tasks were not as strongly associated with prenatal alcohol exposure, which is interesting given the clinical observation that many individuals with FAS are quite talkative, and do relatively well with verbal tasks. The 7-year composite neurobehavioral LV generated by PLS methods was as sensitive to prenatal alcohol dose as was the best neonatal composite performance LV, suggesting that alcohol effects were not attenuating with age. Important covariates included paternal education and family size. See Streissguth, Bookstein, Sampson, and Barr (1989) for more information.

Neuropsychological tests are designed to measure the processes of CNS functioning rather than the products, and so may provide more sensitive measures of the long-term consequences of prenatal alcohol exposure than intelligence or achievement tests. Besides the 7-Year Vigilance Task, tests from the battery that demonstrated alcohol-related effects were the Seashore Rhythm Test (Seashore, Lewis, & Saltveit, 1960), the Seattle Study revision of the Children's Memory Test developed by Dodrill (which included Copying Designs, Memory for Designs, and Verbal Memory), and three tests from the Halstead-Reitan Neuropsychological Battery for Young Children (the Progressive Figures Test, Memory and Location scores of the Tactual Performance Test, and Name-Writing Speed; see Streissguth, Barr, Sampson, Bookstein, & Darby, 1989).

The children's behavior during clinic testing was rated by examiners using a set of 7-point rating scales developed in the Seattle laboratory. PLS analyses of these examiner ratings revealed that the cluster of subjective behavioral variables most highly associated with the Alcohol LV at 7 years included child distractibility, overpersistence, reassurance-seeking, and poor organization (Streissguth, Bookstein, et al., 1989). This problem cluster is similar to a group of problem behaviors rated by the children's teachers using other scales and focusing on the totally different situation of the classroom. Observation of similar behavior problems in different situations, and by different observers, strengthens the conclusions that these behavioral deficits represent intrinsic individual differences among this group of children, rather than responses to situational demands. There is notable congruence between the clinic and school findings, especially considering the fact that the teachers had no knowledge of the children's alcohol exposure background, or even that alcohol was a variable under study.

School-Age Findings at Age 11 Years

When the children had just about reached the age of 11 years, most often while attending fourth or fifth grade, parents and children gave permission to obtain data from their classroom teachers. Questionnaires were mailed to teachers in over 200 schools, and in a range of classroom types, to solicit learning and classroom behavior ratings, as well as five achievement test summary scores. Based on earlier data and on clinical experience with FAS patients, problems were hypothesized in domains of day-to-day classroom behavior and academic performance presumed to be related to prenatal alcohol exposure: attention and activity level at school, classroom conduct, fine motor skill in handwriting, and school achievement (see Figure 1).

Classroom Behavior Ratings and Standardized Achievement Tests   The complete Multigrade Inventory for Teachers (MIT; Shaywitz, 1986; Shaywitz, Shaywitz, Fletcher, & Escobar, 1990) was used as an instrument for the early detection of learning disabilities. The MIT requires teacher ratings on fifty-five 6-point rating scales, such as "Is this child in constant motion—always on the go?" Portions of other scales were used, including the Pupil Rating Scale (PRS) described in the section on 7-year findings, and rating scales created for this study covering untapped dimensions of behavior that were thought to be related to prenatal alcohol exposure. The children's academic performance was quanitified in two ways. First, teachers rated their pupils on how well the child was currently performing in each area of school achievement, as well as rating the child on overall academic function. Second, national percentile scores were obtained on standardized achievement tests administered by the schools in fourth grade to assess reading, mathematics, language, spelling, and overall achievement.

Partial Least Squares methods were applied to the 13 × 77 matrix of correlations between all the alcohol and child outcome variables. This is presented fully in a recent article by Carmichael Olson and colleagues (Carmichael Olson et al., 1992). Tables IV and V show these PLS findings, listing the saliences, or weights, of the component alcohol and school performance items. Much can be learned from this complex picture. In Table IV are the saliences of the 13 alcohol scores. As observed at earlier ages, the most heavily weighted measures in the 11-Year Alcohol LV were the "binge" measures of maternal consumption and, to a lesser extent, measures of drinking in the period prior to pregnancy recognition (thought to represent much of the first trimester). These more strongly predicted decrements in child school performance than did other alcohol consumption measures. In Table V are the saliences of the 77 school performance scores, ranked in order from high to low. The 11-year Child School Performance LV involved a pattern of saliences that was interpreted in light of an LV model that expressed all outcomes as joint, but unequally salient, reflections of a latent alcohol effect on the children's abilities to function at school. Looking at the items with higher saliences, the more highly weighted types of classroom problem behavior included items measuring distractibility, restlessness, lack of persistence, and reluctance to meet challenges. The more highly weighted items of learning problems tapped information processing and reasoning problems, a lack of interest in reading, and the teacher's overall impression that the child had a learning problem and did not do work well.

Surprisingly, teachers' subjective ratings appeared to capture the specific effects of prenatal alcohol exposure on academic performance more fully than did scores on standardized achievement tests. Inspecting the saliences in Table V, teachers' ratings of problems in most areas of academic achievement were salient for prenatal alcohol exposure: decoding and comprehension, associating sounds with letters, spelling and written expression, as well as arithmetic skill mastery and reasoning. As expected, the standardized achievement test score most salient for the effect of alcohol was the arithmetic national percentile. This was followed closely by the total achievement national percentile score, and the language and spelling national percentile scores were of midlevel salience as well.

As shown in Table IV, the pair of Alcohol and Child School Performance LVs explained 96% of the summed squared interblock correlations, adequately summarizing the available correlational information. At age 11, alcohol-related difficulties appeared dose-dependent and consistent in direction, with increasing school performance difficulties beginning in apparent linear fashion with the lowest nonzero alcohol scores and extending across the spectrum of alcohol use. Higher alcohol exposure was related to school performance problems with a correlation between LV scores of 0.22. This was comparable to the correlations of the Child School Performance LV with familiar predictors such as sex ($r = 0.22$) and race ($r = 0.24$). The correlation of Child School Performance LV with paternal education, the best single covariate, was -0.35, with poorer performance related to lower education.

To consider the magnitude and pattern of the alcohol effect, the scatterplots in Figure 3 illustrate and contrast the unadjusted relationships of paternal education and alcohol exposure with 11-year child school performance. The graph on the left portrays the well-recognized and relatively strong association of child outcome with father's education in years. The relationship of child outcome with alcohol exposure presented in the right-

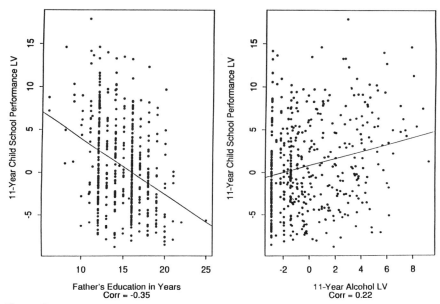

Figure 3 Comparison of associations between the 11-year child school performance latent variable LV and paternal education (left graph; $r = -0.35$) and the 11-year child school performance LV and prenatal alcohol exposure LV (right graph; $r = 0.22$).

hand graph, although weaker, is quite clear. As alcohol dose increased, child performance decreased. There is no clear drinking level threshold below which no effects are found. No model with a sharp transition or jump fits the data better than the line depicted in Figure 3.

The Next Phase of the Seattle Study: Adolescence

The Seattle cohort has now been examined again, during the adolescent years, at age 14. Adolescence is a demanding time, with many developmental advances accompanied by increased societal expectations. Subtle alcohol effects are expected to endure into this stage. Beyond early manifestations in the areas of growth and dysmorphology, alcohol effects are predicted to continue growing more differentiated and cognitive in nature during adolescence, and to appear in several realms: attention, differentiated aspects of cognition and memory (such as spatial problem solving, executive control, or motor memory), refinements of fine motor skill, certain aspects of academic achievement (such as arithmetic skills or more cognitively demanding reading tasks such as phonic analysis), and behavioral adjustment. Because the primary focus of the Seattle project is on lower levels of prenatal alcohol exposure, the alcohol effects under study are likely to continue to be subtle and to appear as specific patterns of deficit. Therefore, the Seattle Study has continued to employ multiple objective measurement tools that are age-appropriate and carefully developed to assess the presumed effects of alcohol on CNS function. One measure being used is the Wisconsin Card Sorting Test, a classic neuropsychological measure of the ability to shift attentional focus and a measure of executive control and frontal lobe function. A second task is the Spatial-Visual Reasoning Task, specially developed for this study to measure the speed and accuracy of visual spatial problem-solving. There is also an age-appropriate sustained attention task, called the Continuous Performance Test. Another task is a Fine Motor Skill battery developed for the Seattle Study that can discriminate subtle decrements in such tasks as the ability to control finger pressure when aiming at targets, and other important and specific aspects of eye–hand coordination related to cerebral dysfunction. Included in the battery are measures that tap areas potentially unaffected by prenatal alcohol exposure, such as grip strength, to begin to clarify the specificity of alcohol effects on development. Also included are behavior ratings by the research examiners, more subjective assessments of adolescent function, as well as caregiver and self-report measures of "real-life" difficulties in behavior and learning. The 14-year phase of the Seattle Study is considering covariates potentially important in the developmental pathway during the period of adolescence, such as the presence of pubertal changes or parental childrearing style. The Seattle research group is continuing to use statistical methodology appropriate for the study of developmental and teratological phenomena. These results are just beginning to be published.

SUMMARY AND CONCLUSIONS: NOT QUITE THE END OF THE STORY

The Seattle Longitudinal Prospective Study on Alcohol and Pregnancy has brought together insights from the field of developmental psychopathology and behavioral teratology to address an issue of major public health importance. Findings of the Seattle Study suggest that lower levels of prenatal alcohol exposure *do* place developing children at risk for subtle learning and behavior problems. Because of the longitudinal nature of the data, alcohol-related difficulties of some consistency could be discerned in several developmental domains in the Seattle cohort, from the neonatal period through age 11 years. These deficits did not attenuate over time, and appeared in developmental tasks important at each age.

A Developmental Perspective on Findings from the Seattle Study

The presence of alcohol-related decrements in a single developmental domain, beginning in the neonatal period and persisting across time, is a powerful argument that these problems have a biological basis. Enduring deficits suggest that a child's development is biologically affected by prenatal alcohol exposure as an important factor in the network of developmental influences described by authors studying developmental psychopathology (Cicchetti, 1984).

Considered in a longitudinal context, alcohol-related difficulties were evident across time in the neuromotor arena. These difficulties appeared in the neonatal period as tremors, inappropriate movement patterns, and a weak sucking response, and were manifested in balance, fine motor speed, and perceptual-motor accuracy difficulties by early childhood. Subtle deficits endured through age 7, appearing as decreased speed of performance or slowed reaction time on neuropsychological tasks during the early school years. True to the course of development, these deficits became more differentiated and cognitive in nature with time.

In the cognitive arena, there has been evidence both of persistent general cognitive difficulties and impairments in specific cognitive processes, all associated with alcohol teratogenesis. Poor operant learning among neonates (at least in those alcohol-exposed infants born to smokers), and poor mental and motor development in the whole cohort at 8 months was followed by no apparent general mental or motor decrements at 18 months resulting from exposure to alcohol. Yet this finding was succeeded by results indicating significant but subtle alcohol-related IQ decrements at ages 4 and 7 years. These decrements were followed at age 11 by results showing ratings from classroom teachers highly salient for alcohol exposure which reflected an overall impression that a child had "a learning problem" and "did not do work well." Specific cognitive processes showing alcohol-related impairments at age 7 included signs of memory difficulties in several modalities and decrements in organization and abstract problem solving (especially with numerical stimuli). At age 11, cognitive process impairments were reflected in teacher ratings, salient for prenatal alcohol exposure, which tapped information processing and reasoning problems. These alcohol-related outcome deficits reflect a pattern of lowered cognitive performance, perhaps in fluid rather than crystallized intelligence, and also may reflect slowness of central processing.

An especially important cognitive process showing alcohol effects is that of attention and its precursors in neonatal behavior. A related skill showing alcohol effects is the ability to inhibit responding. Alcohol-related deficits in the child's ability to attend to and identify redundant stimuli, as well as a tendency to respond impulsively without response inhibition, have been noted in the Seattle data from birth to 11 years. In the neonatal period, alcohol effects emerged in poor habituation and low arousal. This was succeeded by significant but subtle decrements in performance on a sustained attention task at 4 and 7 years, which included more "false alarms" or impulsive responses. At age 7, two of the subscales of the WISC-R subtests most highly related to alcohol exposure (Digit Span and Arithmetic) were those that are adversely affected by distractibility. Examiners saw distractibility and poor cooperation in the clinic at age 7. Moreover, at 7 years, teachers and parents commented on distractibility or impulsivity in their ratings of problem behavior, along with processing and organizational problems. At age 11, problem classroom behavior salient for prenatal alcohol exposure included distractibility, restlessness, lack of persistence, and reluctance to meet challenges.

The effects of prenatal alcohol exposure have also been observed in "real-life" function. By the end of first grade and later on in fourth grade, alcohol effects were apparent in teacher reports of problems in reading and math, and in decrements in tested academic achievement at age 11. Arithmetic skills were a particularly important area of deficit.

It is interesting to note specific domains that do not seem to be affected by prenatal alcohol exposure. Some of these intact skills may be highly canalized or subject to overlearning. Some of these relatively unaffected abilities appear to fall in the realm of crystallized intelligence, which may be more amenable to environmental influence than is fluid intelligence. Some aspects of motor skill appeared relatively unaffected by prenatal alcohol exposure. Early on, neonatal muscle tone, motor maturity, and certain movement patterns appeared relatively unaffected by alcohol exposure before birth, as did motoric strength and gross motor coordination at the preschool level, and at later school age, overlearned fine motor skills such as handwriting. Surprisingly, activity level did not show detectable alcohol-related increases. Preschool and school-age Verbal IQ did not reflect alcohol effects, nor did classroom "rote learning" verbal skills such as spelling.

A Behavioral Teratology Perspective on the Seattle Study Findings

In studying the behavioral teratology of alcohol, the central point is to discover whether there is a dose–reponse relationship between prenatal alcohol exposure and child outcome. This means the following must be determined:

1. Is alcohol associated with a significant deficit in child outcome (after other known causes are adjusted for or controlled)?
2. Are the effects on child outcome larger with increasing alcohol dose?
3. What are the patterns of detrimental prenatal alcohol exposure and associated outcome deficits?
4. Under what modifying conditions do the deficits in child outcome occur?

These questions were answered in the Seattle Study. Alcohol-related deficits in child outcome were detected after other known causes were adjusted for or controlled in the study design, even at the lower alcohol doses primarily targeted in the Seattle Study. These alcohol-related deficits were indeed more severe with increasing levels of exposure, indicating a dose–response effect. Some alcohol effects, such as IQ decrements among the children at age 4, were notable only at the upper ranges of exposure. Other outcome deficits appeared to be linearly related to prenatal alcohol exposure and did not show a "drinking level threshold" below which no effect could be discerned. True of a teratogenic effect, the effect of these lower doses of alcohol exposure (at the level of moderate to heavy social drinking) was only observable by studying a large population-based sample of children with many types of exposure histories. Because not all exposed children are affected by a teratogen, it cannot be assumed that there are deficits associated with particular exposure histories in each individual, and so a large sample is needed to detect the impact of a teratogen.

The evidence from the Seattle Study underlines how widespread is the CNS dysfunction caused by prenatal alcohol exposure, although not all areas of function are affected. The pattern of child outcome deficits associated with alcohol exposure before birth has already been described in this chapter. The pattern of prenatal alcohol exposure most likely to be detrimental is one that involves massed doses or bingelike drinking and drinking that occurs early in pregnancy. This finding is in accord with primate research revealing neurobehavioral offspring effects from a weekly binge model of maternal drinking (Clarren et al., 1990) and with research using rat models that shows that a given amount of alcohol was more damaging when administered in a binge pattern than in regular doses once or twice daily (West, Goodlett, Bonthius, Hamre, & Marcussen, 1990). However, note that the pattern just described is not the only maternal drinking pattern with adverse effects for the offspring. Also note that the effects of alcohol may be exacerbated by certain postnatal environmental conditions ("risk factors" such as less paternal education or larger family size) and ameliorated by others ("protective factors" such as positive mother–child interaction), at least starting at early school age. One of the principles of behavioral teratology is that prenatal injury is subject to postnatal environmental modification.

The precepts of behavioral teratology have brought methodological refinements to a developmental research problem. The Seattle Study demonstrates the importance of using carefully selected, adequately sensitive and specific outcome assessments in an effort to detect teratogenic effects, and demonstrates the need to choose developmentally appropriate outcomes at each age. The Seattle Study clearly illustrates the utility of objective measures, rather than general clinical assessments, for describing low dose teratogenic effects, although teacher ratings seem of value as well. Evident in the Seattle Study is the importance of research design and adequate statistical methodology to control potentially confounding variables and to ensure detection of an effect of the teratogenic agent in question, if indeed one exists. The aim of the Seattle Study to examine dose and response, neither of which can be precisely or directly measured but must be estimated in a variety of ways, has brought to bear the useful methodology of PLS on a thorny problem in developmental research.

FITTING SEATTLE STUDY FINDINGS INTO A BROADER PICTURE: PUBLIC HEALTH IMPLICATIONS

In other laboratories, longitudinal follow-up research on prenatal alcohol exposure across the spectrum of maternal alcohol use has so far been carried out across early childhood, through at most the age of 8 years. The research question is complex, but the body of research is growing and beginning to inform social policy. Four behavioral teratology studies in progress are finding some alcohol-related deficits in early growth and/or behavior, as has the Seattle Study (Brown et al., 1991; Coles et al., 1991; Day et al., 1991; O'Connor, Brill, & Sigman, 1986; Russell et al., 1991). A fifth study reveals deficits that seem to be attenuating over time (Fried & O'Connell, 1987; Fried & Watkinson, 1990), and a sixth research group finds alcohol-related deficits associated primarily with morphology rather than behavior (Boyd, Ernhart, Greene, Sokol, & Martier, 1990; Ernhart et al., 1985; Greene, Ernhart, Ager, et al., 1990; Green, Enrhart, Martier, Sokol, & Ager, 1990). Differences in study design, sample enrollment criteria, and methods of measuring prenatal alcohol use partly underlie this variation in results. Some investigators are beginning to examine developmental transactions that acknowledge not only the direct contribution of prenatal alcohol exposure to infant mental development, but also an indirect contribution involving mediating variables such as infant negative affect and mother–child interaction (O'Connor & Kasari, 1990). This new line of research fits well with findings from the Seattle Study of mother–infant interaction at 18 months (and other family-focused measures) as important covariates in the association between prenatal alcohol exposure and later child outcome.

Research on alcohol-related birth defects includes work on FAS/possible fetal alcohol effects and investigations, such as the Seattle Study, into the effects of more moderate levels of maternal drinking during pregnancy. Such research has been essential in making the public aware of alcohol consumption during pregnancy as a health problem. Public policy efforts to prevent and deal with the problem of alcohol-related birth defects have been stimulated by these research findings. In 1981, based on available data, the U.S. Surgeon General stated that women should refrain from drinking during pregnancy (FDA Drug Bulletin, 1981). In the late 1980s, bills were passed in some states that required warning signs stating that drinking alcohol during pregnancy could cause birth defects to be posted at all points of purchase of alcoholic beverages. The passionate and articulate book, *The Broken Cord*, by Michael Dorris, was published in 1989 and brought FAS research and a parent's perspective on FAS to the public eye (Dorris, 1989). In 1990, the "Healthy 2000" strategies for national health promotion included as a goal the reduction of the national incidence of FAS per 1000 live births from 0.22 to 0.12 (and for Native Americans and Alaska Natives from 4/1000 to 2/1000 live births) by the year 2000 (Department of Health and Human Services, 1990). For the past decade, Native American groups, local communities, and now American states, Canadian provinces, and other countries have been working against alcohol-related birth defects on many fronts. These efforts have been fueled by research data such as that of the Seattle Study, pinpointing prenatal alcohol exposure, even at lower doses, as a potential threat to the health of children.

ACKNOWLEDGMENTS

This research was supported by grant number AA01455-01-17 from the National Institute of Alcohol Abuse and Alcoholism, U.S. Public Health Service, with supplemental support from the University of Washington Alcohol and Drug Abuse Institute and the University of Washington Biomedical Research Fund. We gratefully acknowledge the contributions of the many colleagues, students, researchers, and staff who have worked on this project over the years. In particular, we thank Dr. Joan C. Martin and Donald C. Martin, coinvestigators in the early years of the project, as well as Drs. Sharon Landesman Ramey, Cynthia Herman Ervin, Veronica Buffington, and Betty Darby, psychologists who collaborated on specific components of the study. We also thank Drs. James W. Hanson, John Graham, and Sterling Clarren, pediatric dysmorphologists. We appreciate the extraordinary efforts of Ninia Carpio Ingram in manuscript preparation. Finally, we thank the parents and children who made this project possible. This report updates and extends an earlier chapter "Alcohol Use During Pregnancy and Child Development: A Longitudinal Prospective Study of Human Behavioral Teratology" by Streissguth, Barr, and Sampson, Chapter 10 in *Longitudinal Studies of Children at Psychological Risk: Cross-National Perspectives,* by Greenbaum and Auerbach (Eds.), Norwood, NJ: Ablex, 1992.

REFERENCES

Abel, E. L., & Sokol, R. J. (1987). Incidence of fetal alcohol syndrome and economic impact of FAS-related anomalies. *Drug and Alcohol Dependence, 19,* 51–70.

Barr, H. M., Streissguth, A. P., Darby, B. L., & Sampson, P. D. (1990). Prenatal exposure to alcohol, caffeine, tobacco, and aspirin: Effects on fine and gross motor performance in 4-year-old children. *Developmental Psychology, 26,* 339–348.

Barr, H. M., Streissguth, A. P., Martin, D. C., & Herman, C. S. (1984). Infant size at 8 months of age: Relationship to maternal use of alcohol, nicotine and caffeine during pregnancy. *Pediatrics, 74*(3), 336–341.

Becker, R. A., Chambers, J. M., & Wilks, A. R. (1988). *The new S language: A programming environment for data analysis and graphics.* Pacific Grove, CA: Wadsworth and Brooks/Cole Advanced Books and Software.

Bookstein, F. L., Sampson, P. D., Streissguth, A. P., & Barr, H. M. (1990). Measuring "dose" and "response" with multivariate data using Partial Least Squares techniques. *Communications in Statistics: Theory and Methods, 19*(3), 765–804.

Boyd, T. A., Ernhart, C. B., Greene, T., Sokol, R. J., & Martier, S. (1990). Prenatal alcohol exposure and sustained attention in the preschool years. *Neurotoxicology and Teratology, 13*(1), 49–55.

Brazelton, T. B. (1973). *Neonatal Behavioral Assessment Scale.* Philadelphia, PA: Lippincott.

Brown, R. T., Coles, C. D., Smith, I. E., Platzman, K. A., Silverstein, J., Erickson, S., & Falek, A. (1991). Effects of prenatal alcohol exposure at school age. II. Attention and behavior. *Neurotoxicology and Teratology, 13*(4), 369–375.

Caldwell, B., & Bradley, R. (1979). *Home observation for measurement of the environment.* Little Rock, AK: University of Arkansas.

Carmichael Olson, H., Sampson, P. D., Barr, H. M., Streissguth, A. P., & Bookstein, F. L. (1992). Prenatal exposure to alcohol and school problems in late childhood: A longitudinal prospective study. *Development and Psychopathology, 4,* 341–359.

Cicchetti, D. (1984). The emergence of developmental psychopathology. *Child Development. 55*(1), 1–7.

Clarren, S. K. (1986). Neuropathology in the fetal alcohol syndrome. In J. West (Ed.), *Alcohol and Brain Development* (pp. 158–166). New York: Oxford University Press.

Clarren, S. K., Astley, S. J., Bowden, D. M., Lai, H., Milam, A. H., Rudeen, P. K., & Shoemaker, W. J. (1990). Neuroanatomic and neurochemical abnormalities in nonhuman primates exposed to weekly doses of alcohol during gestation. *Alcoholism: Clinical and Experimental Research, 14*(5), 674–683.

Clarren, S. K., Sampson, P. D., Larsen, J., Donnell, D., Barr, H. M., Bookstein, F. L., Martin, D. C., & Streissguth, A. P. (1987). Facial effects of fetal alcohol exposure: Assessment by photographs and morphometric analysis. *American Journal of Medical Genetics, 26,* 651–666.

Coles, C. D., Brown, R. T., Smith, I. E., Platzman, K. A., Erickson, S., & Falek, A. (1991). Effects of prenatal alcohol exposure at school age. I. Physical and cognitive development. *Neurotoxicology and Teratology, 13*(4), 357–367.

Day, N. L., Robles, N., Richardson, G., Geva, D., Taylor, P., Scher, M., Stoffer, D., Cornelius, M., & Goldschmidt, L. (1991). The effects of prenatal alcohol use on the growth of children at 3 years of age. *Alcoholism: Clinical and Experimental Research, 15*(1), 67–71.

Department of Health and Human Services. (1990). *Healthy people 2000: National health promotion and disease prevention objectives* (DHHS Publication No. PHS 91-50213). Washington, DC: U.S. Government Printing Office.

Dorris, M. (1989). *The broken cord: A family's ongoing struggle with Fetal Alcohol Syndrome.* New York: Harper Collins.

Driscoll, C. D., Streissguth, A. P., & Riley, E. P. (1990). Prenatal alcohol exposure: Comparability of effects in humans and animal models. *Neurotoxicology and Teratology, 12,* 231–237.

Ernhart, C. B., Wolf, A. W., Linn, P. L., Sokol, R. J., Kennard, M. J., & Filipovich, H. F. (1985). Alcohol-related birth defects: Syndromal anomalies, intrauterine growth retardation, neonatal behavioral assessment. *Alcoholism: Clinical and Experimental Research, 9*(5), 447–453.

Federal Drug Administration (July, 1981). Surgeon General's advisory on alcohol and pregnancy. *FDA Drug Bulletin, 11*(2), 9–10.

Fried, P. A., & O'Connell, C. M. (1987). A comparison of the effects of prenatal exposure to tobacco, alcohol, cannabis, caffeine on birth size, subsequent growth. *Neurotoxicology and Teratology, 9*(4), 79–85.

Fried, P. A., & Watkinson, B. (1990). 36- and 48-month neurobehavioral follow-up of children prenatally exposed to marijuana, cigarettes and alcohol. *Developmental and Behavioral Pediatrics, 11*(2), 49–58.

Giunta, C. T., Barr, H. M., Gillespie, J. M., & Streissguth, A. P. (1987). *Techniques for minimizing subject attrition in longitudinal research* (Tech. Rep. No. 87-01). Seattle: University of Washington, Pregnancy and Health Study.

Giunta, C. T., & Streissguth, A. P. (1988). Patients with fetal alcohol syndrome and their caretakers. *Social Casework: The Journal of Contemporary Social Work, 69*(7), 453–459.

Goodlett, C. R., & West, J. R. (1992). Fetal alcohol effects: Rat model of alcohol exposure during the brain growth spurt. In I. S. Zagon & T. A. Slotkin (Eds.), *Maternal substance abuse and the developing nervous system* (pp. 45–75). San Diego, CA: Academic Press.

Graham, J. M., Hanson, J. W., Darby, B. L., Barr, H. M., & Streissguth, A. P. (1988). Independent dysmorphology evaluation at birth and 4 years of age for children exposed to varying amounts of alcohol in utero. *Pediatrics, 81*(6), 772–778.

Greene, T. H., Ernhart, C. B., Ager, J., Sokol, R. J., Martier, S., & Boyd, T. A. (1990). Prenatal exposure to alcohol and cognitive development. *Neurotoxicology and Teratology, 13*(1), 57–68.

Greene, T. H., Ernhart, C. B., Martier, S., Sokol, R. J., & Ager, J. (1990). Prenatal alcohol exposure and language development. *Alcoholism: Clinical and Experimental Research, 14*(6), 937–945.

Hanson, J. W., Streissguth, A. P., & Smith, D. W. (1978). The effects of moderate alcohol consumption during pregnancy on fetal growth and morphogenesis. *The Journal of Pediatrics, 92*(3), 457–460.

Jacobson, J. L., & Jacobson, S. W. (1991). Assessment of teratogenic effects on cognitive and behavioral development in infancy and childhood. *Drug abuse prevention and intervention research: Methodological issues* (NIDA Research Monograph No. 107). Rockville, MD: U.S. Department of Health & Human Services.

Jessor, R., Graves, T. D., Hanson, R. C., & Jessor, S. L. (1968). *Society, personality, deviant behavior: A study of tri-ethnic community.* New York: Holt, Rinehart, & Winston.

Jones, K. L., & Smith, D. W. (1973). Recognition of the fetal alcohol syndrome in early infancy. *Lancet, 2,* 999–1001.

Jones, K. L., Smith, D. W., Ulleland, C. N., & Streissguth, A. P. (1973). Pattern of malformation in offspring of chronic alcoholic mothers. *Lancet, 1,* 1267–1271.

Jöreskog, K. G., & Wold, H. (Eds.). (1982). *Systems under indirect observation: Causality-structure-prediction, Part 1 and 2.* Amsterdam: North Holland.

Ketterlinus, R. D., Bookstein, F. L., Sampson, P. D., & Lamb, M. E. (1989). Partial least squares analysis in developmental psychopathology. *Development and Psychopathology, 1,* 351–371.

Landesman-Dwyer, S., Keller, L. S., & Streissguth, A. P. (1978). Naturalistic observations of newborns: Effects of maternal alcohol intake. *Alcoholism: Clinical and Experimental Research, 2,* 171–177.

Lemoine, P., Harousseau, H., Borteyru, J. P., & Menuet, J. C. (1968). *Children of alcoholic parents: Abnormalities observed in 127 cases.* (A translation from a French journal article. Available from: National Clearinghouse for Alcohol Information, P.O. Box 2345, Rockville, MD, 20852.)

Marcus, J. D. (1987). Neurological findings in Fetal Alcohol Syndrome. *Neuropediatrics, 18,* 158–160.

Martin, D. C., Martin, J. C., Streissguth, A. P., & Lund, C. A. (1979). Sucking frequency and amplitude in newborns as a function of maternal drinking and smoking. In M. Galanter (Ed.), *Currents in Alcoholism* (Vol. 5, pp. 359–366). New York: Grune and Stratton.

Martin, J. C., Martin, D. C., Lund, C. A., & Streissguth, A. P. (1977). Maternal alcohol ingestion, cigarette smoking, and their effects on newborn conditioning. *Alcoholism: Clinical and Experimental Research, 1*(3), 243–247.

Matthews, C. G., & Klöve, H. (1978). *Wisconsin fine motor steadiness battery. Administration manual for child neuropsychological battery.* Madison, WI: Neuropsychology Laboratory, University of Wisconsin Medical School.

Mirsky, A. F. (Speaker). (1991). *The neuropsychology of attention: Implications for the development of neuropsychiatric disorders.* (Cassette Recording). Washington, DC: American Psychological Association.

Myklebust, H. R. (1981). *The Pupil Rating Scale Revised: Screening for Learning Disabilities.* San Antonio, TX: The Psychological Corporation.

Nuechterlein, K. H., & Dawson, M. E. (1984). Information processing and attentional functioning in the development course of schizophrenic disorders. *Schizophrenia Bulletin, 10*(2), 160–202.

O'Connor, M. J., Brill, N. J., & Sigman, M. (1986). Alcohol use in primiparous women older than 30 years of age: Relation to infant development. *Pediatrics, 78*(3), 444–450.

O'Connor, M. J., & Kasari, C. (1990). *Attachment behavior of infants exposed to alcohol prenatally mediating effects of infant affect, mother–infant interaction.* Paper presented at the biennial meeting of the International Conference on Infant Studies, Montreal, Canada.

Posner, M. I., & Petersen, S. E. (1990). The attention system of the human brain. *Annual Review of the Neurosciences, 13*, 25–42.

Porter, R., O'Connor, M., & Whelan, J. (Eds.). (1984). *Mechanisms of alcohol damage in utero* (CIBA Foundation Symposium 105). London: Pitman.

Ragozin, A. S., Landesman-Dwyer, S., & Streissguth, A. P. (1978). The relationship between mothers' drinking habits and children's home environments. In F. A. Seixas (Ed.), *Currents in Alcoholism* (Vol. 4, pp. 39–49). New York: Grune & Stratton.

Reitan, R. M., & Davison, L. A. (1974). *Clinical Neuropsychology: Clinical Status and Applications.* New York: Wiley.

Riley, E. P. (1990). The long-term behavioral effects of prenatal alcohol exposure in rats. *Alcoholism: Clinical and Experimental Research, 14*(5), 670–673.

Rosett, H. L., Snyder, P., Sander, L. W., Lee, A., Cook, P., Weiner, L., & Gould, J. (1979). Effects of maternal drinking on neonatal state regulation. *Developmental Medicine and Child Neurology, 21*(4), 464–473.

Russell, M., Czarnecki, D. M., Cowan, R., McPherson, E., & Mudar, P. J. (1991). Measures of maternal alcohol use as predictors of development in early childhood. *Alcoholism: Clinical and Experimental Research, 15*, 991–1000.

Sampson, P. D., Streissguth, A. P., Barr, H. M., & Bookstein, F. L. (1989). Neurobehavioral effects of prenatal alcohol. Part II: Partial least squares analysis. *Neurotoxicology and Teratology, 11*(5), 477–491.

Sampson, P. D., Bookstein, F. L., Barr, H. M., & Streissguth, A. P. (1993). *Prenatal alcohol exposure and measures of child size from birth to age 14 years* (Technical Report No. 92-03). Seattle, WA: University of Washington Pregnancy & Health Study.

Seashore, C. B., Lewis, C., & Saltveit, J. G. (1960). *Seashore Measures of Musical Talent: Manual.* New York: Psychological Corporation.

Shaywitz, S. E. (1986). *Early recognition of educational vulnerability-EREV* (Technical Report). Hartford, CT: State Department of Education.

Shaywitz, S. E., Shaywitz, B. A., Fletcher, J. M., & Escobar, M. D. (1990). Prevalence of reading disabilities in males and females: Results of the Connecticut longitudinal study. *Journal of the American Medical Association, 264*(8), 998–1002.

Stock, D. L., Streissguth, A. P., & Martin, D. C. (1985). Neonatal sucking as an outcome variable: Comparison of quantitative and clinical assessments. *Early Human Development, 10*, 273–278.

Streissguth, A. P. (1986). The behavioral teratology of alcohol: Performance, behavioral, and intellectual deficits in prenatally exposed children. In J. R. West (Ed.), *Alcohol and Brain Development* (pp. 3–44). New York: Oxford University Press.

Streissguth, A. P. (1992). Fetal alcohol syndrome and fetal alcohol effects: A clinical perspective of later developmental consequences. In I. S. Zagon & T. A. Slotkin (Eds.), *Maternal substance abuse and the developing nervous system.* San Diego, CA: Academic Press.

Streissguth, A. P., Aase, J. M., Clarren, S. K., Randels, S. P., LaDue, R. A., & Smith, D. F. (1991). Fetal alcohol syndrome in adolescents and adults. *The Journal of the American Medical Association, 265*(15), 1961–1967.

Streissguth, A. P., Barr, H. M., Darby, B. L., & Ervin, C. H. (1987). *The MIIS, a simple, reliable method of assessing mother–infant interactions which predicts 4-year IQ* (Technical Report No. 87-02). Seattle, WA: University of Washington Pregnancy & Health Study.

Streissguth, A. P., Barr, H. M., & Martin, D. C. (1983). Maternal alcohol use and neonatal habituation assessed with the Brazelton Scale. *Child Development, 54,* 1109–1118.

Streissguth, A. P., Barr, H. M., Martin, D. C., & Herman, C. S. (1980). Effects of maternal alcohol, nicotine, and caffeine use during pregnancy on infant mental and motor development at 8 months. *Alcoholism: Clinical and Experimental Research, 4,* 152–164.

Streissguth, A. P., Barr, H. M., & Sampson, P. D. (1990). Moderate prenatal alcohol exposure: Effects on child IQ and learning problems at age 7½ years. *Alcoholism: Clinical and Experimental Research, 14,* 662–669.

Streissguth, A. P., Barr, H. M., Sampson, P. D., Bookstein, F. L., & Darby, B. L. (1989). Neurobehavioral effects of prenatal alcohol. Part I: Literature review and research strategy. *Neurotoxicology and Teratology, 11*(5), 461–476.

Streissguth, A. P., Barr, H. M., Sampson, P. D., Darby, B. L., & Martin, D. C. (1989). IQ at age 4 in relation to maternal alcohol use and smoking during pregnancy. *Developmental Psychology, 25*(1), 3–11.

Streissguth, A. P., Barr, H. M., Sampson, P. D., Parrish-Johnson, J. C., Kirchner, G. L., & Martin, D. C. (1986). Attention and distraction at age 7 years and prenatal alcohol exposure. *Neurobehavioral Toxicology and Teratology, 8,* 717–725.

Streissguth, A. P., Bookstein, F. L., Sampson, P. D., & Barr, H. M. (1989). Neurobehavioral effects of prenatal alcohol: Part III. PLS analyses of neuropsychologic tests. *Neurobehavioral Toxicology and Teratology, 11*(5), 493–507.

Streissguth, A. P., Clarren, S. K. & Jones, K. L. (1985). Natural history of the Fetal Alcohol Syndrome: A ten-year follow-up of eleven patients. *Lancet, 2,* 85–92.

Streissguth, A. P., & Giunta, C. T. (1992). Subject recruitment and retention for longitudinal research: Practical considerations for a nonintervention model. In M. M. Kilbey & K. Asghar (Eds.), *Methodological issues in epidemiological, prevention, and treatment research on drug-exposed women and their children.* (National Institute on Drug Abuse Monograph No. 117). Rockville, MD: U.S. Department of Health and Human Services, Public Health Service.

Streissguth, A. P., & LaDue, R. A. (1987). Teratogenic causes of developmental disabilities. In S. R. Schroeder (Ed.), *Toxic Substances and Mental Retardation* (AAMD Monographs 8, 1–32). Washington, DC: American Association on Mental Deficiency.

Streissguth, A. P., Martin, D. C., Barr, H. M., Sandman, B. M., Kirchner, G. L., & Darby, B. L. (1984). Intrauterine alcohol and nicotine exposure: Attention and reaction time in 4-year-old children. *Developmental Psychology, 20,* 533–541.

Streissguth, A. P., Martin, D. C., & Buffington, V. E. (1977). Identifying heavy drinkers: A comparison of eight alcohol scores obtained on the same sample. In F. A. Seixas (Ed.), *Currents in Alcoholism* (Vol. 2, pp. 395–420). New York: Grune & Stratton.

Streissguth, A. P., Martin, D. C., Martin, J. C., & Barr, H. M. (1981). The Seattle longitudinal prospective study on alcohol and pregnancy. *Neurobehavioral Toxicology and Teratology, 3,* 223–233.

Streissguth, A. P., Sampson, P. D., Barr, H. M., Clarren, S. K., & Martin, D. C. (1986). Studying alcohol teratogenesis from the perspective of the fetal alcohol syndrome: Methodological and statistical issues. In H. M. Wisniewski & D. A. Snider (Eds.), *Mental retardation: Research, education, and technology transfer* (pp. 63–86). New York: New York Academy of Sciences.

Streissguth, A. P., Sampson, P. D., & Barr, H. M. (1989). Neurobehavioral dose–response effects of prenatal alcohol exposure in humans from infancy to adulthood. In D. E. Hutchings (Ed.), *Prenatal Abuse of Licit and Illicit Drugs* (Vol. 562, 145–158). New York: Annals of the New York Academy of Sciences.

Streissguth, A. P., Sampson, P. D., Bookstein, F. L., & Barr, H. M. (1993). *The enduring effects* of prenatal alcohol exposure of child development: Birth through seven years (mono-graph). Ann Arbor, MI: University of Michigan Press.

Trites, R. L., & Price, M. A. (1978). *Assessment of readiness for primary French immersion.* Ottawa: University of Ottawa Press.

Ulleland, C. N. (1972). The offspring of alcoholic mothers. *Annals of the New York Academy of Sciences, 197,* 167–169.

Voorhees, C. V. (1986). Principles of behavioral teratogenicity. In E. P. Riley & C. V. Voorhees (Eds.), *Handbook of Behavioral Teratology,* New York: Plenum.

West, J. R. (1986). *Alcohol and Brain Development.* New York: Oxford University Press.

West, J. R., Goodlett, C. R., Bonthius, D. J., Hamre, K. M., & Marcussen, B. L. (1990). Cell population depletion associated with fetal alcohol brain damage: Mechanisms of BAC-dependent cell loss. *Alcoholism: Clinical and Experimental Research, 14*(6), 813–818.

West, J. R., Goodlett, C. R., Bonthius, D. J., & Pierce, D. R. (1990). New approaches to research on the long-term consequences of prenatal exposure to alcohol. *Alcoholism: Clinical and Experimental Research, 14*(5), 684–689.

Wilson, J. G. (1977). Current status of teratology. In J. G. Wilson & F. C. Fraser (Eds.), *Handbook of teratology: Vol. 1. General principles and etiology* (pp. 47–74). New York: Plenum.

Health
Surveillance
and the
Development
of Children

Jack P. Shonkoff

INTRODUCTION

The interdependence of health and development is a concept with substantial face validity. Each reflects a dynamic process that depends on the
mutual impacts of biological endowment and environmental influence. Each
is governed by the principles of adaptation and homeostasis. Each is characterized by considerable variation within a normal range, coupled with a
vaguely defined domain of dysfunction and a distinct realm of frank pathology.

Drawing on the biopsychosocial model formulated by Engel (1977), health
and development may both be viewed as complementary dimensions of a
hierarchical biosystem that extends from the levels of molecules, cells,
tissues, and organ systems to the individual, family, community, and culture.
Within this framework, health and competence, as well as illness and disability, are determined by the relative and interactive functioning of each component system at each hierarchical level. Thus, physical well-being and adaptive

Developmental Follow-up
113

behavior reflect a high level of systemic harmony. In contrast, disease or dysfunction may reflect disruptions at any, or more than one, level, from the molecular to the sociocultural.

Considerable clinical interest and promising empirical research have highlighted the complex relation between health and development in childhood, and multidimensional models have been postulated to explain both the facilitating and the inhibitory effects of illness, discomfort, and pain on the developmental process (Bax, Hart, & Jenkins, 1983; Parmelee, 1986; Pless & Pinkerton, 1975; Rutter, Tizard, & Wightmore, 1970). This chapter examines the potential inclusion of health surveillance within a comprehensive strategy for developmental follow-up of children and youth from early infancy through adolescence. Four major questions are explored. First, what do we know about the interdependence of health and development? Second, what do we know about the developmental consequences of health impairment? Third, how can a child's health status be screened effectively within a comprehensive follow-up strategy? Finally, what can we learn from investigating children's patterns of health care utilization?

WHAT DO WE KNOW ABOUT THE INTERDEPENDENCE OF HEALTH AND DEVELOPMENT?

The concept of health is well understood intuitively, but it has proven to be difficult to define for research or program evaluation purposes (Shonkoff, 1984). Parsons (1972) defined health as a state of optimum capacity for the effective performance of the roles for which an individual has been socialized. The definition formulated by the Constitution of the World Health Organization (1958) specifies "complete physical, mental, and social well-being." Medical research generally has focused most successfully on disease; consequently, when health has been the object of investigation, it has been defined most commonly as "the absence of pathology." The failure to achieve consensus on an objective, nonexclusionary construct for physical or emotional health remains one of the fundamental measurement challenges facing research in this area. Therefore, until this issue is resolved, developmental follow-up programs will have to accommodate to an evaluation model that views health simply as the absence of disease.

Despite the vagueness of its definition, the concept of health as a facilitator (although not a guarantee) of adaptive development has a great deal of intrinsic appeal. For example, whereas persistent illness is characterized by diminished energy and a decrease in stamina, sustained good health generally is accompanied by a level of physiologic vitality that provides a potent substrate for active learning and mastery behavior. Whereas the child with a chronic impairment must deal with varying degrees of recurrent discomfort or pain, the child who remains healthy is free from such distraction. The apathy and irritability that may result from the experience of both acute and chronic disease provide a stark contrast to the positive sense of well-being that is generated by good physical health. Finally, the intrinsic drive toward autonomy and personal efficacy that characterizes the normally developing child may be threatened significantly by the drift toward dependence and regression that often accompanies continuous ill health.

The extent to which a child's developmental trajectory is influenced by health factors depends on his or her sense of well-being, the nature and duration of experienced adverse symptoms, the inherent adaptive capacities of the individual, and the quality of his or her caregiving and social supports. For some, ill health is a source of considerable vulnerability; for others, the process of coping adaptively with disease becomes a source of resilience. Generally speaking, however, it may be useful to think about health as a protective factor and illness as a risk factor in the lives of children.

Beyond the conceptual appeal of these notions, there is a growing body of empirical research that has extended our knowledge of the close relation between health and developmental adaptation across the life span. Psychosocial adversity, for example, has been shown to be associated with higher rates of physical illness (Haggerty, 1980; Rabkin & Struening, 1976; Syme & Berkman, 1976) as well as with behavioral and developmental difficulties (Garmezy, 1983; Werner & Smith, 1977). Conversely, the protective benefits of social support have been shown to correlate positively with both physical health (Boyce, 1985) and emotional well-being (Werner & Smith, 1982). Although these associations have been appreciated for decades, their mediators have not been elucidated. Recent research on the psychobiology of stress, however, provides a promising framework for extending our understanding in this area (Boyce & Jemerin, 1990; Boyce, Barr, & Zeltzer, 1992; Jemerin & Boyce, 1990).

The capacity to deal with stress is fundamental to survival. As an adaptive response, it transcends the domains of health and development, and includes such diverse functions as self-regulation, interpersonal competence, resistance to infection, somatic growth, and physical maturation. Studies of the physiologic correlates of typical behavioral responses to environmental challenge have revealed a complex, interactive process that is mediated largely through neuro-endocrine pathways in the sympathetic-adrenomedullary (catecholamine-releasing) and the hypothalamic-pituitary-adrenocortical (cortisol-releasing) systems. When the level of circulating catecholamines rises, the effects include an increase in heart rate, greater tissue availability of oxygen and glucose, and an increase in mental alertness and anxiety. A rise in cortisol also results in an elevation of blood glucose, in conjunction with a suppression of both inflammatory and immunologic processes.

Individual differences in thresholds of responsiveness and magnitudes of reaction within these systems are considerable, and have been linked to both behavioral and health-related outcomes. Heightened adrenergic reactivity, for example, has been found to be associated with both aggressiveness and behavioral inhibition, as well as with an elevated risk of cardiovascular disease in association with the type A personality. Elevated cortisol levels have long been known to reduce resistance to infection, and more recently have been associated with major affective disorders. Although a comprehensive overview of research on psychobiology is beyond the scope of this chapter, these examples underscore the extent to which further study is likely to extend our knowledge about the mediators of biopsychosocial vulnerability and resilience, and to demonstrate the essential interdependence of health and development.

WHAT DO WE KNOW ABOUT THE DEVELOPMENTAL CONSEQUENCES OF HEALTH IMPAIRMENT?

The potential impacts of impaired health on human development are complex and multidimensional. Three aspects of that influence will be considered in this chapter. The first is the cumulative experience of minor illnesses, with particular interest in their role as facilitators of the normative developmental process. The second issue to be addressed is the contribution of common childhood illness to the emergence of developmental dysfunction. Finally, the consequences of a chronic health impairment will be examined from both a biobehavioral and psychosocial perspective.

Minor Illness as a Facilitator of Normal Development

In his Presidential Address to the Society for Research in Child Development, Parmelee (1986) speculated on the potential benefits of common childhood illnesses as important socializing experiences. Three areas of influence were hypothesized: (a) effects on the development of general behavioral competence, (b) impacts on the development of children's understanding of the concepts of illness and wellness, and (c) effects on the ability of children to understand the relations and differences among physical, emotional, and social causes of distressed feelings and altered physical states.

Although empirical data in this area are sparse, the potential opportunities for fruitful investigation are substantial. In reviewing a range of previous studies, Parmelee (1986) suggested that common childhood illness may play an important role in both affective and cognitive development, as well as in emerging capacities for self-knowledge, empathy, and overall prosocial behavior. Children have multiple opportunities to learn from their own experiences with ill health, as well as from those of their siblings, their friends, and the adults in their environment. During periods of illness, children behave differently, are treated differently by their caregivers (both parental and nonparental), and generally are held less accountable for difficult behaviors (Campbell, 1978; Haskins, Hirschbiel, Collier, Sanyal, & Finkelstein, 1981; Mattsson & Weissberg, 1970). Experience with minor illness can provide an opportunity for either adaptive growth in the parent–child relationship or an exacerbation of caregiver–child dysfunction or maladaptation. The degree to which episodes are enhancing or debilitating may be influenced by a host of cultural and familial factors related to differences in such domains as reaction to pain, acknowledgment of symptoms, and seeking of medical assistance (Mechanic, 1964, 1972; Zborowski, 1952; Zola, 1966).

Common Childhood Illnesses as Risk Factors for Developmental Dysfunction

Although experience with routine childhood illness is universal, evidence suggests that some common health impairments may confer a specific susceptibility to adverse developmental sequelae. One example about which there is growing research interest is the hypothesized association between recurrent or chronic middle ear dysfunction and disorders of language or learning.

Fluid accumulation in the middle ear, with or without frank infection (otitis media), is among the most common medical problems of early childhood. With appropriate clinical management, the risk of significant health complications is low, and most children "outgrow" their susceptibility to ear infections by the time they enter school. However, because of the fluctuating conductive hearing loss that accompanies fluid accumulation in the middle ear, questions have been raised about the adverse impact of this disorder on the process of language acquisition, particularly in the early developmental period (Berko-Gleason, 1983; Paradise, 1981; Teele, Klein, Rosner, et al., 1984). Furthermore, retrospective studies have documented an increased prevalence of early and/or more frequent middle ear disease in the histories of school-aged children with learning disabilities (Bennett, Ruuska, & Sherman, 1980; Zinkus & Gottlieb, 1980). Thus, although there is a need for more methodologically sound research in this area, the collection of reliable data on the timing, frequency, and duration of middle ear dysfunction, as well as on the child's hearing status, should be an important component in any developmental follow-up protocol. A more definitive understanding of the relation between otitis media and language development, however, must await the completion of well designed and carefully conducted long-term prospective studies.

Developmental and Behavioral Consequences of Chronic Health Impairment

Although reliable data are difficult to obtain because of definitional uncertainties, it is estimated that at least 10% of children and youth have a persistent health impairment or chronic disease (Pless & Roghmann, 1971).

This category includes youngsters with a wide variety of conditions, including asthma, diabetes mellitus, cystic fibrosis, arthritis, seizure disorders, congestive heart failure, chronic renal insufficiency, and chronic inflammatory bowel disease.

Although long-term longitudinal data are rare, a substantial number of cross-sectional and short-term studies have been conducted on a broad variety of developmental and behavioral issues for children with chronic diseases or physical impairments that are not associated with mental retardation, learning disabilities, or significant mental illness (Cadman, Boyle, Szatmari, & Offord, 1987; Mattson, 1972; Pless & Pinkerton, 1975; Stein & Jessop, 1984). The range of documented as well as hypothesized influences extends from those that may be considered primarily biomedical (e.g., specific physiological insults secondary to such factors as malnutrition/anemia, chronic hypoxia, or specific medication effects) to a number of broad-based psychosocial sequelae related to such factors as a child's self-concept, peer relationships, and sense of autonomy. Several specific examples will help to illustrate some of these salient concerns.

Iron Deficiency Anemia   The developmental consequences of iron deficiency anemia represent one area of increasing interest. A growing body of data has demonstrated that children with iron deficiency anemia demonstrate greater fatigue, increased irritability, and more frequent affective disturbances in association with decreased motivation, shortened attention span, and deficits in intellectual performance (Deinard, List, Lindgren, Hunt, & Chang, 1986; Lozoff et al., 1987; Lozoff, Wolf, Urrutia, & Viteri, 1985; Oski, Honig, Helu, & Howanitz, 1983). A number of questions have been raised, however, about whether these behavioral differences are secondary to chronic deficits in tissue oxygenation, abnormalities in iron-dependent central nervous system neurotransmitters, the consequences of associated general malnutrition, or the result of environmental influences on children who are both poorly nourished and live under conditions of poverty. Furthermore, additional questions remain regarding the differential effects of iron deficiency anemia that are dependent on age, and whether the behavioral manifestations of iron deficits are reversible after the completion of a course of iron therapy. Recent data suggest that children with moderately severe iron deficiency anemia in infancy are at risk for long-lasting developmental disadvantage extending to the time of school entry (Lozoff, Jimenez, & Wolf, 1991).

Hypoxia   The impact of persistent hypoxia secondary to chronic respiratory disease provides another area of promising investigation. Yet, the results of developmental follow-up studies of premature infants with a history of respiratory distress syndrome and subsequent bronchopulmonary dysplasia (a chronic respiratory condition) have been somewhat inconsistent. For example, in a follow-up study of 26 children with bronchopulmonary dysplasia up to 2 years of age, Markestad and Fitzhardinge (1981) reported that developmental outcomes were predicted with greater accuracy by perinatal factors than by the pulmonary sequelae. In contrast, Meisels, Plunkett, Roloff, Pasick, and Stiefel (1986) found a greater risk for delays in cognitive and language performance among infants with ongoing bronchopulmonary dysplasia than among infants who experienced respiratory distress syndrome in the newborn period without pulmonary sequelae. Moreover, the latter team of investigators found that both the chronicity and the severity of postnatal respiratory illness were significant predictors of cognitive and psychomotor performance (Meisels, Plunkett, Pasick, Stiefel, & Roloff, 1987). Although further study of this complex issue is clearly needed, the potential developmental implications of chronic hypoxia remain worthy of consideration.

Medications　The long-term use of medications by children with chronic health impairments presents another area of potential developmental concern. In fact, the pharmacology of some commonly prescribed substances suggests a particularly high risk for behavioral sequelae. The mood altering properties of corticosteroids (commonly prescribed for a variety of chronic inflammatory conditions) are one striking example. On the other hand, empirical investigations have produced inconsistent findings regarding the nature and extent of some specific drug effects on children with chronic illnesses. Conflicting data on the influence of theophylline preparations (prescribed for children with asthma) on attention and memory illustrate the current uncertainty in this area (Rappaport et al., 1989; Rachelesfsky et al., 1986). Questions regarding the behavioral and cognitive effects of long-term anticonvulsant medications similarly are unresolved (American Academy of Pediatrics Committee on Drugs, 1985). Marked individual differences in susceptibility to pharmacologic "side effects" and limitations in our knowledge of the neurotransmitter mediators of affective/behavioral reactions confound current understanding in this area.

Pain　This is another feature of some chronic health impairments that can be examined within a developmental framework. Although many children cope remarkably well with the assault of persistent or recurrent discomfort, others do not. Among the many variables that may influence an individual's response to pain, age is one important factor to be considered. The infant, for example, will often withdraw and display disturbances in eating, sleeping, and attachment behavior. Similarly, the preschooler who experiences chronic pain generally will exhibit withdrawn behavior that often is accompanied by significant anxiety and behavioral regression. During the middle childhood years, persistent pain often elicits increased aggressiveness and greater anxiety related to loss of control and disturbed peer interactions. Adolescents, on the other hand, commonly respond through depression or extreme oppositional behavior (Schechter, 1985).

Psychosocial Impacts

Overall, the psychosocial impacts of having to cope with multiple aspects of a chronic health impairment can best be understood within the context of an age-referenced developmental model. During the infant and toddler years, the diagnosis of a chronic health condition may have a dramatic impact on the early development of the parent–child relationship. Severe illness and the threat of long-term impairment or a shortened life span may disrupt typical parental feelings of attachment. Problems in growth and early nutrition, with or without specific feeding difficulties or dietary restrictions, may threaten the basic core of early parent–infant interactions. Beyond the initial process of attachment and the establishment of a mutually satisfying relationship, children with chronic health impairments are particularly vulnerable during the normal period of separation and individuation. At a time when increasing autonomy is expected and should be facilitated, such children are susceptible to the infantilization and overprotection that typically accompanies parental concerns about a "vulnerable child" (Green & Solnit, 1964). In fact, the psychosocial consequences of disturbed family relationships during this period can be far more debilitating for the child than the actual physical limitations of his or her chronic disease. When delays in the achievement of specific competencies are found, determining the degree to which they can be attributed to the physical burdens of illness or to the emotional burdens of a stressed family system requires sophisticated clinical skills.

The later preschool years generally represent a period of increasing independence and developmental competence, in association with a growing capacity for symbolic thought. During this period, children begin to move beyond the sole influence of their immediate family and toward the initiation of meaningful relationships with peers and adults in the outside world. For youngsters whose chronic health conditions require close supervision (e.g., special diets, routine administration of medications, activity restrictions, etc.), the attendant psychosocial stresses can be considerable. As their cognitive functioning becomes less egocentric, children with chronic diseases develop an early sense of their own "differentness." The typical magical thinking of the older preschooler makes him or her especially susceptible to the guilt and anxiety that associates illness with punishment. As described for the earlier infant-toddler period, the interplay among the direct effects of physical impairment and the interactive influences of parental restriction and overprotection may result in secondary lags in the acquisition of a variety of developmental skills.

The normative developmental tasks and emotional challenges of the school age years provide a useful framework for examining the psychosocial burdens of chronic illness during middle childhood. The significant growth in independence that normally characterizes this period of development clearly is threatened by the forces of dependence associated with many chronic health impairments. As compliance with medical treatment increasingly becomes an important concern, the degree to which the child is allowed to assume greater responsibility for his or her own management becomes critical. At a time when issues of dependence and independence are becoming more salient for all parents and their children, families with a youngster who has a chronic illness face significant additional challenges.

The importance of peer relationships during the middle childhood years imposes an added strain on many children with a chronic health condition. The stigma of being different and the need to accept such difference-promoting restrictions as special diets and physical limitations may create debilitating psychological barriers. The degree to which physical illness itself compromises performance in such developmentally important areas as athletic competition presents an additional burden.

The consequences of a chronic health impairment also can be detrimental to a child's function in school. Frequent absences, the effects of persistent or recurrent physical symptoms, and the burden of chronic psychological stress can all contribute to academic underachievement. The importance of school performance during middle childhood, and its close link to developing concepts of self-esteem and self-worth, make the arena of school function particularly critical for examining the psychosocial impact of chronic illness during the middle childhood period (Weitzman, 1984).

Beginning with the onset of puberty and extending throughout the teenage years, many early psychosocial themes reemerge with heightened intensity. Issues of autonomy and independence generally are dramatic for all families during this period. Compliance regarding medication, specific therapies, special diets, or activity restrictions often becomes a major battleground between the adolescent with a chronic health impairment and his or her parents. The fact that the onset of puberty is often delayed in children with chronic illness only serves to exacerbate the turmoil that typically surrounds psychosexual developmental issues. Concerns regarding body image and sexual competence are heightened. The impact of disease-associated stigmata may be substantial. As future planning regarding vocational and personal aspirations becomes more salient, specific limitations necessitated by chronic illness or physical impairment may become particularly difficult to accept.

For the family as a whole, although specific issues vary depending on the age of the child, a number of generic concerns persist throughout all developmental periods. On a practical level, daily family functioning may require adaptation to a variety of specific demands related to special diets, the administration of medication, the provision of specific therapies, and other constraints. Such routine tasks serve as a constant reminder of the child's vulnerability and may provide continual fuel for parental emotional struggles around such issues as grief, anxiety, anger, and guilt. The specific burdens of care, or the stigmata attached to some chronic health impairments, often contribute to significant social isolation for all family members. Underlying marital conflicts are often exacerbated by the stresses of rearing a child with a chronic disease. And finally, financial pressures can be substantial for all but the wealthiest families.

Family relationships are often strained as well for the healthy sibling of a child with a chronic health impairment (Drotar & Crawford, 1985). In some cases, the nondisabled child is expected to shoulder additional burdens; in other instances, he or she may be relatively invisible. Depending on their age and psychological predisposition, healthy siblings may feel guilty about the ill siblings' condition, or fear for their own health. Peer relations also may be affected. For many of these stresses, the final common pathway is demonstrated in behavioral difficulties or poor performance in school.

In summary, it is clear that a child with a chronic health impairment and his or her family bear a substantial risk for psychosocial difficulties throughout the childhood and adolescent years. Some of the stresses are long-standing and virtually universal. Others are more idiosyncratic and may have particular salience during certain developmental periods. However, it is important to emphasize that, although some children and families have great difficulty coping with the stresses of a chronic illness, others demonstrate remarkable adaptability and experience minimal difficulties. Individual differences in this area are striking. Although our knowledge base is continually expanding, a great deal more research is needed to understand those factors that result in the greatest vulnerability, as well as those that are associated with highly successful adaptation.

HOW CAN A CHILD'S HEALTH STATUS BE SCREENED EFFECTIVELY WITHIN A COMPREHENSIVE FOLLOW-UP STRATEGY?

The measurement of health status is a complex task that has challenged generations of investigators and policymakers. Assessing the health of children is particularly difficult, because of confounding factors related to the selection of informants (the children or their parents); parent–child differences in perceptions of physical, psychological, and social symptoms; and age-related developmental differences in the ability of children to judge and report their own sense of well-being (Lewis, Pantell, & Kieckhefer, 1989). Two decades ago, Starfield (1974) proposed a multidimensional scheme for evaluating health outcomes that included measurements of activity, comfort, satisfaction, disorder, achievement, and resilience. However, no single instrument has been adopted for widespread use, nor is there consensus on the optimal timing or best sources of information for collecting health-related data during childhood.

As discussed earlier in this chapter, the measurement of disease or of health care utilization has been far easier to operationalize than has the assessment of health or well-being. Consequently, despite continuing debate regarding the selection of the most sensitive and specific indicators of physical and emotional health in children, the marker variables that have been used most frequently include such factors as immunization status, days of hospitalization, and the prevalence of specific categories of illness, injury, or biological vulnerability.

Beyond these conventional measures, the collection of data on somatic growth and physical maturation would provide a useful and simple marker of health status within a developmental follow-up protocol. A normal rate of growth in both height and weight, for example, can serve as a rough indicator of physical well-being, adequate nutrition, and the absence of a significant chronic disease. In contrast, evidence of failure to thrive in the early years of life suggests the possibility of physiological dysfunction and/ or neurodevelopmental vulnerability, and impaired growth and delayed physical maturation in later childhood may reflect the influence of a chronic illness or the biological impact of severe psychosocial adversity. In fact, in follow-up studies of infants born prematurely, post-natal growth in length, weight, and head circumference has been found to correlate positively with neurobehavioral outcomes, even when differences in birth weight are controlled (Hack, Merkatz, & Gordon, 1982; Ross, Krauss, & Auld, 1983).

Growth data are easy to collect and most meaningful when they are recorded and analyzed over an extended period of time. Among the multiple patterns of poor growth that may be observed, three variations can be identified. Based on the relations among chronologic age, height age (defined as the age at which the observed height is average), bone age, and growth velocity, the classification of children into one of the following three categories would provide useful information within the context of a comprehensive developmental follow-up strategy (Schaff-Blass, Burstein, & Rosenfield, 1984).

The first group includes children with intrinsic growth deficiency, on a constitutional or genetic basis, who are relatively small for their chronologic age but who have a normal bone age and who grow and mature physically at a normal rate. In the absence of a specific central nervous system deficit, children with this type of growth "problem" can be expected to achieve developmental skills at a normal rate in all areas. Their small size, however, may have important psychosocial implications as manifested by a greater risk of infantilization or by inappropriately low developmental expectations as a result of the youngster being seen as a younger child.

A second pattern is characterized by delayed growth and slowed physical maturation which may represent a normal variant but which is often second-ary to the consequences of undernutrition or moderate chronic disease. Children in this group characteristically demonstrate normal growth velocity but slower skeletal maturation. Delayed onset of puberty is common, and youngsters in this category generally do not achieve a stature that is com-mensurate with their genetic potential. When chronic illness or undernutri-tion is of sufficient severity to result in such an interference with normal growth and maturation, the risk of developmental dysfunction or psychoso-cial impairment is increased. In such cases, delayed growth can serve as a simple yet potent marker of developmental vulnerability.

The third category of physical impairment is characterized by a diminished velocity and attenuated pattern of growth, in conjunction with significant delay in physical maturation. Such patterns of growth failure are found most commonly as a consequence of severe malnutrition, in association with a specific endocrinopathy or metabolic disorder, or as a result of a severe chronic disease. When an attenuated growth pattern is documented, "the developmental drain" of ongoing illness and/or poor nutrition can be sub-stantial, and the risk of concomitant developmental/psychosocial dysfunc-tion is greatly increased. During the later childhood and early adolescent years, the psychosocial consequences of delayed physical maturation are particularly problematic, especially for boys who experience a delayed ap-pearance of secondary sexual characteristics.

In summary, although a normal pattern and rate of growth and physical maturation does not preclude significant developmental or psychosocial vulnerability, the documentation of poor growth warrants more careful inves-tigation. The broad range of risk factors for which a deficiency in growth may be a marker, and the simplicity of recording growth data, provide a compelling argument for the careful collection, graphing, and analysis of height, weight, and head circumference over time for all children involved in developmental follow-up activities.

WHAT CAN WE LEARN FROM INVESTIGATING CHILDREN'S PATTERNS OF HEALTH CARE UTILIZATION?

Among the health-related behaviors that may be useful to consider as part of an overall developmental follow-up strategy, the level and pattern of use of health care services may provide an interesting window into the psychosocial milieu in which a child is reared. For example, evidence of regular health maintenance and the completion of routine well-child visits to a consistent source of primary care may be viewed as a marker of family organization, and perhaps of its economic well-being. In contrast, the ab-sence of routine health visits, the associated incompleteness of childhood immunizations, and the episodic use of emergency room services for attention to minor illnesses should suggest the need for a more careful look at family resources for childrearing.

Of perhaps greater potential interest for developmental follow-up programs is the observation of a pattern of "excessive" health care utilization as a potential marker of elevated parental anxiety or significant family stress. In this regard, substantial data have been collected that demonstrate direct correlations between the prevalence, duration, and severity of a variety of common childhood illnesses and the presence of family stress (Beautrais, Fergusson, & Shannon, 1982; Boyce et al., 1977; Heisel, Ream, Raitz, Rappaport, & Coddington, 1973; Schor, 1986). This finding has been attributed to greater susceptibility to illness (especially infection) as a result of the association of stress with a number of specific physiological responses, including decreased white blood cell phagocytosis, increased adrenal cortical hormone release (which reduces the inflammatory response), and a reduction in secretory IgA in the pharynx. In addition, high levels of "inappropriate" health care utilization for common concerns have been related to maternal perceptions of increased vulnerability in their young children, which, in turn, have been linked to infantilization, somaticization, and an increased prevalence of later school difficulties (Green & Solnit, 1964; Levy, 1980).

SUMMARY

Conceptual and empirical advances over the past decade have contributed to a growing appreciation of the interdependence of health, behavior, and development. The relations among these domains are complex and the directions of influence are multiple. In a general sense, although physical well-being is neither necessary nor sufficient to ensure normal development, sound health may be viewed as a protective factor for adaptive progress. As such, a state of healthfulness provides a facilitating substrate for growth and development that is free from the relative drain that typically accompanies the experience of illness or disability.

In contrast to the benefits of a healthy state, an impairment of health presents a developmental and behavioral challenge. As a risk factor for adverse sequelae, illness may be associated with a wide variety of physical symptoms (e.g., discomfort, diminished stamina, etc.) and/or psychosocial stresses (e.g., parental overprotection, dysfunctional peer relationships, etc.). The ultimate developmental impact of such stressors, however, generally depends on individual differences in the coping resources and adaptability of affected children and their families. For some, illness will mediate psychosocial dysfunction. For others, the growth-promoting aspects of the stress associated with poor health will serve as a developmental facilitator.

The monitoring of physical health and growth over time adds an important dimension to any strategy for developmental follow-up. As a relatively understudied aspect of the process of human development, health status during childhood provides a promising focus for exploring the biopsychosocial roots of resilience and vulnerability.

REFERENCES

American Academy of Pediatrics Committee on Drugs. (1985). Behavioral and cognitive effects of anticonvulsant therapy. *Pediatrics, 76,* 644–647.

Bax, M., Hart, H., & Jenkins, S. (1983). On the intimate relationship of health development and behavior in the young child. In T. B. Brazelton & B. M. Lester (Eds.), *New approaches to developmental screening of infants* (pp. 259–267). New York: Elsevier.

Beautrais, A., Fergusson, D., & Shannon, F. (1982). Life events and childhood morbidity: A prospective study. *Pediatrics, 70,* 935–940.

Bennett, F., Ruuska, S., & Sherman, R. (1980). Middle ear function in learning-disabled children. *Pediatrics, 66,* 254–260.

Berko-Gleason, J. (1983). Otitis media and language development. Workshop on effects of otitis media in the child. *Pediatrics. 71,* 644–645.

Boyce, W. T. (1985). Stress and social support: Implications for health and childhood. *Pediatric Annals, 14,* 539–542.

Boyce, W. T., Barr, R., & Zeltzer, L. (1992). Temperament and the psychobiology of childhood stress. *Pediatrics, 90,* 483–486.

Boyce, W. T., & Jemerin, J. (1990). Psychobiological differences in childhood stress response. I. Patterns of illness and susceptibility. *Journal of Developmental and Behavioral Pediatrics, 11,* 86–94.

Boyce, W. T., Jensen, E., Cassel, J., Collier, A., Smith, A., & Ramey, C. (1977). Influence of life events and family routines on childhood respiratory tract illness. *Pediatrics, 60,* 609–615.

Cadman, D., Boyle, M., Szatmari, P., & Offord, D. (1987). Chronic illness, disability, and mental and social well-being: Findings of the Ontario child health study. *Pediatrics, 79,* 805–813.

Campbell, J. (1978). The child in the sick role: Contributions of age, sex, parental status, and parental values. *Journal of Health and Social Behavior, 19,* 35–51.

Constitution of the World Health Organization. (1958). In *The first ten years of the WHO.* Geneva: Palais des Nations.

Deinard, A., List, A., Lindgren, B., Hunt, J., & Chang, P. (1986). Cognitive deficits in iron-deficient and iron-deficient anemic children. *Journal of Pediatrics, 108,* 681–689.

Drotar, D., & Crawford, P. (1985). Psychological adaptation of siblings of chronically ill children: Research and practice implications. *Journal of Developmental and Behavioral Pediatrics, 6,* 355–362.

Engel, G. (1977). The need for a new medical model: A challenge for biomedicine. *Science, 196,* 129–135.

Garmezy, N. (1983). Stressors of childhood. In N. Garmezy & M. Rutter (Eds.), *Stress, coping, and development of children.* New York: McGraw Hill.

Green, M., & Solnit, A. (1964). Reactions to the threatened loss of a child: A vulnerable child syndrome. *Pediatrics, 34,* 58–66.

Hack, M., Merkatz, I., & Gordon, D. (1982). The prognostic significance of postnatal growth in very low-birth-weight infants. *American Journal of Obstetrics and Gynecology, 147,* 693.

Haggerty, R. (1980). Life stress, illness and social supports. *Developmental Medicine and Child Neurology, 22,* 391–400.

Haskins, R., Hirschbiel, P., Collier, A., Sanyal, M., & Finkelstein, N. (1981). Minor illness and social behavior of infants and caregivers. *Journal of Applied Developmental Psychology, 2,* 117–128.

Heisel, J., Ream, S., Raitz, R., Rappaport, M., & Coddington, R. (1973). The significance of life events as contributing factors in the diseases of children. *Journal of Pediatrics, 83,* 119–123.

Jemerin, J., & Boyce, W. T. (1990). Psychobiological differences in childhood stress response. II. Cardiovascular markers of vulnerability. *Journal of Developmental and Behavioral Pediatrics, 11,* 140–150.

Levy, J. (1980). Vulnerable children: Parents' perspectives and the use of medical care. *Pediatrics, 65,* 956–963.

Lewis, C., Pantell, R., & Kieckhefer, G. (1989). Assessment of children's health status. *Medical Care, 27,* S54–S65.

Lozoff, B., Brittenham, G., Wolf, A., McClish, D., Kuhnert, P., Jimenez, E., Jimenez, R., Mora, L., Gomez, I., & Krauskoph, D. (1987). Iron deficiency anemia and iron therapy effects on infant developmental test performance. *Pediatrics, 79,* 981–995.

Lozoff, B., Jimenez, E., & Wolf, A. (1991). Long-term developmental outcome of infants with iron deficiency. *New England Journal of Medicine, 325,* 687–694.

Lozoff, B., Wolf, A., Urrutia, J., & Viteri, F. (1985). Abnormal behavior and low developmental test scores in iron-deficient anemic infants. *Journal of Developmental and Behavioral Pediatrics, 6,* 69–75.

Markestad, T., & Fitzhardinge, P. (1981). Growth and development in children recovering from bronchopulmonary dysplasia. *Journal of Pediatrics, 98,* 597–602.

Mattsson, A. (1972). Long-term physical illness in childhood: A challenge to psychosocial adaptation. *Pediatrics, 50,* 801–811.

Mattsson, A., & Weissberg, I. (1970). Behavioral reactions to minor illness in preschool children. *Pediatrics, 46,* 604–610.

Mechanic, D. (1964). The influence of mothers on their children's health attitudes and behavior. *Pediatrics, 39,* 444–453.

Mechanic, D. (1972). Social psychologic factors affecting the presentation of bodily complaints. *New England Journal of Medicine, 286,* 1132–1139.

Meisels, S., Plunkett, J., Pasick, P., Stiefel, G., & Roloff, D. (1987). Effects of severity and chronicity of respiratory illness on the cognitive development of preterm infants. *Journal of Pediatric Psychology, 12,* 117–132.

Meisels, S., Plunkett, J., Roloff, D., Pasick, P., & Stiefel, G. (1986). Growth and development of preterm infants with respiratory distress syndrome and bronchopulmonary dysplasia. *Pediatrics, 77,* 345–352.

Oski, F., Honig, A., Helu, B., & Howanitz, P. (1983). Effect of iron therapy on behavior performance in nonanemic, iron-deficient infants. *Pediatrics, 71,* 877–880.

Paradise, J. (1981). Otitis media during early life: How hazardous to development? A critical review of the evidence. *Pediatrics, 63,* 869–873.

Parmelee, A. (1986). Children's illnesses: Their beneficial effects on behavioral development. *Child Development, 57,* 1–10.

Parsons, T. (1972). Definitions of health and illness in the light of American values and social structure. In E. Jaco (Ed.), *Patients, physicians, and illness* (2nd ed.). New York: Free Press.

Pless, I. B., & Pinkerton, P. (1975). *Chronic childhood disorder: Promoting patterns of adjustment.* London: Henry Kimpton.

Pless, I. B., & Roghmann, K. (1971). Chronic illness and its consequences: Observations based on three epidemiologic surveys. *Journal of Pediatrics, 79,* 351–359.

Rabkin, J., & Struening, E. (1976). Life events, stress and illness. *Science, 194,* 1013–1020.

Rachelefsky, G., Wo, J., Adelson, W., Mickey, M., Spector, S., Katz, R., Siegel, S., & Rohr, A.

(1986). Behavior abnormalities and poor school performance due to oral theophylline usage. *Pediatrics, 78,* 1133–1138.

Rappaport, L., Coffman, H., Guare, R., Fenton, T., DeGraw, C., & Twarog, F. (1989). Effects of theophylline on behavior and learning in children with asthma. *American Journal of Diseases of Children, 143,* 368–372.

Ross, G., Krauss, A., & Auld, P. (1983). Growth achievement in low-birth-weight premature infants: Relationship to neurobehavioral outcome at one year. *Journal of Pediatrics, 103,* 105–108.

Rutter, M., Tizard, J., & Wightmore, K. (1970). *Education, health, and behavior.* London: Longmans.

Schaff-Blass, E., Burstein, S., & Rosenfield, R. (1984). Advances in diagnosis and treatment of short stature, with special reference to the role of growth hormone. *Journal of Pediatrics, 104,* 801–813.

Schechter, N. (1985). Pain and pain control in children. *Current Problems in Pediatrics, 15*(5), 6–67.

Schor, E. (1986). Use of health care services by children and diagnoses received during presumably stressful life transitions. *Pediatrics, 77,* 834–841.

Shonkoff, J. (1984). The biological substrate and physical health in middle childhood. In W. Collins (Ed.), *Development during middle childhood.* Washington, DC: National Academy Press.

Starfield, B. (1974). Measurement of outcome: A proposed scheme. *Millbank Memorial Fund Quarterly, 52,* 39–50.

Stein, R., & Jessop, D. (1984). Relationship between health status and psychological adjustment among children with chronic conditions. *Pediatrics, 73,* 169–174.

Syme, S., & Berkman, L. (1976). Social class, susceptibility and sickness. *American Journal of Epidemiology, 104,* 1–8.

Teele, D., Klein, J., Rosner, B., & The Greater Boston Otitis Media Study Group. (1984). Otitis media with effusion during the first three years of life and development of speech and language. *Pediatrics, 74,* 282–287.

Weitzman, M. (1984). *School and peer relations of chronically ill children.* Pediatric Clinics of North America, February.

Werner, E., & Smith, R. (1977). Kauai's children come of age. Honolulu: University Press of Hawaii.

Werner, E., & Smith, R. (1982). *Vulnerable but invincible: A study of resilient children.* New York: McGraw Hill.

Zborowski, M. (1952). Cultural components in responses to pain. *Journal of Social Issues, 8,* 16–30.

Zinkus, P., & Gottlieb, M. (1980). Patterns of perceptual and academic deficits related to early chronic otitis media. *Pediatrics, 66,* 246–253.

Zola, I. (1966). Culture and symptoms: An analysis of patients' presenting complaints. *American Journal of Sociological Review, 31,* 615–630.

Early Cognitive Development and the Contribution of Peer Interaction: A Piagetian View

Hermina Sinclair

INTRODUCTION

Of all the consequent conditions that one could study using developmental follow-up strategies, cognitive development probably receives the most research attention. Cognitive development provides a good developmental model because it is ongoing, it concerns processes of logical thought that are vitally important to the learning and social development that must take place as children get older, and it can be studied from a wide variety of perspectives. In this chapter, I examine one aspect of cognitive/social development, peer interaction, from a Piagetian perspective, and suggest that observational research on peer interaction can provide valuable data for understanding the social context of the development of important aspects of reasoning, as well as for assessing long-term effects of many possible developmental interventions.

COGNITIVE DEVELOPMENT IN SOCIAL CONTEXT

Cognitive development, with its deep-seated biological roots, embraces the full span of human life and proceeds, according to Piaget, from the ways in which newborn babies, toddlers, children, adolescents, and adults organize—first in deed, then in thought—their interactions with the world of objects and with the world of people. Although in his theoretical works Piaget emphasized the importance of the "world of people" and postulated a strict parallelism between intra- and interpersonal operations, his experimental work as well as his observational studies, with only a few exceptions, bear on knowing subjects' relations with their world of objects. The image many psychologists have retained of Piaget's work is that of "the child as a solitary thinker experimenting as a scientist" (Damon, 1979).

Indeed, despite Piaget's oft-repeated affirmation that cognitive development takes place in a social setting from its very beginnings, and that objective knowledge can only be obtained through discussion and cooperation with others, he did not carry out his own proposal for research aiming at "the determination of the precise form of exchanges between the subject and other people at each level of cognitive development (i.e., sensorimotor intelligence, intuitive intelligence and operatory intelligence)" (Piaget, 1965, p. 90).

In his best-known observational studies, Piaget (1935, 1937, 1945) reported many episodes in which children interact with their parents, but apart from an interesting discussion in the chapter on causality by imitation (Piaget, 1937/1954), as well as in the entire chapter on imitation (Piaget, 1945/1951), the interaction patterns themselves were not analyzed.

In one of his earliest observational studies (Piaget, 1932) we find a long account of 6- to 12-year-olds playing marbles. It describes not only the development of the children's capacities to play the game according to the rules, but also their ideas about the nature of these rules (from their answers to Piaget's questions and from discussions among the children themselves). The parallel between inter- and intraindividual operations that Piaget continued to emphasize in his theoretical writings is, in this work, treated at the hands of observational data that show the close relationship between logical and moral rules, and the elaboration of both with the gradual development of reciprocity and mutual respect in social interaction. The most interesting discussion on social interaction and cognitive development is, however, to be found in a chapter added in 1946 to the third edition of *Le langage et la pensée chez l'enfant* (Language and thought in the child; Piaget, 1923/1946/

1959), at least in my opinion. In this chapter, Piaget reported an analysis carried out by A. Leuzinger of the verbal exchanges between one child (during his fourth year of life) and two friends of the same age, and between the same child and adults (mainly his mother). The results are confirmed by data on three other children, all in their fourth year. This is the only text in which Piaget discussed the differences in social interaction among peers and social interaction between children and adults, and in which he emphasized, for children as young as 3, "the all important part played by cooperation between equals" in development, because "the play-mate . . . in so far as he is himself an individual, presents a new problem: that of continually distinguishing the ego from the other person and the reciprocity of these two views" (Piaget, 1923/1946/1959, p. 278).

Just as infants have to dissociate when acting on objects what belongs to their own action and what belongs to the objects and the way objects behave when acted upon, young children have to dissociate their own thoughts, intentions, and desires from those of others before, in either case, new coordinations and new objective knowledge can be constructed. Young children's conceptions of the physical world are adjusted to its exterior appearance and at the same time endowed with the children's own intentions, wishes, preferences, and dislikes. Similarly, in their conception of other people, children are already aware of the differences and similarities between their own actions and those of others, but the thoughts, the points of view, and the focus of attention of others are still considered to be the same as the children's own. No intellectual relativity, no objective system of reference is possible before a differentiation between one's thoughts and those of others is established: only from then on can problems be considered from different points of view and coordinations be constructed. Interaction of a collaborative kind with others, particularly with peers, is the essential factor in this "decentration," as Piaget called it.

CHILD TO CHILD: A SPECIAL SOCIAL CONTEXT

Adults, who for children are far more different from themselves than are other children, play a less important role in this decentration process: "The adult is at the same time far superior to the child and very near to him. He dominates everything, but at the same time penetrates into the intimacy of every wish and every thought" (Piaget, 1923/1946/1959, p. 257). The adults that children interact with are seen as sources of help and of information, but genuine discussion and collaboration appear earlier among peers and form the basis for the "equilibrated exchanges" that lead to objective knowledge.

The features that characterize what Piaget called an "equilibrated exchange of thought" are essentially the following:

1. The partners in the interaction possess a common frame of reference, a shared system of symbols and definitions, in the sense that they are no longer limited to personal symbols and subjective meanings.
2. The partners "conserve" propositions that have been accepted as valid by mutual agreement, and without authoritarian imposition.
3. The partners show "reciprocity" in their exchanges, that is, "they arrive either at identical propositions or at different, but reciprocal and combinable propositions" (Piaget, 1965, p. 163).

In the last 20 years or so, researchers working in the Piagetian tradition have begun to study interaction among children in its links with cognitive development from two sides: (a) sociocognitive conflict and cognitive development, and (b) spontaneous interaction during free play.

The first line of research received its impetus from work by Doise and his colleagues in Geneva (e.g., Mugny, Doise, & Perret-Clermont, 1975–1976). This line of research has gained considerable importance since the 1970s. It concerns mainly experimental studies in which dyads (and sometimes larger groups) of peers collectively solve problems often inspired by traditional Piagetian tasks such as those concerned with the conservation of length. In several studies it was found that the processes of dissociation, decentration, and recoordination that, in a Piagetian framework, play their part in the construction of new knowledge, are often activated by conflicts of opinion among children, each of whom brings his or her own point of view to the solution of a problem, thus leading to progress in reasoning. This is demonstrated by the comparison of performance between individual pretests and posttests. Although these findings call for further analysis of the particular interactional components that promote development (as shown by Bearis, Magzamen, & Filardo, 1986), the studies on sociocognitive conflict opened up a new area of research that extended Piagetian postulates into the domain of social interaction.

From the more general perspective of sociocognitive development, it should not be forgotten that these studies on sociocognitive conflict were mainly, if not exclusively, carried out with school-age children, who had already constructed a system of intrapersonal and interpersonal operations. The impression one gets from many of the studies is that the subjects already have the "idea of decentration," but that they cannot apply this idea to the particular problem at hand. Interaction with peers then activates decentration, which helps them to construct new coordinations necessary for the solution of the problems. Despite their intrinsic interest, the studies on sociocognitive conflict do not yet correspond to the line of research proposed by Piaget, who wished to determine "the precise form of the exchanges between the subject and other people at each level of cognitive development" (1965, p. 90). From a Piagetian perspective, the development of the "idea of decentering" has a long sociocognitive history. Moreover, the mechanisms of dissociation, decentration, and recoordination do not operate in the same way and at the same time in all problem situations; in many social and cognitive contexts, adults are as incapable of decentering as are young children. The postulate that peer interaction is the most important starting point for the construction of genuine collaboration—that is, an organization of interpersonal operations characterized by reciprocity isomorphic to intrapersonal operations characterized by reversibility—led other Piagetian psychologists into the second line of research previously mentioned: observation of spontaneous interactions among young children in a familiar setting.

OBSERVATIONS OF PEER INTERACTION

Until recently, occasions to observe interaction among young peers in a natural environment (as opposed to laboratory studies) have been rare. With the greater number of child-care centers that have become necessary in many countries, and with the shift in the objectives pursued in these institutions (less a simple safe-keeping of young children, more an opportunity for cognitive development), studies on peer interaction between the ages of 18 months (or even earlier) and 3 or 4 years are becoming more frequent. Moreover, day-care centers also make it possible, at the same time, to study the role of the adult caretakers and their influence on the various modes of peer interaction that can be observed. Such studies have both theoretical and practical importance: they contribute to our understanding of the social context in which the gradual "epistemic shift" in the individual's relationship as a knower toward the object to be known takes place (Piaget, 1923/1946/1959, pp. 268–272) and they provide data that can lead to an optimal organization of child-care centers and nursery schools.

A certain number of studies have recently been carried out with young children interacting in a familiar setting, a day-care setting where the children already know one another and also know the caretakers as well as the locality, with its spatial disposition and its familiar collection of toys. This type of research has greatly benefited from television taping equipment, which provides documents that can be studied over and over again and analyzed from different points of view. We thus are beginning to know more about the modes of interaction of children below the age of about 4 years, but much remains to be done before it becomes possible to analyze particular components of such interactions and, in my opinion, such analyses of naturalistic studies are necessary before useful experimental situations can be constructed. At present, the naturalistic observational studies may be characterized as follows:

1. Most of the studies are limited to a particular age: Very few studies are longitudinal (and even these are only partial), and no follow-up studies on the same groups of subjects exist.
2. No studies exist, to my knowledge, on the topic of the functional and structural differences between early peer interaction and the interaction between very young children and adults, apart from the previously cited study by Piaget (1923/1946/1959), which is limited to the analysis of verbal exchanges.
3. Most studies have been focused on a particular aspect of the interaction patterns; for example, the contents and structure of symbolic play, the use of language, or affective phenomena such as agressivity, frustration, sympathy, and the beginnings of friendship.

My own interest, and the theme of this chapter, is limited to peer interactions as a source of the organizational principles that are at the roots of coherent reasoning. As yet, very few studies have been carried out from this point of view. Nonetheless, it has become increasingly clear that collaboration among children starts far earlier than Piaget appeared to think, that is, well before the age of 3 or 4. Although collaborative episodes between children as young as 1 or 2 years old certainly do not display all the features that, according to Piaget, characterize exchanges between partners who are equal (or at least behave so that they can be considered equal), their roots certainly reach back into early infancy.

In what follows, I mainly refer to those studies of early peer interaction with which I am most conversant. These include the work of Stambak and her colleagues (e.g., Stambak et al., 1983; Verba, Stambak, & Sinclair, 1982). Their observations were carried out in Parisian day-care centers. Those that I discuss here concern interactions between children of 18 and 25 months of age.

The researchers were frequently present in the center and collaborated with the staff. The adults' attitudes, most favorable to the appearance of lengthy (sometimes up to 20 min) and well-structured episodes of interaction between two or more children, were found to be neither directive nor neutral and disengaged. Sustained interest in what the children were doing, expressed verbally or nonverbally, but without interrupting their activities (except in rare cases of conflict or danger) seemed to create the kind of socio-affective climate in which peer interaction flourishes.

The material context, that is, the locality and the presence or absence of certain kinds of toys and of such items as small tables and chairs and mattresses to jump on, also influenced the interaction patterns. As one might expect, and as we have already noted (Sinclair, Stambak, Lezine, Rayna, S.,

& Verba, 1982/1989), toy pots and pans, plates, and spoons led more easily to symbolic play than did bits of string, modeling clay, blocks, and rings; and symbolic play leads more readily to verbal exchanges.

Various types of structured interaction episodes can be distinguished in those observations. Leaving aside collective symbolic play, which starts as early as 18 months (cf. Musatti's description and analysis, Stambak et al., 1983) and which has given rise to much research, the following types of activities were frequently observed.

1. Activities whose very structure demands the collaboration of a partner: object exchange, hide-and-seek, and peek-a-boo. Usually, only two children play together in these activities; very occasionally a third may join. Objects are used, but their properties are not in themselves the focus of attention or a structuring factor in the interaction. In the object exchange format, for example, one child gives a small object (a piece of paper, a small toy) to the other, who hands it back to the first, and this pattern is repeated, sometimes many times. The children's interest is in the actions of giving and taking, and the change of roles: the giver becomes the taker, who becomes the giver; the object is not explored or played with.

2. Shared activities, in which one child performs part of a task several children have set themselves, and others carry out other parts of the task. Stambak et al. (1983, pp. 140–142) gave a striking example of such a division of labor among 13- to 15-month-old children. One child puts an empty cylindrical cardboard container on a box, which serves as a table; another child puts a second container next to it; then several children join in a project to put all the containers (six scattered about the room) on the box. Some children look for and bring the containers to the box; others put them on top and try to arrange them so that they will all fit. This type of activity can, of course, also be performed by one child alone, but it takes on a different character when carried out in collaboration.

3. Activities exploring objects, leading to experimentation and construction or fabrication of new objects. These activities are also observed in children acting alone (cf. Sinclair et al., 1982/1989, pp. 63–121), but when working in a group one child's idea is taken up and developed further by others in various ways, giving rise to new ideas, and so forth. For example (cf. Verba et al., 1982), one of a group of four children of about 20 months, seated around a table with various small objects, shoves a stick into a small cardboard cylinder; another shoves an identical small cylinder into a bigger one; and a third, having intently observed the others, pokes a stick into a ball of modeling clay. All three then push the smaller objects in and out of their containers. Object substitution is thus made visible in simultaneity (cylinders and clay ball as containers), and, even more important, the small cylinder is simultaneously used as content and container. A child acting alone can only carry out these activities sequentially.

These activities present features that may contribute to cognitive development. Two of them are, in my view, particularly important: (a) imitation in direct interaction, and (b) the division of an activity into subparts.

Imitation in Direct Interaction

As we have seen, imitation plays an important part in the different interactional situations related here. Janet (1935, p. 72) considered that "imitation is the simplest of all social acts," and insisted on the double face of all imitation of persons, because it always consists of "an action and a reciprocal action which modify the social act itself" (p. 67) thereby introducing a cybernetic feedback loop. Indeed, in social imitation there is always somebody who imitates, and somebody else who lets herself be imitated (or even elicits imitation). This double character is of the same nature as the more obvious double-facedness of social acts such as give–receive, lead–follow, and speak–listen.

Social imitation has another important characteristic: it allows one to observe an action that one has performed as it is performed by somebody else, and thus as an external object. Veneziano (1986) developed a similar argument concerning the vocal/verbal interaction between mother and infant. Janet (1935, p. 71) also emphasized the importance of imitation as a signaling device: The imitator learns to react as soon as the model starts acting, and reciprocally, the model learns to insist on the beginning of his or her action. Observations of peer interactions show many examples of such almost theatrical insistence on the beginning of an action sequence on the part of the child who wants to be imitated. In Piaget's discussion of causality by imitation, reference is also made to the fact that the child only carries out the beginning of the action he or she wants the other person to perform. The "signaling function" of imitation certainly plays an important part in the construction of shared symbol systems.

Social imitation, in its different forms, thus suggests the appearance of "structures" of reciprocity and correspondence, as well as nascent objectivization of knowledge and conservation of an interactional "theme" that is open to various transformations and elaborations. Last, in reciprocal imitation, both partners signal their acceptance of the other as somebody worthy of interest, and thereby create a relation of bilateral respect.

Division of an Activity into Subparts

One example of the segmentation of a sequential activity into several parts, performed by different children, has already been given: the episode during which some children bring empty containers to other children, who then put them on a box. The ability to segment a goal-directed activity into component activities is considered essential for many cognitive tasks.

Problem solving and planning usually demand such segmentation. The establishment of subgoals, with subprograms for their attainment, organizes the activity and makes it easier to evaluate progress, to correct errors, and, particularly, to use the already constructed subprograms for new goals.

Segmentation of an activity between partners clearly delineates its component parts because there is a change in agents, and can thus lead to greater awareness of its component parts. Such sharing also demands adjustment and coordination between the actions carried out by the different individuals. When performed by only one individual, the activity appears instead as a totality directed toward the main goal.

Both reciprocal imitation and division of labor also appear in interaction between adults and children, but then they seem to have different, though perhaps equally important, features. On the one hand, imitation is often easier among children (they are of the same size and their "ideas" for activities are similar); on the other hand, adults can, and usually do, correct small errors in manipulation committed by children, and make it possible for the shared activity to attain a goal not yet within the reach of the children. As already noted, however, we still do not possess any clear comparison between adult–child and child–child interactions, although differences are easy to observe in everyday life. When a mother and a child build a tower together, each adding a block in turn, the mother adjusts the block put down by the child if it is askew. When two or more children make block constructions, the tower more often falls down than stays erect, but the result may be that the project is changed and agreement is reached to build a garden wall rather than a tower.

COGNITIVE DEVELOPMENTAL ROLE OF PEER INTERACTION: A GOOD APPLICATION OF DEVELOPMENTAL FOLLOW-UP RESEARCH

It appears from the studies already at our disposal that interaction between peers shows, from a very early age onward, the essential features Piaget defined as characteristics of "equilibrated exchanges." Well before the age at which language becomes a privileged mode of interaction, children understand each other's intentions and ideas, communicating by gestures, postures, looks, and actions. They clearly conserve propositions that have been accepted: It would be impossible to construct lengthy episodes of coherent interaction if this were not the case. Their activities show reciprocity-in-action, as in the examples I have given. At later ages, these same characteristics of peer interaction appear in different ways, both as concerns their structure and as concerns their form. The development of these interactive abilities between peers is as yet almost totally unknown, as are their differences with child–adult interactions. Longitudinal and follow-up studies are clearly needed. From a theoretical point of view, such studies should contribute to our understanding of the acquisition of knowledge as a coconstruction between equals; from the practical point of view, they should help to optimize the organization of institutions where very young children of the same age are together for a good part of their daily lives.

REFERENCES

Bearis, D., Magzamen, S., & Filardo, H. (1986). Socio-cognitive conflict and cognitive growth in young children. *Merrill-Palmer Quarterly, 32,* 51–72.

Damon, S. (1979). Why study social-cognitive development? *Human Development, 22,* 206–212.

Janet, P. (1935). *Les débuts de l'intelligence* [The beginnings of intelligence]. Paris: Flammarion.

Mugny, G., Doise, W., & Perret-Clermont, A. N. (1975–1976). Conflit de centration et progrès cognitif [Centration conflict and cognitive progress]. *Bulletin de Psychologie, 29,* 199–204.

Piaget, J. (1923/1946/1959). *Le langage et la pensée chez l'enfant.* Neuchâtel: Delachaux et Niestlé, 1923. 3rd ed., 1946. Trans. M. & R. Gabain, *The language and thought of the child.* London: Routledge & Kegan Paul, 1959.

Piaget, J. (1932). *Le jugement moral chez l'enfant.* Paris: Alcan. Trans. M. Gabain, *The moral judgment of the child.* London: Routledge & Kegan Paul, 1932.

Piaget, J. (1935/1952). *La naissance de l'intelligence.* Neuchâtel: Delachaux et Niestlé, 1935. Trans. M. Cook, *The origins of intelligence in children.* New York: International Universities Press, 1952.

Piaget, J. (1937/1954). *La construction du réel chez l'enfant.* Neuchâtel: Delachaux et Niestlé, 1937. Trans. M. Cook, *The construction of reality in the child.* New York: Basic Books, 1954.

Piaget, J. (1945/1951). *La formation du symbole chez l'enfant.* Neuchâtel: Delachaux et Niestlé, 1945. Trans. C. Gattegno & F. Hodgson, *Play, dreams, imitation in childhood.* Toronto, London: Heinemann, 1951.

Piaget, J. (1965). *Etudes sociologiques* [Sociological studies]. Geneva: Droz.

Sinclair, H., Stambak, M., Lezine, I., Rayna, S., & Verba, M. (1982/1989). *Les bébés et les choses ou la créativité du développement cognitif.* Paris: Presses Universitaires de France, 1982. Trans. M. Sinclair, *Infants and objects: the creativity of cognitive development.* New York: Academic Press, 1989.

Stambak, M., Barrière, M., Bonica, L., Maisonnet, R., Musatti, T., Rayna, S., & Verba, M. (1983). *Les bébés entre eux* [Relations among infants]. Paris: Presses Universitaires de France.

Veneziano, E. (1986). Vocal/verbal interaction and the construction of early lexical knowledge. In M. Smith & J. Locke (Eds.), *The emergent lexicon.* New York: Academic Press.

Verba, M., Stambak, M., & Sinclair, H. (1982). Physical knowledge and social interaction in children from 18 to 24 months of age. In G. Forman (Ed.), *Action and thought.* New York: Academic Press.

Expanding the Boundaries of Evaluation: Strategies for Refining and Evaluating Ill-Defined Interventions

Debra J. Rog

INTRODUCTION

In recent years, the role of program evaluation has broadened. There has been a steady shift away from an exclusive focus on the outcomes and long-term effects of an intervention and a greater emphasis on examining both the underlying theory of the intervention (Bickman, 1987, 1990; Chen, 1989, 1990; Chen & Rossi, 1981, 1983, 1987, 1989, in press) and its implementation and functioning (e.g., Scheirer, 1987). The black box approach to evaluation is increasingly being replaced with a more thorough examination and specification of the independent variable—the intervention itself—before examining its effects.

Developmental Follow-up

This expanding role for evaluation is particularly pertinent for "ill-defined" interventions or interventions in emerging problem areas (Edwards, 1987). Ill-defined interventions are characterized by the lack of an explicit theoretical or conceptual framework and the absence of a well-developed understanding of the problem. Moreover, these interventions, often carried out in complex, chaotic service delivery systems, are challenged by many extraneous variables that can interact or interfere with the intervention in question. Therefore, in these situations, an evaluation focused exclusively on outcomes is either likely to be a premature test of the intervention or one that produces information only on success and failure and not on how to improve and refine the program.

Ill-defined interventions can arise in situations in which the political and social pressures for action inhibit a more linear approach to developing an appropriate knowledge base on the problem. With many contemporary social problems, such as homelessness, it is often necessary to take action long before adequate knowledge of a phenomenon has been obtained, analyzed, understood, and disseminated. Consequently, evaluations of interventions in these areas must take a broader view, incorporating strategies both for acquiring basic knowledge on the problem in question and for evaluating the intervention and its effects.

Homelessness and its effects on children's development is one area in which society is struggling to gain a greater understanding of the problem as it takes action. Although there are the beginnings of a knowledge base on the nature of the problem (e.g., Bassuk, 1990; Bassuk and Rubin, 1987; Bassuk, Rubin, & Lauriat, 1986), the knowledge is far from complete. The preliminary research on children indicates that they are suffering from severe emotional, developmental, social, educational, and health problems (Alperstein, Rappaport, & Flanigan, 1988; Bassuk & Rubin, 1987; Molnar, Klein, Knitzer, & Ortiz-Torres, 1988; Wood, Valdez, Hayashi, & Shen, 1990). Although some children may suffer from these problems prior to becoming homeless, shelter life and the lack of a home appear to exacerbate these problems and may even create additional ones (Bassuk, 1990). Thus, the potential devastating effects of homelessness call for action and intervention before the problem of homelessness itself is fully understood or even defined.

When examining interventions for homeless children, a developmental follow-up perspective must be incorporated within the broader evaluation perspective. The evaluation must be sensitive to the broader context and environment. The differential effects of various types of homeless situations (communal shelters, private family shelters, living on the streets, living "doubled-up") must be taken into account and understood to have a true picture of the context in which an intervention is taking place.

As Molnar and Rubin (1991) have indicated, the effects of homelessness on children can be mediated by a number of ecological conditions and by the effects of these conditions on the family system. Such conditions, or "mediating mechanisms" (Rafferty and Shinn, 1991) include shelter conditions, the nature of the residential instability of the families, and the availability of services. Thus, it is important when examining the efficacy of interventions for homeless children to be cognizant of the many faces of homelessness and the myriad of events that may interact with it.

Within the context of developmental follow-up research for homeless children, I describe in this chapter an expanded role for the practice of program evaluation beyond the traditional boundaries set by questions of effectiveness and outcome. In particular, four areas of evaluation inquiry are discussed:

1. The underlying logic of the intervention. Questions that can be addressed include: Is the intervention conceptually sound? Does it have an underlying logic? Does the program incorporate relevant theoretical and empirical knowledge? Does it match the needs of the intended target population? Can it be implemented as designed with the resources that are available?

2. The nature of the intervention as implemented. This area includes examination of the nature of the population actually served, the specific activities undertaken and their functioning, and the nature of the context in which the intervention is operating. Particular focus is on the nature of the environment in which the intervention is implemented and its effects.

3. The conditions for an outcome study. Evaluation should address to what extent the methodological requirements can be met for conducting an appropriate, rigorous effectiveness evaluation. In developmental follow-up studies, it is particularly important to determine whether the conditions are right for implementing a longitudinal design and for sensitively assessing the possible interactions of developmental growth with the intervention.

4. The effectiveness of the intervention. This area includes determining the extent to which an intervention or components of the intervention (Bickman, 1985) achieve the desired outcomes. For ill-defined interventions, it is particularly important to take a broad look at effectiveness (i.e., multiple outcomes) and the ways in which the treatment alters different developmental trajectories.

In this chapter, I describe each area of evaluation inquiry and discuss how it can help to refine the intervention as well as to increase understanding of the target problem. The chapter closes with a brief summary and discussion of the challenges in taking a broad evaluation approach.

EXAMINING THE LOGIC AND THEORY OF AN INTERVENTION

Attention to the logic underlying programs and interventions has come largely through the work of Joseph Wholey and his colleagues at the Urban Institute during the 1970s (e.g., Schmidt, Scanlon, & Bell, 1979; Wholey, 1979; Wholey, Scanlon, Duffy, Fikumoto, & Vogt, 1971). Disturbed by the lack of influence that program evaluation studies were having, Wholey and his colleagues concluded that many evaluations were being conducted prematurely or on programs that were ill-conceived; that is, evaluations were being conducted on programs that were not yet fully implemented or that were focused on unrealistic goals. They developed "evaluability assessment" with the original intent of serving as a preevaluation examination of the underlying logic of a program and its implementation.

Evaluability assessment was developed to assess a program and determine whether or not there exists (Wholey, 1987): (a) clear operational definitions of the problem addressed, the program and its activities, the program's goals, and expected outcomes; (b) a clear logic linking the resources, goals, activities, and outcomes; (c) agreement among program stakeholders (i.e., those with a vested interest in the program) on the intended uses of the evaluation; and (d) the ability and willingness of those stakeholders in charge to act on the basis of the information produced by an outcome evaluation.

Through such an assessment, it is possible to determine what components of the program are "evaluable," that is, which ones are ready for an evaluation of their outcomes. In practice, however, evaluability assessment often may provide enough information on its own to guide program refinements. In a review of 57 evaluability assessments conducted in the Departments of Health and Human Services and Education between 1972 and 1984, Rog (1985) found that only a handful of the evaluability assessments had been followed by an outcome evaluation, even though in many cases the investigators had determined that at least a portion of the program was evaluable.

Evaluability assessment and continued work on program theory (e.g., Bickman, 1990; Chen & Rossi, in 1992) have created an enhanced focus within evaluation research on the extent to which a program is based on a sound conceptual framework. Although those involved in the development of the program theory perspective have different views as to the nature of program theory and the ways in which it can be developed, the basic perspective is that attention to theory in evaluation can help in understanding a program's implementation, in diagnosing problems in the basic structure of the program, and in increasing the usefulness and actual use of the results (Chen, 1989).

There are several specific aspects of a program's theory or logic (Wholey, 1987) that should be explored as one studies interventions in dynamic, ill-defined problem areas. These are the nature of the target population, the goals and objectives of the program, the program activities and components, the fit between goals and activities, outcome indicators, and resources. These aspects are described in the following paragraphs.

Target Population

Among the first questions that can be addressed by an evaluation is whether or not the target population has been clearly defined. For example, in examining the structure of an intervention for homeless children it would be useful to ask such questions as: How is the construct of homelessness operationally defined? Does it include only persons who are literally homeless—on the streets, in the shelters, and in cars—or does it also include the "precariously housed" (Rossi, 1989), those doubled-up (i.e., living with relatives, friends, or others) or in otherwise temporary housing situations?

To clarify the nature of the target population, one must also determine whether or not the program is indeed designed to reach or enroll the target population adequately. For example, although a program may be targeted to families who are precariously housed as well as to those who are literally homeless, the absence of activities in the program's design to identify and reach persons in doubled-up housing should lead one to question the extent to which the persons addressed in the intervention will actually include those in precariously housed situations. For most interventions in the homeless area that lack an aggressive outreach component, it is likely that only a subset of the population will be reached—typically those most eager and motivated to be involved in the program. Therefore, if the program is intended for the most needy and most troubled, it will need to include aggressive efforts to recruit these hard-to-reach persons.

Other important questions are whether the needs of the persons to be served are known, and whether the program activities appear to meet the needs of those persons. Rog and Bickman (1984), using an example from an evaluation of a stress management program, illustrated how the lack of demonstrated program effectiveness may have been due, in part, to the lack of fit between the target population's needs and the program. The program was designed to reduce stress in a corporation's middle managers who were involved in frequent high stress situations; however, the participants in the program reported only a small number of instances in which they were involved in stressful situations. In addition, the type of stress they experienced was qualitatively different from the type of stress for which the program was targeted. The program emphasized personal coping strategies for individuals who experienced job stress resulting from workload, deadlines, and other work-related stress; the type of stress the managers were confronting, however, involved organizational and internal communication problems and called for broader organizational interventions. Thus, because the program was serving a different population from the one for which it was designed, the evaluation may not have been a fair test of the program's effectiveness.

In areas in which the phenomenon is not well known and the needs of the target population are unclear, it may be important to do a more formal needs assessment before the study itself (e.g., McKillip, 1987), or at a minimum, to collect additional data on the needs of participants as part of the outcome effort. This latter data collection effort will not assist the program developers in targeting the program, but it can allow for a feedback research component. Feedback research involves an internal assessment of the problem and the degree to which the program has adequately addressed the problem (Rog & Bickman, 1984). This type of effort may be particularly important in developmental follow-up research on homeless children. Differences in the types of homeless situations, family environments, and other predisposing and preintervention conditions may indicate the need for different types of interventions.

Goals and Objectives of the Program

The critical questions in this area are (a) whether the program goals are explicit for all levels of the program, (b) to what extent they are clear at the systems, program, and individual participant level, and (c) whether they are based on some existing knowledge or on a sound conceptual scheme.

Goal setting for programs may be particularly difficult in new areas in which there is insufficient information on the phenomenon being studied. For example, it may be difficult to set realistic educational goals for school-based interventions with homeless children without more information on the needs of the different age groups of children, the length of time children are expected to participate in an intervention, who would be responsible for implementing the intervention (e.g., teachers, paraprofessionals, volunteers), and who else might participate in the intervention (e.g., only homeless children, other children, parents, siblings). Moreover, it may be difficult to set realistic goals without information on and control of environmental conditions that could nullify an educational program's effects (e.g., conditions such as chaotic shelter environments and multiple and frequent transitions from shelters; Rafferty & Shinn, 1991).

Program Activities and Components

The following are important questions regarding program activities and components: (a) Are the activities well defined and specified? (b) Are the specific activities measurable and can they be implemented consistently? (c) Have all the activities and subactivities been fully delineated? (d) How have they been selected? Although service providers and program developers generally seek information to guide their efforts, there are often few resources to do this, particularly in areas in which there is great pressure to intervene. In these situations, they often draw on their instincts and own experience as well as the "best practices" of others in tackling a problem. In fact, as Rog and Huebner (1992) have discussed, service providers often have an action orientation and a "service set": They begin with an idea of the services and activities they would like to provide rather than starting with a clear identification of the needs of the population. The result is that the program activities may not be specifically targeted to the needs of the overall population, or to the different needs of various subgroups within a broader, heterogeneous population.

Fit between Goals and Activities

It is important to ask how likely it is that the goals can be achieved, given that the proposed activities will be implemented as designed, and whether some goals are more possible than others. For example, although it is plausible that psychotherapeutic interventions for homeless youth who suffer from emotional problems will increase their self-esteem and insight into their problems and possible solutions, it is less likely that these interventions alone will have the ability to increase the residential stability of these children. Other activities such as case management and family reunification may be needed to assist children in finding new homes or in returning to their parents' homes.

The plausibility of a program also may be affected by other variables that could mediate the effectiveness of the intervention and its activities. For example, a major goal of an intensive case management program may be to have at least 80% of participating homeless families secure stable permanent housing within 3 months of participating in the program. However, the plausibility of the program's ability to accomplish this goal is not only dependent on the underlying logic of the program and the integrity of its implementation, but also on the extent to which affordable, suitable housing is available in the community.

The length of the intervention also may affect its plausibility. The goals of interventions, such as school-based interventions, may be plausible only if a certain "dose" of the program is received by participants. In school-based interventions for homeless children, for example, the children may have difficulty attending school on a regular basis because of their family's movement from one shelter to another and to other temporary housing situations. It may be important, therefore, to include other activities in the program, such as transportation, to ensure that the children can participate regularly and for the requisite period of time regardless of their shelter or housing situation.

Outcome Indicators

Outcome questions are: (a) Is the full range of both short-term and longer term outcomes clearly specified? (b) Are they measurable? (c) Have the program developers considered not only the types of outcomes that are expected but also the magnitude of effects that would be considered meaningful? (d) Have they determined when and how often the measurements should be taken? Part of the overall logic of a program is having a clear sense of what the intervention is designed to accomplish.

An important aspect of determining the evaluability of the program is determining whether it is feasible to measure the effects of the program. Can the outcomes be operationalized and measured with existing technology? Do data currently exist or can they be collected? Measuring the developmental and psychological status of homeless children, for example, is often a difficult enterprise. Many of the instruments available to assess development have not been standardized for poor and minority children (Rafferty & Shinn, 1991); many of those available are inadequate in general and often are difficult to administer validly in the chaotic shelter environments.

Resources

Important questions about resources are (a) Are the necessary resources to implement the program as designed available and sufficient? (b) Will they be available throughout the course of the intervention? Resources include financial resources, personnel with the necessary expertise and skills, and the time needed to implement the intervention fully and to have it in place long enough to achieve the intended individual, system, and community level effects. A program may have a strong conceptual framework but may be implausible if it lacks the resources necessary to implement it as designed. For example, if an infant stimulation program is designed to be conducted for 1 year but funding is available only for 6 months, the plausibility of reaching the original goals of the year-long program is questionable.

The process of examining the conceptual framework underlying a program typically involves the development of a "logic model," depicting the goals and objectives, resources, activities, and outcomes of a program as well as the linkages between them (e.g., Schmidt et al., 1979). The logic model is developed based on written material on the program and interviews with key program staff and other stakeholders in the program. Once the model is developed, it is checked for accuracy and completeness by program staff and revised as necessary.

Reviewing the conceptual structure of a program with the program developers often results in refinements in the underlying program, in the implementation plans for the program, and in the measurement plans. Through the process, program staff become more aware of the need for a well-articulated theoretical basis of the program and the extent to which the program activities require clarification or expansion.

EVALUATING THE IMPLEMENTATION OF THE INTERVENTION

Understanding the process and implementation of an intervention has long been considered an important feature of a thorough and sensitive evaluation (e.g., Scheirer, 1981). The interest has typically been in monitoring the process of a program as it unfolds and in examining what activities have occurred, what has changed from the original plans, and what barriers or problems have been confronted.

Implementation evaluation has matured over the years and gained sophistication in the methods that are being used (e.g., Brekke, 1987; Brekke & Wolkon, 1988). More attention is being given to studying implementation of an intervention at the individual participant level as well as at system and problem levels.

Extensive information on the nature of the population served is critical to collect in the evaluation of programs in emerging problem areas. These data can provide a greater understanding of the needs and characteristics of the population and the various subgroups contained in it. In particular, it is important to understand the extent to which the intended target persons are participating in the program. The importance of knowledge about the population is important not only for judging the external validity of the sample served but also the degree of fit between the objectives and goals of the program and the population. As noted earlier, if the program is serving a different population than was intended, it may not be a fair test of the effectiveness of the program (Rog & Bickman, 1984).

In addition to examining the coverage of the intended population, it is important to examine the biases within the population (Brekke, 1987), that is, the degree to which different subgroups participate to differing degrees. Collecting detailed implementation data per client can permit a more sensitive outcome assessment, especially if there is considerable variability in the intensity of services received by individuals. Dose–response studies can be conducted to determine whether different levels of participation in a program or different levels of service receipt are correlated with different levels of outcome. Of course, motivation for participating as well as other confounding factors need to be considered in an analysis of the outcomes associated with different dosage levels.

Implementation data also can be useful in understanding why variations exist in the service delivery process. It is important to examine the characteristics of the deliverers, the service delivery setting, and the broader community context, and how they may affect what is done as well as what is achieved.

Methods for studying implementation include intense observations of services, detailed activity logs, reviews of process documents such as minutes of meetings, and tracking data on clients and their service use. Data collection methods will vary depending on whether implementation information is being collected on the program level or on the individual client level. At the program level, data can be gathered through site visits, interviews with program staff, reviews of pertinent documents, and record abstractions. At the individual level, data collection can be much more difficult. Data collection on service receipt and participation usually requires the strong involvement of program staff, particularly if data are to be collected routinely or over a long course of time. Tools that can be developed for collecting participation data include activity logs, contact logs, and tracking forms. Less specific information could be collected by the researchers through client interviews.

Implementation data are not only valuable in increasing the understanding of the design and operation of the program, but also in making midcourse corrections to strengthen the probability that the program will achieve its outcome goals. Implementation data coupled with effectiveness data provide a very powerful assessment of a program and also provide the explanatory strength to understand why certain outcomes are or are not achieved. Moreover, data on the population and nature of the intervention are essential for replicating a program or individual program components that are found to be effective.

MEETING THE METHODOLOGICAL REQUIREMENTS OF EFFECTIVENESS EVALUATION

An outcome evaluation is typically viewed as the ultimate test of an intervention. It can provide the key information for determining whether a program should be maintained or discontinued. Not all situations, however, are conducive to an outcome study. Among the conditions that need to be addressed are (a) the evaluability of the intervention and its individual components; (b) the existence, quality, and integrity of control or comparison groups; (c) the ability to design a sufficiently sensitive evaluation to detect meaningful differences; (d) the existence of meaningful, feasible, valid, and reliable outcome measures; (e) sufficient time to conduct the study on the outcomes.

Evaluability

As discussed earlier, the internal logic of an intervention should be examined before studying its outcomes. This is particularly important for long-term evaluations of interventions designed either to prevent or to forestall the negative effects of a problem (such as homelessness) or to produce long-term developmental effects. Unless the intervention is conceptually strong and measurable, it may be unwise to invest the resources needed to conduct a follow-up study.

Comparison Groups

The existence of a basis for comparison is a critical condition for undertaking an outcome study. The evaluator must have the ability either to compare the treatment to a no-treatment or status-quo (minimal) treatment control group, or to one or more comparison groups that are equivalent to the target population.

For interventions that have been mounted in response to social and political pressure, it is often difficult to develop a randomized study and to maintain its integrity. Even if there is initial acceptance of the idea of random assignment, the study may break down for a variety of reasons. For example, there may be pressure to serve all those individuals most in need, despite original plans to assign randomly the entire target population to two or more groups. In addition, there may be conditions that emerge during the intervention that challenge the random assignment, such as differential refusal and attrition among the groups. In areas in which intervention is desperately needed, there also may be an increased chance of spillover from the intervention groups to the control groups; the news of the intervention may spread quickly and control group participants may seek ways to participate in the intervention.

Design Sensitivity

It may not be possible in certain situations to mount an outcome study that is sufficiently sensitive to detect the intended or expected differences. Lipsey (1990) discussed several factors that affect the sensitivity of a study. Three sets of factors especially important in designing an outcome study concern the nature of the independent variable, the type and number of subjects, and the measurement of the dependent variable. Concern about the nature of the independent variable relates to the evaluability of the intervention: What is the strength of the treatment? Can it produce effects large enough to be detected by the evaluation? Is the treatment applied uniformly and consistently to the recipient group?

An intervention that is expected to be weak and to produce small effects will require a much more powerful research design than one in which the treatment is considered strong and able to produce moderate or large effects. In addition, heterogeneity in the implementation of an intervention, resulting in various "doses" of the treatment across participants, complicates the study and potentially weakens the study's ability to detect differences. This may be particularly the case in ill-defined intervention areas in which the treatment is somewhat fuzzy or provided on an individualized basis.

Thought needs to be given to the advisability of conducting an outcome study on the intervention as designed. Is it a wise use of resources to strengthen the statistical power of the evaluation through strengthening the design (i.e., increasing sample size) if the effects are small and may not be practically significant? It might be better to hold off the study until the intervention itself can be strengthened either through standardizing the treatment received or through targeting the intervention to a less heterogeneous population. Again, data from an evaluability assessment or from an implementation study may be helpful in this regard.

The validity of the dependent measures, their sensitivity to small changes, the timing of the measurement to expected changes in the treatment, and the inclusion of short-term and long-term outcomes are all features considered in assessing the sensitivity of a design (Lipsey, 1990). For example, in a school-based intervention targeted to homeless children, it would be important for program developers to have fleshed out a theory of how the intervention will work and the staging of outcomes. Understanding the range of proximal and distal outcomes and how they are linked to one another is critical to conducting a thorough, sensitive test of an intervention.

Achievement of proximal goals may be a key step to progress on more distal goals. If an evaluation of an intervention cannot be conducted for a period of time sufficient to measure its long-term effects, measurement of proximal goals can at least indicate whether the intervention is making progress toward the longer-term goals. In addition, the failure to achieve certain necessary short-term goals may provide important information as to why longer-term goals were not achieved. For example, if a school-based program fails to maintain school attendance, it is unlikely that it will have any effect on children's development and educational achievements.

Sensitivity to Developmental Differences

In developmental followup research, it is important to assess the within-treatment group differences and effects of the intervention as well as those between treatment and control groups. Understanding the developmental differences among the children and the interaction of the treatment with each child's stage of development is key to a comprehensive evaluation of the developmental interventions. Thus, a comprehensive look at the interaction of development with the intervention itself has implications for the comprehensiveness of the data collected, repeated measurement in small enough time intervals to capture developmental changes sensitively, and collecting data on a treatment group large enough to draw implications across a broad span of development.

Time

Finally, in a developmental follow-up study, it is important to consider how long the follow-up period must be to measure the effects of the program, and whether the integrity of the study can be maintained over this period of time. Will resources be available to support a longitudinal assessment? Will there be continued support by the program and other relevant agencies? For example, has there been agreement to the evaluator's continued use of relevant records maintained by key agencies?

In studying the effectiveness of interventions with homeless families, one of the realities is the difficulty of tracking because of frequent movement to a variety of housing and shelter situations. What mechanisms and strategies can be used to track both the program participants and control group participants? Typically, continued support is needed by key community agencies to maintain contact with the families.

EVALUATING EFFECTIVENESS—AND EFFECTS—OF THE PROGRAM

Features important to include in evaluating the effectiveness of programs in an ill-defined program area are similar to those examined in the previous three areas of evaluation inquiry. An expanded evaluation approach suggests an outcome study that can contribute to the knowledge on the phenomenon under study, in addition to knowledge on the effectiveness of the intervention. Other features that are important to include in effectiveness evaluations that go beyond traditional boundaries include the following:

1. Examining a wider range of outcomes than those stated by the program. Guidance in identification and selection of additional outcomes to measure can come from theory and research in the problem area and in similar areas of investigation (Chen & Rossi, 1981).
2. Exploring the differential effectiveness of the intervention for subgroups of the target population. Combined with a detailed understanding of the needs and characteristics of each subgroup, outcome information on each group can aid the evaluator in determining if a program or its individual components are better suited for certain types of individuals.
3. Examining the relationship between implementation data and the effectiveness of the program. This feature is particularly important for disentangling the effects of different doses of the program.

SUMMARY

In evaluating interventions in ill-defined problem areas, a broad approach is warranted. The approach should begin with an understanding of the knowledge that exists to date and an analysis of the underlying logic and theory of the intervention. It is critical to collect implementation data at both the program level and the individual client level throughout the study of the intervention, both for clarifying outcome information and for facilitating later replication. Likewise, taking a sensitive look at the components of the intervention and measuring their proximal as well as distal outcomes may help to bring clarity to intervention studies focused on messy, real-world problems.

The task of designing evaluation strategies for programs in emerging areas is not easy. The need for information to guide a program is great and usually immediate. In addition, the powerfulness of the issue often increases the difficulty of conducting rigorous tests of the intervention. Because an ill-defined intervention is focused on a pressing problem, the feeling may be that "anything is better than nothing." In these situations, efforts to implement an experimental design may be misguided and doomed to failure. Even evaluations that focus on describing an intervention and its implementation may be hindered by barriers in collecting systematic information. In these situations, evaluators often feel challenged and frustrated; the complexities of the problem, the compromises that continue to be made in the original design, and the continuing evolution of the programs may appear incongruent with a scientific approach to evaluation; however, as Rog and Huebner (1992) have noted, one of the key ingredients to working in ill-defined areas may be a strong and continuing relationship between the research and the service providers. Breaking communication barriers and increasing understanding by the providers of the evaluator's role is critical to implementing an evaluation that can be conducted systematically, with the highest quality research design and data, and that is most responsive to the reality of the program as it unfolds and evolves.

REFERENCES

Alperstein, G., Rappaport, C., & Flanigan, J. (1988). Health problems of homeless children in New York City. *American Journal of Public Health, 78,* 1232–1233.

Bassuk, E. (1990). The problem of family homelessness. In E. Bassuk, R. Carman, & L. Weinreb (Eds.), *Community care for homeless families: A program design manual.* Newton Centre, MA: The Better Homes Foundation.

Bassuk, E., & Rubin, L. (1987). Homeless children: A neglected population. *American Journal of Orthopsychiatry, 57,* 279–286.

Bassuk, E., Rubin, L., & Lauriat, A. (1986). Characteristics of sheltered homeless families. *American Journal of Public Health, 76,* 1097–1101.

Bickman, L. (1985). Improving established statewide programs: A component theory of evaluation. *Evaluation Review, 9,* 189–208.

Bickman, L. (1987). The functions of program theory. In L. Bickman (Ed.). Using program theory in evaluation. *New Directions for Program Evaluation* (No. 33, pp. 5–18). San Francisco: Jossey-Bass.

Bickman, L. (Ed.). (1990). Advances in program theory. *New Directions for Program Evaluation* (No. 47). San Francisco: Jossey-Bass.

Brekke, J. S. (1987). The model-guided method for monitoring program implementation. *Evaluation Review, 11,* 281–299.

Brekke, J. S., & Wolkon, G. H. (1988). Monitoring program implementation in community mental health settings. *Evaluation and the Health Professions, 11,* 425–440.

Chen, H.-T. (1989). The conceptual framework of the theory-driven perspective. *Evaluation and Program Planning, 12,* 391–396.

Chen, H.-T. *Theory-driven evaluations.* (1990). Newbury Park, CA: Sage.

Chen, H.-T., & Rossi, P. H. (1981). The multi-goal, theory-driven approach to evaluation: A model linking basic and applied social science. In H. E. Freeman & M. A. Solomon (Eds.), *Evaluation Studies Review Annual, 6,* 38–54. Beverly Hills, CA: Sage.

Chen, H.-T., & Rossi, P. H. (1983). Evaluating with sense: The theory-driven approach. *Evaluation Review, 7,* 106–122.

Chen, H.-T., & Rossi, P. H. (1987). The theory-driven approach to validity. *Evaluation and Program Planning, 10,* 95–103.

Chen, H.-T., & Rossi, P. H. (1989). Issues in the theory-driven perspective. *Evaluation and Program Planning, 12,* 299–306.

Chen, H.-T., & Rossi, P. H. (1992). (Eds.). *Theory-driven evaluation: Analyzing and developing programs and policies.* Westport, CT: Greenwood.

Edwards, P. (1987). Conceptual and methodological issues in evaluating emergent programs. *Evaluation and Program Planning, 10,* 27–34.

Lipsey, M. (1990). *Design sensitivity: Statistical power for experimental research.* Newbury Park, CA: Sage.

McKillip, J. (1987). *Needs analysis: Tools for the human services and education.* Beverly Hills, CA: Sage.

Molnar, J., and & Rubin, D. H. (1991, March). The impact of homelessness on children: Review of prior studies and implications for future research. Paper presented at the NIMH/NIAAA research conference organized by the Better Homes Foundation, Cambridge, MA.

Molnar, J., Klein, T., Knitzer, J., & Ortiz-Torres, B. (1988). *Home is where the heart is: The crisis of homeless children and families in New York City.* A Report to the Edna McConnell Clark Foundation, New York City.

Rafferty, Y., & Shinn, M. (1991). The impact of homelessness on children. *American Psychologist, 46,* 1170–1179.

Rog, D. J. (1985). *A methodological analysis of evaluability assessment.* Unpublished doctoral dissertation. Vanderbilt University, Nashville, TN

Rog, D. J., & Bickman, L. (1984). The feedback research approach to evaluation: A method to increase evaluation utility. *Evaluation and Program Planning, 7,* 169–176.

Rog, D. J., & Huebner, R. (1992). Using research and theory in developing innovative programs for homeless individuals. In H. T. Chen & P. Rossi (Eds.), *Theory-driven evaluation: Analyzing and developing programs and policies.* Westport, CT: Greenwood.

Rossi, P. (1989). *Down and out in America: The origins of homelessness.* Chicago: University of Chicago Press.

Scheirer, M. A. (1981). *Program implementation: The organizational context.* Beverly Hills, CA: Sage.

Scheirer, M. A. (1987). Program theory and implementation theory: Implications for evaluators. In L. Bickman (Ed.). Using program theory in evaluation. *New Directions for Program Evaluation* (No. 33, pp. 5–18). San Francisco: Jossey-Bass.

Schmidt, R. E., Scanlon, J. W., & Bell, J. B. (1979). Evaluability assessment: Making public programs work better. *Human Services Monograph Series,* No. 14.

Wholey, J. S. (1979). *Evaluation: Promise and performance.* Washington, DC: The Urban Institute.

Wholey, J. S. (1987). Evaluability assessment: Developing program theory. In L. Bickman (Ed.). Using program theory in evaluation. *New Directions for Program Evaluation* (No. 33, pp. 77–92). San Francisco: Jossey-Bass.

Wholey, J. S., Scalon, J. W., Duffy, H. G., Fukomoto, J. S., & Vogt, L. M. (1971). *Federal evaluation policy: Analyzing the effects of public programs.* Washington, DC: The Urban Institute.

Wood, D., Valdez, B., Hayashi, T., & Shen, A. (1990). Health of homeless children and housed, poor children. *Pediatrics, 86,* 858–866.

Developmental Psychopathology of Multiplex Developmental Disorder

Donald J. Cohen
Kenneth E. Towbin
Linda Mayes
Fred Volkmar

INTRODUCTION

For more than four decades, clinicians have been aware of children suffering from early, severe, and persistent disturbances that derail the processes underlying socialization and the emergence of personal autonomy (Kanner, 1943; Putnam, Rank, Pavenstedt, Anderson, & Rawson, 1948; Rank & MacNaughton, 1950). The groups that are best defined are those whose disturbances in social relations and communication have been conveyed by the categorical diagnosis of autism. For many of these children, the process of socialization—of entering into the mainstream of social intercourse and reciprocity—is blocked from the first months of life. Burdened by retardation and limited or absent speech, the majority of these children fail to develop a sense of their own internal world or to appreciate the emotional lives of others (Ritvo & Provence, 1953). Although the precise boundaries of the diagnostic concept of autism remain under investigation, its basic validity and major diagnostic criteria are broadly accepted (Volkmar, Bregman, Cohen, & Cicchetti, 1988; Volkmar & Cohen, 1988).

In addition to autistic children, however, there are many other children who have severe developmental difficulties emerging during the first years of life whose symptoms and natural histories share a "family resemblance" to those with autism but who are distinctive from autistic children in various ways, including their more varied social adaptations. These children are described as eccentric, odd, overanxious, aloof, and "weird." Numerous diagnostic labels have been suggested over the years to provide a taxonomic location and to convey the nature of the interferences in the emergence of their sense of themselves and their basic social and emotional capacities to relate to others. These formal designations include borderline, schizotypal, schizoidal disorders, atypical development, childhood psychosis and symbiotic states, pervasive developmental disorders, and, most recently, Asperger's syndrome (e.g., Geleerd, 1958; Mahler & Furer, 1968; Wolff & Chick, 1980; Wing, 1981; Pine, 1982; Robson, 1982; Szatmari, Tuff, Finlayson, & Bartolucci, 1989; Petti & Vela, 1990). The term Pervasive Developmental Disorders—Not Otherwise Specified (PDD-NOS) is used in DSM-III-R (APA, 1987) to refer to children with some, but not all features of autism; by definition no actual criteria for this condition are specified. No term, however, has been fully satisfactory nor broadly accepted for the children we specifically have in mind; and although clinicians have had the sense of a category of such children, no doubt as broad as that of autism and probably more populous, there are as yet no clearly defined diagnostic criteria that could guide systematic studies, including those on the basic validity or utility of such a grouping.

The epistemology of clinical research often starts with an intuitive recognition of a recurrent pattern of features; the pattern may include prominent current clinical symptoms, age of onset, family and social context of symptoms, natural history, laboratory findings, and the like. The broader the domains of observation—past and present symptoms, social, cognitive, and adaptive findings,—and the easier it is to make predictions based on a subset, the more conviction, within clinical epistemology, of the validity of the category. In this chapter, we describe how the longitudinal study of a group of these children, seen early in childhood and followed through early adulthood, has led us to explicate specific criteria for the diagnostic category *multiplex developmental disorder* (MDD). As we outline our own clinical observations and studies, we will suggest ways in which the clinical approach to children with this type of condition may augment and be elaborated by other, more formal studies of developmental psychopathology (Cohen, Paul, & Volkmar, 1986; Cohen, Paul, & Volkmar, 1988). Also, in the course of describing the clinical findings, we will attempt to show how studies of complex, persistent developmental disorders of very early onset can contribute to understanding developmental continuities and discontinuities that relate to the emergence, changes, and maintenance of the intertwined psychological processes that constitute a sense of self.

LONGITUDINAL STUDIES OF DISORDERS OF SOCIAL RELATEDNESS

Clinical and longitudinal studies of children with early onset difficulties affecting social and emotional development started in the Child Study Center at Yale before the Second World War in the work of Gesell. In the early 1950s, Provence and her colleagues began intensive, systematic work on very young children with developmental disorders; over the decades, "younger" colleagues, including ourselves, have joined in the work (Provence & Dahl, 1987). At least 75 to 100 new patients have been seen annually throughout these years. The continuity of this program of research over more than four decades provides us with a breath of clinical observations and opportunities for developmental follow-up of children with a broad range of difficulties. Many of the young children seen during the 1950s and 1960s have grown into adulthood in our community and have remained in affiliated programs. One such patient provided us with a personal account of his development that illuminated the experience of autism (Volkmar & Cohen, 1985).

In the early decades of the research program on young children with developmental disorders, the children with autism were categorized as suffering from "severe atypical development." They satisfied the descriptive features that emerged from many other studies during the 1950s and 1960s for this most severe childhood disorder. A systematic follow-up study by Provence and her colleagues showed that long-term outcome was generally poor for social and adaptive functioning and that adult status was closely related to the severity of the intellectual deficit. Almost all needed long-term care. The families of children with severe atypical development were found to be similar to those of children with other biologically based problems, such as mental retardation; the parents and siblings had their share of emotional difficulties (e.g., mothers frequently became depressed as a result of the strains of the child's illness), but they were not particularly marked by psychiatric illness (Dahl, Cohen, & Provence, 1986).

In addition to the young children with "severe atypical development," Provence and her colleagues distinguished a group of children with atypicalities in social relations, rather than impoverishment, severe disturbances in the modulation of anxiety, and peculiarities in thinking and language rather than delays or absence. These children were diagnosed as "mildly atypical." Their outcome tended to be far more optimistic and varied than seen for autistic individuals (Dahl, et al., 1986). On follow-up over the next years, some of these children with early onset atypicalities of development were functioning within the mainstream, whereas others remained odd and plagued with anxieties and social difficulties (Sparrow et al., 1986; Rescorla, 1986). The families of these children more often had difficulties with anxiety, obsessiveness, and other personality problems.

Children with multiplex developmental disorder are similar, in many ways, to these "mildly atypical children." These youngsters move into the periphery of their families and society and become the "strange uncle" who lives upstairs in his elderly parents' home, the hardworking cleaning man, the somber bachelor who sorts the mail, the stablehand who takes very good care of the horses but who gets enraged by the noise and mess left by the teenagers, and the "borderline" adult who is admitted to the general psychiatry service for detoxification. The children with multiplex developmental disorder may be similar in some ways to those who, most recently, have been diagnosed as suffering from Asperger's syndrome (Wing, 1981), although this latter disorder seems more closely related to higher-functioning autism. Over time, individuals with MDD are vulnerable to more elaborated social and psychiatric problems, even including psychosis, but who, on the other hand, unlike autistic individuals, are able to maintain restricted degrees of social relatedness. The range of outcomes and prognostic predictors for this diagnostic category will become more apparent through the careful study of these individuals through adolescence and early adulthood. Their life histories also illustrate how impaired capacities for social relatedness influence environmental responses which in turn effect facets of the expression of the disorder.

THREE YOUNG MEN

Over the course of their lives, Ezra, Zack, and Jeremiah experienced difficulties with defining their sense of self as the locus of feelings, desires, and intentions; they could not fully understand the relations between their emotional states and their experiences. They had no way to understand why they sometimes felt quite unhappy or anxious, or how to describe their feelings and thoughts to others. Nor could they fully understand the motivations and feelings of others, what really makes other human beings operate as they do. Their imaginations would play tricks on them, and reality and fantasy were blurred. They felt cut off from peers and outside of the normal stream of family life, and they became frightened and suspicious.

Ezra

Ezra's parents became worried about him when he was about 1 year old; so unlike his older siblings, Ezra seemed prematurely subdued and gloomy.

He pulled away, just ever so slightly, from signs of affection or when his siblings tried to play too roughly with him. A thorough pediatric evaluation at that time showed that his motor skills, cognitive capacities, and basic social skills were on track: he was already walking, he knew his parents and responded specifically to them, and he was quite familiar with the routines of daily life (eating, bathing, waving goodbye, etc.). Yet, the pediatrician confirmed the parental sense that Ezra seemed preoccupied and less available to affection than other children his age.

During his second year, Ezra was clinging, and he became tearful and whiny with slight provocation or for no apparent reason at all. His parents were struck by how quickly his mood and relations with them could change: In one instant, he could be transformed from being cheerful and comfortable into being in a state of rigid tension, with clenched fingers and jaw. His parents would try to console him but eventually they learned that the best approach was simply to allow Ezra to find his own way out of a black mood.

During his third year, Ezra developed a variety of unrelated fears (separation from his mother, bugs, ladies with large hats, men in uniforms) which restricted the family's freedom to travel. Activities that his siblings and other children enjoyed greatly would often end in disaster for Ezra. A trip to the park would lead to his whimpering demands to be taken home; his balloon would always break; the noise in the restaurant would upset him to the point where he could not eat or felt like he was going to vomit. His parents thought he was like the comic strip character whose head was covered by rain clouds. He had to be withdrawn from two nursery schools because he wouldn't allow his mother to leave and bothered other children with requests, questions, and temper outbursts. Several times he became so upset he bit another child.

By 6, Ezra asked the oddest questions—about death, disease, the insides of people's bodies—of both strangers and his family. It was sometimes hard to follow precisely what he was wondering about, nor did he seem reassured by the usual answers. He began to walk about the house from room to room as if searching for something but never finding the object in mind. He would spend hours talking aloud to himself in a high, falsetto voice or in a unique Ezra accent, which seemed rather English-Scottish. At school, his academic capacities were acceptable or even excellent, but he dawdled over his work and gave unusual responses which sometimes alarmed the teachers.

At age 10, he told his parents about odd spells in which he suddenly felt that he was in another world, or that this world was not real, or that he deeply worried about being hurt or dying. He frightened his parents with questions about whether someone on the street was real or a dream, and he would awake from sleep wondering if his dreams had actually taken place. He would sometimes explode with rage at his mother or father, or anyone else who might be near, and act as if the other were about to hurt him or had already done something to harm him. He felt certain that others were thinking bad, critical things about him.

Ezra's parents tried to buffer Ezra from experiences that would frighten or confuse him and they worked tirelessly to help him with homework, to make nice school projects, to have successful visits with friends whom they would invite for special treats. This prosthetic environment often succeeded in making Ezra look so normal that relatives sometimes felt that his parents were spoiling Ezra and causing the mild problems they noticed. Parental attempts to help Ezra make friends often ended poorly; he would say something nasty or simply walk out on a friend who was visiting.

Adults found Ezra's humor, sarcasm, and shrewd comments engaging. He enjoyed movies and often accompanied adult relatives to the theater where he was particularly fond of musicals with big dance numbers. At home, he enacted parts, particularly female roles; he was a fine mimic of famous actors. He could be dryly humorous and even make jokes about himself.

With the onset of puberty Ezra spent long hours masturbating in the bathroom or bedroom and was interested in looking at scantily dressed men and women, in photos and in person. His parents could never say or do the right thing in relation to Ezra; when they made suggestions or tried to be useful they often irritated him even further and provoked explosive arguments. Yet, Ezra could not be without them and he would become upset if they were not at home when he returned or if they went away on vacation. During adolescence, he had an increase in his feelings of unreality and his spells of anxiety increased. He sometimes ran out of class when he was overcome by an intense dread, which eluded description but left him in cold sweats.

In his young adult years, Ezra drifted the streets hoping to make friends. He took a series of jobs in small stores and restaurants. At age 24, he felt he had a "sack thrown over his entire life" and that he was "immobile" and without direction; he would sit for hours in front of the television or at the side of his bed; he had no interests; he spoke of "death as liberation from nothing . . . from a bleak future." After many months, he slowly returned to work and, surprisingly, established a friendship with a gentle, young woman who had come to the bookstore where he worked as a book shelver. She found his quiet, dark-eyed intensity appealing and liked to take care of him. Ezra and his new friend spent increasing amounts of time together and a mutually pleasant physical relationship evolved. Ezra enjoyed being hugged and having his back rubbed. For the first time, he had months of good spirits and some pleasure in his work; he enjoyed living independently of his family in a YMCA and spending all his spare time with his girlfriend. She was very understanding of his spells of anxiety and unreality and appreciated his interest in theater and movies as well as his insights about lighting, scenery, and the like. She also knew when to leave Ezra alone and how not to become upset when he became furious about some statement or oversight.

Zack

At age 9, Zack Ross, a tall, wiry, fair, handsome boy, was referred to the state psychiatric hospital after spending two months in a private psychiatric facility. He had been admitted to the private institution after becoming disorganized in his thinking, engaging in compulsive hand washing, and exhibiting frankly paranoid ideas. Although there had been vigorous efforts to maintain him at home while he attended a day treatment program, he began to strike peers and staff and to engage impulsively in dangerous actions like running into traffic hoping he would be hit by an oncoming car. His weight was dropping because, in reaction to fears that his mother had poisoned his food, he had stopped eating. Zack was not responding to efforts to treat him with a combination of hospitalization, medication, psychotherapy, and family therapy.

The private hospitalization at age 8 was not the first psychiatric evaluation Zack received. The Ross' first brought Zack to medical attention when he was 3 years old in response to their concerns about his delay in speaking and withholding stool to the point of becoming impacted. Zack had always been "temperamental," in that he was squirmy, colicky, and difficult to feed. His parents found him active, and literally "bouncy," in the way he most enjoyed moving up and down. The result of the evaluation at age 3 by his pediatrician was that he was thought to be simply an "active boy." Yet his parents thought this unlikely. They recalled that Zack would grab onto them "until it hurt" and that soon after the pediatric evaluation at 3 he began to talk, and then continued to do so incessantly, often asking pointless questions as if to fill every moment of silence. Nevertheless, they were clear that he was attached to them, knew them to be his caretakers, sought them for comfort, reacted with excitement to their arrivals and with tears at their departures.

At age 5, when Zack attended school for the first time, he had great difficulty separating from his mother. He refused to attend for months. Zack was thought to be "odd" by the kindergarten teacher, who reported that he seemed oblivious to disciplinary measures and his difficulties with peers caused him to be picked on and teased routinely. He did not have a single classmate who could be considered a friend. In first grade, he was placed in special education although his academic progress was satisfactory. His father took Zack to and from school each day. His excessive activity was still prominent and Zack was started on methylphenidate (10 mg daily) by his pediatrician, which apparently was helpful, although his parents discontinued the medication within months. At the time Zack entered second grade, his pronounced impulsivity remained, but in addition, he began to hit or slap himself and to push, kick, or hit his classmates. He would run down the school hallways screaming, and made many threats against staff and peers. For weeks he ceased eating anything prepared by his mother and feared the toilet to such a degree that he began to defecate in cups and plastic bags, or in the kitty litter box. He urinated in different corners of the house. Ritualized hand washing followed the conviction that he had germs on his hands that could not be removed. He believed students at school were talking or laughing at him behind his back and he sought revenge. On the street he would spit at passers-by without any definable precipitant.

In the context of this deterioration he was first hospitalized. Evaluation then showed superior verbal skills but low average verbal reasoning within social contexts, restricted emotional reactions, and impaired "reality testing." He was quite guarded. Projective testing showed redundant themes of aggression, sexuality, and violence. Treated with neuroleptic medication in doses ranging from 50 to 200 mg equivalents of chlorpromazine, Zack made little gain but was less aggressive.

In a day hospital setting for several months, he sustained his gains but made no progress. After 2 more months he deteriorated again and concern for his safety and his parents exhaustion from attempting to manage his pressing demands, angry outbursts, and suspicious beliefs led to readmission. Just before admission, he poured a cleaning solvent on the family cat in a deliberate attempt to harm it. He explained that he was jealous of the attention the cat received at home. On this rehospitalization, he seemed even more out of control. His thoughts were quite disorganized and he was barely able to cope with ordinary hygiene.

The Ross' are a hard-working middle-class family; Mr. Ross is a middle manager in a small manufacturing concern and his wife is a clerical worker for a large business. They had little experience raising children prior to Zack, and initially were not sure whether his delays should worry them. The Ross' family history in second-degree relatives was significant for recurrent depression, alcoholism, and disorders in which paranoia is prominent. Some family members may have been frankly delusional and psychotic, although the guardedness of the parents' reports made us cautious in our diagnostic estimates. It was not possible for us to clearly distinguish whether there had been paranoid personality, paranoid schizophrenia, or bipolar mania in several second-degree relatives. Mr. Ross had a personal history of depression, alcohol abuse, and suicide attempts and Mrs. Ross appeared to suffer from a chronic subclinical paranoid disorder with prominent magical thinking, most likely a paranoid personality disorder. Both were deeply concerned and even guilty about Zack's difficulties. They believed that much of his impairment was a consequence of their behaviors. It was very hard for them to sustain rules and a predictable pattern of living at home or a stable residence. The family moved from town to town at 18- to 24-month intervals.

Even with the moves, they held their jobs consistently, but had few social contacts and viewed their neighbors with fear and reproach.

From the day of admission to the state hospital Zack was deeply fearful. He threatened the admitting physician with a piece of furniture on their first interview. He seemed confused about routines and adapted to the behavioral program slowly, but approached staff often and appropriately to ask for help and obtain reassurance. He was sexually approached by another patient and later that day urinated on his belongings. Soon after admission, Zack was withdrawn from all medication. During the evaluation period he took refuge in the unit schedules and became less anxious with his therapist. He seemed only partially aware of the actions of the other patients and of their emotions. He would mimic some of their worst behaviors. Later, as he began to make progress he had the habit of laughingly reminding other patients of behaviors that lead them to receive fines or lose out on favorite activities ("Billy, if you don't clean up, you're going to get a fine "). He would repeat bad news to other patients while giggling, or remind them of their failings during the day—"John, remember yesterday how you tried to hit staff and got put in the Quiet Room?" He would mockingly echo their chants. He seemed to know just what would irritate them and he would tease them.

Assessment of his speech and language functioning showed that his vocabulary was advanced and he had a good appreciation of the pragmatics of communication. At times his diction was very advanced, and he used his words in a wooden manner. For example, he described his feces as "organic human waste." His vocabulary was large, though stilted; he read constantly. In this evaluation, the more structured the testing situation, the better Zack performed. Open interviews were the most difficult. Superior verbal skills and average performance skills were shown again, consistent with his previous evaluations.

After a disappointingly consistent pattern of disorganization, Zack was begun on 1 mg of haloperidol each day. He responded well to this without side effects and with a marked diminution in fears and silliness. However, he continued to display a highly variable and unpredictable level of function. The unit Zack lived in worked on a token economy system. On some occasions he would manage a fine without incident, but on others, when faced with exactly the same fine and consequences, he would loose control and begin to hit, spit, or kick. He might escalate until he required placement in a Quiet Room and there he defecated and smeared his feces while giggling and reciting silly jingles repetitively—but then hours later or the next day he was smiling, attentive, and responsive.

After a sustained period of vigorous attempts by his therapist, he looked forward to their meetings, seemed to develop a genuine affection for her, and to trust many members of the unit staff. He would ask about why other children responded as they did. He noticed who was discharged and whether they were going home or to other living arrangements. In therapy sessions, his interactions progressed from parallel play to more reciprocal and finally even a pleasurable competitive gamesmanship. He began to play with other children in the unit. With his therapist, he requested and learned the rudiments of chess. He maintained his appropriate academic grade level consistently. He began to gain skills in the unit and to make progress in his treatment plan.

Yet even during the periods of his highest functioning and progress, he would have "bad days" during which he was irritable and illogical. Occasionally on these bad days he would report that he had fears. One evening after watching a nationally televised "docudrama," he became convinced that the perpetrators featured in the program, who were now sought by the police, were on the hospital grounds; he crouched in the corner of his room or kept a vigil by his window, reluctant to sleep on his bed or venture out of his room. Days later he seemed reassured and returned to a more relaxed level. Several months later he calmly discussed his beliefs that an alien space colony flourished across the valley from the hospital and that its inhabitants were spying on the patients. At times when he reflected on this, he thought it was just a silly story, but other times he was virtually convinced of its veracity. The strength of his conviction in the story fluctuated throughout days and weeks. Some days he denied having told the story at all. Weeks before his discharge to a therapeutic group home, he expressed relief that he would finally be away from "them" but worried they could locate him in his new residence. At the time of discharge he considered the whole report just silly.

Jeremiah

After many years of trying to have a child, Mr. and Mrs. Schwartz almost gave up hopes of having the family they so much desired and proceeded with an adoption agency. They were an ideal couple—attractive, young, professional, with inherited wealth. The only thing missing from their lives was the son they both had fantasized about since their courtship. Just as the final adoption procedures were being completed, Mrs. Schwartz became pregnant. The pregnancy, however, was a grueling experience with months of nausea followed by high blood pressure and varicose viens. A difficult, 2-day labor finally ended with an emergency C-section. The newborn seemed fatigued by the ordeal: he needed a lot of stimulation to begin crying and was then hypotonic and grey. A few days later he brightened and began to suck well enough to be discharged from the hospital as a healthy newborn. At home, Jeremiah was so irritable and tense that breast feeding was abandoned. A series of different nipples and formulas were tried but he was not a baby who enjoyed eating. Mrs. Schwartz' nervousness and self-doubts increased. Pediatric guidance focused on the ways her tensions were transmitted to Jeremiah at meals, bathing, and when he was upset.

When Jeremiah was 16 months old, the pediatrician agreed with Jeremiah's parents that he seemed to be a child who was too self-contained, self-reliant, and serious. A few months later, the family and physician were commenting that Jeremiah was "aloof" and "distant." When he was 19 months old, his motor skills lagged and he seemed clumsy. For the next 2 years, his parents continued to wait for a "turning point" in Jeremiah's development, but they became increasingly worried that something indefinable but ominous was afflicting their son. A pediatric neurologist who examined Jeremiah when he was 2 felt he was an "autistic-like" child. He especially noted Jeremiah's insistence on maintaining rigid patterns (e.g., how he was fed and bathed, the arrangement of objects in his room) and his perseveration on small details of objects. A child psychiatrist found that Jeremiah was hard to engage socially but found clear indications that Jeremiah was socially attached to his parents and that his language was advanced and unusually well articulated. By age 3, Jeremiah had unexpected mood swings, with periods of dejection followed by dizzying, diffuse overactivity. He would sometimes become bewildered in the middle of an activity and stare ahead with a look of puzzlement. An EEG at this time was normal. By 4, Jeremiah was described as a hyperactive child, a label which would change, over the next decade, into minimal brain dysfunction (MBD) and then attention deficit disorder (ADD). He was too active and easily stimulated to stay in the normal nursery school and was started in a special program at the rehabilitation center where he received communication, gross motor, and social training.

By 5, he had some odd habits which only in retrospect could be called tics. These early habits consisted of rapid finger flicking and little mouth movements, sometimes accompanied by squeaks or sniffing sounds. When he was 8, he had rapid eye blinking that followed an episode of conjunctivitis, but the blinking did not stop when the infection was controlled. Over the next several years, he had an array of motor and vocal tics that came and went: head jerking, shoulder thrusting, arm and leg jerks, sniffing, coughing, and humming. He also said sexual slang words under his breath and interjected them into sentences. By age 10, his pediatrician diagnosed Tourette's syndrome and he was again seen by the pediatric neurologist and child psychiatrist who confirmed the diagnosis.

Jeremiah's school years were one disappointment after another. His terrible problems with concentration and organization prevented him from making full use of his superior intelligence and good language skills in school. His motor and vocal tics and extremely odd social behavior marked him out for teasing by other children. He perseverated about the same topic, endlessly asking for reassurance through questions about his body, his health, and their well-being: "Will this sore heal? Do you think I have an infection? What will happen if it doesn't heal? Are you going to die? Will grandma die?" And he worried about bee stings, small scratches, whether dogs who drooled had rabies. Years later, he worried about the transmission of AIDS from restaurant silverware, from sitting on park benches, and from touching coins handled by beggars.

At age 16, Jeremiah became much less docile and sweet and started to argue with his parents about his "rights." He didn't like their entering his room, looking at his things, or telling him when to come home. More and more, he stayed out after school and walked around teenage hangouts and the local mall. His parents worried about the dangers of his fascination with motorcycle gangs and drugs and they resented his decorating his walls with pictures of tough looking men and women. He would focus his attention on one or another tough youth whom he would meet on the street or in the mall: a few phrases exchanged with this idealized young man would be enough to set off a crush. Jeremiah would then talk endlessly about the man, ask his family if they thought the youth would consider him a friend, and try to watch the boy interacting with others from afar. This preoccupation was similar to the way in which Jeremiah would "hold onto" relationships, both good and bad, for many years. More than a decade after having been teased by a little girl in the second grade, Jeremiah would still speak about how "Louise hurt my feelings. I hate her" or "Do you remember Louise? Where is she now? I hate her." Jeremiah talked about his "idols" and his "demons," discussing or thinking about these individuals could bring a glow or rage to his face. Interestingly, his tics were much less apparent as he moved toward adulthood, although his obsessiveness, perseverations, and occasional stereotypic or tic-like gesture continued.

At age 20, Jeremiah graduated from a special high school and registered in a local junior college that had a program for youngsters with learning disabilities. He began to obsess about suicide and contemplated the various ways he might kill himself. He asked his father how long it took to suffocate with a bag over your head; another time, how long it took to die if a car was left running in the garage. After asking, he then would say something like, "Just joking" or "Don't worry, I would never do anything like that." His parents were, of course, not reassured. When they left him alone at home, they worried they might return to find him hanged, bleeding, or in a coma.

In his midtwenties, Jeremiah decided to move into an apartment with two young men he had met at a restaurant where he had started to work part time. He seemed content to go to work, return home, and cook a meal for himself, and spend the evenings watching television. The men shared a space, rent, and an occasional movie but mostly Jeremiah spent time alone in his room. His family saw him drift into a social class far below their own. Jeremiah found visiting their home uncomfortable but would accept invitations for dinners if there were no other people present. He especially took a dislike to one of his younger siblings who had a brilliant social and academic career and looked, in every way, like his father. If this brother were at home, Jeremiah sullenly would refuse to visit. He might be explicit about his feelings—"I don't need the buzz in my head"—or just excuse himself with "It is not convenient for me. That's all."

THE SPECTRUM OF DISORDERS OF DEVELOPMENT

In trying to make sense out of the lives of children and adults like Ezra, Zack, and Jeremiah, clinicians call on a range of diagnostic categorical lables. Each term captures some fragment of their complex stories, and none completely describes the evolving and changing expression of difficulties from childhood to adulthood. Their troubles with social relations might be captured by the concept of *schizoid* personality, whereas the oddness of their thinking and the blurring between reality and the contents of their own internal world might bring them closer to the diagnoses of *borderline* or *schizotypal* with connotations of the spectrum of *schizophrenic disorders.* Their impulsivity and excessive activity might be seen as arising from *attention deficit hyperactivity disorder.* Their fears and anxieties suggest the diagnosis of an *anxiety disorder*—generalized, phobic, or social—and they often seemed to have episodes of *panic* which might lead to requests for reassurance or withdrawal; their years of sadness and pessimism suggest a diagnosis of *dysthymia* and they occasionally would have longer periods of true hopeless *depression.* The abundance of obsessive thoughts and compulsive actions brings to mind the diagnosis of *obsessive-compulsive disorder* and, for Jeremiah, there was the full-blown diagnosis of Tourette's syndrome as well (Cohen, Bruun, & Leckman, 1988).

Ezra, Zack, and Jeremiah displayed a variety of dysfunctions, most of which had been present in some form for as long as their parents could recall. They were never socially well attuned, free of fearfulness, motorically well coordinated, cheerful, predictable, emotionally stable, or readily understandable to adults or other children who came into contact with them. They were just as impaired in their capacities to understand the feelings of others, particularly how they affected those closest to them. They were immature, disorganized, and strange. Although only Zack became frankly psychotic, all made odd comments about ordinary events for a very long time. Their preoccupations with the contents of their own imaginations—with their elaborate fantasies, daydreams, toy figures, and imagined relationships—were virtually delusional. Also they were sometimes tormented by fears, doubts, and suspicions, by paranoid concerns that others (including sometimes those closest to them, such as a sibling) were set on humiliating, damaging, or in some other way harming them.

A salient characteristic of their mode of thinking, as well as acting, was predictable inconsistency. Over the course of minutes or hours, they could suddenly switch from being mentally clear and even clever to being far off in a foggy world of misperceptions and misunderstanding. For all three young men, psychological testing revealed normal or even above-average intellectual ability. Yet this endowment could not be channeled effectively because of the disruptions that emerged on psychological testing: highly idiosyncratic reasoning, poor reality testing, and an abundance of aggressive and destructive themes which reflected their internal representations of themselves and others. Their inner worlds were densely populated with frightening and incomprehensible spirits which were then projected outwardly on others, especially when they were anxious (Ekstein & Wallerstein, 1954; Geleerd, 1958). Sometimes they could strike out verbally and, when younger, physically; the target of their aggression was most often their parents or siblings, but sometimes also other children whom they felt were tormenting them.

The Ezras and Jeremiahs have profound disturbances in finding regularities in their inner world—in the relations among desires, intentions, and emotional responses—and in the behavior of others. For them, the process of developing a coherent sense of self is disrupted and piecemeal, and the self that is created disintegrates under stress, with separation, and when they experience bewildering anxiety. They are perplexed by ordinary events because they cannot really understand what they are feeling or how their actions (e.g., their silliness, their funny comments, their oppositional activities) make their parents feel. Reality and fantasy, their selves and others, thinking and doing become indistinct.

For children like Jeremiah who are also burdened by disorders such as Tourette's syndrome, the task of developing and maintaining a stable sense of self is particularly difficult. Their capacities are taxed not only by problems in organizing experience, but by the intrusion of the impulses to emit acts (tics) and compelling obsessive thoughts that originate from within but seem alien and uncontrollable (Cohen, Bruun, & Leckman, 1988; Cohen, 1991b). The study of children with Tourette's syndrome and similar conditions may provide a special opportunity for exploring aspects of the emergence of self and the various influences that the self, once formed, requires for the sense of continuity and coherence (Cohen, 1991a).

Jeremiah's situation of having both multiplex developmental disorder and a tic disorder also exemplifies that for many children with early onset disorders there is more than a "single" condition, however this may be defined. "Co-morbidity" is quite common. The entire diagnostic rubric of MDD may, from one perspective, be construed as paradigm of co-morbidity, a combination of several conditions, rather than a disorder in its own right. The range of diagnoses that can be affixed to a child who is anxious, aloof, and socially impaired, as indicated previously, is diverse. Without overstepping the boundaries of the current discussion, we only note in passing that there are many ways in which a child might be led to have more than one diagnosable condition. For example: (a) two or more disorders may represent varying manifestations of the same underlying diathesis, (b) one disorder may cause another, or (c) the two disorders may be associated simply by chance. It is an unusual child, however, who is admitted to a child psychiatry service with only one diagnosable condition; multiple sources of morbidity and co-morbidity are the rule, not exceptions. Whatever the precise nature of the relationships between conditions such as Tourette's syndrome, language disorders, and attention deficit hyperactivity disorder, on one hand, and multiplex developmental disorder, on the other, in the experience of the child, the various conditions merge together and reinforce each other in determining clinical impairment and in shaping the child's sense of himself.

Disorders that arise during the very first year or two of life, especially those involving the emergence of basic competencies, are likely to have a broad range of effects on multiple aspects of development, with multisurface manifestations. Unlike disorders of adolescence or adulthood, which may involve discrete areas of behavior, disorders of early childhood often are more global and involve many lines of development as well as psychophysiological symptoms. Conditions such as Jeremiah's, with a broad spectrum of disturbances during the very first years of life that affect the unfolding of major domains of development—social, emotional, cognitive—thus may be reminiscent of the paradigmatic pervasive developmental disorder, autism, with which they share some surface family resemblances (Volkmar, Cohen, Hoshino, Rende, & Paul, 1988).

Yet, these three individuals were not autistic. In contrast to even high functioning autistic adults, these men were attached to their families and sensitive to the way they were treated by them. They engaged in reciprocal social relations, although these relations were skewed by their profound difficulties in forming trusting and secure relations and by their egocentricity, anxieties, and rages. Their receptive and expressive language was not only normal, but an area of charming giftedness for Ezra and Jeremiah, and their imagination was rich, textured, and a compelling source of both dread and pleasure. Thus, however impaired in the emergence of developmental competencies, these three did not display the cardinal features of autism—impoverished or absent reciprocity, poor communication and use of language, and markedly restricted imagination.

The concept of development disorders captures the core feature that fundamental, underlying processes of development were distorted for Ezra and his peers. The immediate and far-reaching developmental nature of their difficulties is highlighted by placing them on a spectrum of developmental disorders. In this spectrum, children with the multiple and complex difficulties we have been describing would occupy a region midway between the specific developmental disorders that affect a single developmental line (such as the disorders of language, reading, and motor coordination) and those that leave virtually no area untouched (such as autism). The term *multiplex developmental disorder* underscores the multiple interactions among a range of developmental lines.

Within the DSM-III-R (APA, 1987), the most suitable placement for this category would be within the large domain covered by Pervasive Developmental Disorders (PDD). This domain is now occupied by only one disorder with specific criteria, autism. The vast and uncharted remaining domain is denoted as "PDD-Not Otherwise Specified," a phrase reminiscent of the insignia in the margins of an ancient map that indicates territories that remain to be explored. Multiplex developmental disorder is a "candidate" continent within PDD. Children with the types of conditions presented by Ezra and Zack are not new arrivals in the clinical world. They have been recognized for many decades, under various rubrics, such as borderline (Pine, 1982), atypical personality development (Rank, 1955), and childhood schizophrenia (Fish, Shapiro, Campbell, & Wile, 1968). What we now offer is explication of core diagnostic features and a challenge for more systematic, basic, and longitudinal research than these conditions have so far received.

Based on our studies at the Child Study Center of young, mildly atypical children and clinical evaluations of school-age children with this constellation of findings, including children and young adolescents evaluated during inpatient hospitalization, we believe that a systematic approach to diagnosis can be offered as the basis for future investigations of the reliability and validity of the concept of multiplex development disorder (Cohen, Paul, & Volkmar, 1987; Dahl et al., 1986). The criteria (see Table I) fall within three broad areas: affect and anxiety regulation, imparied social behavior, and disturbances in thinking. These criteria are similar to descriptions of children with atypical development and disorders of ego development described over the past decades (e.g., Weil, 1953). At this stage of research, it is not possible to specify the number of symptoms from each category that should be satisfied for the formal assignment of the diagnosis. Rather, the diagnostic criteria serve as descriptions of the characteristic findings described earlier.

PHENOMENOLOGY

From a phenomenological perspective, it would be useful if we could provide a more specific, theoretic account for the basis of the disturbances in children with MDD. What could explain their early onset, persistent, and severe disturbances? What are the relations among the various domains—interpersonal, affective, and cognitive—of their difficulties? Unfortunately, we are far from a theory of pathogenesis based on known deviations in neurobiological processes. The early emergence of difficulties in the regulation of state—irritability, inconsolability, social lack of engagement, colic, sleep problems, lack of pleasure in small acts of caregiving, and the like—suggest that some children with MDD suffer from problems as early as the very first months of life. Our sense is that these neuroregulatory difficulties continue as an important, underlying foundation of the dysfunction and are reflected

Table I Diagnostic Criteria: For Multiplex Developmental Disorder in Three Major Domains of Functioning

I. Regulation of affective state and anxiety is imparied beyond that seen in children of comparable age, as exemplified by several of the following:
   (a) Intense generalized anxiety or tension
   (b) Fears and phobias (often unusual or peculiar)
   (c) Recurrent panic episodes or flooding with anxiety
   (d) Episodes of behavioral disorganization punctuated by markedly immature, primitive, or violent behaviors
   (e) Significant and wide emotional variability with or without environmental precipitants
   (f) Frequent idiosyncratic or bizarre anxiety reactions

II. Consistently impaired social behavior/sensitivity, as exemplified by the following types of disturbances:
   (a) Social disinterest, detachment, avoidance, or withdrawal despite evident competence
   (b) Severely impaired peer relationships
   (c) Markedly disturbed attachments; high degrees of ambivalence to adults (especially parents/caregivers)
   (d) Profound limitations in the capacity for empathy or understanding others affects accurately

III. Impaired cognitive processing (thinking disorder), as exemplified by some of the following difficulties:
   (a) Irrationality, sudden intrusions on normal thought process, magical thinking, neologisms or repetition of nonsense words, desultory thinking, blatantly illogical, and bizarre ideas
   (b) Confusion between reality and inner fantasy life
   (c) Perplexity and easy confusability (trouble understanding social processes or keeping thoughts "straight")
   (d) Delusions, overvalued ideas including fantasies of omnipotence, paranoid preoccupations, overengagement with fantasy figures, grandiose fantasies of special powers, and referential ideation

IV. The syndrome appears during the first several years of life.

V. The child is not suffering from autism or schizophrenia.

later, most clearly, in the broad range of anxiety difficulties (general anxiety, phobias, social avoidance, panic). For normal children, anxiety can be muted by the presence and care of others (Kinnert, Campos, Sorce, Emde, & Svejda, 1983), who become internalized as aspects of the self in its soothing and self-care capacities (Winnicott, 1945, 1951; Loewald, 1977). For children with multiplex developmental disorder, this process does not work adequately (or cannot be activated),and they often require but cannot fully metabolize the reassurance and presence of parents, who may, indeed, also elicit disappointment and become the triggers for rage (Mahler & Furer, 1968).

Indeed, it is typical of children with MDD that their internal portraits of parents are ambivalent. One parent is hated and the other loved; or a parent is clung to and fondled and then, a few moments later, is despised, hit, pinched, or abused. This splitting between good and bad attributions, between idealization and denigration, leaves the child rapidly shifting, for reasons he cannot articulate, between one pole and the other. There are close mutually reciprocal relationships between anxiety and painful affects, on one side, and the construction of ambivalent and unstable representations of others on the other side. The permeating sense of discomfort and tension which cannot be placed by caregivers leads the child to feel that the parent and others are uncaring and inadequate; in turn, the absence of a secure, internalized representation of the caregiver as a caring person makes it quite difficult for the child to create, within himself, a barrier against the intrusion of irrational worries and tensions. This internal structure of self-comfort requires the template of *a constant, caring figure who is fully present and actively provides comfort* (Winnicott, 1945).

These two processes—the regulation of anxiety and the creation of a stable inner and outer world of social relations—are also intimately related to the cognitive difficulties of children with MDD. In some ways, the emergence of rational thought and the ability to use language to express thoughts—the understanding of cause–effect relations, using empirical facts to correct fantasies, discerning the difference between wish and reality, engaging in step-by-step planning, and the like—also take root in the social matrix. Thus, there are dense interconnections among these various processes: (a) rational thinking is shaped by and mapped upon the predictability and orderliness of expereince, and (b) the concepts and language that allow the child to appreciate and represent this sense of orderliness are shaped by the dialogue between parent and child.

Without inborn capacities, how could the child begin the process of metabolizing what the world has to offer in order to synthesize the higher, cognitive and emotional competencies during the course of development? What cognitive capacities and categories are needed from the very start in order for the child to organize experience and make sense of the world, including the social world? Epistemologists since the ancient Greeks have been driven to postulate specific inborn conceptual schemes that allow humans to take the first steps in the process of making sense of their experiences. These inborn capacities serve as fundamental philosophical assumptions, as exemplified by the Platonic Forms and Kant's *a priori synthetic* categories of space and time. Within philosophical schemes, these capacities and concepts function as the "givens" of the system; they are the axioms that allow the child to find sense in his or her first contacts with the world and which start off the developmental program of learning from experience. These inborn capacities originate before experience, yet pertain to the empirical world. They serve as the building blocks for future understanding. In a similar vein, Hobson (1991) postulates the need for "innately determined perceptual-affective sensibilities towards the bodily appearances and behavior of others" and we are led (Mayes, Cohen, & Klin, 1993) to postulate the instinctual, neurobiological underpinnings of early social engagement (Loewald, 1977).

However we conceptualize the relations between the child's actual experiences (including his own actions and the responses they elicit) and the growth of rational thought, the thought processes of the child with MDD are out of harmony with those around him or her; even those closest to the children find their thoughts, comments, and ideas odd, strange, and tortuous. The troubles with affect and social mutuality of children with MDD may impair the ability to learn basic concepts and to think normally (Tager-Flusberg, in press; Tager-Flusberg et al., 1990). The thought difficulties of these children may express themselves early in life first in relation to anxiety and affect and, later, in relation to the sharing of interests and the unfolding of social relations (Sigman, Mundy, Sherman, & Ungerer, 1986; Sigman, Ungerer, Mundy, & Sherman, 1987).

Affective, perceptual, cognitive, and linguistic problems have been proposed, at various times, as candidates for the area of core dysfunction for autism as well as other disorders of social relatedness such as MDD (Cohen & Donnellan, 1987). In trying to clarify the basis for the social dysfunction of the early pervasive developmental disorders, a new area of investigation has extended concepts from research on the development of the normal child's theory of mind (Astington, Harris, & Olson, 1988; Wellman, 1990). Empirical studies on the origins of a child's theory of mind are also related to philosophical investigations of questions about how we know that other people have minds, that their minds work like ours, that they experience things as we do (e.g., that everyone sees the same thing when they view an object, that they mean the same thing when they refer to its colors or qualities, that their intentions are related to their behaviors as ours are, etc.; e.g., Wisdom, 1956; Wittgenstein, 1958). A wide body of findings, using various methodologies, has shown that between ages 3 and 4 years, normal children demonstrate a change in how they understand others' behavior. At this time, they become increasingly aware of and able to describe the beliefs and feelings that guide others' behaviors, that is, that others have minds. They use the language of mental states—beliefs and desires—to explain why adults act in a particular way and they become adept at using this theory in an effort to predict and to change adults' behaviors. For example, children learn how they can manipulate the behavior of others through deception.

Of course, the young child's theory of mind does not burst forth fully developed at age 3. Prior to 3, a child already has ideas about knowing what it is to want an ice cream cone. This desire can guide the child's actions, and he can understand what another child might wish for and do if he saw him eating his cone. The child can discern the difference between a real cone and a pretend cone. All these are based on early concepts and skills. These cognitive competencies help him or her separate appearances from reality, the intention to act from the act itself, the difference between believing and knowing, or perceiving and believing, and the like. The child's ability to think about mental states—believing, imagining, pretending, hoping for, desiring, anxiously awaiting, thinking—comes about through his or her interactions with others who respond reasonably and predictably, his or her feelings toward them, the emergence of related capacities (especially language), basic cognitive endowment, and the underlying neurobiological substrate that makes symbolic thinking, self-reflection, and representation of the material and mental world possible (Hobson, 1991; Astington et al., 1988).

The psychological preconditions for a theory of mind begin to emerge during the first year of life—for example, with attentiveness and concern about the feelings of others—and are crystallized as the child develops an increasingly firm and textured sense of his own wishes and feelings and the emotions and actions of those around him whose affection and care are critical to his own existence. Hand in hand with the child's intuitive under-standing of others as having an inner life that can be described in mental terms, the child develops a sense of himself, as an individual with an inner life that can be understood in similar mental terms (Mayes, Cohen, & Klin, 1993). That is, the child recognizes and represents continuities and regulari-ties in his experience and the relationships between his wishes, his inten-tions, his actions, and his emotions: he registers at some level of awareness that he *wants* his mother's attention, *decides to act* on this desire rather than on a competing or alternate wish, he *approaches* her with the *intention* of showing her something of which he is *proud,* and *he feels warmly cared for* when she takes him up on her lap. He knows he will make her unhappy if he interrupts her while she is talking on the telephone and please her if he brings her a picture he has drawn; he knows that he will feel disappointed if she says no when he asks her to go outside to play and feel angry if she takes away (as she always does) the silver bell he has taken down from the shelf.

These regularities between desires, intentions, and emotions allow the child to develop a sense of coherence within himself. The acquisition of a "theory of mind" is also the construction of the self and representations of others; these representations of others (the caring mother, the angry mother, the forceful father, the competitive and domineering sibling) also, in various ways, become constitutive in the self. Self and other representations are not sharply demarcated, especially in early childhood and in special states of closeness when the boundaries between self and other become more permeable (e.g., when aroused, loving, anxiously regressed, furiously angry, or after states of psychic trauma).

It is exactly capacities such as these—the gradual formation of a stable and integrated sense of the other as someone with feelings, beliefs, inten-tions—that are apparently distorted in children with MDD. An important link between studies of normal development and developmental psychopathol-ogy has been the application of the concepts relating the child's theory of mind to the study of autism (Baron-Cohen, Tager-Flusberg, & Cohen, in press). A large body of empirical findings has demonstrated that autistic children have profound disturbances in precisely the area of commonsense psychology that requires a theory that beliefs and desires guide the behavior of others (Baron-Cohen, Leslie, & Frith, 1985; Baron-Cohen, 1989, 1991). They perform much worse than predicted by their general intellectual abilities on tests that require an understanding that another person can be misled—that he can believe something falsely—and that a person will behave in a predictable fashion as a consequence of this false belief. Indeed, careful study shows that for many autistic children, even those with the necessary equipment, there are remarkable problems in the domain of using and understanding mental concepts in relation to others. Although it is clear that many, if not most, autistic individuals exhibit such deficits, it is quite possible that these difficulties reflect more fundamental problems in social development, many of which are apparent developmentally well before theory of mind capacities develop (Klin, Volkmar, & Sparrow, in press). In this context, the accounts of their inner experiences provided by higher-functioning adults with autism provide illuminating insights into the close relations between emotional, cognitive, and social development (Bemporad, 1979; Volkmar & Cohen, 1985).

It may be that the mapping of developmental psychopathological conditions through study of children's theories of mental functioning could be even more relevant and useful for those conditions that are less pervasive than autism and where language and intelligence are generally well preserved. The concepts that seem so easily acquired by normal 3- and 4-year-olds as they explore how their minds and the minds of others operate are just those domains that are so perplexing for children with multiplex developmental disorders. Indeed, problems in developing a theory of their own and others' beliefs and intentions may be reflected in these children's frequent trouble in organizing their accounts of experiences and using abstract categories of sequence, causality, and hierarchy.

They find it difficult to fully narrate a complicated story (Loveland & Tunali, in press) or to provide the salient information that is most needed or interesting to others. They may focus on small and tangential information and miss the whole. When the family is worrying about a major crisis, they may perseverate on whether they will get to the movies; they will regard father's distress when arranging for the tow truck as a mere nuisance. They cannot get their own or others' priorities straight. Their social incongruence is not simply because they are self-centered but because they have no "center." They operate without the benefit of fully shared, internalized values, concerns, and emotional responses. Whether these problems in theory of mind can be understood as reflecting earlier and more basic difficulties (Hobson, Ouston, & Lee, 1988; Hobson, 1990a, 1990b, 1991; Mayes, Cohen, & Klin, 1993) and the degree to which the disturbances in theory of mind lead to many of the major, presistent core problems found in MDD define a necessary area of research. Studies such as these also address the theme that defines the present volume—how early disturbances in those functions essential to socialization shape the child's place in the social world and continue to influence how he or she responds to others and vice versa.

One of the major advantages of studying children such as Ezra, Jeremiah, and Zack is the challenge of splitting cognitive, affective, and social development into separate domains which then need to be reassembled into a whole person (Caparulo & Cohen, 1983). Although these subdivisions of development are useful for organizing chapters in textbooks and college curricula, they also artifically cleave fundamental processes that subserve humanization for becoming an individual in society. These distortions may be less apparent in relation to children whose development proceeds smoothly and harmoniously, where the multiple lines of development are integrated, and the sense of self is secure. For children with multiplex disorder, however, basic assumptions about the underlying processes in development may be questioned in light of the experiments of nature which these children present. The study of the stability and change in developmental disorders over time underscores fundamental questions about developmental continuities and discontinuities, and provides opportunities for the clincal investigator to contribute to knowledge about the origins and maintenance of basic modes of human functioning, including the unfolding and elaboration of the self and its continuities and discontinuities over the life span.

ACKNOWLEDGMENTS

We are very appreciative of the many years of collaboration with Sally Provence, Kirsten Dahl, and James F. Leckman, and our colleagues in Benhaven and Riverview Hospital, especially Elisabeth Dykens and Geri Pearson, and also appreciate our valuable discussions with Simon Baron-Cohen, Helen Tager-Flusberg, and Ami Klin about theory of mind. This research was supported in part by grants from the National Institute of Mental Health, the National Institutes of Health, and Mr. Leonard Berger.

REFERENCES

Astington, J., Harris, P., & Olson, D. (1988). Developing theories of mind. Cambridge: Cambridge University Press.

Baron-Cohen, S., Leslie, A. M., & Frith, U. (1985). Does the autistic child have a "theory of mind"? Cognition, 21, 37–46.

Baron-Cohen, S. (1989). The autistic child's theory of mind: A case of specific developmental delay. Journal of Child Psychology and Psychiatry, 30, 285–298.

Baron-Cohen, S. (1991). Do people with autism understand what causes emotion? Child Development, 62, 385–395.

Baron-Cohen, S., Tager-Flusberg, H., & Cohen, D. J. (Eds.). (In press). Understanding other minds: Perspectives from autism. Oxford: Oxford University Press.

Bemporad, J. R. (1979). Adult recollections of a formerly autistic child. *Journal of Autism and Developmental Disorders, 9,* 179–197.

Caparulo, B. K., & Cohen, D. J. (1983). Developmental language studies in the neuropsychiatric disorders of childhood. In K. E. Nelson (Ed.), *Children's Language,* (pp. 423–463). New York: Gardiner Press.

Cohen, D. J. (1991a). Finding meaning in one's self and others: Clinical studies of children with autism and Tourette syndrome. In F. Kessel, M. Bornstein, & A. Sameroff (Eds.), *Contemporary constructions of the child: Essays in honor of William Kessen* (pp. 159–175). Hillsdale, NJ: Lawrence Erlbaum.

Cohen, D. J. (1991b). Tourette's syndrome: A model disorder for integrating psychoanalytic and biological perspectives. *International Review of Psycho-Analysis, 18,* 195–209.

Cohen, D. J., Bruun, R. D., & Leckman, J. F. (Eds.). (1988). *Tourette's syndrome: Clinical understanding and treatment.* New York: Wiley.

Cohen, D. J., & Donnellan, A. (Eds.). (1987). *Handbook of autism and pervasive developmental disorders.* New York: Wiley.

Cohen, D. J., Paul, R., & Volkmar, F. R. (1986). Issues in the classification of pervasive developmental disorders. *Journal of the American Academy of Child Psychiatry, 25*(2), 213–220.

Cohen, D. J., Paul, R., & Volkmar, F. R. (1987). Issues in the classification of pervasive developmental disorders. In D. Cohen, & A. Donnellan (Eds.), *Handbook of autism and pervasive developmental disorders* (pp. 20–40). New York: Wiley.

Cohen, D. J., Paul, R., & Volkmar, F. R. (1988). The diagnosis and classification of autism: Empirical studies relevant to nosology. In J. Mezzich & M. von Cranach (Eds.), *International classification of psychiatry* (pp. 99–114). Cambridge: Cambridge University Press.

Dahl, E. K., Cohen, D. J., & Provence, S. (1986). Clinical and multivariate approaches to nosology of pervasive developmental disorders. *Journal of the American Academy of Child Psychiatry, 25,* 170–180.

Ekstein, R., & Wallerstein, J. (1954). Observations on the psychology of borderline and psychotic children. *Psychoanalytic Study of the Child, 9,* 344–369.

Fish, B., Shapiro, T., Campbell, M., Wile, R. (1968). A classification of schizophrenic children under five years. *American Journal of Psychiatry, 124,* 1415–1423.

Geleerd, E. (1958). Borderline states in childhood and adolescence. *Psychoanalytic Study of the Child, 13,* 279–295.

Hobson, R. P. (1990a). On the origins of self and the case of autism. *Development and Psychopathology, 2,* 199–213.

Hobson, R. P. (1990b). On psychoanalytic approaches to autism. *American Journal of Orthopsychiatry, 60,* 324–336.

Hobson, R. P. (1991). Against the "Theory of Mind." *British Journal of Developmental Psychology, 9,* 33–51.

Hobson, R. P., Ouston, J., & Lee, A. (1988). Emotion recognition in autism: Coordinating faces and voices. *Psychological Medicine, 18,* 911–923.

Kanner, L. (1943). Autistic disturbances of affective contact. *Nervous Child, 2,* 217–250.

Kinnert, M., Campos, J., Sorce, J., Emde, R., & Svejda, M. (1983). Emotions as behavior regulators: Social referencing in infancy. In R. Plutchik & H. Kellerman (Eds.), *Emotions in early development: The emotions* (Vol. 2, pp. 57–86). New York: Academic Press.

Klin, A., Volkmar, F. R., & Sparrow, S. (In press). Some limitations of the theory of mind hypothesis in autism. *Journal of Child Psychology and Psychiatry.*

Loewald, H. (1977). Instinct theory, object relations, and psychic structure formation. In H. Loewald: *Papers on psychoanalysis* (pp. 207–218). New Haven: Yale University Press.

Loveland, K., & Tunali, B. (In press). Understanding other persons: Narrative language in autism. In S. Baron-Cohen, H. Tager-Flusberg, & D. Cohen (Eds.), *Understanding other minds: Perspective from autism.* Oxford: Oxford University Press.

Mahler, M., & Furer, M. (1968). *On human symbiosis and the vicissitudes of individuation.* New York: International Universities Press.

Mayes, L., Cohen, D. J., & Klin, A. (1993). Experiencing self and others: A psychoanalytic perspective on theory of mind and autism. In S. Baron-Cohen, H. Tager-Flusberg, & D. Cohen (Eds.), *Understanding other minds: Perspectives from autism* (pp. 450–465). Oxford: Oxford University Press.

Petti, T., & Vela, R. (1990). Borderline disorders of childhood: An overview. *Journal of the American Academy of Child and Adolescent Psychiatry, 29,* 327–337.

Pine, F. (1982). A working nosology of borderline syndromes in children. In E. Robson (Ed.), *The borderline child* (pp. 83–100). New York: McGraw-Hill.

Provence, S., & Dahl, E. K. (1987). Disorders of atypical development: Diagnostic issues raised by a spectrum disorder. In D. J. Cohen, & A. Donnellan (Eds.), *Handbook of autism and pervasive developmental disorders* (pp. 677–689). New York: Wiley.

Putnam, M. G., Rank, B., Pavenstedt, E., Anderson, I. N., & Rawson, I. (1948). Round table 1947: Case study of an atypical two-and-a-half year old. *American Journal of Orthopsychiatry, 18,* 1–30.

Rank, B., & MacNaughton, D. (1950). A clinical contribution to early ego development. *Psychoanalytic Study of the Child, 5,* 53–65.

Rank, B. (1955). Intensive study and treatment of preschool children who show marked personality deviations of "atypical development" and their parents. In G. Caplan (Ed.), *Emotional problems of early childhood* (pp. 491–501). New York: Basic Books.

Rescorla, L. (1986). Preschool psychiatric disorders. *Journal of the American Academy of Child Psychiatry, 25,* 162–169.

Ritvo, S., & Provence, S. (1953). Form perception and imitation in some autistic children: Diagnostic findings and their contextual interpretations. *Psychoanalytic Study of the Child, 8,* 155–161.

Robson, K. (Ed.). (1982). *The borderline child.* New York: McGraw Hill.

Sigman, M., Mundy, P., Sherman, T., & Ungerer, J. A. (1986). Social interactions of autistic, mentally retarded and normal children with their caregivers. *Journal of Child Psychology and Psychiatry, 27,* 647–656.

Sigman, M., Ungerer, J. A., Mundy, P., & Sherman, T. (1987). Cognition in autistic children. In D. J. Cohen & A. Donnellan (Eds.), *Handbook of autism and pervasive developmental disorders* (pp. 103–120). New York: Wiley.

Sparrow, S., Rescorla, L., Provence, S., Condon, S. O., Goudreau, D., & Cicchetti, D. W. (1986). Follow-up of "atypical" children. *Journal of the American Academy of Child Psychiatry, 25,* 181–185.

Szatmari, P., Tuff, L., Finlayson, M. A., & Bartolucci, G. (1989). Asperger's syndrome and autism: Neurocognitive aspects. *Journal of the American Academy of Child and Adolescent Psychiatry, 29,* 130–136.

Tager-Flusberg, H. (In press). What language reveals about the understanding of minds in children with autism. In S. Baron-Cohen, H. Tager-Flusberg, & D. Cohen (Eds.), *Understanding other minds: Perspectives from autism.* Oxford: Oxford University Press.

Tager-Flusberg, H., Calkins, S., Nolin, T., Baumberger, T., Anderson, M., & Chadwick-Dias, A. (1990). A longitudinal study of language acquisition in autistic and Down syndrome children. *Journal of Autism and Developmental Disorders, 20,* 1–21.

Volkmar, F. R., Bregman, J., Cohen, D. J., & Cicchetti, D. V. (1988). DSM III and DSM III-R: Diagnoses of Autism. *American Journal of Psychiatry, 145*(11), 1404–1408.

Volkmar, F. R., & Cohen, D. J. (1985). The experience of infantile autism: A first person account by Tony W. *Journal of Autism and Developmental Disorders, 15*(1), 47–54.

Volkmar, F., & Cohen, D. J. (1988). Classification and diagnosis of childhood autism. In E. Schopler & G. Mesibov (Eds.), *Diagnosis and Assessment in Autism* (pp. 71–89). New York: Plenum Press.

Volkmar, F. R., Cohen, D. J., Hoshino, Y., Rende, R. D., & Paul, R. (1988). Phenomenology and classification of the childhood psychoses. *Psychological Medicine, 18,* 191–201.

Volkmar, F. R., Sparrow, S. A., Goudreau, D., Cicchetti, D. V., Paul, R., & Cohen, D. J. (1987).

Social deficits in autism: An operational approach using the Vineland Adaptive Behavior Scales. *Journal of the American Academy of Child and Adolescent Psychiatry, 26*(20), 156–161.

Weil, A. (1953). Certain severe disturbances of ego development in children. *Psychoanalytic Study of the Child, 8,* 271–287.

Wellman, H. (1990). *The child's theory of mind.* Cambridge, MA: M.I.T. Press.

Wing, L. (1981). Asperger's syndrome: A clinical account. *Psychological Medicine, 11,* 115–129.

Winnicott, D. (1945/1975). Primitive emotional development. In D. Winnicott, *Through Paediatrics to Psycho-analysis* (pp. 145–156). New York: Basic Books. (Original published in 1945)

Winnicott, D. (1951/1975). Transitional objects and transitional phenomena. In D. Winnicott, *Through paediatrics to psycho-analysis* (pp. 229–242). New York: Basic Books. (Original published in 1951).

Wisdom, J. (1956). *Other minds.* Oxford: Basil Blackwell.

Wittgenstein, L. (1958). *Philosophical investigations.* Oxford: Basil Blackwell.

Wolff, S., & Chick, J. (1980). Schizoid personality in childhood: A controlled follow-up study. *Psychological Medicine, 10,* 85–100.

SOURCES
OF
DATA:
PERSONS
AND
INSTRUMENTS

Assessing Child Psychopathology in Developmental Follow-up Studies

Craig Edelbrock

INTRODUCTION

Follow-up studies, whether focused on the development of normal children or children at risk, face complex measurement issues. Nowhere are these issues more vexing than the assessment of child psychopathology. There is a lack of consensus among mental health professionals regarding the nature of child psychopathology. Not surprisingly, there are diverse opinions regarding the best procedures for detecting, describing, and classifying psychopathology in children and adolescents. Many different assessment approaches and procedures are available, but they are not equally well suited to longitudinal studies. There are also unsolved measurement problems and issues in this area that cut across all assessment instruments and procedures.

The goal of this chapter is to review procedures for assessing child psychopathology, with special reference to their use in developmental follow-up studies. The strengths and weaknesses of different procedures will be compared. Some factors to consider in selecting measures for use in follow-up studies will be discussed. Finally, some problems and issues in measuring child psychopathology will be discussed. Attention will be given to problems of measurement equivalence in longitudinal studies of psychopathology. Two very pressing measurement problems will be discussed in detail: (a) the lack of agreement among different informants, and (b) variations in the availability and relevance of different informants at different ages.

REVIEW OF MEASUREMENT PROCEDURES

There are several procedures for assessing child psychopathology. Four procedures that are amenable for use in developmental follow-up studies are brief screening questionnaires, checklists and rating scales, observational coding systems, and structured interviews.

Screening Instruments

Several brief questionnaires have been developed for screening large samples of children for psychopathology. These measures, which usually rely on information from parents, yield a single index of global functioning that can be used to identify children as normal or disturbed. Several brief screening instruments have been developed, most of which are for preschool-aged children. One example is the 12-item Behavioral Screening Questionnaire (BSQ; Richman, 1977). The reliability and validity of the BSQ and other screening devices have been well established (see Earls et al., 1982).

Screening instruments focus on fairly common problems that indicate general disturbances. The ideal item for a screening questionnaire would be very common among disturbed children, but rare among normal children. Rare problems (e.g., visual and auditory hallucinations, sexual disturbances, self-destructive behaviors) would not be considered. There is no question that such items are valid indicators of psychopathology, but they are too rare to be useful on a screening instrument.

Checklists and Rating Scales

Checklists and rating scales are longer and more comprehensive than brief screening questionnaires. The respondent, usually a parent or teacher, simply checks those items that apply to the target child, or rates each item on a simple scale. Many behavioral checklists and ratings scales have been developed (see Barkley, 1988, for a review). Measures such as the Behavior Problem Checklist (Quay, 1983) have been designed to be completed by any informant (e.g., parent, teacher, mental health worker). Other instruments, such as the Child Behavior Checklist (Achenbach, 1991) and Conners'

Ratings Scales (Goyette, Conners, & Ulrich, 1978), have separate versions for different informants.

Rather than trying to tap predetermined diagnostic criteria, checklists and ratings scales tap a very broad range of behaviors that have a high *content validity*. In other words, the items just look like they are reasonable indicators of maladjustment. Items are aggregated into scales using multivariate statistical procedures such as factor analysis. Despite differences in items, rating procedures, samples, and statistical analyses, there has been considerable convergence across factor analytic studies in identifying several syndromes of child psychopathology (see Edelbrock, 1987, for a review).

Checklists and rating scales have the advantage of producing *quantitative scores,* not just a present/absent distinction like screening and diagnostic procedures. Quantitative scores facilitate direct comparisons between individuals or groups, for instance, and can be used to determine changes in behavior over time and in response to interventions. Checklists and rating scales also yield scores on many dimensions, not just one. Scores can be portrayed on a multidimensional profile that provides a more comprehensive picture of the child's functioning in many areas at once. In addition, many checklists and ratings scales have been standardized on large, representative samples of children. Norms provide a means for interpreting how deviant a score is relative to "normal" children.

Observations

Direct observation represents another approach to assessing child maladjustment. Trained raters can observe the child and record behaviors according to a coding system. This can provide more objective and precise information regarding the frequency, duration, and severity of specific behavior problems. Observations can also be used to identify the antecedents and consequences of specific behaviors.

Many different types of observational coding systems have been developed (see Reid, Baldwin, Patterson, & Dishion, 1988). Some coding systems, such as the Direct Observation Form of the Child Behavior Checklist (Achenbach, 1991) are designed for use in *naturalistic settings,* such as home or school. Others, such as the Restricted Academic Situation (Barkley, 1990) are designed for *analogue settings* such as a clinic observation room. In addition, more complicated coding systems have been developed for assessing the *interactions* among two or more people. The Parent–Adolescent Interaction Coding System (PAICS; Robin, 1988), for example, is an analogue measure focused on how adolescents interact with their parents, particularly in problem-solving situations.

Observational assessment procedures are limited to phenomena that are readily observable such as physical aggression or hyperactivity. They are not well suited to assessing internal feelings such as depression and anxiety.

The phenomena to be assessed must also be relatively frequent. Most observational assessments cover less than 1 hr of total observation time, so behaviors that occur rarely, say once a day or less, are likely to be missed.

Interviews

The most common way of gaining information about children's health, development, and behavior is to interview parents. Unfortunately, most interviews are too haphazard to provide reliable information. Different interviewers ask questions in different ways and they vary in how they interpret and record the interviewee's responses. To standardize the interviewing process and boost reliability, structured interview schedules have been developed.

Several structured interviews have been developed for assessing psychopathology in children and adolescents. Most of these were designed to assess diagnostic criteria for child psychiatric diagnoses (see Edelbrock & Costello, 1988, for a review). Some interviews are highly structured and specify the exact order and wording of questions as well as the way responses are recorded. The interviewer has almost no discretion in conducting the interview. The Diagnostic Interview Schedule for Children (DISC) is an example of a highly structured diagnostic interview. The DISC has parallel versions for interviewing either parents or children ages 8–18 (see Edelbrock & Costello, 1988). The DISC is an operationalization of the diagnostic criteria for child psychiatric diagnoses in the revised third edition of the *Diagnostic and Statistical Manual* of the American Psychiatric Association (APA, 1987). The DISC covers diagnoses that are applied to children and adolescents, including Attention Deficit-Hyperactivity Disorder, Conduct Disorder, Anxiety Disorder, Separation Anxiety, and Simple Phobia.

Some interviews are less rigidly structured and allow more flexibility. Some list areas to be covered, for example, but leave the exact wording of questions up to the interviewer. The Child Assessment Schedule (CAS; Hodges, Kline, Stern, Cytryn, & McKnew, 1982) is one example of a semistructured interview. The CAS includes 75 items about school, friends, family, self-image, behavior, and mood. It is organized thematically beginning with questions about family and friends, but interviewers can alter the order of questions if they wish. The CAS can be scored according to diagnoses, content areas (e.g., school, friends, activities), or symptom areas (hyperactivity, conduct disorder, anxiety).

Strengths and Weaknesses

Any of these four assessment procedures can be used to assess psychopathology in developmental follow-up studies. However, they have different strengths and weaknesses.

Screening instruments are inexpensive and require little professional time or resources. They can therefore be used in follow-up studies of relatively large samples of subjects. Of course, screening instruments provide little information, usually a single index of global maladjustment. This is not very useful if the focus of the study is on psychopathology, but if the focus is in another area, say cognitive development, a brief screening instrument can be added at little cost and provide some information about behavioral functioning.

Checklists and rating scales cover much more than screening instruments and are still fairly economical. They cover a wide range of social, emotional, and behavioral problems and yield quantitative scores on several dimensions at once. The availability of norms greatly extends the meaning and utility of the information obtained. They also provide a means for comparing reports by different informants and identifying areas of agreement and disagreement about the child's functioning. For these reasons, checklists and rating scales are often employed in studies where the primary focus is psychopathology.

Checklists and rating scales depend on the informants' aggregate impressions of the child's functioning over a period of time. The chronicity of problems—when problems started and stopped, the order in which they occurred, the number of distinct episodes, and which problem occurred at the same time—is obscured. This is a problem if assessments are repeated infrequently (e.g., once a year or less). It is possible that checklists and rating scales will miss episodes of psychopathology during the follow-up interval. Alternatively, if they detect some psychopathology, they will provide no information about when it started or how many discrete episodes there have been.

If the goal is precise and detailed information about specific target behaviors, then observations are called for. Observations are also well suited to identifying the antecedents and consequences of specific behaviors. But observations are fairly costly and time consuming. Some observational coding systems require extensive training or depend on technical equipment such as videotape recorders or laptop computers for directly entering data. For these reasons, observations are rarely used in developmental follow-up studies involving repeated assessments.

Structured interviews are also costly and time consuming. They are obviously warranted if it is necessary to make psychiatric diagnoses. They also represent one way of obtaining information directly from children. In addition, they provide unparalleled detail about the chronicity, onset, and duration of symptoms. Interviews are of limited value if they yield only diagnostic categorizations. The present/absent nature of diagnosis is of little value for purposes of description or measurement of change.

Summary and Recommendations

In sum, different assessment procedures yield different types of information and are more useful for some purposes than others. A brief screening questionnaire that yields a single summary score reflecting global maladjustment may be a useful addition to developmental studies focused on areas other than psychopathology. There may be times when it is necessary to use a more comprehensive checklist or rating scale to provide broad enough coverage of many areas of functioning.

Checklists and rating scales are the instruments of choice for measuring change. They produce quantitative indices of behavior in many areas and have norms for comparison pruposes. Brief screening instruments are too narrow and too crude. Diagnostic interviews are also ill suited to this purpose. On the other hand, checklists and rating scales cannot be readministered frequently. They are useful for plotting changes only over broad periods of time, such as several months or years. Observations are necessary to measure changes in specific behaviors over shorter periods of time.

PROBLEMS OF MEASUREMENT EQUIVALENCE

In addition to the standard issues of reliability and validity, developmental studies must grapple with the vagaries of measurement equivalence. There are obvious advantages in using the same measures repeatedly during the course of a longitudinal study. Unfortunately, this is not always possible. Researchers often find that their measurement procedures are not feasible or appropriate across the entire age range of interest. Measures have to be altered, or completely replaced, to account for shifts in the phenomena to be assessed. Of course, anytime different measures are used, questions arise as to whether or not they are measuring the same thing. Any doubts about measurement equivalence threaten the validity of inferences regarding developmental stability and change.

Measurement equivalence is more of a problem in some areas than others. Some health indices, for example, can be assessed and interpreted in the same way from birth to maturity. In other areas, separate measurement materials and procedures have been developed to account for developmental shifts. Different measures, for example, can be used to assess the intelligence of preschoolers, school-aged children, and adults (e.g., WPPSI, WISC, and WAIS, respectively). The tasks, problems, and questions used to measure intelligence differ according to age, but the data is scored, aggregated, and interpreted along the same conceptual lines (e.g., verbal and performance IQ), and are scaled and standardized in the same ways. Thus, stability and change in IQ can be plotted across the entire life span. Change in IQ across the life span are attributed to true changes in intelligence, not just measurement shifts.

In other areas, the problems of measurement equivalence have not been completely solved and therefore limit knowledge and hamper progress. One of the most complicated measurement areas is child psychopathology. Assessment of children's social, emotional, and behavioral difficulties is plagued by fundamental problems. As mentioned previously, there is little consensus regarding the nature of child psychopathology. There are diverse opinions about what constitutes psychopathology in children and how it should be assessed. Moreover, the nature of psychopathology changes so much from early childhood through late adolescence that different measurement procedures have to be used for different ages. This creates particularly thorny problems of measurement equivalence.

It is easy to use one or more procedure for assessing child psychopathology in a developmental follow-up study, but problems would be encountered as the subjects grew older. No measures of psychopathology span the age range from birth to maturity. Most measures are designed for one age period such as preschool, middle childhood, or adolescence. Different measures would have to be employed for different ages.

Why cannot the same measures of psychopathology be used across the entire age range? The problem is that the phenomena to be assessed, in this case indicators of psychopathology, change both *quantitatively* and *qualitatively* with age. The frequency and severity of problem behaviors vary widely during childhood and adolescence. In addition, qualitatively different behaviors are relevant at different ages. Behaviors such as clings to parents, gets upset when separating from parents, holds his/her breath, and resists toilet training may be very useful when assessing preschool age children, but they are hardly appropriate for adolescents. Conversely, behaviors such as truancy, vandalism, drug and alcohol use, and sexual promiscuity may be important to assess with adolescents, but would not apply to young children. Because of these developmental shifts, it is not possible to use a single measure of psychopathology for all ages.

Accounting for Developmental Variations

There are several ways to account for developmental differences when assessing maladjustment. One approach has been to use completely separate instruments for different age groups. In the context of a developmental follow-up study, different items, scales, and norms would be used as the subjects grow older. There are separate versions of the Child Behavior Checklist (CBCL), for example, for 2- to 4-year-olds, versus 4- through 18-year-olds (Achenbach, 1991). The items, scales, and norms for the CBCL for 2- to 4-year-olds are highly relevant to the preschool-aged group, but they are not appropriate for older children. The advantage of this approach is that it accounts for both quantitative and qualitative developmental shifts by tailoring the instruments to specific age groups. There is a high price to be paid, however. Because different measures have to be used as the subjects grow older, questions of measurement equivalence arise.

As children are followed out of the age range for one measure and into the age range of another, comparability of items, scales, and norms is lost.

This creates obvious problems if the goal is to plot stability and change in the same behaviors over time. A partial solution is to analyze relations between scales having similar content. Some scales for the two versions of the CBCL, for example, are similar enough in content to have been given the same summary label (e.g., Aggressive). Stability of behavior in such areas can be determined by correlational analyses of scores on such scales. It is difficult, however, to determine change. Analyzing mean differences between dissimilar scales can, of course, be misleading. In other words, correlations between scores on different scales can validly reflect stability, but mean differences between different scales do not necessarily reflect valid changes.

A key methodological problem when analyzing different scales for different ages involves the use of raw scores. When different scales are used, the raw score distributions may differ in mean and variance of scores. Absolute differences between raw scores on the two scales do not necessarily represent true age differences. Such differences may simply be an artifact of using scales that differ in number of items, item content, and so on. Correlational analyses adjust for the mean and variance within each scale and therefore can produce a meaningful index of stability. Analyses of mean differences (e.g., t test, ANOVA), however, do not adjust for the artificial differences in mean and variance created by the use of different scales. The results of such tests will be meaningless, or worse, misleading.

An alternative approach that allows for analyses of both stability and change is to use the same scales for all ages, but standardize them separately for different age groups. The CBCL for ages 4 through 18, for example, is scored on eight core scales that are the same for all ages. The items are identical for all ages, but that does not mean that the raw scores distributions are identical. The normative base rates of many items shift dramatically across the age span, so the distributions of scale scores vary by age as well. Because the same scales are used for all ages, changes are reflected in the absolute differences between raw scale scores. But given the shifting normative baselines, a given raw score may have different meaning at one age versus another. To account for shifting norms, raw scores can be standardized within age groups. For the CBCL, for example, separate norms have been developed for ages 4 through 11 versus 12 through 16.

This approach permits flexibility in analysis. Within an age range, either raw or standardized scores can be analyzed directly for stability and change. As subjects grow older, there will be a shift in norms between ages 11 and 12. However, the scales will remain the same, so absolute differences in raw scores can still be analyzed. To account for shifting base rates in problem behavior, standard scores can be analyzed. In other words, scores for different ages can be analyzed on either *absolute* grounds, using raw scores, or on *relative* grounds, using scores standardized within age groups.

Value of Different Informants

Assessing child psychopathology in developmental follow-up studies is complicated further by problems of informant variance. Information about children's social, emotional, and behavioral functioning can be obtained from many possible informants, including parents, teachers, and the children themselves. No informant is perfectly accurate and comprehensive. Each informant has potential strengths and weaknesses as a source of informaion.

Parents usually have the most comprehensive view of their child's behavior and development and they are almost always involved in the assessment of psychopathology. Parents are the crucial persons involved in (a) instigating child mental health referrals, (b) implementing child treatments, and (c) evaluating child outcomes. Parents may be biased about their children's functioning, but their perceptions must be taken into account, whether biased or not. For information about medical, behavioral, and developmental history, child behaviors at home (e.g., sibling relationships), or behaviors at night (e.g., nightmares, bed-wetting, sleep disturbances), parents are the prime source of information.

Teachers are also widely used as a source of information about child behavior. Teachers have at least some professional training in child behavior and development and the classroom is a relatively standardized environment. A particular strength of teachers is that they can compare children of the same age and developmental level. Teachers are also well positioned to observe certain types of child behaviors, such as ability to follow directions, attention span, distractibility, and peer relationships.

Unfortunately, it is difficult to use teachers as informants in developmental follow-up studies. A given teacher will usually have a child in class for only 1 year. A multiyear follow-up study would therefore involve collecting data from several different teachers for each child. Variations in ratings from year to year might be due to differences in the informants, not variations in the children. In addition, there is a relatively brief window of time each year for obtaining teacher ratings. It is inadvisable to try to obtain teacher data too early in the school year before teachers know their pupils very well, or too late in the school year when there are too many other demands on a teacher's time. In addition, it is usually not feasible to obtain teacher data in the summer months.

For many years, children were overlooked as sources of information about their own behavioral functioning. Assessment of child psychopathology has traditionally depended on reports and ratings by adults, such as parents and teachers. Only recently have the value of children's self-reports been acknowledged. Several assessment instruments have been developed for capturing children's perceptions of their own feelings, behaviors, and social relationships (see LaGreca, 1990). Children are uniquely qualified to report on certain phenomena, including private thoughts and feelings (e.g., fears, anxiety, depression) and behaviors intentionally hidden from others (e.g., alcohol and drug use, sexual behavior, stealing, truancy, vandalism).

Almost everyone in the field of child psychopathology advocates the use of multiple informants based on the argument that no single informant is perfectly comprehensive and reliable, and different informants have different strengths and weaknesses. By using different informants, one can cross-validate findings and converge on the truth. The use of multiple informants has been made possible by the development of assessment instruments having parallel versions for different informants. The CBCL, for example, has separate versions for parents, teachers, and adolescents ages 11–18. The DISC interview also has parent and child versions, and a teacher version is under development.

Using multiple informants is probably better than depending entirely on one informant, but it also causes major problems in developmental follow-up studies. One problem is *informant variance*—different informants do not agree. The other problem involves *developmental relevance*—different informants are not equally available or relevant at different ages.

Informant Variance   A recent review of published studies (Achenbach, McConaughy, & Howell, 1987) found that informants do not agree about children's social, emotional, or behavioral functioning. The average correlation between parent and teacher ratings of the same type of child behavior problems, for example, was only .27. Parent–child agreement averaged only .25 and teacher–child agreement averaged only .20. The problem of low agreement is not caused by unreliability or invalidity of the measures used. It appears that different informants contribute valid and reliable data that simply does not agree with data from other informants. How can this be?

The answer, in part, involves situation specificity. Children's behaviors vary widely according to the situation they are in. Discrepancies between parent and teacher reports, for example, might reflect true differences in the child's behavior at home versus at school. Another factor is the differential effects informants have on child behavior. Differences between mother and father reports of their child's behavior, for example, might vary because the child behaves differently in the presence of one parent versus the other. There are many other factors that influence agreement among informants.

Research on these factors can help explain why discrepancies between informants arise, but they do not necessarily solve the problem of informant variance. Informant variance is particularly problematic in follow-up studies. Stability and change in any behavioral area is likely to vary according to which informant is used. Also, outcomes will vary depending on who is asked about which types of outcomes. Further research is needed on how to best handle disparate data from different informants.

Developmental Relevance   The second problem related to multiple informants involves their availability and relevance at different ages. Parents' reports of their children's functioning can be obtained throughout a child's life. However, *these are not necessarily of uniform quality at all ages.* From birth to about age 5 data from parents are of paramount importance, particularly because other sources of information (e.g., teachers, the children themselves) may not be available during this time. Parents' reports are valuable throughout middle childhood, but they decline in value after the age of 11 or 12. By early adolescence, children's behavioral and social arenas shift outside the home to school and community. Peers become more influential and, in general, parents know less about their children's social, emotional, and behavioral life. Behavioral norms also become more fluid, and what parents may have considered a problem at an earlier age (e.g., smoking, swearing) may be tolerated at an older age. Parents are still a potential source of information through adolescence, but their reports are certainly less comprehensive and possibly less valid than earlier in their children's lives.

The value of teachers as informants also varies by age. Teacher data are not always available before age 5 or 6. As discussed previously, teachers are not available all year round, and they change from year to year—factors that create problems for studies involving periodic reassessments. More importantly, teacher data are useful mostly during the grade school years (roughly ages 6–12) when not only do children tend to have one main teacher, but the teachers themselves seem more oriented toward the behavior, health, and development of "their" students. By middle school or junior high school, students are usually taught different subjects by different teachers. On the average, teachers are less involved and less knowledgeable of individual pupils. One sign of this is the increasing frequency with which junior high and high school teachers decline to provide assessment information because they do not know the target child well enough.

The availability of child self-reports compensates for the declining value of parent and teacher data during the adolescent years. By about age 11, most children can provide reliable information about their own feelings, behaviors, and social relationships. It is possible, of course, to obtain reliable information from children younger than 11, but it is a challenge. Assessment procedures have to be adapted to the child's cognitive level (see Bierman, 1984). Previous studies using structured interviews (Edelbrock, Costello, Dulcan, Kalas, & Conover, 1985) found that children below the age of 11 were not reliable in reporting their own psychiatric symptoms. Reliability increased markedly with age and by mid-to-late adolescence, children's self-reports were as reliable as parents' reports.

In sum, the value and availability of parent, teacher, and child reports depends largely on the child's age. Parents are crucial informants from birth to early adolescence, but then their value as sources of information about their children's functioning begins to diminish. Teachers are important sources for certain types of information, but their value depreciates rapidly after grade school. Child self-reports become more valid and reliable during early adolescence. There is only a brief period of time (around age 11–12) when all three informants are valuable. (Unfortunately, the levels of agreement among informants is no higher during that period than any other.)

Implications

No single informant can provide uniformly good data throughout child-hood and adolescence. Different informants, and combinations of infor-mants, must be used with children of different ages. This creates many problems in developmental follow-up studies. As subjects are followed through various transition points (e.g., beginning school, finishing grade school), assessment of psychopathology will depend on different informants. This will greatly complicate the analysis of stability and change. If different informants are used at different ages, it will not be possible to analyze stability and change in child functioning in any direct or simple way. Chang-ing informants inevitably raises questions about measurement equiva-lence—just as changing assessment instruments does. Any observed insta-bility in scores, for example, might be due to changes in the measures or informants used, as opposed to true changes in the phenomena being assessed.

There are no simple solutions to these measurement problems, and there does not appear to be any way to avoid them. Optimal assessment of child psychopathology will require that different informants be used at different ages—and these informants will not agree. The best advice one can offer is to use the best measures available, use more than one way of assessing the same constructs, and use multiple informants when they are relevant. The problems of measurement equivalence and low informant agreement will have to be dealt with statistically. More complex multivariate statistical procedures (e.g., structural equation modeling), for example, show promise in addressing both measurement issues and developmental stability and change simultaneously.

CONCLUSION

There are several procedures for assessing child and adolescent psycho-pathology that could be used in developmental follow-up studies. The value of studies focusing on other areas (e.g., health, cognitive development, language) could be increased by adding some quick and inexpensive mea-sures of psychopathology, such as a screening questionnaire or a behavioral checklist. Follow-up studies focusing on psychopathology can utilize more extensive checklists, rating scales, interviews, and observations. Checklists and rating scales are the most psychometrically developed and are well suited to the analysis of stability and change. Interviews are costly and time consuming, but they are essential if psychiatric diagnoses are required. Observations are also expensive, but they provide unparalleled levels of precision and are uniquely well suited to the identification of antecedents and consequences of specific target behaviors.

Whatever assessment procedures are used in developmental follow-up studies, problems of measurement equivalence will be encountered. No assessment instruments exist that account for the quantitative and qualitative shifts in manifestations of psychopathology throughout childhood and adolescence. Different measures and different informants must be used at different ages. In addition, different informants will not agree. This causes many problems for studies aimed at determining stability and change over time. The best advice at this time is to use multiple measures and multiple informants and save all the pieces. Multivariate statistical procedures may ultimately succeed in putting the pieces together and solving the puzzle of developmental psychopathology.

REFERENCES

Achenbach, T. M. (1991). *Manual for the Child Behavior Checklist/4–18 and 1991 Profile.* Burlington, VT: University Associates in Psychiatry.

Achenbach, T. M., McConaughy, S., & Howell, C. (1987). Child/adolescent behavioral and emotional problems: Implications of cross-informant correlations for situation specificity. *Psychological Bulletin, 101,* 213–232.

American Psychiatric Association. (1987). *Diagnostic and statistical manual of mental disorders* (3d ed., rev.). Washington DC: Author.

Barkley, R. (1988). Child behavior rating scales and checklists. In M. Rutter, A. H. Tuma, & I. S. Lann (Eds.), *Assessment and diagnosis in child psychopathology.* (pp. 113–155). New York: Guilford.

Barkley, R. (1990). *Attention Deficit-Hyperactivity Disorder: A handbook for diagnosis and treatment.* New York: Guilford.

Bierman, K. (1984). Cognitive development and clinical interviews with children. In B. Lahey & A. E. Kazdin (Eds.), *Advances in clinical child psychology* (Vol. 6, pp. 217–250). New York: Plenum.

Earls, F., Jacobs, G., Goldfein, D., Silbert, A., Beardslee, W., & Rivinus, T. (1982). Concurrent validation of a behavior problem scale for use with three-year-olds. *Journal of the American Academy of Child Psychiatry, 21,* 47–57.

Edelbrock, C. (1987). Psychometric research on children. In C. Last and M. Hersen (Eds.), *Issues in diagnostic research* (pp. 219–240). New York: Plenum.

Edelbrock, C., & Costello, A. J. (1988). Structured psychiatric interviews for children. In M. Rutter, A. H. Tuma, & I. S. Lann (Eds.), *Assessment and diagnosis in child psychopathology* (pp. 87–112). New York: Guilford.

Edelbrock, C., Costello, A. J., Dulcan, M., Kalas, R., & Conover, N. (1985). Age differences in the reliability of the psychiatric interview of the child. *Child Development, 56,* 265–275.

Goyette, C. H., Conners, C. K., & Ulrich, R. F. (1978). Normative data on revised Conners Parent and Teacher Rating Scales. *Journal of Abnormal Child Psychology, 6,* 221–236.

Hodges, K., Kline, J., Stern, L., Cytryn, L., & McKnew, D. (1982). The development of a child assessment interview for research and clinical use. *Journal of Abnormal Child Psychology 10,* 173–189.

LaGreca, A. (1990). *Through the eyes of a child.* New York: Guilford.

Quay, H. (1983). *Manual for the Revised Behavior Problem Checklist.* Coral Gables, FL: Author.

Reid, J., Baldwin, D., Patterson, G., & Dishion, T. (1988). Observations in the assessment of child disorders. In M. Rutter, A. H. Tuma, & I. S. Lann (Eds.), *Assessment and diagnosis in child psychopathology* (pp. 156–195). New York: Guilford.

Richman, N. (1977). Short-term outcome of behavior problems in preschool-aged children. In P. Graham (Eds.), *Epidemiological approaches in child psychiatry* (pp. 165–180). London: Academic Press.

Robin, A. (1988). *Parent–Adolescent Interaction Coding System—Revised (PAICS-R) training manual.* Detroit, MI: Author.

Parents as Scientific Observers of Their Children's Development

John E. Bates

INTRODUCTION

Much of developmental research, especially social development research, relies on caregivers' descriptions of children. There is strong ambivalence about the reliance on parental questionnaires and interviews. On the one hand, parents' reports are relatively easy to obtain and easy to process, and they are widely accepted. On the other hand, they are sometimes viewed by editors and other arbiters of science as having dubious value. This negative view is supposed to be a guide toward improved science, and must be carefully considered; however, it should not be accepted uncritically any more than one accepts uncritically the view that parents' reports are highly valid. Either view might impede scientific progress. In this chapter, I argue that both acceptance and doubt are in order; and I argue that parental ratings can make major contributions to research if scientists do their own tasks properly. I offer reasons for this optimistic view of parent reports, as well as some more personal observations on the general scientific context within which parental reports and other data are often interpreted.

Developmental Follow-up
197

That caregivers' reports are doubted is not the key problem; the key problem is that they are usually doubted more informally than formally. They are most typically disparaged by assumption or as an aside. One frequently hears the warning that maternal reports are not to be trusted. I have read and heard comments about parent reports being "just parent perceptions," especially in conference discussions and in evaluations of journal articles and grant proposals. By "just parent perceptions" is usually meant that the data are distorted and of questionable worth (see Thomas, Chess, & Korn, 1982).[1]

The alternative sources of information, naturalistic and structured observation (including psychological tests), are regarded as offering greater empirical rigor than parental reports. Like parental reports, however, observation methods have limitations. There are good developments in naturalistic and structured observational tests, but such observations are costly and have their own validity problems. All social behaviors have multiple meanings. Neither parents nor the best professional observers will be able to see all the important patterns. Operational definitions for professional coding systems are unavoidably ambiguous. One behavior code could represent multiple meanings and a particular meaning could be represented by rather different behavior codes (Rizzo, Corsaro, & Bates, 1992). The real question is how to capitalize on the complementary perspectives of parents and formal observers. This chapter argues that it is both scientifically justifiable and practical to use parent report data and worthwhile to learn more about what parents perceive. Parents do have extensive knowledge about their children's development, even if it may not yet fully fit scientific concepts of objectivity. In this view, parents and researchers are allies in efforts toward eventual improvements in practice.

THE MEANINGS OF CAREGIVER REPORTS

Caregiver reports are social perceptions. Social perceptions are unlikely to be completely a reflection of the child being described; they will have a subjective element. This is the biggest reason to distrust caregiver reports. An earlier review of the literature on temperament (Bates, 1980) challenged a previous, often tacit assumption by some researchers that operational measures of temperament mainly revealed things within the child and that subjective factors in the parent were not important in data interpretation. The collection of empirical studies at that time showed generally small correlations (at best) between parent reports and measures assumed to be

---

[1] A friend disclosed that at a convention of the Society for Research in Child Development he had several times heard apologies for the use of caregiver reports, and mother and teacher informants "blamed" several times for nonsignificant or confusing findings. My friend takes methodology very seriously, and in the face of such widespread disapproval, it was a struggle, he reported, to maintain his respect for his wife, who is both a mother and a teacher.

more highly objective, such as observer records of behavior. On the other hand, the research also showed that parent reports of temperament overlap with parent characteristics such as self-reported anxiety level or social desirability response set. The accumulated data were interpreted in different ways, with different implications for constructs of temperament. One reaction was to object that current validity information was insufficient, to reassert that indeed temperament does exist within the child, and to argue the wrongness of denigrating parental objectivity. Another reaction was the opposite, to conclude that parent report of temperament is invalid and that "mere perceptions" do not constitute a scientific measurement. The implication was that the caregiver's bias is so strong that practically nothing of the child is revealed by the report. Statements resembling these two views can still be found. Each polar position holds danger, with the rejection of parent reports holding at this time perhaps the greater danger to scientific progress. Luckily, there is a large middle ground. This chapter presents evidence that parent reports do have externally verifiable components and that the apparent subjective components do not eclipse the objective components.

RESEARCH ON VALIDITY OF MATERNAL REPORTS

Summarized here, are the findings on the objective and subjective elements of parental reports from the Bloomington Longitudinal Study and related studies of our laboratory. We have considered a large amount of data, and have obtained a complex, but fairly clear picture of the network of validity.

Consistent Dimensionality in Mother Reports

Through factor analyses of items on individual questionnaires (e.g., Bates, Freeland, & Lounsbury, 1979) and scales from a variety of questionnaires (e.g., Bates & Bayles, 1984), it can be seen that the perceptions of the mothers are differentiated in an interpretable, consistent way. For example, in temperament, the first domain we focused on, analyses showed several, relatively independent temperament dimensions. These included difficultness (defined primarily by frequent and intense fussing, crying, and attention demanding), unadaptability (negative reactions to new people and situations), and resistance to control of activity (not stopping when told no). The first two of these dimensions had factor counterparts at 6, 13, and 24 months, and the latter had counterparts at 13 and 24 months (the only ages where it was assessed). Moreover, these cross-age counterpart scales loaded together on the appropriate second-order factors (Bates & Bayles, 1984), showing that mothers were consistent over time in giving complex, organized pictures of their children.

Objective and Subjective Components

Early results supported a part subjective, part objective model of mother perceptions, but these results were mostly restricted to perceptions on one construct—difficultness (Bates, 1980). Analyses (mostly bivariate) showed that the mother reports of difficultness were confirmed by observer counts and ratings of infant fussing and crying behaviors, and even spectrographic analyses of recorded crying sounds. The correlations were low (in the .20s and .30s), but they were replicated in different samples and at different infancy ages (Bates et al., 1979; Bates, 1980; Lounsbury & Bates, 1982; Bates, Olson, Pettit, & Bayles, 1982; Pettit & Bates, 1984). These same studies showed that the mother reports of infant difficultness were correlated, to comparable degree, with the mother's own characteristics, such as social desirability reported on a personality questionnaire. These findings were consistent with the assumption that there are both objective and subjective components in maternal perceptions; but our data would allow analyses that were at the same time more conceptually precise and generalized. Our goal therefore became to test the generality of the simple, subjective–objective model across a wide variety of mother perception constructs.

Second-Order Factors in Multiple Mother Report Scales   The first step, then, was to explore the organization in the full range of maternal report scales collected on 6-month-olds to 36-month-olds in our longitudinal study (Bates & Bayles, 1984). We performed a second-order factor analysis of 27 scales from the 6-, 13-, and 24-month versions of our main temperament questionnaire, the Infant Characteristics Questionnaire (ICQ; Bates et al. 1979), the 13- and 24-month versions of the Maternal Perceptions Questionnaire (MPQ; Olson, Bates, & Bayles, 1982), which was designed to assess some child social and developmental characteristics not well assessed by the ICQ, and two questionnaires given at 3 years, the Preschool Behavior Questionnaire (PBQ; Behar, 1977) and the Minnesota Child Development Inventory (MCDI; Ireton & Thwing, 1974).

The second-order factor analysis showed eight conceptually clear, cross-age consistent dimensions. These are listed in Table I. Of course, factors derived depend on researcher interests and measures included. They also depend, especially for the smaller factors, on the sample of families tested. It would not be expected that all eight factors would reappear in another sample, even in the somewhat unlikely event that the same questionnaires would be used. However, there are hints in the literature that some dimensions may qualitatively reappear, even when different scales were used (Bates, 1990). All eight of the factors are listed to show the range of constructs surveyed. They reflect amounts of various kinds of social friction—difficultness, unadaptability, and misbehavior—as well as levels of positive affective responsiveness such as unexcitability and unresponsiveness, and development of language and other forms of competence.

Table I   Second-Order Factors in Mother Reports over the First 3 Years

1. Difficult and Demanding
   Concerns fussing and crying and attention-demandingness at 6, 13, and 24 months (ICQ[a]).
2. Negative Adaptation
   Concerns negative reactions to new persons and situations, 6–24 months (ICQ and MPQ[b]).
3. Noncompliant
   Indexes child's resistance to control and unpredictability of biological functions as a toddler (ICQ and MPQ).
4. Unexcitable
   Indexes (inversely) the extent to which the 6- to 24-month-old is active and socially excitable (ICQ).
5. Problem Behavior
   Most precisely defined by the Hostile, Anxious, and Hyperactive scales of the 36-month PBQ,[c] but also by the Troublesome scale from the 24-month MPQ, which itself loaded significantly also on the first factor.
6. Language Competence
   Mother ratings of language development at 13 and 24 months (MPQ) and general competence at 36 months (MCDI[d]).
7. Unresponsiveness to Mother
   Inversely indexing the extent to which the infant or toddler acts glad to see the mother and affectionate toward her (MPQ).
8. Psychomotor Incompetence
   A small factor defined only by the 13-month MPQ scale of concerns about the infant's general rate of development.

Note. From "Objective and Subjective Components in Mothers' Perceptions of Their Children from Age 6 Months to 3 Years" by J. E. Bates and K. Bayles, 1984, Merrill-Palmer Quarterly, *30*, 111–130.

[a] Infant Characteristics Questionnaire. (Unless otherwise indicated, all questionnaires developed and published by our laboratory.)

[b] Maternal Perceptions Questionnaire.

[c] Preschool Behavior Questionnaire (Behar, 1977).

[d] Minnesota Child Development Inventory (Ireton & Thwing, 1974).

Multiple Regressions within Domains   The next step was to test the array of possible correlates of the mother report scales via hierarchical multiple regressions (Bates & Bayles, 1984). In each case, the dependent measure was one of the mother report scales, and the predictor variables were various observational, father report, mother personality, and demographic variables. The validity of parent reports was not checked equally well in each of the eight domains, but in each of these domains the evidence supported the same basic model: Variance in mothers' reports about their young children can be divided into components attributable to subjective and objective factors.

To illustrate the data, results are reviewed for three of the domains: Difficult and Demanding, Negative Adaptation, and Language Competence. Each of these domains consisted of more than one high-loading scale. Each scale in the domain served as a separate, dependent measure in a regression analysis. Results were summarized within domains by averaging percents of variance accounted for by the different kinds of variables in the several analyses.[2]

The first variables to be entered in all equations were those of background, including socioeconomic status, number of previous children, and sex of the target child. These were entered first because although they may reflect subjectivity in mother perceptions, they are conceptually the most distant from the child's temperament and adaptational characteristics and one would want to see whether there was variance left to be explained by the more theoretically relevant predictors after these components were removed. Entered second were mother personality indexes—variables that would more clearly pertain to the hypothetical subjective component, mother social desirability set and defensiveness, anxiety problems, externalizing problems, and outgoingness. For neither the background nor the personality variables can it be said that they are purely representing the subjective factor, inasmuch as such variables can logically influence the child's actual characteristics, at least in the relationship with that parent. Parent personality and patterns of behavior with the child have both been demonstrated, moreover, to have heritable components, for example, in the amount of self-reported neuroticism or observations of warmth shown the child (Plomin & Bergeman, 1991). To the extent that these things represent parent temperament, overlap between parent personality/behavior and child temperament could reflect shared genes influencing shared behavior patterns.[3] Nevertheless, it can still be assumed that personality variables represent that subjective factor to some degree, and probably to a greater degree than those in the next group of variables.

The third group of variables, then, were those representing the objective component, including the most pertinent home observation, lab observation, and structured test indexes. Here, too, the interpretation of objectivity is one of assumed degree, inasmuch as the background and mother personality characteristics might have influenced either the objective component of the observers' perceptions, via the ways the mother's personality-derived patterns of action frame the child, or the subjective component, via halo effects based on how the mother has related to the observer. Nevertheless, one would still assume that these measures would be more highly objective than subjective, given the professionalism of the observers and the standard controls of the data collection process (independent reliability checks, etc.). Further-

---

[2] We chose to average together the various effect sizes regardless of significance level of the effect. Some effects were significant; others were not. The resulting averages are generally substantial.

[3] Nor can it be assumed that the characteristics of the child do not influence the adjustment of the mother. Shroff, DelaFlor, and I presented data at the 1990 University of Toronto Psychology Symposium ("The Challenges of Parenting") that showed that mothers with both temperamentally unadaptable children and unsupportive husbands were more apt to show a worsening of their personal adjustment from the child's age of 6 months to 3 years, and were less likely to improve in adjustment than the other groups of mothers.

more, some of the linkage between mother personality and observer perceptions might have been removed by entering the mother characteristics earlier
in the equation.[4]

Entered last were the perceptions of the father on the particular mother
report scale that served as the dependent measure. It is harder to categorize
the fathers' reports as objective in the same way as observers' reports because
they are potentially influenced by some of the same subjective factors that
influence the mothers' perceptions. However, in the design of the analyses,
these hypothetical influences, such as the mother's need for social desirability, were removed at an earlier step in the equation. Father ratings entered
last also allowed us to see whether some portion of the mother–father
correlation was accounted for by the observational data.

Findings for the example domains are summarized in Figure 1, adapted
from Bates and Bayles (1984). The three scales that defined the Difficult and
Demanding dimension were on the average predicted to a modest extent,
as previously shown, by mother background and personality variables. This
was shown by previous bivariate analyses. However, the predictions from
the "objective" indexes of observer and father reports were stronger in this
instance than the ones from the "subjective" indexes of mother and child
demographic background and mother personality; the background and personality variables combined explained only an average of 10% of the variance
in the temperament measures, whereas the observer indexes accounted for
an additional 15% and the father reports a further 25%. The father reports
were more highly correlated with the corresponding mother reports than
were the observer reports. This pattern repeated itself across the full array
of multiple regressions.[5] However, across the full array of scales, the father
variables were only slightly more highly predictive of the mother scales than
the weighted sums of the observational indexes. Observer indexes of child

---

[4] In constructing our overall web of validation, an important consideration was the meaning-
fulness of the home observations used to represent the objective side of the equation. The
home observation data have as a set shown adequate interobserver reliability, short-term
stability, especially for the mother codes (e.g., Bates, Olson, Pettit, & Bayles, 1982), meaningful
factor structure in the codes (Bates, Olson, Pettit, & Bayles, 1982; Lee & Bates, 1985; Pettit &
Bates, 1984), cross-age coherence of individual differences in rates of behaviors from 6–24
months and even to 4 years (Pettit & Bates, 1984, 1989; Olson, Bates, & Bayles, 1984), and
meaningful patterns of correlation between mother–child interaction variables and developmental outcomes (Bates & Bayles, 1988; Bates, Maslin, & Frankel, 1985; Frankel & Bates, 1990;
Olson, Bates, & Bayles, 1984, 1989, 1990; Olson, Bayles, & Bates, 1986).

[5] We thought that we might find that a substantial component of the overlap between father
and mother reports was attributable to the child characteristics that an observer could see.
However, across all the scales, when father variables were entered before any other variables,
they predicted an average of 22% of variance in mother reports, and when entered last, after
the observer reports, they still accounted for an average of 18%, less reduction than if the
mother–father overlap were attributable to easily observed child behavior. So whether the
substantial agreement between mother and father is due to their extensive, objective experience
with the child or whether the father partly sees the child through the mother's eyes must remain
in doubt.

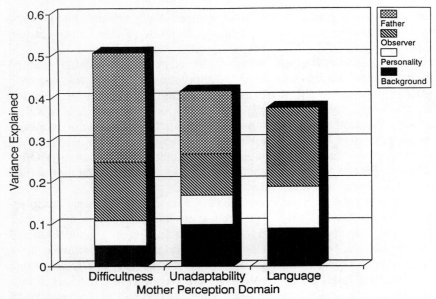

Figure 1   Portions of variance attributable to the four components of model of mother perceptions: Squared multiple correlations averaged within domains of child characteristics across 3-5 separate, hierarchical regressions. Adapted from Bates & Bayles (1984).

negative affect expression, for example, predicted maternal perceptions of difficultness well, even in the comparison with the father scales.[6]

The second example, Negative Adaptation, represented five different regression analyses. It was more clearly predicted from demographic characteristics than was Difficult and Demanding, and there was a little less contribution from observer and father variance.[7] Even here, however, the subjective

---

[6] It should be emphasized that these comparisons of the relative amounts of variance accounted for by the different domains are impressionistic, even though many of the differences mentioned are actually statistically significant. What makes true significance so uncertain is that the numbers and qualities of the particular predictors vary across domains. Nevertheless, I am not aware of any existing evidence better suited to the kind of speculation presented in this chapter.

[7] The amount of variance charted here does not appear to be caused by a few large effects, but rather by the cumulation of small effects that largely failed to reach statistical significance. One significant bivariate relationship suggested, however, that the lower socioeconomic status (SES) mothers tended to see their infants as more unadaptable than higher SES mothers. Whether or not this reflects differences in experience or inborn temperament that covary with class must be determined by further research. When the link between unadaptability and SES (Bates & Bayles, 1984) is replicated, it will be interesting to test various explanations. One possible SES scenario would be a greater likelihood of chronically high levels of stress in any given family in the lower socioeconomic classes, which elevates the fear responsiveness of predisposed children from repeated elicitation of fear in threatening circumstances. In a related vein, Kagan (1983) suggests that high levels of stress-response hormones in the pregnant mother will neuro-developmentally tune up the fetus' fearful/inhibited responses by affecting the development of cholinergic versus adrenergic ganglia.

component could not be said to dwarf the objective component. The implications of Negative Adaptation indexes have become clearer in our long-term follow-ups: Evidence suggests that these scales are differentially indexing some aspect of anxiety-proneness because they tend to predict later internalizing styles of adaptation (as perceived by the parents) more than they predict externalizing (Bates & Bayles, 1988; Bates, Bayles, Bennett, Ridge, & Brown, 1991). One source of this cross-age linkage may be continuity in the underlying characteristics of the child; fearful reactions to novelty mark a preparedness for anxiety that is manifested later as internalizing symptoms. Evidence for this hypothesis comes from Kagan, Reznick, & Snidman (1989), who have shown in cases of infants extremely inhibited in the face of novelty versus those who are extremely uninhibited that the fearfulness perceived by the parent has a component of physiological reactivity, can be seen in structured testing situations, and shows continuity into middle childhood. Another possible source of linkage is continuity of the parent's perceptual style; the parent's own tendency to see the child's adaptation as fearful is what persists. Evidence for this is not as clear as for the first interpretation. The notion of a perceptual style suggests that both self and others would be perceived in parallel ways, whether this is based on the organizing effects of the parent's environment or the genetically shared tendency to be anxious. There is evidence in our research (e.g., Bates & Bayles, 1988) that parent self-reported psychopathology is correlated with perceived internalizing symptoms of the child. However, these linkages do not show the same differentials of continuity seen for internalizing and externalizing types of behaviors perceived in the child; both the internalizing and externalizing symptoms of the parent are predictive of both internalizing and externalizing perceived in the child (Bates & Bayles, 1988; Bates et al., 1991). If the continuity were largely due to parental perceptual style, one might expect to see some differential.

Analysis of the third example domain, Language Competence, suggests the interesting point that there may be both subjective and objective components even in the perception of child characteristics that are not regarded as part of personality. Mothers' ratings of their children's language competence were considerably more convergent with observer impressions than was the case for temperament qualities; for example, mother ratings of language competence at 24 months correlated .71 with observer ratings of mature child communication and .45 and .50, respectively, with the Peabody Picture Vocabulary Test and the Bayley Mental Development Index (Olson et al., 1982).[8] One would expect that background would influence the child's language competence, as Figure 1 indicates was the case. However, we were surprised by the lack of significant predictiveness of socioeconomic status in the multiple regression, which we know from other studies and

---

[8] Sample sizes for these analyses were 107–117.

analyses of our own to have significant bivariate correlations with tests of language development (Olson, Bayles, & Bates, 1986).

What did predict mother ratings of language development, however, was the child's birth order. Firstborns were seen as more advanced in their language development. It is possible that first-time mothers would be biased to rate their infants' development higher, but in fact, the first-time mothers did tend to provide more of the kind of stimulation that forecasts advanced language development (as shown by Olson et al., 1984), both at 6 and 13 months of age (Bates et al, 1982; Pettit & Bates, 1984).[9] Moreover, the finding of greater perceived language competence in first borns was paralleled by modest, but significant negative correlations between child birth order and the observer, Bayley, and Peabody indexes. Finally, in predicting Language Competence, the mother personality variable of social desirability made a significant contribution here too, just as it did to Difficult and Demanding and to Negative Adaptation. Although social desirability can be interpreted as a bias factor, it may also reflect positive social adjustment.

Data-Based Interpretations and Speculations

The differentiation in cross-age continuities in our measures of mother perceptions is taken as a basic form of validity. At the very least, the mothers' questionnaire responses do not simply reflect some global bias or personality trait such as social desirability or negative affectivity (Watson & Clark, 1984), even though such characteristics do play a limited role in how the parent describes the child. Parents use questionnaires to depict their children as having multiple facets, and also as having complexly ordered, fairly consistent patterns of individuality. The Bates and Bayles (1984) study showed this with a sample followed over the first 3 years of life.

The differentiated paths of temperament and adjustment styles are also seen in development beyond the first 3 years. There are comparable links also with behavior problems at ages 4 through 8 (Bates & Bayles, 1988; Bates et al., 1991; Pettit & Bates, 1989). The links even make conceptual sense, especially for unadaptability predicting later internalizing better than externalizing (reflecting perhaps the anxiety system being tuned high), and resistance to control predicting externalizing better than internalizing (reflecting perhaps high levels of stimulus seeking or aggressiveness). In the case of difficultness, which overall predicts both types of symptom dimension more equally, my hypothesis is that difficultness reflects two separable components. First is demand for social mediation of the environment.[10]

---

[9] The social class variable's prediction of child intellectual competency is mediated by the practices of the mother: When mother's warm and educative involvement is controlled for, the effect of SES is sharply reduced (Olson, Bates, & Bayles, 1984).

[10] In a study of mothers with 4- to 6-month-old infants, we found that mothers of difficult infants tended to see them as socially demanding (Bates, Miller, & Bayles, 1984).

Social demandingness could reflect a high need for stimulation—social stimulation tends to be more intense for an infant than nonsocial stimulation. It could also reflect chronic fatigue caused by sleep deprivation. Weissbluth, a pediatrician, has described how the stress of chronic sleep loss impairs emotional and cognitive functioning (Weissbluth, 1989). My clinical observation is that it is not unusual for parents and children to have difficulty establishing optimal schedules of sleep (Bates, 1989). The second hypothetical component of difficultness is irritability, or high sensitivity to minor aversive stimuli. This could reflect the anxiety system being tuned high, or perhaps even chronically high levels of general stress in the child's environment.[11] These speculations are plausible, but need to be empirically tested.

Aside from the basic validity implied by coherent and conceptually interesting paths in mothers' perceptions of their children, the evidence just described has shown other kinds of validity as well. Across a wide variety of mother report scales, wherever we have made an effort to observe the children in parallel to the mothers, whether in the home or the lab, we have found at least minimal support for the ratings. Father reports tend to be more closely related to the mother reports than are the corresponding observer reports, as would be expected on the basis of the fathers having more extensive knowledge either of the child or of the mothers' views, but it is not such an impressive superiority when considered across a range of scales, using multiple observer indexes. In addition, the father scores are still about as highly correlated with the mother scores even after controlling for the characteristics rated by trained observers, which shows that it is not necessarily the easily seen patterns of infant behavior that account for the overlap in mother and father perceptions.

Finally, it is clear that the likely representatives of subjectivity in parental perception do not dwarf the representatives of objectivity in explaining the variance in parent reports. The obtained correlations are generally small, even when multiple personality and background indexes are used in parallel. Moreover, there are suggestions that some of the overlap between parent characteristics and perceptions of the child could turn out to be due to objective similarities.

FUTURE DIRECTIONS

Some interesting future research awaits us in testing the assumptions just presented. Let me emphasize that although the conclusions of this chapter are based on research, they are far from a complete resolution. The measures

[11] Tellegen (personal communication, Jan. 1991) suggested that the chief marker of difficultness, crying, is both operant and respondent. Thus, the two components of difficultness could reflect the synergistic effects of operant (attention-demanding) versus respondent (physical/emotional distress) processes.

and constructs are far from a noise-free level of precision. The work summarized here is in many respects an effort to improve the precision of our interpretations of parent report data. Similar data need to be collected from replication samples and the same kind of summary is needed for the other windows on the developmental process—the various types of formal observation.

Although the evidence shows parent reports valid to an extent, substantial uncertainties remain about their use. There are some things that might be done to reduce uncertainty. One direction to try is improving scientists' understanding of how people perceive and interact with their children, and how they interpret the scientist's questions. The parent does not necessarily construe reality in the same terms as the researcher, or even the clinician. On the one hand, researchers need to keep trying to find ways to communicate their ideas clearly to parents by experimenting with how items are worded. On the other hand, parents need to keep teaching us how they construe the process they participate in. We can design better interviews and questionnaires, ones that capitalize on what parents perceive well and that do not ask them to judge things they are inaccurate in perceiving. This is one approach to making parent reports better scientific data.

Another possible way is for the scientist to try to train parents in observation. If there is a construct that parents often do not perceive clearly, the scientist might provide some definitional training to see if this intervention produces better attention to key details, and hence better data from parents. It should also be worthwhile to be able to adjust the picture given by the parent by factoring in the parents' own characteristics. Even if one accepts that, on the average, parent reports are neither simply nor overwhelmingly slanted, one might still suggest that there are some individuals whose perceptions will be highly inaccurate from bias or ignorance. This does seem likely in some cases. We can improve our ability to identify and eventually predict such cases. If biases ran in predictable directions, we could then correct, say, for lack of contact with the child, or for personality tendencies that would compromise observational ability or interpretation of rating scales. Such statistical corrections would be like computer enhancement of the video images we receive from interplanetary probes. The principle here is an old one in some adult personality tests. The Minnesota Multiphasic Personality Inventory, with its correction for defensiveness, is the best-known example. Within our limits to conceive of and measure the relevant characteristics, why should something analogous not be possible with parental descriptions of their children?[12]

[12] It must be mentioned here that the resolution of the picture does not simply rest on technological improvements in the questions and contextual interpretations of parent reports. It also depends on efforts to improve the technology of other forms of measurement of children's development, including observation. Interpretation and validation are always a process of triangulation, exploring the complementarity of alternate perspectives of reality (Rizzo, Corsaro, & Bates, 1992).

In writing about the meanings of parent reports, I have discussed the most widely used kind of caregiver report and the kind whose validity has been most vigorously investigated. However, I would expect research to show the same general principles in what other caregivers, for example, teachers, say about the children in their care. Of course, different kinds of caregivers would be expected to have different kinds of perspective and to differ in their insights and biases. One would expect that they would also differ in the degree of objectivity brought to the task; for example, the average teacher ought to be in a better position to describe children in relation to general norms than the average parent.

REASONS TO USE CAREGIVER REPORTS

I hope it will be conceded, based on the foregoing arguments and evidence, that the following reasons for the use of caregiver reports on children are not simply rationalization to cover the widespread reliance on this method. I can list four good reasons to use caregiver reports in research about children's development.

1. Expertise of the caregiver. Researchers are interested in children's behaviors that occur in the relationship that encompasses the largest part of the young child's life. Parents would have to be recognized as the most knowledgeable members of that setting. This review provides some empirical support for parental expertise. Of course, the parent does not construe events in the same language as the researcher, but they can partially adapt to the researcher's framework, and vice versa. The remaining differences in perspective can help us to appreciate different aspects of complex social reality.

2. Cultural expectation. It is culturally and ethically appropriate to treat parents (or teachers) with respect. Parents are responsible for the care and activities of their children. At the least, it would be considered impolite not to ask them their opinions and observations on research issues pertaining to their children. Even more, it would be a waste of the insight into the meanings of child behavior held by the family. Not only are parents and their views of their children key in defining the contexts of children's social development, they are also already essentially partners of the research enterprise. Parents are major consumers of developmental research. They pay for much of the research, via federal and state taxes, and for the empirical knowledge acquired by consultants, child and family therapists, and teachers. Researchers' communications that recognize parent perceptions of reality will tend to have greater practical impact, even if in fact they are challenging those perceptions. So, beyond being impolite and wasteful of insights, it might even be politically self-defeating to attempt to learn about children without learning anything about how parents see their children.

3. Familiarity of method. Both researchers and subjects are accustomed to questionnaires and interviews. Questions do not arouse as much resistance as more intrusive methods such as observation.[13] Parents are more used to being asked a series of questions (see reason 2) than having a stranger or near-stranger in their home for hours at a time, watching and not interacting.

4. Relative economy. Asking caregivers is relatively easy and inexpensive, especially in questionnaire form. It is expensive to provide laboratory assessments, to code videotapes, and to keep observers in the field. Designing and checking observation systems and training and retraining observers are very time-consuming tasks, and even the most highly trained observers may be unable to sample important behaviors that occur infrequently. There are certainly occasions when the more standardized and objective observational data would be needed. However, given the complexity of patterns researchers tend to be interested in and their sensitivity to context, they often are unable to get by with structured, laboratory observations. Also, naturalistic observations of sufficient length to sample all the relevant situations could be expensive. Although parent reports have some ambiguities of meaning, given the demonstrated merits of parent reports and the overall lack of greater validity for observational measures, the modest cost of parent reports is a reason for their use.

PITFALLS IN THE USE OF CAREGIVER PERCEPTIONS

One major pitfall in the use of caregiver perceptions is failing to keep in mind the source of the data. Forgetting the source of an assertion, even when that source is distrusted, is common. This is one source of the "sleeper effect" in attitude change (McGuire, 1969). It is apparent that it can happen with scientists, too, and has resulted in some overinterpretations in studies of early childhood personality development. One common form of overinterpretation is confusing a variable's label with its meaning. For example, the concept of temperament is usually taken to refer to biological characteristics, even though patterns of behavior must also reflect environment; consequently, operational measures of temperament take on this meaning, even though this interpretation can only be a temporary expedient. The "objective" components in operational indexes might allow parent reports to predict independent criterion variables. However, as previously suggested, the par-

---

[13] We found that when observations focus on a young infant, mothers are relatively comfortable. However, as the focus of observation becomes more extensively linked to the parents via interactions, parents show more signs of concern about the violation of privacy boundaries. Of course, many parents are still not obviously reserved even when the children are old enough to be embarrassing, and some parents are reserved about observation even when their child is a young infant.

ents' perceptions of child characteristics are actually complex phenomena, reflecting reality as others see it, background characteristics, personality characteristics, and probably, although not as well described, relationship characteristics. For some purposes, especially in clinical science, this rich mixture is probably useful even with our rudimentary knowledge of its complex meanings (Bates, 1980). For others, especially for more basic science goals, there needs to be further analysis of the perceptions.

Perhaps, it should seem easy to remember that measures have only operational, provisional meanings. However, it is in fact sometimes difficult to do so. One wants a comprehensive and comprehensible model of how biological and social processes combine to produce personality and competencies. Limited tolerance for cognitive complexity, as well as limited resources for research, force simplified thinking.

Because I am preaching good habits in the scientific usage of parent reports, I will briefly suggest several other practices I find useful in avoiding the overinterpretation pitfalls. First, it helps when those who use a measure test its validity frequently, even for supposedly objective, structured observations, but especially for questionnaire measures. This suggests the need for multivariate, multimethod research in which one keeps trying to assess both parallel and contrasting constructs in alternative ways. This leads to a second suggestion: It can be useful to know about nonrelationships between variables. Replicated nonrelationships among otherwise valid measures can enrich understanding in a way that complements findings of significant correlations. In a similar way, it is also instructive to look at the actual sizes of correlations, not just whether they are significant or not. If something is related to two similar variables, but is consistently more related to one variable than to another, this could suggest fruitful distinctions between two variables previously regarded as vaguely similar.[14] It would probably be worthwhile for different researchers to share multiple data sets with similar measures. The nomological nets could be larger and more definitive. There do seem to be increased efforts at research consortia. The problems of research tradition, highly individual reward systems, and limited communication are not to be taken lightly, but are probably not insurmountable.

---

[14] A good example of research comparing patterns of relationships between personality variables is Tellegen's (1985). This work, done with adults, considered the nature of the relationship between anxiety and depression, two variables that are often found correlated with each other and both loading on a broader dimension of negative affectivity. Tellegen looked at the relationships of anxiety and depression with the negative affectivity dimension, but also looked at them in relation to another second-order dimension, independent of the first, positive affectivity. The results provide a more precise description, one that allows distinctions that happen to fit with clinical common sense: Anxious people as a group have fewer positive emotional responses than nonanxious people, but this is not as salient as their frequent emotional distress. Depressed people have more emotional distress than nondepressed people, but this is less salient than their lack of positive affect.

Having commented on the interpretation pitfall, there is only one other related pitfall that will be discussed here, the issue of reliability. The pitfall in this basic psychometric principle is in its double-edged nature. On the one side, one would always prefer a more reliable questionnaire (or observational measure), but this sometimes comes at a cost; it often takes repeated testing and revision of a measure to optimize its reliability. If one is on the track across development of an emerging concept of individual differences, and following a longitudinal sample, one may not have the time to polish up the psychometric properties of a series of measures. Nevertheless, relatively rough measures in a multivariate, longitudinal context can still reveal important threads of the developmental process, assuming that they have at least minimal reliability. Even if speed of development is not a problem, there is the problem of taxing one's resources—parents' patience with the demands of researchers only goes so far. If one wants to assess many different constructs, one has to assess any particular construct with a shorter scale, which often (but not always) implies a reduced level of internal consistency and test–retest reliability. One solution is to focus one's interests more tightly and assess in a highly reliable way. Another is, reliability be damned, full speed ahead. In actual practice, as usual, the two approaches form a spectrum, and most researchers are in the middle ranges. Either side of the spectrum can be productive. Kraemer (1989) has made a case for measuring fewer concepts and measuring them well. My own work tends to be, though not invariably, on the side of the center region where one sacrifices some points of reliability for breadth of measurement.

To illustrate, I will comment on the domain of temperament scales. The various measures of temperament do vary somewhat in their reliability (e.g., see Hubert, Wachs, Peters-Martin, & Gandour, 1982). However, despite there being differences, my own perspective is that there is actually a rough comparability among the scales, with only moderate losses in reliability for using shorter lists of items rather than longer scales. It is not that the scales are all so good, it is more that they are all so mediocre—but they are proving useful nevertheless. To cite the body of our studies (as partly summarized previously), some of the ICQ scales are short but have proved predictive despite limited reliability. Their connections and nonconnections with a variety of other measures of the longitudinal study have advanced our understanding of several concepts, both temperament and nontemperament ones.

Other things being equal, I would rather have good reliability, and certainly make efforts to get it. However, other things are often not equal, and one sometimes may wish to risk lower reliability for the sake of a wider network of comparison measures. The principle that reliability limits validity is an important one. However, validity trumps reliability. The fact that lowered reliability makes it more difficult to find effects does not mean that it makes it impossible. When a connection or pattern holds despite only moderate reliability, one still can add substance to the understanding of development.

Substantively valuable indexes may be refined further, and ones with little success will be abandoned. One tries always for reliable measures, but frequently risks non-optimal reliability for the sake of being able to make additional, conceptually important comparisons. This brings up a more general issue about how one is to pursue scientific goals.

THE CONTEXT OF PHILOSOPHICAL METAPHOR

There must be many interesting patterns of developmental diversity, regularity, and change yet to be described. Parent reports could play a big role in their discovery, but that will not be the point of this section. This section is concerned with the general nature of data in science. The field is generally aware of the philosophical complementarity of the context of discovery and the context of confirmation in science (e.g., see Achenbach, 1982). Some science is directed at predicting what will happen under tightly constrained circumstances. This confirms models of nature. Other, more explorative science is directed at the description of more and more features of the phenomenon. Features are observed and related to previously described phenomena and theories. This stretches models of nature. In the ideal, research should move back and forth between these philosophical contexts, even within a particular study. Nevertheless, one detects, in colleague's informal reactions, in published writings, and especially in grant and journal reviews, a general preference for theory-driven, hypothesis-testing research over descriptive and exploratory work. Theory-driven work seems to cross the gulf from one individual researcher to another more easily. In the field of parent–child relations and children's social development, however, I would argue that fairly basic description of the phenomena of development is also quite important now.

For some people, measures are primarily to be used to test prior hypotheses. These people tend to be distrustful and/or disinterested in reports of research that lack such structure. It would be hard not to appreciate work that empirically tests critical hypotheses derived from competing abstract models. This is a powerful way of demonstrating what is and is not known about the phenomena. Some of my own work does have hypothetical undergirding. However, much of it has to be explorative. Longitudinal studies of social development would probably not be worth the trouble if we actually had to restrict ourselves to analyzing only to evaluate prior hypotheses. We do not even know all the variables that should be assessed, much less how they should all influence each other.

Actually, I do not think that many longitudinal researchers in the area of social development fully accept hypothesis testing as the ideal. However, I do think that the ideal does often constrain researchers' analytic strategies. The questions talked about in the literature tend to be the ones that more easily lend themselves to hypothesis testing language, and "fishing expeditions" are disparaged (Bates et al., 1991). When one disparages some research as a fishing expedition, one is implying an ideal that is opposite to fishing; perhaps that would be farming. Is the area of social development research really at a state of knowledge where our analytic strategies should be bounded by agricultural science metaphors, planting seeds of known variety, nurturing them, and then harvesting what had been expected? In many instances, failures to confirm hypotheses—nonfindings—might be important clues in describing phenomena, and so might unexpected or incompletely expected phenomena. The area of social development is more of a jungle (or wild prairie) than a garden plot. Exploratory metaphors such as fishing or hunting probably are more accurate metaphors for what scientists in our area are actually doing, and the inherent dangers of explorative research are no worse nor less avoidable than those of the alternative style of research (Bates et al., 1991). Following advice to test a limited number of relationships keeps one's "experimentwise error rate" to a minimum; but just because one has not tested a relationship does not mean that the relationship is not actually there.

CONCLUSION

In this chapter, I have discussed the interpretation of parent reports. I conclude that caregiver reports should not simply be dismissed or accepted as TRUTH. They can be seen in a more complete, complex light. The research summarized supports a model of parent reports comprising social perceptions with both objective and subjective components. This model is reassuring in the sense of confirming the potential value of a very widely used kind of data. However, it is more a reminder of the complexity of social developmental phenomena than a truly practical guide for theory or practice. One kind of direction for further research is to look for additional substantive distinctions in the perceptions of parents. Another involves methodological thrusts. I suggest that not only might the scientist learn to appreciate more fully how the parent (or other caregiver) perceives the child's qualities and developmental process, the parent-observer might be guided to give more sophisticated reports. The philosophical underpinnings of these directions of research, like many other topics in the area of social development, should be from both the confirmation and the discovery contexts. In fact, this probably is how most researchers are operating, but there does seem to be a stronger bias to appreciate hypothesis testing methods than to appreciate more descriptive or explorative methods. Especially for the goal of understanding the rich array of meanings of parents' perceptions of child development, increased emphasis on explorative research will be productive.

REFERENCES

Achenbach, T. M. (1982). *Developmental psychopathology* (2nd ed.) New York: Wiley.

Bates, J. E. (1980). The concept of difficult temperament. *Merrill-Palmer Quarterly, 26,* 299–319.

Bates, J. E. (1989). Applications of temperament concepts. In G. A. Kohnstamm, J. E. Bates, & M. K. Rothbart (Eds.) *Temperament in childhood* (pp. 321–355). Chichester: Wiley.

Bates, J. E. (1990). Conceptual and empirical linkages between temperament and behavior problems: A commentary on the Sanson, Prior, and Kyrios study. *Merrill-Palmer Quarterly, 36*(2), 193–199.

Bates, J. E., & Bayles, K. (1984). Objective and subjective components in mothers' perceptions of their children from age 6 months to 3 years. *Merrill-Palmer Quarterly, 30,* 111–130.

Bates, J. E., & Bayles, K. (1988). The role of attachment in the development of behavior problems. In J. Belsky & T. Nezworski (Eds.), *Clinical implications of attachment* (pp. 253–299). Hillsdale, NJ: Lawrence Erlbaum.

Bates, J. E., Bayles, K., Bennett, D. S., Ridge, B., & Brown, M. M. (1991). Origins of externalizing behavior problems at 8 years of age. In D. Pepler & K. Rubin (Eds.), *Development and treatment of childhood aggression* (pp. 93–120). Hillsdale, NJ: Lawrence Erlbaum.

Bates, J. E., Freeland, C. B., & Lounsbury, M. L. (1979). Measurement of infant difficultness. *Child Development 50,* 794–803.

Bates, J. E., Maslin, C. A., & Frankel, K. A. (1985). Attachment security, mother–child interaction, and temperament as predictors of behavior problem ratings at age three years. *Society for Research in Child Development Monographs,* special issue, *Growing points in attachment theory and research,* I. Bretherton & E. Waters (Eds.), Serial No. 209.

Bates, J. E., Shroff, J. M., & DelaFlor, M. G. Parental adaptation to the child's temperament. Presented at "The Challenges of Parenting," Scarborough Psychology Symposium, University of Toronto, March 30, 1990.

Bates, J. E., Miller, E., & Bayles, K. (1984). Understanding the link between difficult temperament and behavior problems: Toward identifying subtypes of difficultness. Paper presented in the symposium *Difficult temperament: Toward an integration of parental, clinical, and research perspectives* at ICIS, New York, April.

Bates, J. E., Olson, S. L., Pettit, G. S., & Bayles, K. (1982). Dimensions of individuality in the mother–infant relationship at 6 months of age. *Child Development, 53,* 446–461.

Behar, L. G. (1977). The preschool behavior questionnaire. *Journal of Abnormal Child Psychology, 5,* 265–275.

Frankel, K. A. & Bates, J. E. (1990). Mother–toddler problem-solving: Antecedents in attachment, home behavior, and temperament. *Child Development, 61,* 810–819.

Hubert, N. C., Wachs, T. D., Peters-Martin, P., & Gandour, M. J. (1982). The study of early temperament: Measurement and conceptual issues. *Child Development, 53,* 571–600.

Ireton, H., & Thwing, E. (1974). *Manual for the Minnesota Child Development Inventory.* Minneapolis: Interpretive Scoring Systems.

Kagan, J. (1983). Stress and coping in early development. In N. Garmezy & M. Rutter (Eds.), *Stress, coping, and development in children.* New York: McGraw-Hill.

Kagan, J., Reznick, J. S., & Snidman, N. (1989). Issues in the study of temperament. In G. A. Kohnstamm, J. E. Bates, & M. K. Rothbart (Eds.), *Temperament in childhood* (pp. 133–144). Chichester, England: Wiley.

Kraemer, H. (1989). Measurement/assessment issues and problems in developmental follow-up. Presented at NICHD conference: *Developmental follow-up strategies.* Bethesda, MD, June 29, 1989.

Lee, C. L., & Bates, J. E. (1985). Mother–child interaction at age 2 years and perceived difficult temperament. *Child Development, 56,* 1314–1325.

Lounsbury, M. L., & Bates, J. E. (1982). The cries of infants of differing levels of perceived temperamental difficultness: Acoustic properties and effects on listeners. *Child Development, 53,* 677–686.

McGuire, W. J. (1969). The nature of attitudes and attitude change. In G. Lindzey & E. Aronson (Eds.), *The handbook of social psychology (2nd ed.): Vol. 3. The individual in a social context* (pp. 136–314). Reading, MA: Addison-Wesley.

Olson, S. L., Bates, J. E., & Bayles, K. (1982). Maternal perceptions of infant and toddler behavior: A longitudinal, construct validation study. *Infant Behavior and Development, 5,* 397–410.

Olson, S. L., Bates, J. E., & Bayles, K. (1984). Mother–infant interaction and the development of individual differences in children's cognitive competence. *Developmental Psychology, 20,* 166–179.

Olson, S. L., Bates, J. E. & Bayles, K. (1989). Predicting long-term developmental outcomes from maternal perceptions of infant and toddler behavior. *Infant Behavior and Development, 12,* 77–92.

Olson, S. L., Bates, J. E., & Bayles, K. (1990). Early antecedents of childhood impulsivity: The role of parent–child interaction, cognitive competence, and temperament. *Journal of Abnormal Child Psychology, 18*(3), 317–334.

Olson, S. L., Bayles, K., & Bates, J. E. (1986). Mother–child interaction and children's speech progress: A longitudinal study of the first 2 years. *Merrill-Palmer Quarterly, 32,* 1–20.

Pettit, G. S., & Bates, J. E. (1984). Continuity of individual differences in the mother–infant relationship from 6 to 13 months. *Child Development, 55,* 729–739.

Pettit, G. S., & Bates, J. E. (1989). Family interaction patterns and children's behavior problems from infancy to age 4 years: Validation of a new method of naturalistic observation. *Developmental Psychology, 25,* 413–420.

Plomin, R., & Bergeman, C. S. (1991). The nature of nurture: Genetic influence on "environmental" measures. *Behavioral and Brain Sciences, 14,* 373–427.

Rizzo, T. A., Corsaro, W. A., & Bates, J. E. (1992). Ethnographic methods and interpretive analysis: Expanding the methodological options of psychologists. *Developmental Review, 12,* 101–123.

Tellegen, A. (1985). Structures of mood and personality and their relevance to assessing anxiety, with an emphasis on self-report. In A. H. Tuma & J. D. Maser (Eds.), *Anxiety and the anxiety disorders* (pp. 681–716). Hillsdale, NJ: Lawrence Erlbaum.

Thomas, A., Chess, S., & Korn, S. J. (1982). The reality of difficult temperament. *Merrill-Palmer Quarterly, 28,* 1–20.

Watson, D., & Clark, L. A. (1984). Negative affectivity: The disposition to experience aversive emotional states. *Psychological Bulletin, 26,* 465–490.

Weissbluth, M. (1989). Sleep-loss stress and temperamental difficultness: Psychobiological processes and practical considerations. In G. A. Kohnstamm, J. E., Bates, & M. K. Rothbart (Eds.), *Temperament in childhood* (pp. 357–375). Chichester, England: Wiley.

Assessment of Cognitive and Language Functioning: A Developmental Perspective

Linda S. Siegel

INTRODUCTION

The assessment of cognitive and language functioning is an important part of longitudinal studies. In this chapter, I will discuss some of the conceptual and methodological issues involved in the measurement of cognitive and language functioning in longitudinal studies. I will also review some of the major assessment devices that are available at each age and discuss the advantages and disadvantages of each. Because one of the purposes of longitudinal studies is to examine continuities in development and compare cognitive and langauge functions at different points in time, I will also describe some of the possible ways of analyzing the relationship between two or more measures administered at various points in a longitudinal study and discuss the conceptual and statistical aspects of each method.

GLOBAL SCORES VERSUS ASSESSMENTS OF
SPECIFIC FUNCTIONS

As our knowledge of cognitive and language development has expanded, we have moved away from the idea of an overall developmental level, represented by one score, such as an IQ score (Siegel, 1991). We have become aware that there are many different kinds of cognitive skills. Children may have different levels in each of these skills so an overall score is not a useful way of conceptualizing the functioning of an individual.

One of the most important principles of assessment should be the assessment of specific functions, rather than one general score, should be used. The measurement of specific functions is particularly necessary for assessments of school-age children, but it is relevant at any age. Global scores, such as IQ scores, are not particularly useful and do not provide any information about specific abilities. It is important to recognize that an IQ score is derived from a number of diverse functions and represents a statistical average, but not a particularly meaningful one, of the functioning of an individual. Two individuals may have identical IQ scores but one may have above average language skills and below average visual-spatial skills, whereas the other may be average in both. Obviously, we need to consider the pattern of performance as well as the overall score. The IQ score may be useful as a screening device to isolate individuals at the extremes of the distribution, but it does not provide detailed measures of cognitive processes. In this chapter, the measurement of specific functions will be discussed in detail, with attention to some appropriate measures at each age.

TYPES OF ASSESSMENT

The dilemma faced by investigators in longitudinal studies is whether or not to use standardized tests or experimental tasks that measure much more specific functions. The obvious advantage of standardized tests is that there are norms and procedures that are available. The disadvantage is that often it is not clear what function is being measured, and a particular test may measure several functions at the same time. Therefore, if a child achieves a low score it is not clear what is causing the low score. Specifically, consider a language test such as the Reynell Developmental Language Scales (Reynell, 1985). The child might be asked to "Put the brown cow next to the pink pig." Successful performance means that the child must both understand the terms used in the sentence and must remember the sentence. Suppose the child puts the *white* cow next to the pink pig. We might conclude that the child doesn't understand the sentence, but this conclusion could be incorrect. If the child fails, we do not know whether it is because he or she did not understand the words or, alternatively, forgot some of the critical words in the sentence, such as the color of the cow. Or consider the child who is required to define words on any one of a number of tests such as the McCarthy Scales of Childrens Abilities (McCarthy, 1972) or the Wechsler Intelligence Scale for Children—Revised (WISC-R; Wechsler, 1974). Suppose the child fails a particular item. It may be that the child does not know the meaning of the word or it may be that he or she cannot find the words to express an idea. This kind of expressive language problem is quite common among certain types of learning disabled individuals and could interfere with an understanding of the child's performance. Failure may reflect an inability to find the correct expressive language or it may indicate a lack of knowledge about the word.

Another conceptual issue is how to measure different functions at different ages. The nature of development in the early years is such that abilities change very rapidly over time and one cannot use the same measurement devices at different points in development. For example, consider the case of language development. Early in development, language consists of babbling, responsiveness to voices, and imitation of sounds, whereas later in development, the child understands and produces complex sentences. The diverse abilities are measured in different ways and, on the surface, do not resemble each other. However, they are manifestations of the same underlying language function and although they do not seem to be like each other, are strongly related. I have found that there are significant correlations between measures of language development early in infancy and measures of language development at school age, although, on the surface, these measures do not seem to be similar to each other. For example, there are statistically significant correlations between the Imitation-Comprehension and the Vocalization-Social Scales of the Kohen-Raz analysis (Kohen-Raz, 1967) of the Bayley Scales of Infant Development (Bayley, 1969) at 12 months, and language comprehension and expression scales of the Reynell Developmental Language Scales at 2 years (Siegel, 1981a, 1981b) and 3 years (Siegel, 1979), and the McCarthy Verbal Scale at 5 years (Siegel, in press-b).

There are other examples of this apparent lack of structural correspondence between early and later abilities, but similarity in the deep structure of behavior. I have found that there is a correlation of .41 ($p < .001$) between the Beery Developmental Test of Visual Motor Integration (VMI), a measure of eye–hand coordination administered at 6 years, and the Psychomotor (PDI) scale of the Bayley administered at 4 months. The Bayley PDI measures such abilities as grasping, reaching, and head control. The Beery VMI (Beery, 1967) measures the ability to preserve spatial and size relationships when copying shapes. Obviously, these abilities are quite different on the surface and it may seem curious that a relationship should exist between them. However, it is possible that these measures, the Bayley PDI and the Beery

VMI, are both different reflections of the level of maturation of fine-motor coordination. A delay early in development may be evidence of the slow maturation of that function and this slow rate of development may be reflected in aspects of that function that mature at a later time. We cannot ask a 4-month-old infant to copy shapes, but we can measure behaviors that, on the surface, do not resemble the later behavior but share the same underlying process.

Similarly, I have found that motor behavior, as measured in the first year of life, is more highly correlated than cognitive functioning with language behavior at 3 and 5 years. Although this seems like a paradox because cognitive and language development are closely related, it is not surprising. There is evidence that language is related to the development of certain structures in the brain. It is probably the case that early motor development, as measured by the Bayley PDI, provides an indication of the level of early brain development and a clearer picture than cognitive function because we know more about how to measure motor development more precisely, and it may be less sensitive to attentional effects that create measurement errors. Assuming continuity of function and that early delays will be related to later delays, then the more sensitive and accurate measure, in this case motor development, should show a stronger relationship to later functioning. Investigators need to be wary of assuming that behaviors must resemble each other to be related. Behaviors may be manifestations of the same underlying structure, but appear quite different. It is probably best to approach the measurement of cognitive and language function without any assumptions that behaviors must share the same surface structure to be related. We need to look beyond the surface structure to the deep structure of behavior. Of course, it cannot be assumed that behaviors that are correlated share the same deep structure. The correlation between two variables does not mean that they necessarily are manifestations of one underlying process. However, it is important that investigators consider the possibility of relationships among processes and behaviors that appear to be quite different.

SUGGESTED ASSESSMENT PROCEDURES

Experimental tasks, if properly designed, can be used to achieve a clearer definition of functional abilities. However, as noted earlier, norms and procedures for experimental tasks are not available and must be developed in pilot work. To measure a broad range of functions at different ages, there are a variety of standardized tests that are available. The following suggestions for specific assessments are made in reference to standardized tests and represent a developmental perspective.

Infancy—Birth to 2 Years

The Bayley Scales (Bayley, 1969) provide useful measures of infant development. The Bayley scales are composed of two scales, the Mental Development Index (MDI) that measures cognitive and perceptual development and the Psychomotor Development Index (PDI) that measures motor development. There is also a technique to analyze smaller subsets of items on the MDI into more homogeneous scales, the Kohen-Raz scalogram analysis developed by Kohen-Raz (1967). To assess more specific functions, the Kohen-Raz analysis of the Bayley MDI items is useful.

The Kohen-Raz analysis separates many of the Bayley MDI items into five subscales: Eye–Hand Coordination (e.g., "reaches for dangling ring," "puts three or more cubes in cup"), Manipulation (e.g., "simple play with rattle," "fingers holes in pegboard"), Conceptual Relations (e.g., "uncovers toy," "exploitative paper play"), Imitation-Comprehension (e.g., "responds to verbal request," "imitates crayon strokes"), and Vocalization-Social (e.g., "repeats performance laughed at," "says da-da or equivalent").

I have used the Kohen-Raz analysis (Siegel, 1979, 1983a, 1983b, 1989b) to show that certain subsets of items are differentially predictive at different times in development, with the functions that are the developing most quickly at a particular point in time becoming the most predictive. For example, in Siegel (1979), I examined the relationship between the Kohen-Raz subscales of the Bayley MDI and performance on the Reynell Developmental Language Scale and the Stanford Binet at 30 and 36 months. In examining the relationship between the Kohen-Raz subscales and the performance on the Stanford Binet at 30 and 36 months, the Eye–Hand and Manipulation scales, early in development (at 4, 8, and sometimes, 12 months), showed the highest and most significant correlations with the later IQ scores, whereas at 8 and 12 months, the Conceptual Relations scale showed the strongest relationship. At 18 and 24 months the two language scales, Imitation-Comprehension and Vocalization-Social, became the most predictive, although the Eye–Hand Coordination subscale was also significantly correlated with the later developmental scores. A similar pattern was noted for language comprehension and expressive language skills as measured by the Reynell Developmental Language Scales when the relationship was examined between the Kohen-Raz subscales and the Reynell scores at 3 and 4 years (Siegel, 1979, 1982a).

In Siegel (1989b), the relationship between the Kohen-Raz subscales and a variety of skills at 6 and 8 years, including WISC-R IQ, reading, arithmetic, understanding of syntax, and fine motor coordination skills, was studied. The pattern of results indicated that for IQ scores at 6 and 8 years, the two perceptual motor scales of the Kohen-Raz, Eye–Hand Coordination and Manipulation scales, were predictors throughout infancy, the Conceptual Abilities scale was the most predictive at 8 and 12 months, and the two language scales of the Kohen-Raz were the most predictive at 18 and 24 months. Thus, the results that I have noted earlier—that different developmental functions predicted IQ test scores and language comprehension and expressive language scores at 3 and 4 years—were replicated with a variety of developmental functions in middle childhood, indicating the value of this type of more detailed developmental analysis as opposed to using only global scores. Eventually, it will become possible to analyze these patterns for an individual child by examining which subscale scores significantly deviate from each other, thus increasing our knowledge of the child's performance and providing a sounder basis for remediation, if it is necessary.

There is another useful feature of the Kohen-Raz analysis. Ross (1985) used the Kohen-Raz analysis to assess the differences and similarities between full-term and preterm infants and found that the preterm infants had deficits in language expression and comprehension, imitation, and eye–hand coordination. The use of subscales, rather than global scores, made possible the analysis of specific strengths and weaknesses.

One note of caution is in order concerning the use of the Kohen-Raz system. The Kohen-Raz provides only raw, not age adjusted, scores. Therefore, it is not possible to compare children at different ages. There are probably more detailed subscale analyses that could be developed. Apparently, a new revision of the Bayley intends to categorize the items to subscales and will be more useful (Gyurke, 1990). It should be noted that the Bayley motor scale (PDI) is quite useful and, unfortunately, often omitted from analyses of infant functioning. I have found that the Bayley PDI scores in the first year of life were more predictive than the MDI scale of later language scores (Siegel, 1979, 1981a, 1981b). I would like to add one additional practical note about data analysis. If there are the resources to do so, it is better to enter the scores from individual items, in addition to total scores, into the computer when conducting the analyses of tests. This procedure allows grouping the items into meaningful units after the data are collected and will provide the most useful analyses.

DOMAIN SPECIFICITY

The use of the Kohen-Raz exemplifies the concept of domain specificity, namely, that it is important to measure different functions separately and to not assume that relationships and findings are characteristic of all processes. Studies of low-birthweight and very-low-birthweight children typically report that visual-spatial, perceptual, and motor functioning is more impaired than language functioning. (For a detailed review, see Barsky & Siegel, 1992). Often, receptive vocabulary is not impaired in premature children when compared to full-term comparison groups, but expressive language skills, syntactic awareness, and memory are problematic.

I have also shown that it is useful to analyze more specific skills at points in development other than infancy (Siegel, 1989b). There is some specificity in functions both for the predictions and the outcome measures, that is, certain of the Kohen-Raz subscales predicted some specific skills but did not predict other skills. For the language-related skills of reading and spelling, for the direct measures of language skill (i.e., understanding of syntax), and for the Vocabulary subscale of the WISC-R, the Kohen-Raz language subscales, Imitation-Comprehension and Vocalization-Social, were significantly better predictors than the two perceptual motor scales, Eye–Hand Coordination and Manipulation. For visual-spatial skills as measured by the Block Design subtest of the WISC-R (a computational arithmetic test—the Wide Range Achievement Arithmetic subtest), and the fine-motor coordination as measured by the Beery Developmental Test of Visual-Motor Integration, early perceptual-motor scales were more predictive than later scales of language function. These results indicate both domain specificity in the predictive nature of infant tests and the value of studying more detailed functions than global test scores. The Kohen-Raz analysis of the Bayley seems to be quite useful in understanding the cognitive fine-motor perceptual, receptive, and expressive language processes of the young child.

Although they did not use the Kohen-Raz system, Largo, Graf, Kundu, Hunziker, and Molinari (1990) conducted similar analyses with the subscales of the Griffiths Test for infants. Largo et al. found that the Social and Language Scales of the Griffiths were more highly correlated with the WISC-R Verbal than Performance Scale, but that in some cases scores of the Locomotor Scale were more highly correlated with the WISC-R Performance IQ score than were the Social and Language scores.

Two Years

The Bayley scales and the Language Expression and Comprehension scales of the Reynell Development Language Scales-Revised (Reynell, 1985) are useful at 2 years. The comprehension scale assesses the child's understanding of words, phrases, and sentences. The child is presented with verbal instructions and a set of objects and asked, for example, to "Put the spoon in the cup" or "show me the longest pencil." The expression scale measures the child's ability to name objects, for example, sock, car, and doll, to name pictures, for example, chair, flower, and window, and to describe a scene in a series of pictures. The Bayley MDI scale contains some items that are quite indicative of language development. Cooper, Fitzhardinge, Siegel, and Ash (1989) found that certain of the language items of the Bayley showed a stronger relationship than the total Bayley MDI score to other language measures such as the Reynell scales taken at the same time. This small subset of language items was more accurate than the overall Bayley MDI in detecting language problems of 2-year-old children. Cooper et al. (1989) found that a low score (< 85) on the Bayley MDI predicted language delay as measured by the Reynell. However, there were a number of children who were identified as being in the average range on the Bayley MDI who had scores indicating language delay on the Reynell. These percentages were 26% when the corrected MDI score was used, and 20% when the uncorrected MDI score was used. When the language items from the Bayley were scored separately as a subscale, failures on these language items identified 90% of the language-delayed children that the Bayley MDI score had failed to identify. In addition to demonstrating that a more detailed analysis of items rather than global scores can yield meaningful results, this analysis also shows that the measurement of specific functions, rather than global scores, can yield a more accurate picture of the functioning of the child.

Three and 4 Years

At 3 years, the Reynell (described earlier) is a useful measure of language development. The Stanford-Binet and the McCarthy may also be helpful. The McCarthy Scales of Children's Ability (MSCA; McCarthy, 1972) are composed of five subscales that measure various aspects of the young child's cognitive and language abilities. The MSCA is appropriate for children in the age range 2 1/2 to 8 1/2 years. The Verbal Scale measures language abilities and is composed of tasks such as defining words, producing the opposites of words, and remembering words and sentences. The Perceptual Performance Scale includes tasks such as copying block structures, assembling puzzles, and copying designs and the Quantitative Scale is designed to measure knowledge of numbers and quantitative terminology. The Memory Scale measures verbal and nonverbal short-term memory. The Motor Scale measures gross and fine motor skills, for example, walking on a narrow line, hopping on one foot, and imitating arm movements. The advantage of the McCarthy is that it samples a wide range of cognitive functions and that young children particularly enjoy doing the test as it involves some motor activity. The difficulty, however, is that it is impossible to calculate deviation, age-adjusted scores on the individual subtest scales from the McCarthy. One can calculate scores from the five scales, but the individual subtests do not provide scale scores in the manner of the WISC-R. It would be useful if the McCarthy had this feature.

The Stanford-Binet (Thorndike, Hagen, & Sattler, 1986) measures verbal skills, for example, defining words, comprehension of social situations, short-term memory for words and visual patterns, number concepts, and visual-spatial skills such as copying shapes. Unlike the earlier version, it is divided into subscales. There is, however, a problem with the Stanford-Binet in that if a child does not achieve a baseline on a particular subtest, the score for the subtest cannot be counted. This scoring system makes for some difficulty of interpretation of the total score.

The Illinois Test of Psycholinguistic Ability (ITPA) Grammatic Closure subtest (Kirk, McCarthy, & Kirk, 1968) is a useful measure of language development and appropriate for 3- to 7-year-olds. In cases of delayed language development, we have found that it is useful at least until the age of 12 years (Siegel & Ryan, 1988).

Five Years

The Stanford-Binet and the McCarthy can be used at 5 years and also the Florida Kindergarten Screening Battery, nonword repetition subtest of the Goldman Fristoe Woodcock (Goldman, Fristoe, Woodcock, 1974) and perhaps the McCarthy or the Wechler Preschool and Primary Scale of Intelligence (WPPSI). The Lindamood Auditory Conceptualization Test (Lindamood & Lindamood, 1971) measures phonemic analyses and synthesis skills, and may be a good indicator of the level of development of prerequisites for basic literary skills.

Six to 12 Years

The WISC-R (Wechsler, 1974) is a useful measure of overall cognitive functioning, although, as noted earlier, it is a composite score and does not provide information about specific problems. The WISC-R also underestimates IQ in the case of children with learning disabilities because it involves tests of long- and short-term memory, expressive language, and fine-motor coordination, and learning disabled children may have problems in one or more of these areas. It is a mistake to think that the WISC-R is a pure measure of cognitive ability independent of educational influences. For an extended discussion of these issues, see Siegel (1988a, 1989a, 1989b, 1990).

The Wide Range Achievement Test (WRAT-R; Jastak & Wilkinson, 1984) provides a measure of early reading, spelling, and arithmetic skills. At ages 7 and up, writing, word recognition, nonword reading, spelling, and arithmetic should be measured. The WRAT is useful at any age from 7 years into adulthood. There are norms for 6-year-olds but they are probably not very useful because of the variability in exposure to reading, spelling, and arithmetic that children receive in the first years of instruction in these subjects.

It is often thought to be important to measure reading comprehension. Although reading comprehension is an important construct, reading "comprehension" tests, as they are currently constructed, have a number of serious conceptual and methodological problems. First of all, most of the questions do not really involve an inference, but merely searching the text for the correct verbatim phrase (Tal & Siegel, 1990). A number of the questions can be answered without reading the passage (Tal & Siegel, 1990). As these tests are timed, speed rather than quality of reading is probably being measured. For example, Biemiller and Siegel (1990) found that by giving children a little extra time, their reading scores increased dramatically. However, the most serious problem with the use of a low score on reading comprehension tests is that children with a low score of a reading comprehension test and good word recognition skills are not different from good readers on syntax and phonological processing tasks, whereas children with poor word recognition skills have significantly poorer phonological processing, syntactic awareness, and short-term and working memory skills than normal readers. For these reasons, it would seem to be important to emphasize word recognition and pseudoword reading skills, and not poor "comprehension" skills, in the study of reading.

The Beery Test of Visual Motor Integration is a good measure of fine motor coordination and is most useful in the 5- to 13-year-old age range. The Connors Parent and Teacher checklists (Goyette, Connors, & Ulrich, 1978) are useful. The Achenbach Child Behavior Checklist (Achenbach & Edelbrock, 1983) is also useful and well validated.

LIMITATIONS OF ASSESSMENT

There are many extraneous factors that may limit the value of the assessment. Some of these factors reside in the test devices; they may be inadequately normed, inappropriate for the particular subjects being used, and/or sample a limited set of behaviors. They may confound different processes, such as memory and language factors as discussed earlier in this chapter. Although these processes may co-occur in, for example, understanding discourse, investigators should exercise some degree of caution in interpreting test or task scores as measuring only *one* process. Some of the limitations may be a function of child variables, such as inattention and distractibility, limits on the amount of time that a child will sit still and be cooperative, practice effects, difference in test-taking strategies, and so on. It seems to me that the critical factor is to be aware of these limitations and try to minimize them.

CORRECTION FOR PREMATURITY

If there are premature children in the sample, there is a special problem. This problem is the issue of whether or not to correct the scores of the premature child for the degree of prematurity. The issue is whether to calculate age based on the date of their birth (chronological age) or whether to correct the chronological age for the degree of prematurity (corrected age).

Thus, a child who is born 2 months early (e.g., 32 weeks conceptional age instead of the normal 40 weeks) can be considered either a 4-month-old or a 2-month-old when the child is assessed 4 months after the date of his or her birth. The question is an important one because the determination of the normality or deviance of a child's performance on a particular test may depend on which age measure is used. There is a great deal of debate and concern about what constitutes the appropriate score. In a study of correction, I found that for the first year of life, the corrected scores correlated more highly with subsequent scores but after that point, the *uncorrected* scores were better predictors (Siegel, 1983a). Until we have definitive answers to the question of correction, the most reasonable solution would seem to be to use both scores in the reporting of the outcome. Both these types of scores can be calculated from the age norms on standardized tests.

SOME ALTERNATIVE APPROACHES TO DATA ANALYSIS

Once all these data are collected, the investigator is faced with the task of analyzing it. I will deal with some alternative data analyses that are useful in the case of studies attempting to find the nature of the relationships that may exist between measures taken early in development and those obtained at a later time.

For years developmentalists have used certain traditional methods for analyzing data of this nature. The usual method is to use the correlation coefficient, a statistic that measures the relationship between two variables, and it is assumed that this statistic is the most appropriate one to use. However, I would like to argue that the correlation coefficient is inadequate for the examination of the questions about continuity in development. One of the major problems is that the correlation coefficient does not provide information about an individual child.

For example, let us imagine that the following distribution of scores is obtained on Time 1 and Time 2 for five children: child 1, 120, and 128; child 2, 122 and 120; child 3, 124 and 126; child 4, 126 and 122; and child 5, 128 and 124. The correlation between these two sets of scores is − .33. Yet, all of these scores are actually within a narrow range, and the 10 scores would indicate that all these individuals were in the above-average range at both Time 1 and Time 2. In a sense, this is a perfect prediction for each individual, but the correlation is not statistically significant. The correlation coefficient by itself would not allow the determination of the relationship for an individual.

The correlation is particulary sensitive to the characteristics of the distribution. For example, if the range of scores is narrow and the distribution of scores is fairly homogeneous, the correlation will be spuriously low. An illustration from a study of the predictability of infant tests will demonstrate this problem. Lewis and Brooks-Gunn (1981) reported a nonsignificant correlation between the Bayley scores in the first year and scores on the Bayley at 2 years. However, the mean scores at 3 months in the Bayley for their Sample 2 was 126.9 (SD = 15.44) and 24 months 152.0 (SD = 6.74). Obviously, with such high scores and such a narrow range, it is unlikely that there will be significant correlations. Furthermore, it could be said that the actual prediction was quite good if outcome within a range was used. It appears that all the children who had above-average scores at Time 1 also had above-average scores at Time 2. If this is the case, the prediction is perfect. It should be noted that the scores were not as high for their Sample 1, but on the 24-month MDI, M = 126.42 and SD = 18.90, so that virtually all the 2-year-old children had scores at least one standard deviation above the mean. Illingworth (1967) has also noted that a number of studies of the predictability of infant tests have this problem of range restriction and that the correlation coefficient is an inadequate statistic to represent what is actually happening to an individual child.

In this chapter, I will deal with some alternative data analysis methods. Specifically, I will deal with two types of problems, how we compare groups and how we study the relationships between two measures at different points in time.

For virtually all developmental tests and tasks, the scores obtained form a continuous distribution; the assumption is that the scale is an equal interval one, that is, the magnitude of the difference between scores at all points of the scale is equal. This assumption is problematic because differences at different points in the scale do not necessarily mean the same amount of difference in function. For example, most developmental tests probably make finer distinctions and the differences are more important at both ends of the scale, most particularly at the lower end—the difference between an IQ of 75 and 85 is probably more meaningful than the difference between an IQ of 100 and 110, primarily because of what these differences will predict. In terms of actual functioning, we are more concerned with the children at the lower end who are having problems, and the differences in the middle are of very little significance in terms of the diagnosis of a problem, educational practice, or the provision of remedial services.

In the comparison between tasks, the assumption is that the relationship is a linear one; that is, the relationship does not change throughout the distribution. Consistent with what has been noted earlier in this chapter, there may be a stronger relationship between low scores at different points in time but no strong relationship between scores in the middle range. The assumption of linearity inherent in the correlation coefficient would not capture this curvilinear relationship.

I suggest that the following alternative strategies be used rather than the correlation coefficient, which is the typical method of analysis. One alternative strategy is to compare the children who are doing well on the outcome measure in question with those who are not. These groups can be compared on the earlier measures to determine the mean and distribution differences that are obtained between the two groups. This strategy may be quite useful in providing information about the measure in question. An example of the use of this method is illustrated in Miller and Siegel (1989). We have compared the Bayley scores of groups of children who showed a language delay at 3 years with those who did not. There was a significant difference between these groups in their Bayley scores, even as early as 4 months. For example, the 3-year-old normal Language Comprehension group had a mean of 99.02 on the Bayley PDI scale at 4 months, whereas the mean at 4 months of those who would subsequently show a delay at 3 years in Language Comprehension was 78.60. This difference was significant ($p < .001$), with relatively no overlap between the two groups, indicating that the Bayley PDI is capable of discriminating between children who will subsequently show language delay and those who will not. The correlation between the Bayley PDI at 4 months and the Reynell Language Comprehension Scale at 3 years was .40, which was statistically significant but indicated only a moderate relationship. In this case, the alternative analysis gave a different picture than the correlation. This strategy has also been used in Siegel (1979, 1981a, 1982a, 1982b, 1983b).

It should be noted that when we are examining differences between groups, we really should be comparing the overlap of the distributions. If the overlap of the distributions is considerable, then even though there may be significant mean differences, it is not clear that these differences are clinically significant.

THE CATEGORIZATION APPROACH

There is an alternative approach that can be called the *categorization approach.* The type of analysis that is most meaningful allows the determination of prediction of accuracy for the individual child. This type of analysis involves a type of "truth table." Children are classified into one of the following categories: *true negatives* who have a score in the normal range in childhood and had an average score in infancy; *false negatives* who have a low score in childhood but who had an average score in infancy; *true positives* who were selected as having low scores in both infancy and childhood; and *false positives* who had low scores in infancy, but not in childhood. This type of prediction also allows for a statement about the individual child; correlations, on the other hand, are based on group data and cannot tell us about an individual child. I have used this approach in Siegel (1982a, 1982b, 1982c, 1984, 1985a, 1985b, 1988b, 1989a) and Siegel and Cunningham (1984) and found that infant tests are typically quite successful in predicting category membership.

Illingworth (1967) also proposed this type of approach in which it is determined if a child remains in a particular category of functioning throughout the course of the time period being studied. Illingworth argued for the use of categories rather than exact scores. In a review of a number of studies of the stability of infant assessments, Illingworth showed that in all of the studies, most of the infants remained in the same category, and that low scores in infancy predicted problems later in development. Illingworth reports data to suggest that assessments done in infancy were quite predictive of school age functioning when categories such as above average, average, below average, and inferior were used.

Using this categorization analysis, Largo et al. (1990) have shown that Griffiths test scores at 9–24 months predicted general category of functioning at 7–9 years and recommend this categorization approach, "From a clinical point of view, categorizing children according to their level of mental performance is a more appropriate method of studying prediction than correlation analysis" (Largo et al., 1990, p. 41).

A related approach is to examine patterns of change and stability for an individual child. If there is no stability, it is important to examine the reasons for this. For example, I have shown that when the home environment scores of the false negative and true negatives were compared, the false negative came from less stimulating environments, and when the false positives and true positives were compared, the false positives came from more stimulating environments (Siegel, 1981a, 1982a,c). These findings suggest that good environments may be able to partially counteract the effects of whatever is causing the problem in the development of the infant, and that there is an interaction between developmental status and environment such that prediction should take into account the environment as well as the infant test scores or the risk factors. Bradley et al. (1989) have used this approach to analyze individual change and stability. Combining data on the Home Scale and the Bayley Scale (MDI), they found that developmental outcomes were poorer for those children who had low HOME scores and low Bayley scores than children who had low scores on only one of these measures.

Finally, in terms of comparing tests or tasks at two points in time, particularly when one is concerned about predictive validity, a 2 × 2 table should be used in which the proportion of true and false positives and negatives is calculated. This will tell us much more about the predictive ability of a test. This procedure involves the use of cut-off scores. As cut-off scores are arbitrary and it is difficult to know which is the correct one, consideration should be given to the use of multiple cut-off scores in deciding whether or not there is a problem. With the advent of computer technology, it is possible to analyze the same data with a variety of methods and to try different cut-off scores to see which gives the best picture. We need to consider these alternative data analysis techniques to examine both group differences and the relationship between test scores at different ages.

SUMMARY

In summary, I suggest that the following strategies are useful in developmental assessment: (a) analyze specific cognitive processes, (b) pay careful attention to the requirements of the test or task, (c) recognize the limitations of the correlational analysis, (d) analyze individual patterns of response, and (e) analyze the factors related to the patterns of stability and change for individual children. It is important to recognize both the value and the limitations of assessment.

ACKNOWLEDGMENTS

The preparation of this chapter was supported by grants from the Ontario Mental Health Foundation and the Natural Sciences and Engineering Research Council of Canada. The author wishes to thank Sonia DePasqua and Letty Guirnela for secretarial assistance.

REFERENCES

Achenbach, T. M., & Edelbrock, C. (1983). *Manual for the Child Behavior Checklist.* Department of Psychiatry, University of Vermont, Burlington, Vermont.

Barsky, V. E., & Siegel, L. S. (1992). Predicting future cognitive, academic, and behavioral outcomes for very low birthweight (<1500 grams) infants. In S. L. Friedman & M. Sigman (Eds.), *The psychological development of low birthweight children: Advances in applied development psychology.* (275–289) Norwood, NJ: Ablex.

Bayley, N. (1969). *Bayley Scales of Infant Development.* New York: Psychological Corp.

Biemiller, A., & Siegel, L. S. (1990). *The role of speed, accuracy, syntactic awareness, and working memory: A developmental study.* Unpublished manuscript.

Bradley, R. H., Caldwell, B. M., Rock, S. L., Ramey, C. T., Barnard, K. E., Gray, C., Hammond, M. A., Mitchell, S., Gottfried, A. W., Siegel, L. S., & Johnson, D. L. (1989). Home environment and cognitive development in the first three years of life: A collaborative study involving six cites and three ethnic groups in North America. *Developmental Psychology, 25,* 217–235.

Beery, K. (1967). *Developmental Test of Visual Motor Integration.* Chicago: Follett.

Cooper, D. C., Fitzhardinge, P., Siegel, L. S., & Ash, A. (1989). *Using the Bayley Scales of Infant Development to diagnose language delay in two-year-old high risk infants.* Paper presented at the International Neuropsychology Society meeting, Vancouver, B.C.

Goldman, R., Fristoe, M., & Woodcock, R. W. (1974). *GFW Sound-Symbol Tests.* Circle Pines, MN: American Guidance Service.

Goyette, G. H., Connors, C. K., & Ulrich, R. F. (1978). Normative data on the revised Connors parent and teacher rating scales. *Journal of Abnormal Child Psychology, 6,* 221–236.

Gyurke, J. (1989). Personal communication. San Antonio, TX: The Psychological Corporation.

Illingworth, R. S. (1967). *The development of the infant and young child: Normal and Abnormal.* Edinburgh: Livingstone.

Jastak, S., & Wilkinson, G. S. (1984). *The Wide Range Achievement Test—Revised.* Wilmington, DE: Jastak Associates.

Kirk, S., McCarthy, J., & Kirk, W. D. (1968). *Illinois Test of Psycholinguistic Abilities.* Urbana: University of Illinois Press.

Kohen-Raz, R. (1967). Scalogram analysis of some developmental sequences of infant behavior as measured by the Bayley Infant Scale of Mental Development. *Genetic Psychology Monographs, 76,* 3–21.

Largo, R. H., Graf, S., Kundu, S., Hunziker, U., & Molinari, L. (1990). Predicting developmental outcome at school age from infant tests of normal, at-risk and retarded infants. *Developmental Medicine and Child Neurology, 32,* 30–45.

Lewis, M., Brooks Gunn, J. (1981). Visual attention at three months as a predictor of cognitive functioning at two years of age. *Intelligence, 5,* 131–140.

Lindamood, C. H., & Lindamood, P. C. (1971). *Lindamood Auditory Conceptualization Test—Revised Edition.* Allen, TX: DLM Resources.

McCarthy, D. (1972). *McCarthy Scales of Children's Abilities.* New York: Psychological Corp.

Miller, J., & Siegel, L. S. (1989). Cognitive and social factors as predictors of normal and atypical language development. In S. von Tetzchner, L. S. Siegel, & L. Smith (Eds.), *The social and cognitive aspects of normal and atypical language development.* New York: Springer-Verlag.

Reynell, J. K. (1985). *Reynell Developmental Language Scales—Second Edition.* Windsor, UK: NFER-Nelson.

Ross, G. (1985). Use of the Bayley Scales to characterize abilities of premature infants. *Child Development, 56,* 835–842.

Siegel, L. S. (1979). Infant perceptual, cognitive, and motor behaviors as predictors of subsequent cognitive and language development. *Canadian Journal of Psychology, 33,* 382–395.

Siegel, L. S. (1981a). Infant tests as predictors of cognitive and language development at two years. *Child Development, 52,* 545–557.

Siegel, L. S. (1981b). The use of a Piagetian analysis of infant development to predict cognitive and language development at two years. In M. P. Friedman (Ed.), *Intelligence and learning.* New York: Plenum.

Siegel, L. S. (1982a). Early cognitive and environmental correlates of language development at 4 years. *International Journal of Behavioral Development, 5,* 433–444.

Siegel, L. S. (1982b). Reproductive, perinatal and environmental factors as predictors of development of preterm (<1501 grams) and full-term children at 5 years. *Seminars in Perinatology, 6,* 274–279.

Siegel, L. S. (1982c). Reproductive, perinatal, and environmental factors as predictors of the cognitive and language development of preterm infants. *Child Development, 53,* 963–973.

Siegel, L. S. (1983a). Correction for prematurity and its consequences for the assessment of very low birthweight infant. *Child Development, 54,* 1176–1188.

Siegel, L. S. (1983b). Predicting possible learning disabilities in preterm and full-term infants. In T. Field & A. Sostek (Eds.), *Infants born at risk: Physiological, psychological, perceptual processes.* (295–315) New York: Grune & Stratton.

Siegel, L. S. (1984). Home environmental influences on cognitive development in preterm and full-term children. In A. W. Gottfried (Ed.), *Home environment and early mental development.* New York: Academic Press.

Siegel, L. S. (1985a). Biological and environmental variables as predictors of intellectual functioning at 6 years. In S. Harel & N. Anastasiow (Eds.), *The at-risk infant: Psycho/socio/medical aspects.* (pp. 65–73). Baltimore, MD: Brookes.

Siegel, L. S. (1985b). A risk index to predict learning problems in preterm and full-term children. In W. K. Frankenburg, R. N. Emde, & J. W. Sullivan (Eds.), *Early identification of children at risk: An international perspective.* (pp. 231–243) New York: Plenum.

Siegel, L. S. (1988a). Evidence that IQ scores are irrelevant to the definition and analysis of reading disability. *Canadian Journal of Psychology, 42,* 201–215.

Siegel, L. S. (1988b). A system for the early detection of learning disabilities. *Canadian Journal of Special Education, 4,* 115–122.

Siegel, L. S. (1989a). Detection of learning disabilities in infancy using a risk index. In N. W.

Paul (Ed.), *Research in infant assessment.* (119–126) White Plains, NY: March of Dimes Birth Defects Foundation.

Siegel, L. S. (1989b). A reconceptualization of prediction from infant test scores. In M. Bornstein & N. Krasnegor (Eds.), *Stability and continuity in mental development.* (pp 80–94). Hillsdale, NJ: Lawrence Erlbaum.

Siegel, L. S. (1990). IQ and learning disabilities: R.I.P. In H. L. Swanson & B. Keogh (Eds.), *Learning disabilities: Theoretical and research issues.* Hillsdale, NJ: Lawrence Erlbaum.

Siegel, L. S. (1991). On the maturation of developmental psychology. In F. Kessel, M. Bornstein, & A. Sameroff (Eds.), *Festschrift for William Kessen.* Hillsdale, NJ: Lawrence Erlbaum.

Siegel, L. S. (1992). Infant motor, cognitive, and language behaviors as predictors of achievement at school age. In C. Rovee-Collier & L. Lipsitt (Eds.), *Advances in infancy research,* Vol. 7. New York: Ablex.

Siegel, L. S. (1994). The long-term prognosis of preterm infants: Conceptual, methodological and ethical issues. *Human Nature, 5,* 103–126.

Siegel, L. S., & Cunningham, C. E. (1984). Social interactions: A transactional approach with illustrations from children with developmental problems. In A. Doyle, D. Gold, & D. S. Moskowitz (Eds.), *Children in families under stress.* (pp. 85–98) San Francisco: Jossey-Bass.

Siegel, L. S., & Ryan, E. B. (1988). Development of grammatical sensitivity, phonological, and short-term memory skills in normally achieving and learning disabled children. *Developmental Psychology, 24,* 28–37.

Tal, N. F., Siegel, L. S., Mardun, M. (in press). Reading comprehension: The role of question type and reading ability. *Reading and Writing: An Interdisciplinary Journal*

Thorndike, R. L., Hagen, E. P., & Sattler, J. M. (1986). *The Stanford-Binet Intelligence Scale: Fourth Edition.* Chicago: Riverside.

Wechsler, D. (1974). Manual for the *Wechsler Intelligence Scale for Children-Revised.* New York: Psychological Corp.

Environmental Issues in Developmental Follow-up Research

Bettye M. Caldwell
Robert H. Bradley

INTRODUCTION

Among the most notable advances in child development research in the past generation has been the delineation of the relation between children's development and the environments in which that development occurred. During the middle third of this century, sociologists, psychologists, and educators, among others, began focusing attention on the deleterious consequences of growing up in a "deprived environment" (Skeels & Dye, 1939; Dennis, 1973; Deutsch and associates, 1967; Bowlby, 1951; Hunt, 1961; Bloom, 1964; Caldwell, 1968). During the past decade, ideas from the physical and biological, as well as social, sciences have fused so that human development is now most often viewed within the framework of ecological or general systems theories (Bronfenbrenner, 1979; Ford & Lerner, 1992; Lerner, 1984; Ramey, MacPhee, & Yeates, 1982; Sameroff, 1983). Each human being is viewed as both guest and host in a dynamic and complexly organized aggregate of interleafing and evolving systems. Despite the indeterminacy

Developmental Follow-up

present in ecological models, they are now generally considered to have both theoretical and practical advantages as operating scientific metaphors (e.g., single factor and interactionist models, to use the nomenclature of Sameroff, 1982). Lerner (1984), for instance, describes human beings as ontogenetically advanced (i.e., highly individualistic) and quite plastic in their developmental trajectories, those trajectories being intimately bound up with their own idiosyncratic history of experiences. Such views have particular significance in understanding development at times of transition, such as the transition from infancy to early childhood or from middle childhood to adolescence. As biological and societal forces create new pressures for intraindividual change, there is increased lability and openness in the system. The actual direction of change becomes more dependent on the organism's specific pattern of experiences.

The literature on environment/development relations indicates that developmental problems can arise as a result of factors at all levels of the ecological system, from the general cultural and economic conditions to very specific transactions, objects, and events (Wachs, 1992). How ecological factors such as the availability of social support operate to buffer stress and improve parenting and thereby to assist development in children is of significant interest (Cohen & Wills, 1985). Similarly, of major clinical significance is information pertaining to ways in which stressful life events operate to impair parenting and whether participation in mutual parent support networks or the receipt of high quality educational or social services can improve parenting. Ecological/developmental models suggest that interaction among such ecological variables is likely to be complex, with variables acting to mediate and moderate the effects of other variables (see Barron & Kenny, 1986, for a discussion of this issue).

What is essential for this ecological model to guide significant research is a variety of procedures for measuring the critical components of the environment. Reliance on status and structural measures of the family environment poses significant problems for researchers and for those who wish to customize interventions to meet a family's real needs. Wachs (1992), in his recent book, *The Nature of Nurture*, offers a useful historical perspective on the evolution of our thinking (and presumably our practice) about how children's experiences affect their health and development. He divides this area of inquiry into three broad phases. Phase I is concerned with research and theory using social address models. Actual environments are not directly assessed; rather, comparisons are made between children from different sociodemographic groups with the presumption that different social addresses adequately reflect differences in real experiences. The yield from this approach was limited—and sometimes counterproductive. Families from every social strata and area of residence vary widely in the types and amounts of stimulation and support afforded their children (Bradley & Caldwell, 1978). Phases II and III are overlapping in time, though different in approach to the relationship between experience and development. Phase II is concerned with delineating the environment and determining which aspects of it are salient for particular aspects of development. Theoretically, one component of development (e.g., the formation of a secure attachment) may be highly dependent on one class of experiences (e.g., parents who are socially and emotionally responsive), whereas another component of development (e.g., fine motor skills) may be more highly dependent on a quite different class of experiences (e.g., the availability of toys and other small manipulable objects). Phase III is concerned not just about which aspects of the environment are important for development but also about determining the process by which "variability in the environment translates into variability in development" (Wachs, 1992, p 8).

The development of HOME (Home Observation for Measurement of the Environment) and our research with it bridges these last two phases—delineating the environment and determining the process through which variability in the environment is reflected in variability in development. In our research we have attempted to identify those components of caregiving in the proximal environment that need to be measured in reference to children's development (Bradley, Caldwell, & Rock, 1990). It delineates particular aspects of caregiving associated with optimal development (Caldwell, 1968). As complex organisms with several separable psychobiological systems, human beings need a variety of different types of inputs to sustain the systems and facilitate maximum development. Humans also need a pattern of inputs (care) that is both fitted to their own particular needs at a given moment and facilitative of life-span growth and development (Lerner, 1984; Sameroff, 1982). The inputs must be provided with regard for personal characteristics and contextual conditions (Bronfenbrenner, 1979). Sameroff and Friese (1990) discuss the notion of transactional regulation of human development, "Just as there is a biological organization, the genotype, that regulates the physical outcome of each individual, there is a social organization that regulates the way human beings fit into society" (p. 124). From a systems theory perspective, the idea of experience as a regulator of growth and development is useful. What the child brings to encounters with the environment and what the child experiences during those encounters mutually regulate the course of development. Regulation is a goal-oriented activity aimed at achieving fit with an agenda set by the regulatory system (presumably to maintain and enhance its own functioning). The idea of caregiving as regulating a child's experiences reminds one of child and environment in constant transaction and of the purposive nature of those transactions.

We have defined caregiving as a set of environmental actions and conditions that assist or impede the organism in carrying out its own functions. From a systems perspective, it seems reasonable to assume that optimal development results when the organism has to expend the least amount of energy to maintain its integrity amidst the demands placed on it by its living conditions. If so, then optimal development consists of those objects and actions that permit such development (i.e., achieving an optimal fit with the least effort or stress). To promote optimal development in a living organism, a caregiving (regulatory) system must do four things: (a) help sustain the organism (ensure its viability); (b) stimulate activity in the organism directed at the organism's enhancement; (c) support the organism's self-sustaining capacities and tendencies; and (d) control the amount and patterns of experiences (inputs) that reach the organism so that there is an optimal fit between the organism's own agenda and the agenda of those systems of which the organism is a part.

It is our purpose in this chapter to describe the development of HOME and to discuss its use as a means of understanding the relationship between environment and development and in planning effective strategies for children and families.

DEVELOPMENT OF THE HOME INVENTORIES

Recognizing the shortage of measurement instruments for environmental variables, one of us (Caldwell) began work some 28 years ago on the development of a scale that would bring at least a modicum of metric sophistication into the realm of environmental measures. At that time, some index of social class status (Warner, Meeker, & Eells, 1949; Hollingshed & Redlich, 1958) was about the only metric available for describing quantitatively the environment in which development was occurring. It was a time when rating scales of parent attitudes and presumed parent practices were commonplace and legion (Sears, Maccoby, & Levin, 1957; Schaefer & Bell, 1958; Baldwin, Kahlhorn, & Breese, 1949), but generally not summative into any one index of home environmental adequacy. The researchers who used them presumably thought of them as environmental measures, and, whenever the research sample permitted it (as in Sears et al., 1958), social class differences were described and interpreted.

A major aim of our own early efforts was the development of a measure that would be sensitive to variations within social class groups. To quote the first paper (Caldwell, Heider, & Kaplan, 1966), which described the instrument that was emerging:

> Major contributions have been made in recent years in terms of documentation of long-suspected differences between the home environments of children reared in middle class as opposed to lower class homes. But the size of the unit in such a classification is a large one, and it implies more homogeneity of the units of the dichotomization than is probably warranted. . . . Intraclass variation has been dealt with as experimental error, a quantitative irritant that precludes a delineation of the "true" class picture. . . .
>
> With the exception of characteristics of the physical environment and specific child-rearing practices, most of the aspects of the child's environment which have

been assumed to be significant influences on development have been somewhat removed from the actual day-to-day transactions between the infant and the environment. Information about these daily experiences, which might be thought of as a cumulative series of learning trials, is necessary before we can be more specific about the factors associated with developmental progress. (pp. 1–2)

The result of this early effort was the development of a 73-item inventory for infants and toddlers, shortly thereafter reduced to 68 items, which was known as the Inventory of Home Stimulation and generally abbreviated as the Stim Inventory. Information for scoring was collected by sending someone into the home when the baby was awake, conducting a brief interview, observing the interaction between the mother and baby, and taking note of some of the physical attributes of the home. Major findings from this first version of the Inventory were that a high degree of interobserver reliability (95% agreement) could be obtained after fairly short periods of training, that means were higher for middle class than lower class families, that the variability was greater within the lower class, that there was a high correlation (.69) between scores on the Inventory and on social workers' ratings of degree of deprivation in the families, and that there was an extremely high correlation (.87) between scores on the Inventory and the magnitude of positive change in IQ for children participating in an early infant enrichment program (Caldwell et al., 1966). These early data, based on small numbers of subjects and possibly subject to one or another sort of contamination, offered more than enough encouragement to warrant continued work within the same conceptual framework.

Fortunately that became possible 19 years ago, when the second author (Bradley) became a colleague and brought to the work a degree of sophistication about the design and standardization of psychometric instruments that otherwise would not have been possible. The result of this collaboration has been the complete revision of the original instrument and the publication of a sequence of environmental inventories that cover the entire age range (infancy, early childhood, middle childhood, and adolescence) likely to be included in longitudinal follow-ups. The name of the Inventory was changed to HOME (Home Observation for the Measurement of the Environment), and each version has been carefully standardized and examined for qualities of psychometric adequacy.[1]

Except for deliberately designed variations (Casey, Bradley, Nelson, & Whaley, 1988), all editions of the Inventory are administered by having a trained person go into the home at a time convenient for the mother (with no restrictions except that the child be present and awake), make the observations necessary to code certain items, and conduct an informal, minimally

[1] There are currently three standardized forms of the HOME: the Infant-Toddler HOME, the Early Childhood HOME, and the Middle Childhood HOME. Work is currently in progress on an adapted version for the home environment of disabled individuals and on a form for the home environment of adolescents.

structured interview to obtain data for the remaining items. All items are binary (yes or no) and are worded in such a way that a positive code indicates desirable environmental conditions (e.g., "Parent does not express annoyance with or hostility to child"). The degree of precision specified by the binary items has contributed to the ease of achieving above 90% interobserver reliability on all forms of the inventory with a minimum of training.

All items in the Inventories could be described as assessing proximal rather than distal aspects of the environment (i.e., direct encounters between the child and some person, object, or event in the environment that might directly influence the course of development). The difference between belonging to a church and actually attending a church service is an example of the difference between distal and proximal aspects of the environment. Although church membership, because of the conceptual gestalt associated with it, may mean a great deal to an adult regardless of frequency of attendance, it would mean little or nothing to a young child unless it involved specific concrete experiences in which the child participated.

Table I presents a summary of the subscales identified for all editions of the Inventory as designated by separate factor analyses (using varimax rotation with an eigen root cutoff of 1.0). It will be noted, possibly with puzzlement, that in the different editions, factors assigned the same labels (with some items worded identically in all forms) do not have the same factor position. This is because we have followed the tradition of numbering the factors (and the items within the factors) in the order of their power, both in terms of the extent of variance accounted for and orthogonality.

If one examines the 13 factors that have emerged from the different analyses, one finds a set of characteristics certain to be regarded as important in any process theory of environmental influence. Contained here is a pattern of both stimulating and responding to children, of providing variety without chaos, of demonstrating what is acceptable through one's own behavior, of maintaining an emotional climate that does not overwhelm, of providing toys and objects that function as tools for learning, and of offering the kind of family stability through which identity and a sense of competence can be forged. Not a bad environment, if a child can be lucky enough to have it.

As this volume is concerned with strategies for follow-up designs rather than with results per se, no attempt will be made here to offer a comprehensive summary of findings from studies that have utilized the HOME as a measure of the environment. Several such summaries are already available (Elardo & Bradley, 1981; Bradley, 1982; Bradley & Caldwell, 1984, 1987), and we engage in a continuing effort to update them. Rather, our purpose is to illustrate how the HOME has functioned as a cornerstone in increasingly elaborate studies of environmental action based on increasingly complex models of environment/development relationships. The four main sources

Table I Factor Labels and Brief Definitions for All Subscales on the Infant/Toddler (IT), Early Childhood (EC), and Middle Childhood (MC) HOME Inventories

Factor number			
IT	EC	MC	Name and brief description of factor
1	4	1	Responsivity. Extent to which parent responds to child's behavior verbally, emotionally, and physically.
2	8	3	Acceptance. Parental acceptance of less than optimal behavior and avoidance of undue restriction and punishment.
3			Organization. Regularity and predictability (without monotony), safety of physical environment, and access to family and community supports.
4	1	4	Learning materials. Provision of play and learning materials capable of stimulating development.
5			Involvement. Active involvement of the parent in child's learning and stimulation of mature behavior.
6	7		Variety. Inclusion in daily life of manageable extrafamily stimulation.
	2		Language stimulation. Attempts by parents to encourage language by conversation, modeling, and direct teaching.
	3	7	Physical environment. Extent to which the physical environment is safe, sufficiently roomy, and perceptually appealing.
	5		Academic stimulation. Parental encouragement of the child's acquisition of skills and knowledge.
	6		Modeling. Demonstration by parents of desirable behaviors.
		2	Encouragement of maturity. Extent to which parents expect the child to behave responsibly and conform to family rules.
		5	Enrichment. Parents consciously utilize family and community resources via hobbies, recreation, museums, libraries, etc.
		6	Family integration. Inclusion of the child in parental activities providing mutual enjoyment, and availability of a father-figure and a consistent primary family group.

Note. IT = Infant/Toddler HOME; EC = Early Childhood HOME; MC = Middle Childhood HOME.

of these illustrative findings are our Little Rock Longitudinal Study (see Bradley & Caldwell, 1987), a longitudinal study of children with disabilities (Bradley, Rock, Caldwell, & Brisby, 1989), the Consortium Study (Bradley et al., 1989), and most recently, the multisite Infant Health and Development study (IHDP, 1990).

Relationships between HOME and Children's Development

Environment in Infancy and Infant Development Although we refer to the Infant/Toddler (IT) HOME as covering the age range of birth to 3 years, we do not recommend its use with children younger than 6 months. In general, we have found only a low correlation between the home environment measured when the baby was 6 months of age and mental development measured at 1 year (correlations never higher than .4). Correlations between the Infant/Toddler HOME at 6 months and IQ at 3 and 4 years tend to be higher, remaining within the .3 to .5 range (nature's preferred correlations, according to Clarke and Clarke, 1988, as cited by Horowitz, this volume). The 12-month Infant/Toddler HOME does not correlate any better with the Bayley Mental Development Index at 12 months than did the 6-month HOME. However, the Infant/Toddler HOME administered at either 12 or 24 months correlates impressively (total score roughtly .6–.7, subscale scores lower but all generally significant) with IQ at 3 and at 4 years of age. The consistency of these correlations—nonsignificant with mental development as measured at 1 year but significant and meaningful thereafter—validates the premise that mental development as we can measure it at 1 year, is simply not the same as that which we measure a few years later. It is also consistent with the notion that mental development is more highly canalized in the first year or so of life as compared to later developmental periods (McCall, 1981).

There are differences in the accuracy of prediction achieved by different subscales. Although most studies have found significant correlations for all six subscales on the Infant/Toddler version (administered toward the end of the first year of life) and IQ measured during early childhood, the correlations vary widely in magnitude. Although it is difficult to offer a generalization that comfortably embraces all published findings, it is probably safe to say that Responsivity, Learning Materials, and Involvement are the three workhorses of the Infant/Toddler version. Correlations for these subscales generally cluster around the .5 range. Acceptance, Organization, and Variety rarely do as well, seldom showing correlations with IQ higher than .4.

The approximate .4 correlation we find between Variety and IQ may seem a bit low given the general finding in the literature that variety of experience is a significant factor in intellectual development (e.g., Kagan, 1984). Certainly in item construction we anticipated an important role for this subscale. The probable explanation for this seeming discrepancy is that the Variety subscale on the Infant/Toddler HOME does not contain all the items representing variety of experience that appear in the Inventory. Clustered together into this subscale are various encounters with key persons in the young child's life. Elsewhere in the Inventory are found other aspects of variety, such as the availability of different types of toys and learning materials. These are contained in the Learning Materials subscale and thus cannot contribute to the predictive validity of the subscale assigned the Variety label.

Adding HOME scores to data on infant mental test scores improves prediction regarding which infants will show a rise in test scores, which are likely to remain in the same range, and which ones will decline. When prediction deals with only the lower end of the distribution—the area about which there is likely to be the greatest concern—the sharpening of predictive accuracy is especially noteworthy (Bradley & Caldwell, 1976, 1984).

One important general finding from those longitudinal data is that the level of the home environment is not necessarily stable throughout the childhood years (coefficients for various subscales generally ranging from .4 to .7). This finding will come as no great surprise, in that many parents can joke about being "good with babies but terrible with 4-year-olds," or any other combination of support for and interference with their children's developmental progress. Although some components of status environmental measures—those which rely on distal attributes such as income and type of residence—may well fluctuate with general economic conditions, the more significant components of these indexes (such as education and occupation) tend either to remain stable or to rise. But proximal attributes can and do fluctuate (e.g., frequency of punishment might well increase if an older child is judged to be difficult to manage). Thus when longitudinal research uses such environmental measures, as we are advocating, constancy of relative position within a sample should not be expected. The ability to detect such inconstancy is essential if follow-ups are to reflect both contemporary and prior influences.

Studies Using More Complex Hierarchical Models   If one views the environment as a set of concentric circles and moves along the radius from the part most proximal to the child (the microenvironment, to use Bronfenbrenner's, 1979, nomenclature) to the most distal (the macroenvironment), there is a tendency for the distal segments to be more stable across time. For example, cultural prescriptions (distal) tend to change more slowly than parental behavior (proximal), which can change with the parent's mood and the child's behavior. (Cataclysmic macroenvironmental changes such as war, with major implications for microenvironmental conditions, obviously represent an exception to this generalization.) The younger the child, the more the influence of the distal environment is mediated through the more proximal; if nothing else, infants simply are not exposed to the larger environment as much as are older children.

As Bronfenbrenner has shown (1979), we live in a multifaceted, multilayered environment, each facet and each layer exerting its influence on the behavior and development of children. The pressures exerted by various components of the child's environmental context converge at the point of parent and home for very young children. As the child gets older, the pressures become more diffused. These myriad influences interact in often mysterious, sometimes conflicting ways. Nonetheless, most of the pressures on the child from the total environment to act in a certain way come from those encounters in the most intimate environment. Thus, if we are to understand continuities and discontinuities in children's development, we must regularly assess children's microenvironments to determine what is continuous and what is discontinuous about the actual opportunities they afford and the pressures they exert.

Dealing with Discontinuities and Interactions in Follow-up Designs

Data indicative of the sensitivity of cognitive functioning to changes in home conditions go back a long way in the psychological literature (Honzik, 1967). Such findings, plus many others over the years (McCall, Appelbaum, & Hogarty, 1973; White, Watts, Barnett, Kaban, & Shapiro, 1973; Wachs & Gruen, 1982) clearly indicate the need in longitudinal follow-ups to assess the environment at basically all the time points at which development is assessed. Such assessments will identify both continuities and discontinuities in development, which can help clarify the role of specific influences at different times in the life history.

Data from Bradley, Caldwell, & Rock (1988) illustrate the necessity to assess both development and environment simultaneously at all evaluation points. We located 42 10- and 11-year-old children whose home environments and mental development had been assessed during their infancy. The children were rated on the Classroom Behavior Inventory (CBI) of Schaefer and Aaronson (1977) and were given the Science Research Associates (SRA) achievement test battery as a routine part of the school district's evaluation program. Families were administered the relativley new Middle Childhood (MC) HOME. This availability of both early and late HOMES and data on achievement and general behavioral functioning in middle childhood gave us an opportunity to examine the issue of the priority of early versus contemporary environment in relation to school achievement and behavior.

Using the technique of partial correlations, we examined for the association between the home environment at both time points and school functioning. Specifically, we sought to test the explanatory power of three models: the primacy of early experience (Model I), the primacy of contemporary experience (Model II), and the explanatory power of environmental congruence across time (Model III).

Primacy of early experience (Model I) was tested by examining the correlation between the Infant/Toddler HOME and the 10-year school measures with the 10-year HOME, partialed out for those measures where there was a significant bivariate correlation. This was done for each subscale separately, matching identical or highly similar factors on the different forms of the instrument (e.g., Parental involvement on the IT version and Family Companionship on the MC form). There was some support for Model I (primacy of early experience), in that all of the subscales measured during infancy showed significant correlations with at least one of the 10-year measures when the effects of the contemporary environment were controlled. However, the correlations were not high.

Contemporary experience (Model II) as the more powerful influence received substantial support in our analysis. Partialing out the effect of HOME at either 6 or 24 months left significant correlations with at least one of the 10-year school measures and five of the eight subscales on the MC HOME.

Especially relevant for our concern with follow-up strategies is the question of stability of the environment over time (Model III). Again, it is common to look for such correlations in functions measured in the child but rare to do so with regard to environmental variables. Our data indicated that, for all subscales, the correlations across this decade of time were moderate, rarely exceeding .5. This summary finding in itself has profound implications for how we measure environmental variables. Status variables, as previously discussed, are very likely to fall in the same categories at all measurement points. It is also of interest to note which of the subscales retained the greatest predictive efficiency when the stability coefficient was partialed out: it was the one describing active family interaction (called Involvement on the IT form and Integration on the MC form). Such involvement was found by McCall et al. (1973) to be related to increasing IQ profiles in the Fels longitudinal sample. Our data would suggest that such a relationship of family involvement in the life of the child is significant at least in part because it tends to be a stable dimension with a cumulative impact over time.

The lesson from these data for those conducting follow-up studies in which both individual behavior and environmental support can vary across time is clear: Both sets of variables need to be measured at all relevant assessment points. Early experience may have primacy in some instances, but the contemporary environment will invariably have some influence. In part, this influence will be enhanced if the environmental variable has operated consistently from the early years onward.

Organism–Environment Interaction   In most longitudinal studies of development, we are primarily interested in the organismic variables. Yet to understand both how they appear and how they are sustained or weakened over time, we need to understand how these variables interact with relevant environmental variables at several points along a time dimension. A child whose early developmental progress appears weak and slow might react differently to a nonsupportive environment during infancy than would one whose early functioning is more robust. The latter child might be able to extract from the environment more nutrients for the sustenance of growth than the former. These two hypothetical children characterize end points along the two continua of development and environment. If the environment does indeed interact with intrinsic factors, the first child is at double jeopardy for developmental problems and the second child has a double advantage. Sameroff and Seifer (1983) demonstrated that the probability of a negative developmental outcome increases multiplicatively as the number of risk factors for a child increases.

The availability of an environmental metric provides a perfect opportunity to test this hypothesis, and we did so using data from our Consortium project (Bradley et al., 1989). Table II shows the distribution of 3-year IQs in standard scores as a function of both 1-year HOME and 1-year Bayley scores. With only one exception, those children who scored one standard deviation or more above the mean on both the Bayley and the HOME, scored above the mean on the Stanford-Binet at age 3. Similarly, only two of the children with 1-year Bayleys and HOMEs one standard deviation below the mean scored at or above the mean for 3-year IQ. The children with inconsistent directions of deviation covered the full range of IQ scores. These data clearly support the concept of organism–environment interaction and demonstrate the relevance of the double-risk or double-advantage concept.

Such results are consistent with a transactional view of development: The course of development is life's tango, truly a dance in which organism and environment anticipate and direct the moves of the other. Bell (1969) marshaled convincing evidence for bidirectional influence between child and environment; and, more recently, Scarr and McCartney (1983) have

Table II Distribution of 36-month IQ Scores for Children Who Scored in Extreme Ranges on Both the HOME Inventory and Bayley Scales of Infant Development at 12 months

IQ 36-month standard scores	12-month MDI and HOME scores			
	Both at least 1 *SD* below the mean	No more than one extreme score in the same direction	Both at least 1 *SD* above the mean	Total *N*
−3.0 to −2.5	1	2	—	3
−2.5 to −2.0	1	7	—	8
−2.0 to −1.5	4	25	—	29
−1.5 to −1.0	5	41	—	46
−1.0 to −0.5	5	68	—	73
−0.5 to 0	9	115	1	125
0 to 0.5	1	95	5	101
0.5 to 1.0	1	77	7	85
1.0 to 1.5	—	63	7	70
1.5 to 2.0	—	21	7	28
2.0 to 2.5	—	2	1	3
2.5 to 3.0	—	1	1	2
3.0 to 3.5	—	2	—	2
TOTAL *N*	27	519	29	575

theorized about the changing nature of this mutual influence process, with children evolving from passive elicitors of environmental inputs to active seekers of their own environmental niches.

We examined bidirectional influence during the first 2 years of life using cross-lagged panel analysis. Specifically, we examined two types of cognitive stimulation (in our case Parental Involvement and Learning Materials) and their relation to early cognitive performance (e.g., the Mental Development Index (MDI) from the Bayley Scales). Results for Learning Materials indicated the primary direction of effect is from MDI to Learning Materials from 6 to 12 months, followed by a period of mutual influence from 12 to 24 months. Regarding Parental Involvement, results indicated that during the period from 6 months to 1 year, more capable children elicit more Parental Involvement; whereas during the second year of life, parents who consciously encourage their children's development tend to produce children who have higher MDI scores (Bradley & Caldwell, 1976).

Bell (1969) contended that children's behavior (or characteristics) influence parental behaviors particularly when the child's behavior falls outside the parent's "comfort zone" or tolerance. As the behavior or characteristic becomes more extreme, parents are more likely to move from a self-imposed behavioral agenda to an agenda driven by the demands, concerns, and limitations imposed by the child. We investigated this hypothesis in a study of children with disabilities and found that the more severe a child's disability, the less likely parents were to provide age-appropriate materials, enriching experiences, and facilitative communication (Bradley, Rock, Caldwell, Whiteside, & Brisby, 1991).

Environment–Environment Interaction   Among the new frontiers in the study of the influence of the environment is one concerning environment–environment interactions, which may well be critical determinants of developmental outcomes. At least three types of such interactions can be designated. The first pertains to interactions between the child's most proximal environment (the home/family) and other types of primary care settings (child care) in which the child spends significant periods of time. Just as is true for the same home at different times, these different contemporary settings may be either consonant or dissonant and thereby mediate the effect of any specific type of home influence. For example, the lack of maternal responsiveness may have negative consequences for the child's development if there are no other caregivers in the home to provide responsive care (single parent households) or no responsive caregivers outside the home (extended family or child-care workers) with whom the infant has a significant number of interactions. However, consequences of such a maternal pattern may be more benign if the child receives a certain amount of responsive care from persons other than the mother in alternate care settings.

A second type of environment–environment interaction is an interaction between the macro (or meso) environment and the microenvironment. We examined such an interaction using children from the Infant Health and Development Program (IHDP, 1990). These children, all premature and low birthweight, were randomly assigned to either an intensive 3-year intervention or a follow-up (no intervention) group. From the follow-up group, we identified 243 children living in poverty. Information was available on the health status, growth status, intelligence, and adaptive social competence of all children at age 3. We used this information to determine which children were functioning within the normal range for each domain and which were showing problems in health, growth, or development. Only 26 children met the criteria for functioning within the normal (nonrisk) range in all four domains. We labeled these children resilient against the dual risk of poverty and prematurity. We then attempted to identify factors in the children's microenvironments that served to protect them against this dual risk. Six protective factors were identified: low crowding in the home, a safe play area in and around the home, and above-average scores on the Acceptance, Learning Materials, Variety, and Responsivity subscales (receiver operating curves were used to optimize cutoff scores on all variables). Children with three or more protective factors at age 1 had a 15% probability of being resilient; children with three or more protective factors at age 3 had a 20% probability of being resilient. Without these protective factors, the probabilities were 2% and 6%, respectively. In sum, conditions in the microenvironment (protective experiences) interact with conditions in the macroenvironment (poverty) to influence the course of health and development.

The third type of environment–environment interaction involves interactions between process aspects of the same home environment. This type can be illustrated by data from a study by Parks and Bradley (1991). They found that babies who had *both* a greater number of play materials available to them and parents who were involved in encouraging developmental advances did better on the Griffiths Scales than babies who only had involved parents or an abundance of useful play materials.

The Home Environment as Mediator of Parental Characteristics and Family Structure   A review of studies using the HOME reveals that HOME scores are related to a variety of family contextual and structural factors and parent characteristics including parental IQ (Plomin & Bergeman, 1991), parental personality (Crockenberg, 1987), single parent status (Allen, Affleck, McGrade, & McQueeney, 1984), parental substance abuse (Ragozin, Landesman-Dwyer, & Streissguth, 1980), family structure (Bradley & Caldwell, 1984), parental coping styles (Bradley et al., 1991), and socioeconomic status (Gottfried & Gottfried, 1984). However, none of these factors fully accounts for the variations observed in home environments. A study that reveals something of the complexity of parenting and family ecology was conducted by Wandersman and Unger (1983). It was designed to determine if adolescent mothers with good social support whose first babies had perinatal complications or difficult temperaments are better able to adjust to mother-hood and provide more adequate caretaking than young mothers with less supportive networks. Among mothers who had few obstetric complications, HOME was not related to maternal resources or social support. In the high complications group, HOME was significantly related to age of mother, feelings about pregnancy, preparation for childbirth, knowledge about babies, availability of relatives, support from the baby's father and support from friends. For babies rated as producing little caregiving stress, HOME was related to age of mother and feelings about pregnancy. In the high baby-stress group, HOME was related to age of mother, knowledge about pregnancy, knowledge about babies, social support from father, and having relatives nearby.

The study by Wandersman and Unger (1983) begins to reveal something of the complexity of relations between the family ecology and the quality of parenting that occurs. What it does not show, however, is how all these factors interrelate to affect the course of development (Phase III studies, to use Wachs' framework). Ecological/developmental models such as Belsky's (1984) parenting process model or our own proximal ecological model depict how such relations might obtain—that is, they suggest how contextual factors might act on the home environment and how the home environment might, in turn, act on development. One type of action implied by these models is mediation: Contextual factors change what happens in the home, and it is through these changes that contextual factors ultimately influence the course of development (see Barron & Kenney, 1986, and Walberg & Marjoribanks, 1976, for discussions of conceptual and analytic techniques pertaining to mediation). We have tested these models of environmental action with respect to family socioeconomic status (SES) (Bradley et al., 1990) and maternal IQ (Bradley et al., in press) using HOME subscale scores as mediators and child IQ as outcome. Using structural equation models to analyze the data, we observed that part of the influence of SES on child IQ is mediated through the kinds of cognitive stimulation (Learning Materials, Parental Involvement) found in the home, but it is not mediated by parental control techniques (Acceptance). Similarly, part of the influence of maternal IQ on child IQ is mediated through the same types of cognitive stimulation factors in the home environment. HOME affords a useful means of examining complex relations between family characteristics, family context, and child development the array of particular home environment aspects it indexes (see, e.g., the elegant analyses using behavior genetics techniques done by Plomin & Bergeman, 1991).

What Type of Variable?

A final point we would like to touch on relates to the way in which the environment should be conceptualized in developmental follow-up studies. Elsewhere (Bradley et al., 1988), we have lamented the absence of a taxonomy of the environment that can cover all types of research questions. Certainly all research done within an ecological framework (Bronfenbrenner, 1979) recognizes the necessity of conceptualizing the relevant environmental experiences in which development is embedded. Without such a taxonomy, however, one does the best one can.

The environment, broadly conceived, is often the independent variable in developmental research. A contemporary research issue which perhaps illustrates this as well as any is the question of whether spending some time during infancy in day care has deleterious developmental consequences (see Belsky, 1986). If, in such a study, the environment is conceptualized as the independent variable, various developmental outcome measures are identified as dependent variables (e.g., attachment, aggression, problem-solving, etc.) and their association with exposure of significant duration to a particular quality and quantity of environment is assessed.

Such conceptualization has helped us begin to produce a body of knowledge in this area. But greater progress will be made via research with more complex designs which allow more than one variable to covary simultaneously. For example, young children often have to adapt to both a home environment, the only environmental variable we have dealt with in this chapter, and one or more alternate environments (child-care center 2 days a week, staying with a relative 3 days, and all other sorts of possible patterns) at the same time. These other environments should also be measured in follow-up research designs, as they, too, will undoubtedly vary in quality. This variability can easily be demonstrated when an adequately standardized measure of the alternative care environment, such as the procedure developed by Harms and Clifford (1980), is used. When this is done, it is easy to demonstrate, as McCartney (1984) did, that social and language development vary as a function of quality within the day-care environment, just as we have shown such attributes to vary as a function of home care quality. Such measurement allows us to move beyond an oversimplified designation of the environmental variables (e.g., day care versus no day care) and examine instead the effects of significant variation within several of the relevant developmental environments.

The measurement of more than one aspect of a child's developmental environment allows interaction effects to appear. Many longitudinal designs would be greatly enriched by the adoption of a paradigm that casts the quality of the home environment as a moderating variable between developmental outcomes and other types of environmental influences. Again, research on the association between different types and amounts of day care on behavioral outcome variables will illustrate this point beautifully. A child who spends time in child care can have a pattern of environmental influence offering double advantage (good home care and high quality day care), double risk (poor home and poor day care), or a mixed pattern. It appears to us to be naive to try any longer to assess the effects of day care on the development of children without considering the home environment as a variable that can moderate the effects of an alternate environment. Likewise, for approximately half of our children, it is equally naive to examine for effects of in-home care without simultaneously considering the quality of alternate care in which the child might be spending significant amounts of time. Howes, Galluzzo, Hamilton, Matheson, and Rodning (1989), for instance, found that among children using extensive amounts of day care, social competence was more highly related to the children's attachment to their caregivers than to their attachments to their mothers. The Steering Committee of the NICHD Study of Early Child Care has built this opportunity for interaction between the home and the alternate environment into its design for the longitudinal study. Accordingly, data from this study should have a significant methodological advantage over most research conducted within this gene.

Finally, we suggest that, in longitudinal studies, some aspect of the environment is often the most meaningful dependent variable. Take, for example, an intervention study in which the parent is the main target of the intervention. This is a model that has had great popularity for the past two decades (Gordon, 1970; Levenstein & Sunley, 1968; Bronfenbrenner, Belsky, & Steinberg, 1977). In such interventions, the major aim is generally enhanced development in the children, and the main dependent variables are those which measure some aspect of the child's functioning. However, absence of effect in such efforts is difficult to interpret. Does it mean that the parent-targeted intervention did not really affect the development of the child? Or does it mean that the intervention did not significantly change the behavior of the parent in relation to the child? Addition of a measure of the home environment as a dependent variable can answer these questions.

Some years ago, Hamilton (1972) used the HOME as a dependent variable to show that a Parent and Child center program had indeed changed parent behavior in ways considered conducive to more optimal development in the children. This study was basically a clinical description, however, with no control group used. Since Hamilton's study, several other investigators (Barkauskas, 1983; Barrera, Rosenbaum, & Cunningham, 1986) have used the HOME as an outcome measure to evaluate the effectiveness of a parent-oriented intervention program. It is our conviction that environmental metrics need to be used regularly in such designs. In parent education and family-focused early intervention programs, it is the parent who is a primary target of the intervention, and it is through the parent that the impact on a child is presumably mediated. Thus, it is impossible to know precisely how and whether intervention "works" in the absence of a direct assessment of the environment provided by the parent.

Early data from the Infant Health and Development Program (IHDP; 1990), a highly visible early intervention program for low-birthweight babies, provide information on the value of environmental measures used as a dependent variable in longitudinal designs. In this project, assignment to intervention and control groups was random, and all assessment was done by persons blind to the subjects' group assignments. For the first 12 months of life, weekly home visits offering both suggestions for stimulation of the babies and problem-solving activities for the mothers were made. From 12 to 36 months, the intervention children were enrolled in a high quality day-care center, whereas the control children did not have this experience. Even though the children were assigned randomly to the two groups at the time of birth, theoretically they should not have been entering day care equally matched. That is, if the home-based intervention of the first year had an effect, the children in the two groups should have had different environmental histories at the time they were enrolled in the alternate care setting. Thus, the HOME data obtained on these families when their children were 1 year of age comprise a perfect dependent variable pertaining to the effects of intervention during the first year of life and a vital link in the understanding of how various experiences will interact with the child's intrinsic developmental attributes to produce the effects seen in later childhood.

Casey, Bradley, Caldwell, & Gross (1990) analyzed data from the IHDP files specifically to address this question. Contrary to prediction, there were no differences between the experimental and control groups on the HOME when the project children were 12 months of age. By contrast, there was a significant difference favoring the intervention group at 36 months on the HOME, just as there was on the Stanford-Binet. The difference appeared on the subscales Learning Materials, Academic Stimulation, Modeling, Variety, and Acceptance. These findings demonstrate again the way in which measuring the environment over time increases our understanding of how and for whom complex interventions work. It also increases our chances of fine tuning intervention so that it fits the needs and characteristics of the recipients.

SUMMARY

In this chapter we have described the development of the HOME Inventories and have attempted to make a case for the necessity of including repeated measures of the developmental environment in longitudinal research. The availability of the HOME has significantly increased the knowledge base about patterns of home environmental influence on many developmentally relevant outcome measures.

Follow-up studies using the HOME have established the long-term predictability of some environmental measures made during the first 2 years of life. However, data have also been cited to demonstrate the crucial nature of contemporaneous environmental descriptions at all follow-up points. Such an approach facilitates the interpretation of both continuities and discontinuities in long-term developmental histories. Analyses of data sets that include HOME, plus an array of other child and family variables, has made it possible to map the patterns of relations that obtain between environment and development and to explore the adequacy of the kinds of elaborate ecological models that have come to characterize the field (Lerner, 1986; Sameroff, 1983).

Finally we have suggested that simplistic one-way designs, always conceptualizing the environment as the independent variable, may not lead to the most theoretically relevant data about environment/organism relationships. There are multiple environments in which young children function, and these interact with one another and with developmental characteristics of the children. Further, the direction of presumed cause and effect should not always be thought of as going from the environment to the organism. The environment is influenced, just as it influences. Changes in the environment are themselves highly significant outcomes of human interventions, and creative follow-up research paradigms will embrace this dynamic quality of the environments in which development occurs.

REFERENCES

Allen, D., Affleck, G., McGrade, B., & McQueeney, M. (1984). Effects of single parent status on mothers of their high-risk infants. *Infant Behavior and Development, 7,* 347–359.

Baldwin, A., Kahlhorn, J., & Breese, F. (1949). The appraisal parent behavior. *Psychological Monographs, 63,* No. 299.

Barkauskas, V. (1983). Effectiveness of public health nurse home visits to primiparous mothers and their infants. *American Journal of Public Health, 73,* 573–580.

Baron, R., & Kenny, D. (1986). The moderator–mediator distinction in social psychological research: Conceptual, strategic and statistical considerations. *Journal of Personality and Social Psychology, 51,* 1173–1182.

Barrera, M., Rosenbaum, P. & Cunningham, C. (1986). Early home intervention with low-birthweight children and their parents. *Child Development, 57,* 20–33.

Bell, R. (1969). A reinterpretation of the direction of effects in studies of socialization. *Psychological Bulletin, 75,* 81–95.

Belsky, J. (1984). The determinants of parenting: A process model. *Child Development, 55,* 83–96.

Belsky, J. (1986). Infant day care: A cause for concern? *Zero to Three, 6,* 1–7.

Bloom, B. (1964). *Stability and change in human characteristics.* New York: Wiley.

Bowlby, J. (1951). *Maternal care and mental health.* Geneva: World Health Organization.

Bowlby, J. (1969). *Attachment and loss: Attachment,* New York: Basic Books.

Bradley, R. H. (1982). The HOME Inventory—A review of the first 15 years. In W. Frankenburg, N. Anastasiow, & A. Fandal (Eds.), *Identifying the developmentally delayed child.* Baltimore: University Park Press.

Bradley, R. H., & Caldwell, B. M. (1976). Early home environment and changes in mental test performance in children from 6 to 36 months. *Developmental Psychology, 12,* 93–97.

Bradley, R. & Caldwell, B. (1978). Screening the environment. *American Journal of Orthopsychiatry, 48,* 114–130.

Bradley, R. H., & Caldwell, B. M. (1984). The relation of infants' home environments to achievement test performance in first grade: A follow-up study. *Child Development, 55,* 803–809.

Bradley, R. H., & Caldwell, B. M. (1987). Early environment and cognitive competence: The Little Rock study. *Early Child Development and Care, 27,* 307–341.

Bradley, R., Caldwell, B., & Elardo, R. (1977). Home environment, social status and mental test performance. *Journal of Educational Psychology, 69,* 697–701.

Bradley, R. H., Caldwell, B. M., & Rock, S. L. (1988). Home environment and school performance: A ten year follow-up and examination of three models of environmental action. *Child Development, 59,* 852–867.

Bradley, R., Caldwell, B., & Rock, S. L. (1990). A system for describing elements of the environment: Model for assessing the home environments of developing children. *Early Education and Development, 1*(4), 237–265.

Bradley, R. H., Caldwell, B. M., Rock, S. L., Barnard, K. E., Gray, C., Hammond, M. A., Mitchell, S., Siegel, L., Ramey, C. T., Gottfried, A. W., & Johnson, D. L. (1989). Home environment and cognitive development in the first three years of life: A collaborative study involving six sites and three ethnic groups in North America. *Developmental Psychology, 25,* 217–235.

Bradley, R., Rock, S., Caldwell, B., & Brisby, J. (1989). Uses of the HOME Inventory for families with handicapped children. *American Journal of Mental Retardation, 94,* 313–330.

Bradley, R., Rock, S., Whiteside, L., Caldwell, B., & Brisby, J. (1991). Dimensions of parenting in families having children with disabilities. *Exceptionality, 2,* 41–61.

Bradley, R., Whiteside, L., Caldwell, B., Casey, P., Kelleher, K., Pope, S., Swanson, M., Barrett, K., & Cross, D. 1993. Maternal IQ, the home environment, and child IQ. *International Journal of Behavioral Development, 16,* 61–74.

Bronfenbrenner, U. (1979). *The ecology of human development.* Cambridge, MA: Harvard University Press.

Bronfenbrenner, U., Belsky, J., & Steinberg, L. (1977). Day care in context: An ecological perspective on research and public policy. *Policy issues in day care: Summaries of 21 papers.* Washington, DC: DHEW.

Caldwell, B. (1968). On designing supplementary environments for early child development. *BAEYC Reports, 10,* 1–11.

Caldwell, B. M., Heider, J., & Kaplan, B. (1966). *The Inventory of Home Stimulation.* Paper presented at the annual meeting of the American Psychological Association, New York.

Casey, P., Bradley, R. H., Caldwell, B. M., & Gross, R. T. (1990). *Enhancing the home environment of low birthweight, premature infants.* Paper presented at the 7th International Conference on Infancy Studies, Montreal, April 19–22.

Casey, P., Bradley, R., Nelson, J., & Whaley, S. (1988). The clinical assessment of a child's social and physical environment during health visits. *Developmental and Behavioral Pediatrics, 9,* 333–338.

Clarke, A. M., & Clarke, D. B. (1988). The adult outcome to early behavioral abnormalities. *International Journal of Behavioral Development, 11,* 3–20.

Cohen, S., & Willis, T. (1985). Stress, social support, and the buffering hypothesis. *Psychological Bulletin, 98*(2), 310–357.

Crockenberg, S. (1987). Predictors and correlates of anger toward and punitive control of toddlers by adolescent mothers. *Child Development, 58,* 964–975.

Dennis, W. (1973). *Children of the creche.* New York: Appleton-Century-Crofts.

Deutsch, M. & associates. (1967). *The disadvantaged child.* New York: Basic Books.

Elardo, R., & Bradley, R. (1981). The Home Observation for Measurement of the Environment: A review of research. *Developmental Review, 1,* 113–145.

Ford, D., & Lerner, R. (1992). *Developmental systems theory. An integrative approach.* Newbury Park, CA: Sage.

Gordon, I. (1970). Early child stimulation through parent education. *Childhood Education, 46,* 247–249.

Gottfried, A. E., & Gottfried, A. W. (1988). *Maternal employment and children's development: Longitudinal research.* New York, NY: Plenum.

Hamilton, M. (1972). Evaluation of a parent and child center program. *Child Welfare, 51,* 248–258.

Harms, T., & Clifford, R. M. (1980). *Early Childhood Environment Rating Scale.* New York: Teachers College Press.

Hollingshed, A., & Redlich, F. (1958). *Social class and mental illness: A community study.* New York: Wiley.

Honzik, M. (1967). Environmental correlates of mental growth: Predictions from the family setting at 21 months. *Child Development, 38,* 337–364.

Horowitz, F. D. (1989, June). *Developmental perspectives and developmental follow-up strategies.* Paper presented at the NICHD Conference on Developmental Follow-Up Strategies, Bethesda, MD.

Howes, C., Galluzzo, D., Hamilton, C., Matheson, C., & Rodning, C. (1989). *Social relationships with adults and peers within child care and families.* Paper presented at the Biennial Meeting of The Society for Research in Child Development, Kansas City, MO, April.

Hunt, J. (1961). *Intelligence and experience.* New York: Ronald.

Infant Health & Development Program. (1990). Enhancing the outcomes of low-birth-weight, premature infants: A multisite, randomized trial. *Journal of the American Medical Association, 263,* 3035–3042.

Kagan, J. (1984). *The nature of the child.* New York: Basic Books.

Lerner, R. (1984). *On the nature of human plasticity.* New York: Cambridge University Press.

Levenstein, P., & Sunley, R. (1968). *Aiding cognitive growth in disadvantaged preschoolers: A progress report.* Freeport, NY: Mother-Child Home Program of Nassau County.

McCall, R. (1981). Nature–nurture and the two realms of development: A proposed integration with respect to mental development. *Child Development, 52,* 1–12.

McCall, R., Appelbaum, M., & Hogarty, P. (1973). Developmental changes in mental performance. *Monographs of the Society for Research in Child Development, 38* (3, Serial No. 150).

McCartney, K. (1984). The effect of quality of day care environment upon children's language development. *Developmental Psychology, 20,* 244–260.

Parks, P., & Bradley, R. H. (1991). The interaction of home environment features and their relation to infant competence. *Infant Mental Health Journal, 12,* 3–16.

Plomin, R., & Bergeman, C. S. (1991). The nature of nurture: Genetic influence on "environmental" measures. *Behavioral and Brain Sciences, 14,* 373–385.

Ragozin, A., Landesman-Dwyer, S., & Streissguth, A. (1980). *The relationship between mothers' drinking habits and children's home environments.* (Report #77-10). Seattle: University of Washington, Alcoholism and Drug Abuse Institute.

Ramey, C., MacPhee, D., & Yeates, K. (1982). Preventing developmental retardation: A general systems model. In L. Bonds and J. Joffe (Eds.), *Facilitating infant and early childhood development.* Hannover, NH: University Press of New England.

Sameroff, A. (1982). The environmental context of developmental disabilities. In D. Bricker (Ed.), *Intervention with at-risk and handicapped infants* (pp. 141–152). Baltimore: University Park Press.

Sameroff, A. (1983). Developmental systems: Context and evolution. In W Kessen (Ed.), *Handbook of child psychology: Vol. I. History, theories, and methods* (pp. 238–294). New York: Wiley.

Sameroff, A., and Friese, B. (1990). Transactional regulation and early intervention. In S. Meisels & J. Shonkoff (Eds.), *Handbook of early intervention* (pp. 119–149). Hillsdale, NJ: Lawrence Erlbaum.

Sameroff, A. J., & Seifer, R. (1983). *Sources of continuity in parent–child relations.* Paper presented at the meeting of the Society for Research in Child Development, Detroit, MI.

Schaefer, E., & Aaronson, M. (1977). *Classroom Behavior Inventory.* Unpublished manuscript, University of North Carolina, Chapel Hill.

Schaefer, E., & Bell, R. (1958). Development of a parental attitude research instrument. *Child Development, 29,* 339–361.

Sears, R., Maccoby, E., & Levin, H. (1957). *Patterns of child rearing.* Evanston, II: Row, Peterson.

Skeels, H., & Dye, H. (1939). A study of the effects of differential stimulation on mentally retarded children. *Proceedings of the American Association on Mental Deficiency, 44,* 114–136.

Wachs, T. (1992). *The nature of nurture.* Newbury Park, CA: Sage.

Wachs, T., & Gruen, G. (1982). *Early experience and human development.* New York: Plenum.

Walberg, H., & Marjoribanks, K. (1976). Family environment and cognitive development: Twelve analytic models. *Review of Educational Research, 45,* 527–552.

Wandersman, L., & Unger, D. (1983). *Interaction of infant difficulty and social support in adolescent mothers.* Paper presented at the biennial meeting of the Society for Research in Child Development. Detroit, MI.

Warner, W. L., Meeker, M., & Eells, K. (1949). *Social class in America: A manual of procedure for the measurement of social status.* Chicago: Science Research Associates.

White, B., Watts, J., Barnett, I. C., Kaban, B., & Shapiro, B. (1973). *Environment and experience: Major influences on the development of the young child.* Englewood Cliffs, NJ: Prentice-Hall.

EXPERIMENTAL DESIGN AND DATA ANALYSIS

Special Methodological Problems of Childhood Developmental Follow-up Studies: Focus on Planning

Helena Chmura Kraemer[1]

INTRODUCTION

Developmental follow-up studies pose special methodological problems for a variety of reasons: financing, investment of time and resources, and career impact for the investigators. In this era of restricted research funding, the funding of each long-term developmental follow-up study precludes the funding of several short term cross-sectional studies. Where should funding agencies, particularly federal funding agencies, invest their money for great-

[1] This work was supported by the Infant Health and Development Program, funded by grants to the Department of Pediatrics, Stanford University; the Frank Porter Graham Child Development Center, University of North Carolina; and the eight participating Universities by the Robert Wood Johnson Foundation. Additional support for the National Study Office was provided to the Department of Pediatrics, Stanford University, from the Pew Charitable Trusts; the Bureau of Maternal and Child Health and Resources Development and the National Institute of Child Health and Human Development, HRSA, PHS, DHHS (Grant MCJ-060515); and the Stanford Center for the Study of Families, Children and Youth.

est value and should this investment be in long-term developmental follow-up studies?

Certain important questions cannot be answered using cross-sectional studies, specifically those questions requiring knowledge and understanding of developmental processes that differentiate one individual from another. It is essential that long-term developmental follow-up studies, costly though they may be, be funded to obtain clear and unambiguous answers to such research questions. However, no developmental follow-up study should be funded unless it gives promise of providing *clear* and *unambiguous* answers to *specific and important* research questions. Thus, the criteria for review and evaluation of such proposed studies should be more stringent than for short-term or cross-sectional studies.

Many follow-up studies done in the past have provided neither clear nor unambiguous answers. How can one recognize which proposed studies give promise of providing such answers and which will not? What can the investigators do to ensure that their proposal will be viewed as providing such answers? These are the questions addressed in this chapter; but first, a few preliminary comments.

Cross-sectional studies are inexpensive, relatively easy to do, and produce rapid results. They are essential even in situations where they cannot produce definitive answers to research questions. From such studies, hypotheses can be generated and clarified, pilot studies of measurements, technology, and design executed, and a firm base for research planning laid. More fundamental, the decision as to whether or not the time and expense of a follow-up study is necessary and justified can only be empirically based on a series of well done cross-sectional studies. Such empirical justification is essential in deciding whether or not a proposed costly developmental follow-up study is timely and holds promise.

Developmental follow-up studies can be either *prospective* or *retrospective*. The focus here is on planning prospective studies, but a preliminary word about retrospective follow-up studies is in order. A retrospective follow-up study is one in which the subjects are recruited into the study at a time when the outcomes of interest either are occurring or have already occurred. For example, a study of risk factors for obesity in children might be conducted by recruiting children already clinically obese along with a control sample of normal-weighted children. In such a case, the patterns of growth leading to the present clinical state and the factors associated with the development of obesity can only be ascertained using recall and report, or extant records, because such information predates entry into the study. In such circumstances, missing data are frequent and the quality of data may be both very poor and inconsistent from one subject to another. Worse yet, missing and poor quality data may be more frequent with subjects having certain outcomes (e.g., for obese children rather than their control counterparts). This results in a major potential source of bias in the results. Thus, as is the case with cross-sectional studies, few questions concerning the processes of development can be definitively answered using retrospective studies. However, retrospective follow-up studies incur less cost in time and resources and should be exploited to assess the necessity of prospective developmental follow-up studies and to be a basis for sound research planning in such studies.

For the purposes of this discussion, the focus is on well-justified prospective developmental follow-up studies, that is, studies in which (a) subjects are measured repeatedly over a period of time, (b) the period of time is one during which subjects are expected to change substantially, (c) it is reasonable to expect that there will be individual differences among subjects in the pattern of change, and (d) there is a basis of cross-sectional, retrospective, and other nonconclusive studies sufficient to document empirically the need for a costly follow-up study and to serve as a basis of cost-efficient planning for such a study proposal.

The methodological literature is replete with papers and books dealing with various aspects of developmental follow-up studies (e.g., McGlashan, Carpenter, & Bartko, 1988; Bartko, Carpenter, & McGlashan, 1988). Little that will be dealt with in this discussion is new. The focus is not on novel issues, but on those issues that, despite extensive discussion in the methodological literature, continue to be problematic. Problems arise because of the lack of a clear and specific conceptualization of the goals of a study, and the substitution of charismatic approaches for scientific ones (subjective beliefs for objective, empirically documented knowledge). Most can be avoided with *tough* research planning, and prevented by *tough* reviews of proposal submissions.

Such problems are modeled by Alice in conversing with the Cheshire Cat:

"Would you tell me, please, which way I ought to go from here?"
"That depends a good deal on where you want to get to," said the Cat.
"I don't much care where . . ." said Alice.
"Then it doesn't matter which way you go," said the Cat.
". . . so long as I get *somewhere*," Alice added as an explanation.
"Oh, you're sure to do that," said the Cat, "if you only walk long
    enough."

                    (Lewis Carroll, *Alice's Adventures in Wonderland*)

Unless we propose to wander for a long time (however pleasurably) with only the hope of sooner or later serendipitously reaching some place (perhaps unpleasant), it is essential that the destination be clearly and specifically defined a priori, that all that is known about the possible paths to that destination be evaluated, that the mistakes made in past attempts be recognized and avoided, and that planning for the journey be rigorous, clearly thought out, as well as realistic.

This stance runs afoul of those who would prefer to theorize and explore rather than to plan and confirm: those who see themselves as "hunters" and "fishers" rather than "farmers," as "architects" rather than "builders," as theoreticians or hypothesis generators rather than hypothesis testers. In each case, the former role appears to be a more free-spirited one, less bound by formal limits of some kind, more creative and innovative. In fact, most scientists would agree that much of what is most pleasurable about scientific research lies in the theorizing and the exploration. In contrast, the procedure of putting oneself on the line by articulating specific goals a priori, the process of following strict protocols to achieve those goals, and the ever-present risk of failure in such a process, is undoubtedly the least pleasant part of science.

However, *successful* hunters, fishers, and architects, as well as *successful* farmers and builders and scientists, identify their goals and plan. Defining goals and developing specific strategies to achieve such goals is part of every successful endeavor. Sad indeed must be the hunter who brings along a bear-hunting gun and pulverizes his quail, and even sadder is he who has only a bird-hunting gun when he is facing a grizzly. It is only the casual weekend fisherman, whose livelihood does not really depend on whether or not he catches a fish, whose goal is as much the pleasure of the process of fishing as it is the catching of a fish, who can afford to be casual about goals and planning. Hence the origin, I suspect, of the derisive phrase "fishing expeditions" applied to unplanned or ill-planned studies, those whose results may well be due to a combination of chance and serendipity.

I am not opposed to funding theoretical studies, although the past record of the theoretician in producing empirically validated theories must be a consideration. In any case, such studies do not usually involve long-term developmental follow-up. I am certainly not opposed to funding well-planned exploratory studies, even those involving long-term follow-up. I do not even object to funding loosely planned exploratory studies, even "fishing expeditions," but only as long as the period of funding is short and the amount of funding small. Such studies have their value as pilot studies for future well-planned long-term and costly studies of all kinds. However, my bias is clear: Developmental follow-up studies, particularly those that last beyond a year, and those whose cost exceeds that of a good cross-sectional or retrospective study, should be goal-directed and well planned.

In what follows, without making any distinction between exploratory and confirmatory studies, I delineate several general aspects of planning necessary for sound, definitive, and efficient developmental follow-up studies, and also focus on a few particular problems that seem to recur in many such studies.

CONCEPTUAL FRAMEWORK: SPECIFIC A PRIORI GOALS

The specification of a goal must include considerations of who, where, what, how, when, and why:

1. *Who? Where?* To what population of subjects are the results of a developmental follow-up study to apply? From this decision flow the definitions of the inclusion and exclusion criteria, the decision of whether the study can be a single site or must include multiple sites, and decisions about proper recruitment of subjects and proper sampling methods.

2. *What?* What information about the subjects in the population is needed to answer the research questions of interest? Will adequate measures of such information be available for subjects in that population? Which ones will be used and with what justification?

3. *How? When?* When are the subjects to enter the study? When are they to exit the study? How frequently should they be seen in the course of the study? Must the measurements be blinded or are other controls on bias necessary given the nature of the research questions, the population, the measures, and the information needed? Is a control group necessary? If so, how should it be constituted? How is the study to be implemented? What are the protocols for the design and for the measurements? What quality control procedures are necessary? Once the data are collected, how are they checked for accuracy and completeness? Where are they to be stored? How are they to be retrieved? What analytic approaches are needed?

4. *Why?* Why are the research questions reasonable and important? What is already known about them? What other information has been gathered about them? If other information has been gathered, why has the question not already been answered? Or has it? What, from other studies, are the effect sizes of interest? How large a sample size is thus indicated for the present study? Is there enough preliminary information already available to ensure that the proposed study can be well designed and executed and is likely to yield the necessary answers?

In short, adequate specification of the research goal is not merely an expression of a laudable sentiment, for example, that we want to know about the effects of day care on the health of children. Until we know exactly what is meant by "children," "health," "day care," and "effects," have examined all that is previously known about related issues, and have done a thorough evaluation and critique of all related previous studies and the methods they used—their successes and failures—only then can we begin to specify our own research goals and to plan our own research study. Until then, we are only, as Alice explains, hoping to get to a nebulous "somewhere."

POPULATION/SAMPLING

The first crucial issue in planning the study is the definition of the population to which the results of a developmental follow-up study are meant to apply. Such a definition leads to the articulation of the inclusion/exclusion criteria and plays a key role in all the decisions concerning appropriate sampling procedures, sample size determination, and accretion in the study.

If the inclusion/exclusion criteria are set too narrowly, the population to which the results apply may be so narrow as to have no general interest. In such a case, also, the size of the recruitment pool is likely to be small; it is difficult to amass even minimally sufficient numbers of subjects. A great deal of effort may be expended in screening out subjects who will *not* be studied. The power of tests in the study may be low and estimates of parameters may be quite imprecise. One may end up working long and hard, and expending a great deal of money, to achieve only equivocal results on a limited spectrum of subjects. On the other hand, overly inclusive criteria may produce such heterogeneous samples as to limit the power of tests and precision of estimates as effectively as overly exclusive criteria. One then works much harder gathering data, expending even more time and resources, with just as equivocal results. Thoughtful, careful planning based on extensive evaluation of what is already known and what has already been done is the key to avoiding such problems. No exclusion criterion should be set unless it can be justified as important for the clarity and interpretability of the outcome.

One specific and recurrent issue related to sampling is the need for a multisite study design. The usual argument for multisite studies is based on access to a wider pool of subjects for recruitment. Of course, that remains an incentive. However, an even greater incentive to multisite studies (even when a large enough pool might be available at a single site) is the added generalizability of the results from such studies, at least when the data such studies produce are properly analyzed (Fleiss, 1986).

In my experience, site differences should always be anticipated, even when the entry criteria seem very restrictive. Some site differences arise from sources of heterogeneity in the population that are unknown and uncontrollable. Subjects very similar in health, ethnic and socioeconomic status in New York and San Francisco, for example, may be very different from one another in a variety of other characteristics that may be important to the outcome. Some site differences arise from policy differences: Medical, social, and educational policy may vary from one site to another and these may have impacts on the outcome. Some site differences arise from research staff differences: How the criteria for selection and measurement are interpreted and applied may differ from site to site (and even from one evaluator to another within a site). So also may the level of adherence to protocols and the quality of interaction of staff with subjects. All of these factors, and more, may have impact on the outcome.

Some may argue that such site-to-site differences are merely extraneous heterogeneity that should be "controlled" in research design. I would argue instead, that if the results are truly meant to generalize beyond a single site in which a study is executed, such heterogeneity is not "extraneous," nor should it be "controlled" by eliminating sites. To do so would only ignore facts and limit the generalizability of the results. Instead, sites should be expressly selected to be heterogeneous enough to give some sense of the site-to-site variation likely in the population to which the results are expected to generalize. Then, every effort should be made to control only that portion of the variability caused by staff differences (by clearly defined and strictly enforced protocols, training to promote consistency across sites, and monitoring for strict adherence to protocols).

If a multisite *design* is used, however, it is essential that the *analysis* attempt to seek out any possible site differences in drawing conclusions. Currently, what often happens in multisite studies is that site differences are simply ignored in the analyses. Because it is known that ignoring such effects can produce serious statistical artifacts (Simpson's Paradox: Wagner, 1982; Simpson, 1951; Bickel, Hammel, & O'Connell, 1975; Hand, 1979), ignoring the possibility of site differences in a multisite study is one step *less* desirable than doing a single-site study that precludes the possibility of seeing site differences. Statistical artifact alone might produce the appearance of effects where there are none, or, at the other extreme, conceal effects where there are strong and important ones.

The primary argument against multisite studies is what appears to be the enormous cost of such studies. Indeed, multisite studies are logistically more difficult, but it is not clear that the cost per subject per annum in such studies is different from that for single-site studies (Meinert & Tonascia, 1986). The perceived difference may result from the fact that the research issues addressed in multisite studies tend to be perceived as more important. The consequent larger sample sizes, longer follow-up spans, and more careful execution result in a greater *total* investment of resources. If so, this only enhances the value of multisite studies, inasmuch as such studies are likely to be better and more carefully done, and produce more convincing and sounder results.

Funding one multisite study might well yield clearer and more definitive results, whereas expending the same funds on multiple single-site studies might merely generate inconsistent and conflicting results. One of the most frequently encountered statements in the discussion section of papers reporting single-site research studies is some variation of "Our results indicate the necessity of further studies of this issue." If the primary result of studies is only to foster the need for yet more studies, the wisdom of the investment of funds to support such studies should be carefully reconsidered.

INFORMATION/MEASURES AND DATA

What data should we collect? It is essential to obtain the following information:

1. All necessary administrative information (names, addresses, telephone numbers, social security numbers, etc.).
2. Information to describe adequately the characteristics of the sample, and hence the population to which the results can generalize (baseline information).
3. Information necessary to answer the specific research questions.
4. Information necessary to check the validity of such answers to the specific research questions.
5. Information necessary to elucidate the possible mechanisms underlying the phenomena related to the specific research questions (process measures).

Essential to *omit*, on the other hand, are data that do not amplify the information base, or data that are irrelevant to the specific research questions—data that are collected "while we're at it," or "in case anyone might be interested." Note that in all the preceding statements, I am drawing an essential distinction between *information* and *data*.

Every bit of data comprises Signal (relevant information about the subject of interest) and Noise (irrelevant information about the subject, information about others involved in the measurement process, and random error of measurement). Every bit of data collected adds Noise to the data set. The question is, however, whether that bit of data adds enough Signal to counteract the Noise it inevitably adds. The largest and most poorly constructed data sets are sometimes referred to as "rich in data." Indeed, they may be rich in data, but are they rich in Signal? or merely rich in Noise? Generally, the quantity of data in a data set tends to be inversely proportional to its quality. There are several reasons for this. When researchers are collecting only a few strategic bits of information about each subject, each measure related to that information can be given the attention it deserves to assess a priori its validity, reliability, and sensitivity. During data acquisition, close attention can be paid to completeness and accuracy.

When, on the other hand, thousands of bits of data are to be collected about each subject at each point of time, few bits are accorded that kind of close and thoughtful scrutiny. Data lacking validity can yield incorrect and misleading results. Data lacking reliability and sensitivity diminish sizes of effects, attenuate correlations and power of tests, and produce less convincing results. Incomplete data sets (missing data) may further compromise the representativeness of the sample. Diffusion of attention over thousands of bits of accumulating data compromises close scrutiny for completeness and correctness. Both subjects and data collectors can be overwhelmed by excessive demands for data and be less careful and accurate in reporting, collecting, and recording data. Thus, the quality of the data may deteriorate.

The end result of collecting too much data is that research results are more likely to be unclear, misleading, and ambiguous. Such data sets can and do mislead the field by generating inconsistent and conflicting results between multiple studies on the same issue. The ironic aftermath of all this is the increase in the cost of the study resulting from such excessive data gathering. This is one case in which doing good, careful science costs less.

An essential step, then, in planning sound research is to identify what information (not yet measured) is *necessary* to answer the research questions. The next step is to assess for each such bit of information, how many different ways there are of obtaining it (i.e., different measures), to canvass what is available on the quality of each of these possible measures (reliability, validity) in the population in which they are to be applied, and to assess any previous use of such measures in a similar population and the successes or failures others have experienced. When all this is done, the best possible choice of measure is made on the basis of that material.

This choice should be based on the *demonstrated* qualities of the measures and the experiences others have had with the measure in the field, not because a particular measurement is currently the most popular in the field. There are two reasons for this. First, it may be that the reason the research question has not hitherto been clearly and unambiguously answered is because the currently popular measure has some problems. Second and more important, by the time a follow-up study is completed and the results are ready for presentation, any weaknesses of the currently popular measure may well have already been exposed. To argue, then, that the choice of measure only reflected the same error others in the field were making at the time the study began offers little solace when the results become irrelevant or unconvincing. There must be some assurance that the choice of measure will "age well."

Researchers often include too many measures related to the *same* information, assuming such redundancy affords some extra protection. I would argue the opposite. With more than one measure related to the same information, there is no *addition* of Signal to the data set: At best, the same Signal is repeated. However, because each measure carries along its own Noise, there is the risk of a substantial addition of Noise. The Signals are harder (not easier) to detect clearly in the face of all the static and interference caused by the additional Noise. Such redundant data might be combined, producing a single measure for the desired information with greater reliability (less Noise) than any of its combined components or the best single measure (uni- or multidimensional) selected. One way or another, redundant data should *not* be included in the data set.

In this regard, a distinction must be drawn between a multidimensional measure and multiple measures of a single dimension (redundant data).

Each component of truly multidimensional data should bring into the data set a new Signal, an additional Signal that outweighs the additional Noise it inevitably adds. Five different measurements of age, for example, do not constitute five dimensions of information, just five repeated measurements on the same dimension, five sources of error, and five times as much data to gather, store, and process, at perhaps five times the cost of one such bit of data. When you add the possibility that assessors required to collect five bits of data may be just a little less careful than those required to collect only one, and that respondents, tired of answering multiple essentially repetitive questions, may be just a little less thoughtful in their answers, the cost of too much data becomes clearer.

To use redundant data in statistical tests is to incur the risk of false positive results (from multiple tests of the same hypotheses) as well as false negative results (because each test is based on less than optimally reliable data). Whether in statistical tests or in descriptive statistics, redundant data generate conflicting and confusing results.

Selection and deselection of measures is a painful decision for researchers, but it is more painful *after* one has spent the time and effort to collect data than before such commitment is made. However, such decisions should be made—preferably a priori. Even more painful: In the process of identifying measures related to information necessary to approach the research questions, it may emerge that *no* adequate measures are currently available for some necessary information. For example, in a proposed study of children, information on health may be available only using maternal recall and report. Such measures may carry far more information on the mothers than they do on the health of their children in some populations. If so, the research questions should be reevaluated. Perhaps the report of the mother, indicating the mother's sensitivity and attention and her ability to recall and report about her child's health, is itself of research interest even if the measure relates poorly to the actual health of the child. Alternatively, the research question should be set aside until the technology of measurement advances sufficiently to produce an appropriate measure of the information needed for the child. It does occasionally happen that during the planning process, one finds that certain research questions cannot be answered well, frequently because of inadequate current methodology. Such questions should be set aside until they can be answered well, lest wrong answers mislead the field. It is not true, I believe, that any answer, no matter how wrong, is better than no answer. We must know enough and be honest and courageous enough to admit it when we do not yet have the technology adequate to address a research question. Such admissions may even promote the kinds of research necessary to fill in the gaps in methodology.

If measures are carefully selected, retained only if necessary to answer the research hypotheses, nonredundant to other measures in the data set, and of documented quality, the size of data sets, even in the most complex developmental follow-up studies, will be smaller than they typically are now. However small they might become, such data sets are, by their nature, complex. Considerable effort should be invested in the design of data forms, pretesting forms, training observers and monitoring their performance, and checking completed forms for completeness and accuracy. Error detection procedures should be regular and formal, providing documentation of error rates as well as assurance of consistency over time. There should be documentation of every protocol related to data acquisition, checking, storage, and retrieval. Every analysis reported in a presentation or paper should be archived, along with the identification of the specific set of subjects and the specific set of data to which the analysis was applied.

Finally, it should not be merely assumed that when the time comes the investigators will deal with these problems well. How such problems will be dealt with, and who will deal with them, is an essential part of the planning, and is essential to adequate evaluation of any proposal for a long-term developmental follow-up study.

DESIGN ISSUES

Ideally, every follow-up study should enter subjects at birth and follow them to death—but neither subjects nor investigators can last that long. It is perhaps superfluous to argue the point in seriousness. However, for completeness, let us consider why not. An attempt at that ideal is virtually doomed by several factors. First, subjects tend to drop out and typically do so nonrandomly. As a result, the sample studied at one time point may not represent the same population as the sample studied at a later time point. This criticism, usually levied against repeated cross-sectional studies, also applies to follow-up studies where there is serious attrition.

Second, diagnoses and measures considered "state of the art" today are sometimes unacceptable only a few years from now. Research questions that are urgent now will have been well answered several years from now or will no longer be a topic of interest to the field. If this happens, the investigators have the choice either to continue gathering information on issues in which there is no longer interest or to switch to better measures and more timely issues. In the latter cases there will be missing early data and the value of the study may be no greater than that of much less costly cross-sectional or retrospective studies.

Whatever the ideal may be, the more *practical* strategy is to plan follow-up studies in more manageable blocks of time, perhaps 3 to 6 years of follow-up. This would be a period of time during which it is anticipated that the current research questions remain of interest and moment and the technology will not have shifted too excessively, but a long enough time to observe patterns of change within the subjects. Toward the end of that period, a continuation follow-up study might be independently planned and evaluated, taking into account the shifts in the research hypotheses of interest and what has been learned in the first phase and throughout the rest of the field during the first phase.

But with such a narrow follow-up window, some major decisions involve the time of subject entry, the time of exit, and the frequency with which subjects are seen between entry and exit. Even with the narrow window, some subjects will drop out, and these must be adequately dealt with in the analysis. Singer and Willet's chapter (this volume) presents one powerful analytic approach, relatively new to the behavioral and social sciences, that carries enormous potential for answering many questions in those fields, an approach applicable with an outcome measure that can be defined as a latency, a duration, or, in the standard parlance, a "survival time."

Let me bring to your attention another body of analytic approaches in which the outcome is a *quantitative* measure, not a survival time, with a developmental course that may differ from subject to subject. To illustrate both the problem and a solution, let me present a hypothetical example (loosely modeled after testosterone development in adolescent boys). If one followed a boy from the age of 10 to the age of 20, the pattern of development might appear somewhat like that of Figure 1. For some span of time, one would see a juvenile level response; at some point, there would be a *rapid* rise to an adult level. The general pattern would be the same for all normal boys, but the juvenile level, the adult level and, most important, the time of the rise might differ from boy to boy.

If one did a series of cross-sectional studies in such a case, sampling the same population at each age, what one would see is described in Figure 2. What the results suggest is that the response of boys is a smooth, *gradual* increase in the response that extends from a juvenile level response at about 11 years to an adult level response at about 19 years (the times of the earliest rises to the latest). The variability is least at both ends of the age period (reflecting only variations in the juvenile and adult levels) and maximal in the mid range (where variation in the juvenile and adult levels as well as variation in the time of the rise are expressed). The answer that is obtained has the distinction of being 100% wrong—the conclusion of a slow and gradual rise in response inaccurately describes the process in every individual boy. Using age-standardized scores at each age compounds the problem as seen in Figure 3, which shows the age-standardized values for the boy in Figure 1. Averaging data age by age in a long-term follow-up study also yields incorrect results (Figure 2). Merely doing long-term follow-up is not the answer. The answer lies in how such long-term follow-up data are analyzed.

What is needed is to do a long-term follow-up and use an analytic approach that examines the *pattern* of responses for *each* boy that summarizes the pattern on an individual basis (here by observed juvenile level, time of rise, and observed adult level), and that uses these summary indices to answer

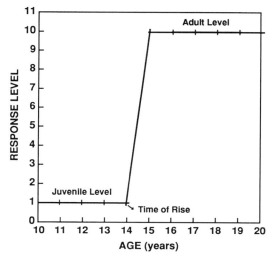

Figure 1 The response of one hypothetical boy over the adolescent years. Each boy in the population has exactly the same general pattern, but they differ in the juvenile level, the time of rise, and the adult level.

any further research questions of interest. Here, for example, we might want to know to what extent the time of the rise is governed by the weight or height of the boy or how the time of the rise relates to the emergence of various secondary sex characteristics, or whether those with low juvenile levels are also those with low adult levels.

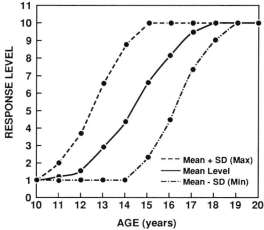

Figure 2 The mean response (and standard deviation SD) in the population of boys, each having the pattern of response shown in Figure 1.

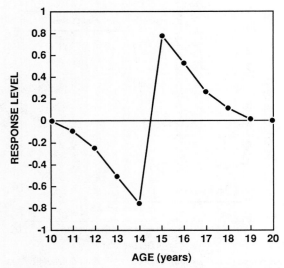

Figure 3   The standardized response curve in the population of boys, each having the pattern of response shown in Figure 1.

This is a simple example of a *random regression model*. What such models seek is a mathematical representation of the developmental course that is as mathematically simple as possible, and that approximates the behavior of the process for individual subjects (here, for example, by a step function). The mathematical model is structured so that the parameters of the model represent identifiable features of the process (here, juvenile and adult levels and the time of the rise). The parameters for *each* individual subject are estimated from that subject's follow-up data. Further analysis focuses on the individual parameter estimates rather than the raw data. Because moving from raw data to parameter estimates per subject usually involves a reduction in the number of data points to be used in analysis, this is consistent with my previous recommendations to utilize strategies to reduce the Noise by removing redundancy, thus clarifying the Signals in the data set.

Such an approach has several other advantages (Kraemer & Thiemann, 1987). Because models are fitted individually, missing data are less of a problem. Data that are available only at irregular intervals are easier to use in analysis. The parameter estimates, usually representing combinations of directly observed values, often are more reliable than the separate, directly observed values. The challenge, of course, is to identify an appropriate mathematical model for the process under study, but frequently simple models, such as straight lines or low-degree polynomials, do quite nicely.

ANALYSIS

Unfortunately, elegant statistical analysis cannot repair poor sampling, measurement, design, or inadequate protocol compliance. On the other hand, a well-planned, well-executed study frequently requires only the simplest and most straightforward analytic methods to produce valid, powerful, and easily understood results. In many ways, the goal of good research planning should be to produce a study plan so that no fancy statistical analyses will be necessary to obtain results that will be clear and convincing to all.

An often quoted barb is the one suggesting that if you need a statistician to tell you what is going on in your data, they must be pretty poor data. Perhaps it is surprising that, as a statistician, I agree with the spirit of this barb. As a statistician, my role is not at the end of a possibly methodologically flawed study to try to elicit some conclusions from possibly flawed data using esoteric statistical methods. It is in the planning phases of a study to help researchers avoid as many flaws as possible and to make it as easy as possible to get the best possible and clearest results. Here, I will focus on one such analytic problem to be avoided that is long recognized, long warned about, but that continues to cause serious problems. It requires "fancy" statistical analyses with the most elusive results: multiple regression models with collinear independent predictors. Redundant data are extreme collinearity, but the focus here is not only on redundant measures, but on measures of conceptually different Signals that Nature has chosen to closely intertwine.

The simple fact is that what Nature has entwined mere statisticians cannot disentwine. To illustrate why this is so, let me use a schematic (Figure 4) rather than the usual mathematical demonstrations (cf. Fleiss, 1986). Suppose the question of interest is that of ascertaining the effects of low birthweight and prematurity on an outcome (such as IQ at age 5). What seems obvious (and is wrong) is that one can answer this question by using multiple linear regression with an IQ score as the dependent variable, with birthweight, gestational age, and perhaps their interaction, as the independent variables. In any population, birthweight and gestational age are highly correlated and are more highly correlated in populations in which such a question is likely to seem most relevant (low birthweight or preterm groups).

In Figure 4, the correlation between birthweight and gestational age in the population is schematically represented by the overlap between the circles representing a measurement of birthweight and a measurement of gestational age (Areas 2 + 4). The outcome (IQ) is represented by a rectangle. If the outcome is correlated with birthweight, it overlaps the circle representing birthweight (Areas 1 and 2), and if it is correlated with gestational age, it overlaps the circle representing gestational age (Areas 2 and 3). In fact, because birthweight and gestational age are themselves so highly correlated

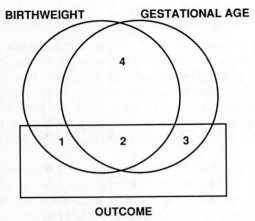

OUTCOME

Figure 4   A schematic representation of the correlational structure of birthweight, gestational age, and an outcome measure. Overlap between figures indicates shared variance or correlation.

(Areas 2 and 4), it would be no surprise that the correlations against either one of these alone would be of very similar magnitude (Areas $1+2$ = Areas $2+3$) because most of the overlap between the outcome rectangle and the circles must be with that portion common to both circles (Area 2). Now, is the correlation represented by Area 2 due to birthweight or is it due to gestational age?

When a multiple regression model of any kind is used (even assuming exact model fit, which is rare), the model tries to pull apart Area 2 and to assign distinct portions to either birthweight, to gestational age, or to their interaction. What the model does is arbitrary. What emerges depends strongly on which computation algorithm is used. If one forced birthweight in first, it may well be that the conclusion would be that gestational age added no information, only birthweight mattered. If one forced gestational age in first, the conclusion would be reversed. If the procedure were done stepwise, either forward or backward, which of the two entered first might well be a matter of chance and the result might be reversed if the study were replicated. Thus, what one concludes would depend on the vagaries of the samples, of the measurements, of the particular algorithm, and of the mathematical model selected. What must be remembered is that the statisticians who formulated the mathematical model, the programmers who put together the computer algorithms, and the researchers who direct that one or another of the available models and algorithms are used, are not privy to what nature intended in this particular case. The answers one gets, consequently, also may not reflect what Nature intended.

This example used only two independent variables, birthweight and gestational age. If more than two were included and these comprised further sets of collinear variables, as well as more variables collinear with the original two (e.g., race and other socioeconomic variables), the results become even more problematic. The conclusions with respect to the role of birthweight and gestational age would also vary according to what other variables the researchers chose to include.

My recommendation is to formulate *answerable* research questions by avoiding collinearity problems. The analytic method may well be a multiple regression analysis, but there must be much greater care in the choice of independent variables, their measurement, and the interpretation of results. In the illustration, for example, we can never know how much of the outcome is due specifically to gestational age or to low birthweight. Because of their collinearity, we might choose to include one or the other, but not both, keeping in mind that in either case developmental status at birth is the Signal being assessed. That Signal is reflected in either birthweight or gestational age, as well as in many other indices that might be proposed such as birth length, measures of pulmonary adequacy, or neurological maturity. Alternatively, we might take one (e.g., gestational age) as the primary indicator of developmental status at birth and use relative weight (birthweight relative to gestational age) to indicate adequacy of intrauterine growth as a second variable. These two are noncollinear, yet use all the information in birthweight and gestational age.

CONCLUSIONS

To summarize: I cannot overemphasize the importance of *planning*. Most common problems in research, particularly the prevalence of conflicting and ambiguous reports in the research literature, can be averted, or at least alleviated, by careful, thoughtful and, most of all, *tough* planning decisions. We cannot trust luck or serendipity. We cannot expect that a decision hard to make in planning will become simpler with time. Above all, we cannot flout the basic rules and dictates of science and hope to achieve scientifically credible results.

Otherwise, I close with four lines (copied from the blackboard of Dr. Lincoln Moses) that might well be titled: "Lament at the Conclusion of a Softly Planned Follow-up Study":

Where is the wisdom we have lost in knowledge? Where is the
    knowledge we have lost in information?

—T.S. Eliot

Where is the information we have lost in data? Where are the data
we have lost?

—Anonymous

REFERENCES

Bartko, J. J.,Carpenter, W. T., Jr., & McGlashan, T. H. (1988). Statistical issues in long-term followup studies. *Schizophrenia Bulletin, 14*(4), 575–587.

Bickel, P. J., Hammel, E. A., & O'Connell, J. W. (1975). Sex bias in graduate admissions, Data from Berkeley. *Science, 187,* 398–404.

Fleiss, J. S. (1986). Analysis of data from multiclinic trials. *Controlled Clinical Trials, 7,* 267–275.

Hand, D. J. (1979). Psychiatric examples of Simpson's Paradox. *British Journal of Psychiatry, 135,* 90–91.

Kraemer, H. C., & Thiemann, S. (1987). *How many subjects?* Beverly Hills, CA: Sage Publications.

McGlashan, T. H., Carpenter, W. T., Jr., & Bartko, J. J. (1988). Issues of design and methodology in long-term followup studies. *Schizophrenia Bulletin, 14*(4), 569–574.

Meinert, C. L., & Tonascia, S. (1986). Single-center versus multicenter trials. In *Clinical trials: Design, conduct, and analysis* (pp. 23–29). New York: Oxford University Press.

Simpson, E. H. (1951). The interpretation of interaction in contingency tables. *Journal of the Royal Statistical Society, B, 13,* 238–241.

Wagner, C. H. (1982). Simpson's Paradox in real life. *The American Statistician, 36,* 46–48.

Methodological Considerations and Strategies for Studying the Long-term Effects of Early Intervention

Carl J. Dunst
Carol M. Trivette

INTRODUCTION

Researchers interested in the long-term developmental follow-up of infants and young children face many conceptual and methodological challenges. Those interested in the long-term developmental outcomes of infants and toddlers who participated in early intervention programs are doubly challenged. On the one hand they must attend to a number of key concerns and requirements that are unique to developmental sciences (Appelbaum & McCall, 1983; Baltes, Reese, & Nesselroade, 1977; Burchinal & Appelbaum, 1991; Nesselroade & Baltes, 1979; Wohlwill, 1973), and on the other hand they must be able to separate out the effects (or lack) of early intervention from the influences of other causal, mediating, moderating, and intervening variables (Baltes et al., 1977; Turner & Reese, 1980).

The purpose of this chapter is to describe the potential utility of two different, but complementary, methodological strategies for the long-term developmental follow-up of young children who have participated in early intervention. Both approaches permit inferences about the nature of behavioral change and factors associated with change. The first is a particular method for estimating individual developmental growth curves and for studying the correlates of intrasubject variations in behavioral change (Bryk & Raudenbush, 1987; Bryk, Raudenbush, Seltzer, & Congdon, 1989). The second method is a particular way of defining the meaning of both risk and opportunity factors that affect behavioral development (Garbarino, 1982; Sameroff, Selfer, Barocas, Zax, & Greenspan, 1987; Werner, 1985), and empirically relating indices of each to variations in developmental outcomes. The description of either strategy is neither new nor unique. What is innovative, is the possible combination of the two as part of the same research program aimed at understanding behavioral change and the environmental factors that promote or impede developmental growth. In addition, we describe possible extensions of both approaches and how these extensions might contribute to a better understanding of the developmental sequel of children who have received early intervention.

The usefulness of both methodological strategies is illustrated with data from three longitudinal studies being conducted in our laboratory. The first is a large-scale follow-up study of adolescents and young adults who participated in an early intervention program, and who either had disabilities or were at risk for poor developmental outcomes (Cornwell, Lane, & Swanton, 1975; Dunst, 1985; Dunst & Trivette, 1988a). The second is a prospective longitudinal study of pregnant women and their offspring that focuses on the influences of intrafamily and extrafamily resources on a number of aspects of child, parent, and family functioning. The third is a longitudinal study of child maltreatment and the environmental correlates of different rates of abuse and neglect. Although these are studies in progress, the illustrative points we wish to make can be done with these different data sets. The use of these data for purposes of this chapter focuses specifically on the implications of several methodological strategies for contributing to an understanding of the course of human development and the factors associated with different developmental trajectories.

This chapter is divided into four major sections. In the first section, we briefly outline the particulars of the developmental model that guides our approach to studying the sequel of children who participate in early intervention. The second section includes a description of (a) hierarchical linear modeling and its application to the study of the correlates of change, and (b) the major features of a risk–opportunity framework, which considers a range of environmental factors that both impede and facilitate development. In the third section, we describe and illustrate the utility of both strategies for studying human development in general and the long-term follow-up of children who participate in early intervention in particular. The fourth section is devoted to a discussion of possible extensions of both strategies and how they may be applied to advancing our knowledge about human development, and the role early intervention plays in developmental rates and outcomes.

A DEVELOPMENTAL ORIENTATION TOWARD LONG-TERM FOLLOW-UP

To place the material in this chapter in proper perspective, we begin with a brief outline of the core features of a particular approach to the study of behavioral change that undergirds our research. The developmental model that we have adopted is best described as a merging of different, but complementary perspectives of developmental psychology (e.g., Bronfenbrenner, 1979; Garbarino, 1982; Piaget, 1983; Wohlwill, 1973). More specifically, the integrated model provides a basis for describing both qualitative and quantitative changes in development over time and for studying the manner in which a variety of determinants, including ecological factors, influence rates and patterns of change. Consequently, there is major "concern for the progressive accommodations between a growing human organism and its immediate environment, and the way in which this relation is mediated by forces emanating from remote regions in the larger physical and social milieu" (Bronfenbrenner, 1979, p. 3).

Our research has been guided by the following broad-based definition of developmental psychology: "Developmental psychology deals with the description, explanation, and modification (optimization) of intraindividual change in behavior across the life span, and with interindividual differences (and similarities) in intraindividual change" (Baltes et al., 1977, p. 4). Stated more simply, this means the description of both individual and group developmental change across time, the specification of differences between and similarities among persons with respect to these changes, and the delineation of both intervention and nonintervention correlates of change. The focus of the material described next is on a particular way of thinking about and operationalizing the study of individual change, and conceptualizing the investigation of factors associated with differences in patterns of development.

Developmental Functions

The study of *individual change* across time or over age is what makes developmental psychology a unique science (Appelbaum & McCall, 1983; Wohlwill, 1973). A true developmental science requires repeated measures of the *same* construct, attribute, or behavior across time on the *same* individual. When data are collected in this manner, the pattern of development can be specified in terms of a developmental function (Wohlwill, 1973). A developmental function defines the form of the relationship between chronological age and the changes in the manifestation of the attribute or construct of interest. For example, the form of the relationship between mental age and chronological age defines one particular developmental function.

According to Wohlwill (1973), two conditions must be met in order for developmental functions to be used as part of the study of intraindividual change:

> First, the behavior variable must be one that can be expected to lead to age changes of sufficient magnitude to be revealed consistently in the face of the "noise" from variance associated with situational factors, stimulus conditions, and errors of measurement. Second, these age changes must remain roughly invariant over differences in specific experimental and environmental conditions so as to make possible the determination of a modal prototype function representing their expected form under "normal" conditions of development. (pp. 33–34)

The particular behavioral variables and constructs (characteristics, attributes, etc.) that meet these conditions provide a basis for mapping change across time, discerning variations in change among individuals having different developmental functions (trajectories), and examining the correlates of change.

The reader is referred to Appelbaum and McCall (1983), Brim and Kagan (1980), and Wohlwill (1973) for in-depth discussions of the characteristics of and underlying assumptions that guide the use of development functions as indices of change and patterns of developmental processes. We note, however, a useful distinction made by Burchinal and Appelbaum (1991) between two general schools of thought that focus on either "strong" or "weak" views of development. According to these theorists,

> The "strong concept of growth" view is based on the idea that a single [prototypical] developmental function can adequately describe the growth of all individuals from some population on a given attribute. . . . The other view has been called the "weak concept of development" model (Nesselroade & Baltes, 1979). Advocates of this view are interested in identifying intraindividual patterns of change and interindividual differences in the intraindividual patterns of change. (p. 25)

Whereas the former view implies that individual developmental functions are minimally influenced by environmental factors, the latter view implies that variations in individual functions may, to a large degree, be associated with differing kinds of experiences, including those that deliberately attempt to positively influence change (see e.g., Hunt, 1987). The "weak view" by its very nature requires the description of change in relationship to one or more explicative factors, and most intervention-oriented research is inherently guided by this perspective of developmental processes.

Developmental Functions and Long-term Follow-up   Life-span developmental psychology is concerned with the study of psychological processes over the entire life span, or at least with that portion of the life span during which attributes under study would be expected to show change (Baltes et al.,

1977). Data on the long-term follow-up of children who participated in early intervention are amenable to a life-span approach if at least two conditions are met. First, the attribute or construct being investigated is the same across all measurement occasions; that is, "the attribute must maintain the same dimensions across measurement occasions (e.g., the attribute is defined by the same 'latent constructs' over time)" (Burchinal & Appelbaum, 1991, p. 24). Second, the analysis of behavior must focus on the description of patterns of intraindividual change in the latent variable. This requires that one ascertain the form of the prototypical growth rate as well as individual deviations in patterns of growth. The latter is accomplished not by examination of developmental outcomes at a particular point in time (e.g., 12th grade performance), but rather by investigation of the shape and patterns of intraindividual growth across the period of time under investigation. Such an orientation, as we will see, differs considerably from the manner in which the developmental sequel of children who participated in early intervention has until now been typically examined (e.g., Consortium for Longitudinal Studies, 1983).[1] Moreover, because this approach emphasizes the study of intraindividual development rather than group change, it provides a more direct way of studying the relationship between early and later development for individual children, and the extent to which early intervention shows conditional or unconditional relationships with subsequent developmental outcomes.

Correlates of Change

Proponents of a "weak concept of development" concern themselves as much with the study of correlates of change as they do with the identification of patterns of development. The term *correlate* is used broadly to refer to a host of factors that might be associated with variations in intraindividual change. Terms like mediators, determinants, moderators, and predictors all fall into this class of correlates. They may be causal or noncausal, distal or proximal, experimental or nonexperimental, conditional or unconditional, and interventive or noninterventive (see e.g., Achenbach, 1978; Baltes et al., 1977; Cohen & Cohen, 1983). The particular correlates that are the focus of investigation will differ depending on the developmental attribute of interest, but, in general, their selection is guided by theory or previous research, or preferably both. Regardless of the basis for the particular correlates that an investigator chooses to include in his or her study, the focus is on the relationship between the correlates as independent variables and developmental functions as dependent variables. Depending on the design of the

[1] It should be noted that this is the case not because these investigators failed to adequately adhere to appropriate design and analysis considerations, but rather because the types of strategies described in this chapter were not yet readily available when these investigations were completed.

study and the conditions under which the data were collected, any number of methodological strategies may be employed for analyzing the data (Appelbaum & McCall, 1983).

Paradigms for Studying Change   The relationship between developmental functions and correlates are often described by equations like: $B = f(A)$, which is read: behavior (B) varies as a function of one or more A variables. Lewin's (1935) classic equation: $B = f(PE)$, where P = Person Variables and E = Environmental Variables is another example of how this relationship has been stated (see also Cohen & Cohen, 1983; Longstreth, 1968). As noted by Baltes et al. (1977), these paradigms are simply statements of hypothesized or expected relationships between variables on both sides of the equations, and in no way are they assertions that the independent variables are necessarily causally related to either a specific aspect of behavior or behavioral change. These types of equations nonetheless provide useful frameworks, or at least mnemonics, for thinking about development and studying its relationship to correlates of change.

The extent to which correlates can be considered causal variables depends to a large degree on whether experimental conditions can be introduced into the study of developmental functions (Appelbaum & McCall, 1983; McCall, 1977). For example, there is no reason why children participating in an early intervention study could not be randomly assigned to begin participation "early versus late," and the effects of this manipulation specifically studied with respect to its influence on patterns of development. Even when this is not possible, age of intervention can still be assessed as a nonexperimental correlate and nonetheless contribute to our understanding of influences indexed by this age variable (Baltes et al., 1977). In either case, "age of entry" becomes a target of empirical investigation, and when included as part of the analysis of factors affecting patterns of development, provides a basis for advancing knowledge about how different factors are related to the long-term sequel of children.

METHODS FOR STUDYING GROWTH AND ITS CORRELATES

There are many approaches for studying development (Appelbaum & McCall, 1983; Baltes et al., 1977; Burchinal & Appelbaum, 1991) and its correlates (Bronfenbrenner, 1979; Longstreth, 1968). Two approaches are described next that have utility for studying life-span development in general and the long-term follow-up of children who received early intervention in particular. One is hierarchical linear modeling, a procedure for estimating intraindividual change and correlates of change (Bryk & Raudenbush, 1987). The other is a strategy for capturing the influences of both risk and opportunity factors on individual differences in rates of change (Garbarino, 1982). Both are currently being used in several longitudinal investigations we are conducting. We make no claims that these are the only or even the best approaches for studying developmental follow-up. They do, however, permit interesting approaches to data analysis that shed considerable light on the nature of the course of human development and factors associated with intraindividual differences in develomental trajectories.

Estimating Intraindividual Developmental Functions

Most previous research on the course of human development has relied on repeated measures analysis of variance for approximating the characteristics of developmental functions (Appelbaum & McCall, 1983). Such approaches, however, have been criticized as being indirect and often biased estimates of intraindividual change (McCall, 1977; McCall & Appelbaum, 1973).

There are now available a host of mathematical models and statistical methods for estimating the key features of prototypical and intraindividual developmental functions (see Bock, 1989; Burchinal & Appelbaum, 1991; Bryk et al., 1989; Nesselroade & Baltes, 1979). One of these is hierarchical linear modeling (Bryk & Raudenbush, 1987). Hierarchical linear modeling (HLM) is a highly flexible, yet sophisticated, technique for estimating linear, polynomial, and nonlinear growth curves (Burchinal & Appelbaum, 1991), and therefore has special utility for use with developmental data that may take on different forms and patterns at different stages of development. As described by Burchinal and Appelbaum (1991), HLM employs a two-stage model for assessing change:

> At the first, or within-subject stage, an individual's status on some trait is modeled as a function of an individual growth trajectory plus random error. At the second, or between-subject stage, the parameters of the individual growth trajectories vary as a function of differences between subjects in background characteristics, instructional experiences, and possibly experimental treatments. (p. 147)

The application of HLM to the study of change necessitates longitudinal data "because only the repeated observation of the same subjects over time allows study of intraindividual change across time in a manner that is uncontaminated by interindividual differences" (Burchinal & Appelbaum, 1991, p. 24). However, it is worth noting that in using HLM, "each subject's growth can be measured at different ages and a different number of times. Thus, the within-subject model does not assume a uniform data collection design across subjects" (Bryk & Raudenbush, 1987, p. 148). It does require at least three data points per subject, but the larger the number of data points over the period of time being investigated, the greater the likelihood that a reliable estimate of individual developmental functions will be obtained.

Hierarchical linear modeling has been used by Bryk and Raudenbush (Bryk & Raudenbush, 1987, 1988; Raudenbush, 1988) in a number of studies examining intraindividual change on various measures of behavior and competence, and on both the experimental and nonexperimental correlates of change. The use of HLM requires that certain statistical and model assumptions be met, and the reader is referred to Bryk and Raudenbush (1987) for technical discussions of these requirements (see also Burchinal & Appelbaum, 1991). Our descriptions are limited to a nontechnical presentation of the methodology.[2] An HLM analysis yields a number of statistics useful for depicting and understanding the nature of developmental change and examining how intervention and nonintervention variables may be related to change. Table I summarizes some of the information produced by an HLM analysis for both the within-subject and between-subject stages of application. Two major features of the within-subject part of the analysis are identification of the structure (linear, nonlinear, etc.) of the average (prototypical) growth pattern for all subjects combined, and an assessment of the extent to which individual growth trajectories differ from the prototypical developmental function. The major features of the between-subject part of the analysis are assessment of the relationship between initial status and change rates, and the correlates of both initial status and patterns of change. Following a presentation of one method of classifying correlates of change, we illustrate the use of HLM for analysis of developmental change among children who participated in an early intervention program.

Classifying Correlates of Change

One task of the developmentalist is to discern the developmental functions of age-related attributes and behavioral characteristics. Another is to account for interindividual variations in acquisition of developmental capabilities. The latter is typically done by studying the various factors that account for individual differences in developmental change (Baltes et al., 1977). When the factors studied include both experimental and nonexperimental variables, the investigation combines and mixes approaches central to the different realms of developmental psychology (Appelbaum & McCall, 1983).

There are many ways of conceptualizing, classifying, and operationalizing the correlates of developmental change. Early classificatory correlate schemes simply divided explicative factors into genetic and nongenetic influences (e.g., Fisher, 1918; Hogben, 1933). Jones (1954), among others (e.g., Bayley, 1970), advanced our knowledge of the determinants of variations in development by producing lists of factors that were found to influence certain behavioral capabilities. Such factors included parental education

---

[2] It is taken as a given here and in subsequent sections of the chapter that in the use of HLM, and possible variations and extensions of the methodology, that the necessary statistical and model assumptions are met.

Table I Within- and Between-Subject Parameters Assessed by a Hierarchical Linear Modeling (HLM) Analysis

Parameter	Description
Within-subject stage	
Mean growth trajectory	Indexes the degree of polynomial to be fitted to the data for the prototypical growth curve.
Intraindividual growth trajectories	Indexes the nature and degree of deviations of intraindividual growth curves from the prototypical growth trajectory.
Reliability estimates	Summary indices of the reliability of the instrument used to measure the growth parameters of the subjects.
Between-subject stage	
Correlates of initial status and change	Statistical relationships (regression coefficients) between the predictor and outcomes measures (initial status and growth rates).
Total variance explained	Total percentage of variance accounted for in intraindividual variations in growth rates by the aggregate set of correlates.
Parameter variance explained	Percentage of parameter variance (total variance minus variance due to sampling error) explained by the aggregate set of correlates.

levels, social class, father's occupation, family income, race, environmental and physical impoverishment, and "the 'general goodness' of community life" (Jones, 1954, p. 649). Longstreth (1968), in his text on the development of child behavior and competence, organized determinants according to past environment, present environment, and heredity influences, and provided lists of variables influencing behavior and development in each category of correlates.

The various classification systems proposed during the early part of this century, which are still employed, are much alike, albeit with slight variations. In the past decade, however, there has been a shift in interest in classifying determinants that has moved away from concern with genetic explanatory factors toward classificatory schemes that focus primarily on different classes of environmental influences. One now finds in both the developmental and nondevelopmental sciences, frameworks that organize correlates into two broad environmental factor classes, which have been termed by different investigators as risk and protective factors (Dubow & Luster, 1990; Rae-Grant, Thomas, Offord, & Boyle, 1989; Roosa, Beals, Sandler, & Pillow, 1990), potentiating and compensatory factors (Cicchetti, 1989; Cicchetti & Rizley, 1981), vulnerability and protective factors (Werner, 1985), vulnerability and resiliency factors (Garmezy, 1987, 1991), resilience and protective factors (Rutter, 1985, 1987), and risk and vulnerability factors

(Barocas, Seifer, & Sameroff, 1985). The major foci of each of these approaches, with the exception of the system proposed by Werner (1985), is the study of factors that prevent negative outcomes, the consequences of negative factors on development, or factors that buffer (protect) individuals from unsupportive environments. The use of these risk-oriented frameworks has proven especially valuable for discovering the cumulative, interactional, and transactional influences of environmental factors that retard behavior and develoment (see, e.g., Sameroff et al., 1987). However, as noted by Bond (1982), such "approaches presume that disaster is impending in our lives [and that of children] and that our efforts should be focused upon its diversion. . . . Protecting ourselves from negative influences is, at most, a narrow perspective on the course of growth and well-being" (p. 5). Because risk-oriented frameworks focus on environmental factors that have either negative effects on development or buffer children against the effects of negative influences, they tend to minimize, and in some cases simply fail to consider, factors related to positive outcomes. Risk-oriented frameworks provide, at best, a limited perspective for studying the correlates of change.

An expanded framework proposed by Garbarino (1982) provides a wider lens for viewing correlates of change, which on the one hand includes all that is central to the various risk-oriented frameworks just listed, and on the other hand, places equal emphasis on environmental factors that enhance and facilitate positive outcomes. Garbarino (1982) labels influences that impede and enhance development, respectively, sociocultural risk and opportunity factors. Risk factors include intrafamily and extrafamily influences that are impoverishing, and therefore undermine a family's ability to nurture child development. Opportunity factors include intrafamily and extrafamily influences that are facilitating, and therefore support and strengthen a family's ability to promote child competence. The Garbarino model is rooted in ecological theory, which considers a range of possible negative and positive factors that might function as determinants and which influence human development at a number of levels of influence (Bronfenbrenner, 1979).

Garbarino's notions of risk and opportunity share key features with the defining characteristics of prevention and promotion models of intervention (Bond, 1982; Cowen, 1985; Dunst, Trivette, & Thompson, 1990; Hoke, 1968; Rappaport, 1981; Seeman, 1989; Stanley & Maddux, 1986; Surgeon General, 1979; Zautra & Sandler, 1983). The primary orientation of prevention models is protection against either actual or perceived events that are likely to result in negative reactions or outcomes. Major emphasis is placed on the deterrence or forestalling of otherwise negative consequences (Cowen, 1985). This is accomplished by "reducing and/or coping with harmful or otherwise threatening events (using) defense as the primary orientation" (Zautra & Sandler, 1983, p. 39). In contrast, promotion models are characterized as having a mastery and optimization orientation. Major emphasis is placed on the facilitation, enhancement, and elaboration of a person's competencies and capabilities (Bond, 1982). This is accomplished by actions that support human functioning in ways that strengthen people's adaptive capabilities. The aim of promotion models is akin to what Baltes et al. (1977) describes as the optimization goal of developmental psychology; namely, the use of interventions that modify individual development in a robust, long-lasting manner.

A central tenet of most risk factor classification schemes is the implicit (and sometimes explicit) contention that the absence of problems (risk factors), or the prevention of poor outcomes by removal of risk factors, may be taken as evidence for the presence of positive functioning or the optimization of development. It is assumed that if risk factors are absent or removed, children's development as measured on any number of developmental tasks will represent optimal performance. We have presented elsewhere evidence indicating the untenableness of this argument (Dunst & Trivette, 1992; Dunst et al., 1990). Fundamentally, our own research as well as that of others (see Dunst et al., 1990, for a review) leads to the conclusion that

> the absence of negative functioning or problems cannot be considered a necessary condition for arguing that a person's behavior will reflect positive (optimal) functioning. Extrapolating from this evidence, a strong case can be made for the argument that the prevention of poor outcomes will not necessarily result in enhancement and strengthening of positive functioning. (Dunst et al., 1990, p. 38)

Garbarino's (1982) risk–opportunity framework has been incorporated into our research as one way of studying factors that either impede or facilitate development. Table II lists various sets of variables that represent targets for investigation as risk and opportunity factors, respectively. The list was generated from a review of both theory and research with an emphasis on those risk and opportunity factors that have been found or hypothesized to have influences on a number of aspects of individual, family, and child functioning in addition to child development (e.g., Antonovsky, 1981; Barocas et al., 1985; Bond, 1982; Brim & Kagan, 1980; Bronfenbrenner, 1979; Cochran & Brassard, 1979; Cohen & Syme, 1985; Dunst & Trivette, 1992; Dunst, Trivette, & LaPointe, 1992; Dunst et al., 1990; Garbarino, 1982; Nesselroade & Baltes, 1979; Rappaport, 1981; Seeman, 1989; Stanley & Maddux, 1989; Werner, 1985; Zautra & Sandler, 1983).

Several things are worth noting about the sets of factors listed in the table. First, they index a wide range of possible intrafamily and extrafamily factors that would be expected to influence various aspects of functioning (e.g., Beavers & Hampson, 1990; Bronfenbrenner, 1979; Cohen & Syme, 1985; Dunst et al., 1990). Second, the factors listed would be expected to have either or both direct and indirect influences on human development depending on the outcome behavior being studied and the manner in which the correlates were hypothesized to be related to dependent measure (e.g., Cochran &

Table II A Proposed List of Risk and Opportunity Factors Influencing Human Development and Functioning

Variables	Risk factors	Opportunity factors
Mothers' age	Younger or older than normal childbearing years	Within optimal childbearing years
Parent education	Low educational attainment	High educational attainment
Income	Inadequate income	Adequate income
Occupation status	Low occupation status of head of household	High occupation status for head of household
Socioeconomic status (SES)	Low SES	High SES
Job stability	Repeated job changes or unemployment	Stable job
Pregnancy	Unplanned	Planned
Number of siblings	More than four children	One or two children
Residential stability	Repeated relocations	None or few relocations
Marital status	Absence of spouse or partner	Supportive spouse or partner present
Marital relationship	Conflictive	Harmonious
Marital stability	Repeated changes in a conjugal relationship	Stable conjugal relationship
Child temperament	Avoidant, difficult	Warm, responsive
Infant separation	Prolonged separation in first year	Limited separation in first year
Parental health	Poor physical health	Excellent physical health
Parental mental health	Repeated occurrences of mental health related problem	Stable emotional well-being
Parental self-esteem	Low self-esteem	High self-esteem
Parental locus of control	External	Internal
Parental social skills	Poor	Good
Coping strategies	Reactive	Proactive
Quality of primary caregiver/ child interaction	Controlling and emotionally unavailable	Stimulating and warm
Parenting style	Authoritarian/Directive	Responsive/Facilitative
Toxic substances	High exposure	No exposure
Nutritional intake	Inadequate	Adequate
Accidents	Frequent	Infrequent
Infections/illnesses	Frequent	Infrequent
Alternative caregivers	No	One or more
Presence of extended family	None or few available	Many and supportive
Extrafamily support	Poor/Unsupportive	Good/Supportive
Life events	Negative life events	Positive life events

Note. Sources: Barocas et al., 1985; Beavers & Hampson, 1990; Bronfenbrenner, 1979; Cicchetti & Rizley, 1981; Cohen & Syme, 1985; Dubow & Luster, 1990; Dunst et al., 1990; Dunst & Trivette, 1992; Egeland & Stroufe, 1981; Garmezy, 1987; Kopp, 1983; Rac-Grant, 1989; Roosa et al., 1990; Rutter, 1987; Sameroff et al., 1987; Werner, 1985.

Brassard, 1979). Third, the correlates listed as risk and opportunity factors are, for the most part, not dichotomous, but rather represent specifiable levels of a factor (e.g., inadequate vs. adequate income) or constitute different aspects of a particular construct (e.g., internal vs. external locus of control). Fourth, the particular variables selected as possible correlates would be expected to differ depending on the outcomes being investigated (see, e.g., Dunst & Trivette, 1992; Sameroff et al., 1987). Fifth, the methods used to assess risk and opportunity factors, should, to the maximum extent possible, be uncorrelated or minimally correlated so as to be able to assess the differential and cumulative influence of the variable or outcome of interest. (More is said about this later.) We have described elsewhere (Dunst & Trivette, 1992; Dunst et al., 1990) several of these kinds of measures and the manner in which positive (opportunity) and negative (risk) correlate variables are related to other positive and negative aspects of behavior. In the next section, the relationships between a subset of the factors listed in Table II and child development are described to illustrate the utility of the risk–opportunity framework for understanding the correlates of child behavior and competence.

APPLICATION TO THE STUDY OF DEVELOPMENTAL OUTCOMES

The use of HLM and the risk–opportunity framework is now illustrated with data from two longitudinal studies currently being conducted in our laboratory. Study 1 is an investigation of the developmental sequel of children who participated in an early intervention program. The sample includes nearly 1000 children with Down syndrome and other chromosomal abnormalities; children with cerebral palsy, brain damage, and other physical impairments; children with sensory impairments; children with cranial anomalies; children who were premature, low birthweight, or had other medically related problems; children who were mentally retarded or developmentally delayed for unknown reasons; children who were at-risk for developmental delays because of environmental and socioeconomic factors; and children with various other etiologies and diagnoses that placed them at-risk for poor developmental outcomes. All of the children were assessed repeatedly as part of their participation in the early intervention program on a number of instruments measuring the sensorimotor, mental, social–adaptive, communication/language, and physical aspects of development. The sample is currently being investigated as part of a long-term follow-up study of the effects of early intervention. Repeated measures of the mental, social–adaptive, and communication/language competence of the children are being collected on four to six measurement occasions during the elementary, junior high, and high school years.

Study 2 is an investigation of the influences of intrafamily and extrafamily resources on child, parent, and family functioning. The final sample will include approximately 300 families from all socioeconomic backgrounds, both married and unmarried mothers, and mothers who have less than a high school education as well as those with advanced graduate degrees. In the initial phase of the study, pregnant women were recruited during the second trimester of their pregnancies and were followed until their children were 2 years of age. The second phase of the study will involve the continued assessment of the mothers and their children throughout the preschool years. As part of this investigation, instruments are used that measure one or more aspects of the personal resources of the mothers (e.g., education level, coping strategies, and social competence), intrafamily (e.g., partner) and extrafamily (e.g., friends and co-workers) support, the psychological health of the mothers, family well-being, mother–child interactions, and child behavioral and developmental competence.

The data from Study 1 are used primarily to illustrate the usefulness of HLM for studying the developmental functions of the children, whereas the data from Study 2 are used primarily to illustrate the utility of the risk–opportunity influences scheme for identifying the determinants of child development. We also discuss the implications of both approaches for assessing the long-term developmental sequel of the children being investigated in both studies.

Estimating the Characteristics of Developmental Functions

We illustrate the use of HLM for estimating both the prototypical and individual growth curves of five groups (subsamples) of children included in Study 1. The groups include children with chromosomal abnormalities (predominately Down syndrome), mental retardation of unknown etiology, physical impairments (predominately cerebral palsy), medically fragile conditions (mostly prematurity and low birthweight), and developmentally at-risk for environmental and socioeconomic reasons. The dependent measure used for estimating the developmental functions of the groups was mental age (MA) measured by the Bayley Scales of Infant Development and the Stanford-Binet Intelligence Scale. For purposes of the analyses reported here, we examined the developmental characteristics of the five groups of subjects between birth and 48 months of age (± 6 months), the time period during which the majority of the sample received early intervention.

Table III provides a summary of selected characteristics of the data collection scheme and child and family descriptive characteristics at the time of entry into the early intervention program. Each child had, on the average, between four and five sets of data. The characteristics of the mothers were, for the most part, much alike in each group, whereas the child characteristics differed in a predictable manner. For example, the children with chromo-

Table III Selected Characteristics of the Five Groups of Subjects (Study 1)

	Chromosomal abnormalities	Mental retardation	Physically impaired	Medically fragile	Developmentally at-risk
Number of subjects	66	121	94	56	81
Number of observations					
3	16	41	40	23	43
4	13	36	32	23	20
5	13	25	13	7	12
6–10	24	19	9	3	6
Total	345	518	379	216	315

	Chromosomal abnormalities		Mental retardation		Physically impaired		Medically fragile		Developmentally at-risk	
Variable[a]	M	SD	M	SD	M	SD	M	SD	M	SD
Child age (mos.)	12.26	10.08	18.11	9.85	16.65	9.26	16.94	9.89	19.27	11.19
Child mental age (mos.)	6.88	5.14	7.99	6.05	11.88	8.45	9.54	7.95	14.74	8.45
Child DQ	65.14	23.98	42.86	18.54	71.06	21.87	54.77	25.55	78.91	16.87
Mothers age (years)	27.82	7.04	26.22	5.26	26.14	6.11	25.43	5.44	25.50	5.46
Mothers education[b]	11.60	2.17	11.59	2.18	11.42	2.13	11.00	2.33	10.65	2.20
Mothers married	91%		80%		78%		59%		70%	
Mothers working	34%		40%		41%		36%		27%	

[a] At child age of entry into the early intervention program.
[b] Number of years completed.

somal abnormalities were, on the average, younger at age of entry compared to the other four groups, presumably because the physical features associated with syndromes caused by chromosomal aberrations are so easily recognizable at birth or shortly thereafter (Robinson & Robinson, 1976). Likewise, it was not unexpected that the children at-risk for developmental delay had the highest DQs, and the children with mental retardation due to unknown etiology had the lowest DQs.

Growth Curve Model The first aspect of development that we considered was the structure of the average growth trajectory for each group of subjects. We fit the data to both linear and polynomial growth models with the intercept set at zero under the assumption that when chronological age (CA) equals zero, so does mental age (MA). Accordingly, because initial MA status at the CA = 0 point in time must be the same for all subjects, the y-intercept (initial status) feature of HLM was not examined in our analyses. (See Bryk & Raudenbush, 1987, for a description and discussion of this aspect of an HLM analysis.) The evaluation of the linear and curvilinear trends in the data showed that for all five subsamples, the data fit only a linear model. More will be said about this in a moment, especially with respect to how this is ascertained using HLM.

Second, we tested whether the linear trends for each group of children indicated that their mean growth rate differed significantly from zero (i.e., did the children make statistically significant progress over the period of time studied). This was done by ascertaining the ratio of each prototypical linear growth curve estimate to its standard error. The result is statistically assessed using a simple Z test. Table IV presents the results from the analyses for each of the subsamples. The findings indicated that each of the groups made statistically significant progress over the period of time under investigation, although the mean growth rates differed between groups ($F(4, 413) = 68.41, p < .0001$), as one would expect. The children with mental retardation

Table IV   Estimated Mean Growth Parameters (Rates) for the Five Groups of Subjects

Group	Mean growth parameter estimate	SD	SE	Range	Z
Chromosomal abnormalities	.536	.186	.023	.046–.874	23.72*
Mental retardation	.365	.208	.019	.042–1.007	19.42*
Physically impaired	.727	.213	.023	.050–1.347	31.50*
Medically fragile	.567	.289	.039	.034–1.167	14.23*
Developmentally at-risk	.819	.151	.017	.463–1.182	49.35*

* $p < .0001$.

of unknown etiology had the smallest growth rates, whereas the at-risk group had the largest.

The third aspect of development we considered was the extent to which intraindividual growth curves deviated from one another (i.e., did the children within groups demonstrate different rates or patterns of development). This was determined by comparing variations in individual growth parameters (rates), which is a test of the hypothesis that there are no differences among the children's developmental functions. The findings from the analyses are reported in Table V, and in all cases, the result led us to reject the hypothesis that there was no variation in the linear growth curves between subjects. This is important because if no variation existed in the data, there would be no basis for studying correlates of individual change. Herein lies the practical as well as scientific value of this aspect of HLM.

The final feature of change that is examined as part of the within-subject stage of HLM is the reliability of the growth rate estimates. The reliability of the individual developmental functions is the ratio of the true parameter variance to the total observed variance. This, by definition, is reliability as specified by classical measurement theory (Nunnally, 1967). The average of the individual reliability estimates for n subjects measured repeatedly, provides an index of the measurement scale's reliability for detecting the developmental growth parameters inherent in the data. The reliability estimates are important for two reasons. First, they provide a basis for knowing whether the data fit a particular model (see preceding discussion) in a reasonable manner. Second, if the psychometric characteristics were found to be unreliable and one proceeded to stage two of HLM (identifying correlates of change) and discovered no covariation between change and the predictors, one would possibly make an erroneous conclusion of no relationship when in fact the likelihood of finding covariation was minimal at best.

Table VI shows the reliability estimates for the growth rates. We present the growth rate reliabilities for both the linear and polynomial models for illustrative purposes. As can be seen, the reliabilities for the linear growth

Table V   Estimated Parameter Variance Associated with Deviations in Individual Growth Rates

Group	Estimated parameter variance	X^2	df
Chromosomal abnormalities	.032	2152.9*	65
Mentally retarded	.043	4325.4*	120
Physically impaired	.048	3122.5*	93
Medically fragile	.093	3133.6*	55
Developmentally at-risk	.019	824.3*	80

* $p < .0001$.

Table VI   Reliability Estimates for Two Different Growth Models

Group/Model	Estimated parameter variance	Estimated total variance	Reliability[a]
Chromosomal abnormalities			
Linear	.03328	.03479	.955
Polynomial	.00001	.00003	.130
Mentally retarded			
Linear	.04168	.04333	.964
Polynomial	.00002	.00005	.438
Physically impaired			
Linear	.04332	.04545	.958
Polynomial	.00005	.00009	.452
Medically fragile			
Linear	.08344	.08629	.971
Polynomial	.00002	.00010	.186
Developmentally at-risk			
Linear	.01914	.02282	.839
Polynomial	.00003	.00013	.204

[a] Proportion of total variance that is the estimate of the parameter variance.

rates are quite high, whereas, in contrast, those for the curvilinear trends are quite low. This indicates that a polynomial model is not very useful for depicting the nature (form) of the growth rate parameters, but that a linear model is quite adequate for representing the underlying dimensions of change in the mental development of the subjects.

Collectively, the results from the within-stage HLM analyses produced evidence indicating that the data fit a linear model of growth, the growth rates differed significantly from zero, there were individual differences in growth rates, and the methods for measuring growth rate estimates were highly reliably. The necessary conditions were therefore met to proceed with an investigation of the correlates of intraindividual differences in rates of development.

Relating Correlates of Change to Developmental Outcomes

As previously noted, a major task faced by the developmentalist beyond the description of the course of change is pursuit of knowledge about the correlates of intraindividual patterns of development (Baltes et al., 1977). The introduction of experimental methods and interventions into the study of correlates of change brings one closer to a fuller understanding of the causal mechanisms and environmental conditions best suited for optimization of development. In this section of the chapter, we describe two approaches for investigating the factors related to individual variations in development. The first is the second stage in performing an HLM analysis. The yield, although enlightening and informative, nonetheless is limited because of the ways in which correlate variables are typically conceptualized and operationalized. The second approach illustrates the usefulness of the risk–opportunity framework for conceptualizing and studying the differential influences of factors that impede (risk) and enhance (opportunity) development. The yield, as we shall see, is rich and considerably more informative in comparison to the traditional way of studying the influences of correlates.

Unidimensional Approaches to the Study of Correlates   The second stage application of HLM focuses on relating differences in growth rates to both intervention and nonintervention variables. This is typically accomplished through study of correlates conceptualized as a unidimension set of variables. For illustrative purposes, we used five family background (mothers' education, marital status, occupation, family income, and number of siblings), two stressor-related (number of family members and relatives with mental health problems and number of child hospitalizations), and two intervention (age of entry and length of intervention) measures as correlates. All of the variables, except the intervention measures, were selected because they parallel the indices used by Sameroff et al. (1987) as risk-factor correlates of child competence. The extent to which the correlates were related to differences in individual growth curves was examined with two groups of subjects, those with Down syndrome and those with physical impairments. The results for these two groups were selected because the analyses produced a combination of both similar and different kinds of findings.

The two major purposes of the between-subject feature of HLM are discerning the amount of variance accounted for in the outcome measure (intraindividual growth curves) by all correlates taken together, and assessing the contributions of individual variables to observed effects. Basically, this is accomplished through regression procedures using the correlates as the independent variables and the intraindividual growth rate estimates as the dependent measure. Selected results from the analyses of the two sets of data are presented in Table VII.

First, consider the percentage of variance accounted for in intraindividual differences by the nine correlates. Two measures of R^2 can be calculated from a set of HLM results, the percentage of total variance accounted for by the predictors, and the percentage of parameter variance accounted for by this same set of variables. The former statistic is the one most often used for ascertaining the relationship between a set of independent variables and an outcome measure in a regression analysis, but it fails to take into consideration the fact that part of the total variance is sampling error, and by definition 100% of the variance cannot be explained by the correlates. Hierarchical linear modeling can be used to compute the parameter variance that covaries with the correlates, which is the percentage of explainable variance accounted for by the dependent variables. In our example, both

Table VII   Effects of Three Sets of Correlate Variables on Mental Age
Growth Rates

| | Group | | | |
| | Chromosomal abnormalities | | Physically impaired | |
Correlates/effects	Coefficient	*SE*	Coefficient	*SE*
Background variables				
Mothers' education	.0225**	.0119	.0357****	.0143
Marital status	.0221	.0765	.1306***	.0656
Occupation	.0094	.0232	.0216	.0254
Race	−.0800	.0870	−.0716	.0473
Number of siblings	−.0212	.0158	.0144	.0195
Stressor-related variables				
Family-related mental health problems	−.0265*	.0150	.0066	.0142
Number of child hospitalizations	.0053	.0148	−.0326***	.0144
Intervention variables				
Age of entry	−.0062***	.0029	−.0020	.0030
Length of intervention	−.0068*	.0036	−.0036	.0029
R^2: Percentage of total variance explained	30****		17**	
R^2: Percentage of parameter variance explained	35****		22**	

* $p < .08$. ** $p < .06$. *** $p < .05$. **** $p < .01$.

the total and parameter variances are significant, but not very much different.
This is the case because the measurement scale is so highly reliable (see
Table VI) that most of the variance associated with intraindividual change
is true variance. If the measurement scale was somewhat less reliable, the
sampling error would be larger, and the amount of parameter variance
accounted for by correlates would be higher as well (see Bryk & Raudenbush,
1987, Table 5).

We next consider the individual contributions of the correlates to the
observed effects. Table VII shows the regression coefficients, their standard
errors, and indicates which variables were significantly related to the outcome measure. In both analyses, mother's education was significantly related
to growth rates. As one would expect, the children's rates of development
were greatest in cases where their mothers had completed more years of
school. Except for this finding, the results were quite different for the two
groups.

Examination of the findings for the children with chromosomal abnormalities indicated that the presence of mental-health-related problems had negative effects on growth rates, whereas age of entry had positive influences.

In comparison, inspection of the results from the analysis of the data for the children with physical impairments showed both number of child hospitalizations and maternal marital status related to the outcome measure. The more hospitalizations a child had, the slower his or her rate of progress. In contrast, the children's rates of progress were greater if their mothers were married. Thus, whereas hospitalizations had negative effects on rates of development, marital status had positive influences.

The findings reported in Table VII, and briefly described here, illustrate the yield from an HLM analysis that was specifically concerned with the correlates of and relationships between three sets of predictor variables and intraindividual development functions as outcome measures. Hierarchical linear modeling, as can be seen, is a fruitful way of testing individual growth and relating the parameters of growth to relevant correlate variables.

A Multidimensional Approach to Studying the Influences of Correlates   The material presented next illustrates the potential yield from employing the risk–opportunity framework as a basis for conceptualizing and operationalizing correlates of development. This multidimensional approach, as previously described, considers factors that are either impediments or enhancers of growth, and has been constructed from the viewpoint that the absence of problems or risk factors is not a sufficient condition for accounting for factors related to optimization of development (Dunst et al., 1990).

The data used to illustrate the usefulness of the multidimensional approach comes from a prospective study of the naturalistic course of adaptation to the birth and rearing of a child, with a specific focus on the influences of intrafamily and extrafamily resources on child, parent, and family functioning (Dunst & Trivette, 1992). The sample for the analyses reported here included all families ($N = 123$) for which we had complete data prenatally up until their children were 18 months of age. Table VIII lists the background characteristics of these parents and families. The mothers are recruited from private obstetric practices, Lamaze classes, public health departments, and county departments of social services, so that the participants differ considerably in their socioeconomic backgrounds as well as on other demographic measures. As can be seen from the table, the participants are quite heterogeneous on the majority of measures.

As part of their involvement in the study, each mother participates in an interview and completes a number of self-report measures during the second and third trimesters of her pregnancy and at 1, 6, 12, 18, and 24 months postpartum. At 6, 12, 18, and 24 months, mother–child interaction measures are also obtained, and the children are administered the Bayley Scales of Infant Development (1969). Several observational measures are used as well to assess a number of aspects of both maternal and child behavior.

The self-report measures used in the study include the Personal Assessment of Social Support Scale (Dunst & Trivette, 1988b), Parental Locus-of-

Table VIII   Descriptive Characteristics of the Study 2 Sample

Continuous variables	Mean	*SD*	Range
Mothers' age	25.42	5.29	14–40
Mothers' education (years)	13.24	2.45	7–19
Fathers' age	28.75	5.33	17–42
Fathers' education (years)	13.65	2.57	8–21
Gross family income (monthly)	1975.16	1045.12	0–5000

Categorical variables	Number	Percentage
Mothers' married	101	82
Mothers' working	64	52
SES: Very low	6	5
Low	36	29
Middle	34	28
High	27	22
Very high	20	16

NOTE. $N = 123$.

Control Scale (Campis, Lyman, & Prentice-Dunn, 1986), Personal Assessment of Intimate Relationships Index (Olson & Schaefer, 1981), and Psychological Well-Being Index (Bradburn, 1969; Bradburn & Caplovitz, 1965). The interview scales include the Personal Assessment of Coping Experiences Scale (Dunst, Trivette, Jodry, Morrow, & Hamer, 1988) and Personal Assessment of Life Events Scale (Trivette, Dunst, Morrow, Jodry, & Hamer, 1988b). The observational measures include the Social Skills Rating Scale (Jodry, Hamer, Trivette, & Dunst, 1988), Personal Well-Being Rating Scale (Trivette, Dunst, Hamer, & Jodry, 1988a), and Maternal Styles of Interaction Scales (Mahoney, Finger, & Powell, 1985).

The instruments used in this study were selected to measure one or more aspects of the personal resources of the mothers (e.g., coping strategies and social competence), intrafamily (e.g., partner) and extrafamily (e.g., social organization) support, the psychological health of the mothers, family well-being, mother–child interaction, and child behavior and development. Additionally, a number of measures were specifically selected or developed for the study (Bradburn, 1969; Dunst et al., 1988; Trivette et al., 1988a, 1988b) because they measure both positive and negative aspects of functioning (e.g., reactive vs. proactive coping, positive vs. negative psychosocial health) and could be used to assess whether measures of risk and opportunity had differential effects on other aspects of parent, family, and child behavior.[3]

The analyses reported next used a set of 10 variables measured prenatally and at 1 and 6 months postpartum as independent variables and 18-month

---

[3] The instruments listed in this section that we developed specifically for this study will be made available to other investigators as soon as reliability and validity analyses are completed.

Bayley Scale Mental Development Indices as the dependent measure. The 10 correlate variables included mother's education; father's occupation (or the mother's if no spouse or partner was present); marital status; mother's social skills, psychosocial health, locus-of-control, and mental health status; mother–child interaction; social support; and positive and negative life events. These particular measures were selected because they have been previously found to have either negative or positive influences on one or more aspects of child development (see e.g., Bronfenbrenner, 1979; Cochran & Brassard, 1979; Dunst & Trivette, 1992; Garbarino, 1982; Sameroff et al., 1987).

Data summary and analysis proceeded through a number of steps to ascertain the presence of risk and opportunity factors and assess their relationship to the children's mental development. First, because data on the same measurement scales were available on more than one occasion for most variables, a procedure similar to that used by Sameroff et al. (1987) was employed for aggregating multiple measures of the same constructs as independent variables and computing risk as well as opportunity scores from these measures. For measures obtained on more than one occasion, a total score was computed by summing the individual scale scores. Second, the distributions of the summed scores for all the correlates except marital status were used for determining whether each mother was considered to have a risk or opportunity status on each variable. The variables and the criteria used to establish risk and opportunity status are shown in Table IX. Third, a total risk score and a total opportunity score were computed for each mother by summing the number of times the mother was assigned to a risk or opportunity group, respectively. The range of scores for both measures varied from 0 to 10. Fourth, a composite risk–opportunity score was computed for each subject because most mothers ($N = 93$) had combinations of both risk and opportunity scores when the cumulative indices were calculated. A composite score was computed by subtracting the cumulative risk scores from the cumulative opportunity scores. The results obtained varied from -10 to $+9$.

The first two analyses we considered were the relationships between the cumulative risk and opportunity factor scores and child mental development. The data were analyzed for both linear and nonlinear (cubic and quadratic) trends between the independent and dependent variables using two one-way analyses of variance with the risk and opportunity scores (0 to 6+) as blocking variables, respectively. The analysis of the risk data produced a significant main effect demonstrating a linear trend ($F(1, 116) = 8.87, p < .004$), as did the analysis of the opportunity factor data ($F(1, 116) = 5.34, p < .03$). The data from these analyses are displayed in Figure 1.[4] As can

---

[4] It should be noted that recent evidence indicates that there has been an upward shift in Bayley scale MDIs so that the normative mean is probabilistically closer to 110 than 100 (Campbell, Siegel, Parr, & Ramey, 1986). This "shift" is evident in the data presented in Figures 1 and 2.

Table IX Variables and Criteria for Ascertaining Risk and Opportunity Status

| Variable | Number of measures[a] | Risk status | | Opportunity status | |
		Measure	Criteria	Measure	Criteria
Mothers' education	1	Less than 11 years	Lo Q	More than 15 years	Hi Q
Occupation (head of household)	1	Unskilled	Lo Q	Professional	Hi Q
Marital status[b]	3	Partner absent	—	Partner present	—
Maternal social skills	3	Low	Lo Q	High	Hi Q
Maternal psychosocial health[c]	3	Negative affect	Hi Q	Positive affect	Hi Q
Maternal mental health[c]	3	Depression	Hi Q	Well-being	Hi Q
Maternal locus of control	2	External	Lo Q	Internal	Hi Q
Personal social network size	3	Small network	Lo Q	Large network	Hi Q
Mother–child interaction	1	Directive	Lo Q	Facilitative	Hi Q
Life events[c]	3	Negative	Hi Q	Positive	Hi Q

NOTE. Risk and opportunity status was determined from the distribution of scores for each variable using the criteria that a mother was either in the highest or lowest quarter (Q: Quartile) of the group.

[a] Number of assessments used to calculate risk and opportunity status.

[b] Partner absent during the entire time period from third trimester to six months postpartum; partner present during the same time period.

[c] Risk and opportunity status measured using separate scales or subscales of this construct.

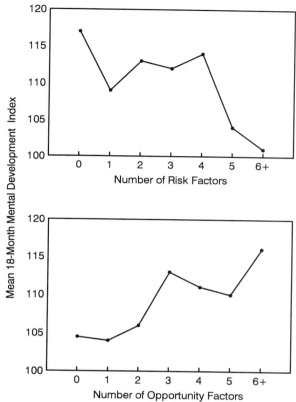

Figure 1   Influences of the number of risk and opportunity factors on child mental development.

be seen, increases in the presence of risk factors had negative effects on child development, whereas increases in the presence of opportunity factors had positive influences.

The findings displayed in Figure 1, although particularly revealing, are partly confounded by the fact that the two sets of analyses do not include independent samples of subjects. The analysis of the composite risk–opportunity score avoids this problem, however, by accounting for overlap by adjusting for the presence of both risk and opportunity factors. The results of the analysis of the composite scores produced a significant main effect demonstrating a linear trend ($F(1, 114) = 9.25, p < .003$). Figure 2 shows the data graphically, and as can be seen, the presence of large numbers of risk factors is associated with the lowest mean MDI scores and the presence of large numbers of opportunity factors is related to the highest mean MDI scores. But this only tells part of the story. More important is the fact that the presence of opportunity factors beyond the absence of risk factors (zero

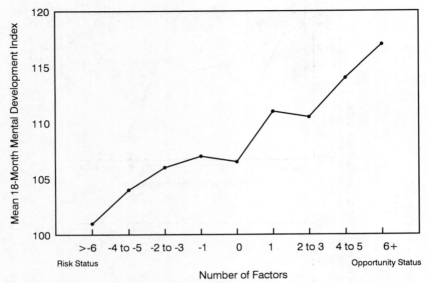

Figure 2 Child mental development as a function of the composite risk and opportunity factor scores.

score) continues to have enhancing influences on child development. These data are highly suggestive with respect to the contention that the absence of problems does not constitute a necessary condition for claiming optimization in development. Additionally, the strategy demonstrates the usefulness and rich yield from employing the risk–opportunity framework for conceptualizing and assessing correlates of behavioral development.

Implications for Studying Long-term Follow-up

The data from Study 1 were used to illustrate the utility of HLM for studying patterns of change and correlates of intraindividual variations in change. The data from Study 2 were used to illustrate the influences of both risk and opportunity factors on child competence and to empirically establish the fact that the absence of problems (risk factors) does not adequately consider the environmental conditions related to optimal performance. The implications of both HLM and the risk–opportunity framework for studying long-term follow-up appear quite diverse.

An HLM analysis can easily be applied in situations where data of the same attribute or latent construct have been collected repeatedly on the same individuals across time. For example, in Study 1, we actually have longitudinal data over the entire preschool years, and currently are collecting similar data during the elementary, junior high, and high school years as part of a follow-up study of these individuals. To the extent that sufficient amounts of data are available at enough points in time between birth and approximately 18 years of age, HLM can be used for estimating intraindividual patterns of change and then for assessing the correlates of variations in rates of development.

As part of the data collection scheme being used in Study 1, a variety of intervention-related measures are coded as correlate variables. These include measures such as child age of entry, length of involvement, frequency of intervention, hours of intervention, intensity and type of intervention, and so on. These, as well as nonintervention variables (e.g., family background characteristics) are used as correlates in an HLM analysis to ascertain their influences on intraindividual variations in rates of development over the 18-year age span under investigation.

In addition to coding the intervention-related variables in the manner previously described, the specific interventions provided the children (as specified in written reports and documents) are individually coded on a series of 7-point rating scales as to whether they were directive versus responsive (Dunst et al., 1987), corrective versus promotional (Dunst et al., 1990), functional versus nonfunctional (Dunst et al., 1987), routine-based versus nonroutine-based (Dunst et al., 1987), strengths-based versus deficit-oriented (Dunst, 1985), and so on. These data are used to calculate risk–opportunity scores in a manner much like that just described, and their influences as correlates are assessed as part of an HLM analysis.

Other potentially important correlate variables are being coded using the risk–opportunity scheme as a framework as well. For example, one measure of intrafamily support is the presence of a supportive spouse or partner versus the presence of a unsupportive spouse or partner. This information is collected for every 6- to 12-month period of time during the preschool years, and the aggregate data for all time periods is used to assign each family either a risk or opportunity status score on this measure. The scores are then used as possible correlates of intraindividual variations in development.

To the best of our knowledge, neither HLM nor the risk–opportunity framework have been used in combination as part of the same investigation of the course of developmental change and factors associated with variations in change. Both strategies, when used separately, have a wide range of applications as part of the study of the long-term sequel of children who participated in early intervention—in combination, the range of applications is multiplied.

POSSIBLE EXTENSIONS OF THE STRATEGIES

In this final section of the chapter, we briefly describe several possible extensions of the strategies described thus far. The following examples were selected because they seem to have special value as methodological approaches for unraveling the complexity of growth and its correlates.

Hierarchical Regression Analysis Approach to HLM

The term hierarchical, as used by Bryk and Raudenbush (1987, 1988), is actually quite different from how it is used by Cohen and Cohen (1983) in describing a particular approach to multiple regression analysis. The within-stage part of HLM actually employs a simultaneous model for assessing the combined influences of all correlate variables of interest at once, without regard to any temporal ordering or causal priority among the independent variables. An HLM analysis produces results that provide the best linear (or nonlinear) estimate of the relationship between the outcome measure and the correlates, but the nature of the interrelationships among the variables cannot be readily identified by the results produced by a simultaneous regression analysis.

In cases where there is theoretical reason or previous research, or both, to suggest a presumed causal priority among the independent variables, there is no reason why HLM cannot be used for analyzing the within-subject aspects of the data, while hierarchical multiple regression analysis used to assess the contributions of a set of correlates to intraindividual variations in patterns of change. In a hierarchical approach to multiple regression, as described by Cohen and Cohen (1983), a set of

> k IVs [independent variables] are entered cumulatively in a prespecified sequence and the R^2 and partial coefficients are determined as each IV joins the others. . . . This leads to an ordering of the variables that reflects their presumed causal priority—ideally, no IV entering later should be a presumptive cause of an IV that has been entered earlier. (Cohen & Cohen, 1983, p. 120)

Thus, for example, family background variables would almost always be entered before one or more intervention-related variables because the latter, in most cases, would not be expected to be a presumptive cause of family characteristics. A hierarchical multiple regression approach to HLM would almost certainly yield findings that make substantive contributions to both theory and research as well as add to our knowledge about the independent contributions of early intervention as a correlate of development change.

Developmental Functions as Correlate Variables

In all of what we have said, as well as what has been written about developmental functions (e.g., Baltes et al., 1977; Burchinal & Appelbaum, 1991; Nesselroade & Baltes, 1979; Wohlwill, 1973), patterns and rates of change have been treated as outcome or dependent variables. But there is no reason why the statistic used to index age-related change during a particular period of time (e.g., when children participate in early intervention) cannot be used as a correlate of either a developmental function for another time period (e.g., from age 10 to 18) or for a developmental outcome measured on another, single occasion (e.g., developmental status at the completion of elementary school). Moreover, there is no reason why a set of HLM-produced individual growth trajectory statistics cannot be used as a set of correlates, and their relationship with subsequent patterns of development or a developmental outcome obtained at a particular age of interest assessed in the various ways described here.

There is actually a rather straightforward and pragmatic reason why one might employ developmental functions as predictors for children who participated in early intervention. Although available evidence indicates there is long-term positive effects of early intervention (e.g., Consortium for Longitudinal Studies, 1983), one would hypothesize, based on a weak-concept view of development (Nesselroade & Baltes, 1979), that one might find different patterns of development during different age periods because of variations in environmental influences. Additionally, there is no reason to believe or contend that even the best interventions possible during the earliest years of life are an inoculation against unsupportive environments that children might experience during the post-preschool years. This can easily be accommodated into an analysis that considers intervention-rated developmental functions as correlates of nonintervention-related patterns of change. The assessment of repeated measures data collected in this manner on the same individuals during the preschool years and the post-preschool years may be considered a special case of an interrupted time-series analysis (Cook & Campbell, 1979). But as proposed here, HLM would be used for estimating individual developmental functions during the preschool years and such estimates would be used as predictors of the developmental functions (also computed from HLM) during the post-preschool years. This type of strategy can be useful for assessing the relationship between earlier and latter *patterns of change,* and data obtained from such an analysis would provide a more direct test of the extent to which there was stability or instability in development (Brim & Kagan, 1980).

The possibility of using developmental function type indices as correlate variables is briefly illustrated next, with data from a third longitudinal study we are conducting. This is an investigation of substantiated cases of child maltreatment (abuse and neglect) in the 100 counties in North Carolina during the 11-year period from 1980 to 1991. Over this time period, incidents of abuse and neglect have been found to increase each year for all counties combined, and for most individual counties examined separately. As part of our study of these observed increases, the patterns of child maltreatment were examined to ascertain both the structure of the average growth trajectory and the extent to which individual county rates of abuse and neglect differed from the mean growth curve. This was accomplished using HLM as described in Table I and as previously illustrated.

A set of seven ecological and social context correlate variables were included in the analysis because they have been found or hypothesized to be factors influencing episodes of maltreatment (e.g., Garbarino, 1977, 1981), and we found that they could be reliably measured from our data. The number of occurrences (per year for each county) of the following seven measures were employed as our independent variables: arrests, violent crimes, AFDC recipients, per capita income, divorces, children born with low birthweights, and teenage pregnancies. However, instead of using a single-year measure of these variables as predictors, we employed HLM to obtain intracounty growth rate estimates, which were then used as correlate variables.

Data analysis proceeded through a series of steps. First, we considered the extent to which the mean growth parameters, variability in growth parameters for individual counties, and the reliability of the measures for both the predictor and outcome variables met the criteria as required by HLM. The statistics from these analyses are shown in Table X. In all cases, for both the predictor and outcome measures, the results indicated that there was significant variation in individual county change rates, and that all the measures had acceptable reliability estimates. For all the variables except the numbers of AFDC recipients and teenage pregnancies, the mean growth rates showed statistically significant changes during the 11 years of investigation. Rates of AFDC recipients and teenage pregnancy were retained in the analysis because there was significant variation in individual county rates which were reliably measured. In instances where the mean growth rates were not significant, the predictor functionally becomes the average of the 11-year measures for those variables.

Second, we considered the relationship between the social context variable change rates as predictor measures, and child maltreatment as the dependent measure. Table XI details the statistics from this part of the

Table X HLM Parameter Estimates for the Study 3 Predictor and Outcome Measures of Child Maltreatment

Measures	Parameter estimates		
	Mean growth parameter	Parameter variance	Reliability
Predictor variables			
Arrests	112.830****	73.401×10^3****	.940
Violent crimes	10.897*	32.619×10^2****	.962
AFDC	8.947	43.831×10^2****	.826
Income	672.269****	24.689×10^3****	.962
Divorce	4.777****	10.415×10^1****	.884
Low birthweight	1.562****	12.874****	.798
Teenage pregnancies	.591	44.591****	.725
Outcome variable			
Child maltreatment	15.16****	612.11****	.898

$^*p < .05.$ $^{**}p < .01.$ $^{***}p < .001.$ $^{****}p < .0001.$

Table XI Effects of the Correlate Variables on Child Maltreatment Growth Rates

Correlates/effects	Coefficient	SE
Arrests	− .018**	.007
Violent crimes	.131***	.040
AFDC	.009	.024
Per capita income	.005	.010
Divorce	.362*	.150
Low birthweight	1.795*	.822
Teen pregnancies	− .315	.272
R^2: Percentage of total variance explained	37***	—
R^2: Percentage of parameter variance explained	59***	—

$^* p < .05. ^{**} p < .01. ^{***} p < .001.$

analysis. As can be seen, statistically significant amounts of both total and parameter variance were accounted for in the rates of child maltreatment by the correlate variables. Examination of the seven regression coefficients showed that higher rates of abuse and neglect were found in counties that had higher violent crime rates, higher divorce rates, and high rates of low birthweight children. (The reason why arrest rates were inversely related to child maltreatment is not readily apparent; but perhaps arrests somehow functioned as a deterrent.)

The data presented in Tables X and XI, and briefly described here, illustrate the potential utility for employing developmental function indices as correlate measures. One can readily think of many applications of such a strategy for studying development in general and the long-term follow-up of early intervention in particular.

Measuring Risk and Opportunity Status

In an example previously presented, risk and opportunity status was determined according to whether a mother's score on each variable placed her in the bottom or top quartile of the total sample for the measures used as correlates. The number of times a mother fell into the risk quartiles was considered her cumulative risk score, and the number of times a mother fell into the opportunity quartiles was considered her cumulative opportunity score. A composite score was computed as the difference between a mother's risk and opportunity scores. Both the cumulative indices as well as the composite scores were found to be related to child mental developmental status. These ways of measuring risk and opportunity status, although enlightening, nonetheless have at least one major shortcoming. Because risk and opportunity status was determined for most variables by placement along a single, continuous measure (e.g., mother's education and social skills), the risk and opportunity scores by necessity must be correlated. This therefore prevents a direct test of the differential and independent relationships between risk and opportunity factors and developmental outcomes.

The solution to this problem is having independent measures of the same construct that are uncorrelated or minimally correlated. A number of such measures are available (Bradburn, 1969; Bradburn & Caplovitz, 1965; Kammann, Christie, Irwin, & Dixon, 1979; Kammann & Fleet, 1983; Kanner, Coyne, Schaefer, & Lazarus, 1981; Kanner, Feldman, Weinberger, & Ford, 1987; Orden & Bradburn, 1968; Reich & Zautra, 1983; Warr, Barter, & Brownbridge, 1983), including several instruments developed in our laboratory (Dunst et al., 1988; Trivette et al., 1988a, 1988b). Research using these scales has consistently produced evidence indicating that the contrasting behavioral dimensions measured by these instruments (positive and negative affect, daily hassles and uplifts, proactive and reactive coping strategies, etc.) are, on the one hand, minimally correlated with each other, and, on the other hand, show differential relationships with other aspects of behavior (see Dunst et al., 1990, for a review of these studies). There is a rich database showing that positive aspects of functioning tend to be related to other aspects of positive but not negative functioning, and that negative aspects of functioning tend to be related to other negative but not positive aspects of functioning (see e.g., Diener, 1984). Additionally, other research provides evidence that positive and negative aspects of functioning operate relatively independently and make separate, incremental contributions to the relationship between positive and negative aspects of functioning as predictor variables, and other behavioral measures, as dependent variables. These types of studies have employed hierarchical multiple regression techniques (as described earlier) where negative (risk) measures of functioning were entered into the analysis first followed by the positive (opportunity) functioning measures. For example, Kanner et al. (1987), using hassles and uplifts as independent measures and a set of seven adaptational measures as outcomes (e.g., depression, self-worth), found that in nearly every analysis, hassles accounted for a significant amount of variance in the outcomes, and uplifts accounted for additional significant amounts of variance in the outcome measures. In a similar study, Reich and Zautra (1983) used demands and desires as predictor variables, and quality of life, positive and negative mood, and psychosocial symptomatology as outcome measures. For two separate samples of subjects, they found that demands accounted for significant amounts of variance in all eight sets of analyses, and desires accounted for additional significant amounts of variance in six of the eight analyses.

The use of risk and opportunity measures as correlates of developmental outcomes beyond that described in a previous section of this chapter depends to a large degree on whether factors that impede and promote development can be measured as independently as possible. The extension of the risk–opportunity framework, and its application to the study of behavioral change, will require considerable attention to measurement considerations that have generally not been a major focus in the developmental psychology or early intervention fields.

SUMMARY AND CONCLUSION

The purposes of this chapter were to illustrate several approaches for studying developmental change and correlates of change, to describe the possible combination of different strategies as part of the same investigation, and propose possible extensions of the strategies for future research. More specifically, we described and illustrated the use of (a) hierarchical linear modeling for estimating intraindividual developmental functions and for studying correlates of intraindividual differences in growth rates, and (b) a risk–opportunity framework for classifying and investigating the infuences of environmental factors that function as either impediments or enhancers of developmental competence. As part of the description of the latter, we presented evidence to indicate that the absence of risk factors is not sufficient for specifying those conditions associated with optimal functioning. Our findings strongly indicate a need to move beyond the study of only risk-related factors if environmental influences that optimize developmental outcomes are to be identified and subsequently translated into interventions for promoting positive features of development.

Our major aim in discussing HLM and the risk–opportunity framework, and both their combinations and extensions, was to point out possible ways of studying the long-term sequel of children who participated in early intervention, and the extent to which early intervention, as an independent variable, was related to differences in long-term outcomes. The research that we described to make our points provided suggestive but most certainly not conclusive evidence regarding the applicability of the strategies we described. The utility of the strategies nonetheless are quite apparent, and the potential scientific yield from their use most certainly deserves further investigation. In many respects, the strategies constitute breakthroughs in methods that can add to the knowledge base about the course of human development, its correlates, and the identification of interventions that contribute to optimization of behavioral competence. Our intent was to describe their application in ways that make the procedures available to researchers interested in developmental sequel in general and the long-term effects of early intervention in particular.

ACKNOWLEDGMENTS

The research reported in this chapter was supported, in part, by grants from the National Institute of Child Health and Human Development (#HD23038) and the U.S. Department of Education, Office of Special Education Programs (#G008630143 and #H023C00062), and the North Carolina Department of Human Resources, Division of Mental Health, Developmental Disabilities and Substance Abuse, Research Section (#82A22). Appreciation is extended to Debbie Hamby for assistance with data analysis, Pat Condrey and Norma Hunter for preparation of the manuscript, Sam Allen for assistance with compilation of the reference material, and Wilson Hamer for preparation of graphic material.

REFERENCES

Achenbach, T. M. (1978). *Research in developmental psychology concepts, strategies, methods*. New York: Free Press.

Antonovsky, A. (1981). *Health, stress and coping*. San Francisco: Jossey-Bass.

Appelbaum, M. I., & McCall, R. B. (1983). Design and analysis in developmental psychology. In P. Mussen (Ed.), *Handbook of child psychology* (Vol. 1, pp. 415–476). New York: Wiley.

Baltes, R., Reese, H., & Nesselroade, J. (1977). *Life-span developmental psychology*. Monterey, CA: Brooks/Cole.

Barocas, R., Seifer, R., & Sameroff, A. J. (1985). Defining environmental risk: Multiple dimensions of psychological vulnerability. *American Journal of Community Psychology, 13*, 433–447.

Bayley, N. (1969). *Bayley Scales of Infant Development*. New York: Psychological Corporation.

Bayley, N. (1970). Development of mental abilities. In P. Mussen (Ed.), *Carmichael's manual of child psychology* (pp. 1163–1210). New York: Wiley.

Beavers, W. R., & Hampson, R. B. (1990). *Successful families: Assessment and intervention*. New York: Norton.

Bock, R. D. (Ed.). (1989). *Multilevel analysis of educational data*. San Diego, CA: Academic Press.

Bond, L. (1982). From prevention to promotion: Optimizing infant development. In L. Bond & J. Joffe (Eds.), *Facilitating infant and early childhood development* (pp. 5–39). Hanover, NH: University Press of New England.

Bradburn, N. M. (1969). *The structure of psychological well-being*. Chicago: Aldine.

Bradburn, N. M., & Caplovitz, D. (1965). *Reports on happiness*. Chicago: Aldine.

Brim, O. G., & Kagan, J. (1980). *Constancy and change in human development*. Cambridge, MA: Harvard University Press.

Bronfenbrenner, U. (1979). *The ecology of human development*. Cambridge, MA: Harvard University Press.

Bryk, A. S., & Raudenbush, S. W. (1987). Application of hierarchical linear models to assessing change. *Psychological Bulletin, 101*, 147–158.

Bryk, A. S., & Raudenbush, S. W. (1988). Toward a more appropriate conceptualization of research on school effects: A three-level hierarchical linear model. *American Journal of Education, 97*, 65–108.

Bryk, S. A., Raudenbush, A. W., Seltzer, M., & Congdon, R. T. (1989). *An introduction to HLM: Computer program and user's guide*. Chicago: Scientific Software, Inc.

Burchinal, M., & Appelbaum, M. I. (1991). Estimating individual developmental functions: Methods and their assumptions. *Chld Development, 62*, 23–43.

Campbell, A. K., Siegel, E., Parr, A. C., & Ramey, C. T. (1986). Evidence for the need to renorm the Bayley Scales of Infant Development based on the performance of a population-based sample of 12-month-old infants. *Topics in Early Childhood Special Education, 6,* 83–96.

Campis, L. K., Lyman, R. D., & Prentice-Dunn, S. (1986). The Parental Locus of Control Scale: Development and validation. *Journal of Clinical Child Psychology, 15,* 260–267.

Cicchetti, D. (1989). How researching child maltreatment has informed the study of child development: Perspectives from developmental psychopathology. In D. Cicchetti & V. Carlson (Eds.), *Child maltreatment: Theory and research on the cause and consequences of child abuse and neglect* (pp. 377–431). Cambridge: Cambridge University Press.

Cicchetti, D., & Rizley, R. (1981). Developmental perspectives on the etiology, intergenerational transmission, and sequelae of child maltreatment. *New Directions for Child Development, 11,* 31–55.

Cochran, M. M., & Brassard, J. A. (1979). Child development and personal social networks. *Child Development, 50,* 601–616.

Cohen, J., & Cohen, P. (1983). *Applied multiple regression correlation analysis for the behavioral sciences* (2nd ed.). Hillsdale, NJ: Lawrence Erlbaum.

Cohen, S., & Syme, S. L. (Eds.). (1985). *Social support and health.* New York: Academic Press.

Consortium for Longitudinal Studies. (1983). *As the twig is bent: Lasting effects of preschool programs.* Hillsdale, NJ: Lawrence Erlbaum.

Cook, T., & Campbell, D. (1979). *Quasi-experimentation.* Chicago: Rand McNally.

Cornwell, S., Lane, A., & Swanton, C. (1975). A home-centered regional program for developmentally impaired infants and toddlers. *North Carolina Journal of Mental Health, 7,* 56–65.

Cowen, E. L. (1985). Person-centered approaches to primary prevention in mental health: Situation-focused and competence-enhancement. *American Journal of Community Psychology, 13,* 31–48.

Diener, E. (1984). Subjective well-being. *Psychological Bulletin, 94,* 542–575.

Dubow, E. F., & Luster, T. (1990). Adjustment of children born to teenage mothers: The contribution of risk and protective factors. *Journal of Marriage and the Family, 52,* 393–404.

Dunst, C. J. (1985). Rethinking early intervention. *Analysis and Intervention in Developmental Disabilities, 5,* 165–201.

Dunst, C. J., Lesko, J., Holbert, K., Wilson, L., Sharpe, K. L., & Liles, R. (1987). A systemic approach to early intervention. *Topics in Early Childhood Special Education, 7*(2), 19–37.

Dunst, C. J., & Trivette, C. M. (1988a). A family systems model of early intervention with handicapped and developmentally at-risk children. In D. R. Powell (Ed.), *Parent education as early childhood intervention: Emerging directions in theory, research, and practice, 3,* 131–179. Norwood, NJ: Ablex.

Dunst, C. J., & Trivette, C. M. (1988b). *Personal Assessment of Social Support.* Unpublished scale, Center for Family Studies, Western Carolina Center, Morganton, NC.

Dunst, C. J., & Trivette, C. M. (1992, March). *Risk and opportunity factors influencing parent and child functioning.* Paper presented at the Ninth Annual Smoky Mountain Winter Institute, Asheville, NC.

Dunst, C. J., Trivette, C. M., Jodry, W. L., Morrow, J. B., & Hamer, A. W. (1988). *Personal Assessment of Coping Experiences.* Unpublished scale, Center for Family Studies, Western Carolina Center, Morganton, NC.

Dunst, C. J., Trivette, C. M., & LaPointe, N. (1992). Toward clarification of the meaning and key elements of empowerment. *Family Science Review, 5*(1/2), 111–130.

Dunst, C. J., Trivette, C. M., & Thompson, R. B. (1990). Supporting and strengthening family functioning: Toward a congruence between principles and practice. *Prevention in Human Services, 9,* 19–43.

Egeland, B., & Sroufe, A. (1981). Developmental sequelae of maltreatment in infancy. *New Directions in Child Development, 11,* 77–92.

Fisher, R. A. (1918). The correlation between relatives of the supposition of Mendelian inheritance. *Transcripts of the Royal Society of Edinburgh, 52,* 399–433.

Garbarino, J. (1977). The human ecology of child maltreatment: A conceptual model for research. *Journal of Marriage and the Family, 39*, 721–727.

Garbarino, J. (1981). An ecological approach to child maltreatment. In L. Pelton (Ed.), *The social context of child abuse and neglect* (pp. 228–267). New York: Human Sciences Press.

Garbarino, J. (1982). *Children and families in the social environment*. New York: Aldine.

Garmezy, N. (1987). Stress, competence and development: Continuities in the study of schizophrenic adults, children vulnerable to psychopathology, and the search for stress-resistant children. *American Journal of Orthopsychiatry, 57,* 159–174.

Garmezy, N. (1991). Resiliency and vulnerability to adverse developmental outcomes associated with poverty. *American Behavioral Scientist, 34,* 416–430.

Hogben, L. (1933). *Nature and nurture*. London: Allen and Unwin.

Hoke, B. (1968). Promotive medicine and the phenomenon of health. *Archives of Environmental Health, 16,* 269–278.

Hunt, J. McV. (1987). The effects of differing kinds of experience in early rearing conditions. In I. C. Uzgiris and J. McV. Hunt (Eds.), *Infant performance and experience: New findings with the ordinal scales* (pp. 39–57). Urbana: University of Illinois.

Jodry, W. L., Hamer, A. W., Trivette, C. M., & Dunst, C. J. (1988). *Social Skills Rating Scale*. Unpublished scale, Center for Family Studies, Western Carolina Center, Morganton, NC.

Jones, H. E. (1954). The environment and mental development. In L. Carmichael (Ed.), *Manual of child psychology* (pp. 631–696). New York: Wiley.

Kammann, R., Christie, D., Irwin, R., & Dixon, G. (1979). Properties of an inventory to measure happiness (and psychological health). *New Zealand Psychologist, 8,* 1–9.

Kammann, R., & Fleet, R. (1983). Affectometer 2: A scale to measure current level of general happiness. *Australian Journal of Psychology, 35,* 257–265.

Kanner, A., Coyne, J., Schaefer, C., & Lazarus, R. S. (1981). Comparison of two modes of stress measurement: Daily hassles and uplifts versus major life events. *Journal of Behavioral Medicine, 4,* 1–39.

Kanner, A., Feldman, S., Weinberger, D., & Ford, M. (1987). Uplifts, hassles, and adaptational outcomes in early adolescence. *Journal of Early Adolescence, 7,* 371–394.

Kopp, C. B. (1983). Risk factors in development. In P. H. Mussen (Ed.), *Handbook of child psychology: Infancy and developmental psychobiology* (pp. 1081–1188). New York: Wiley.

Lewin, K. (1935). *A dynamic theory of personality*. New York: McGraw Hill.

Longstreth, L. E. (1968). *Psychological development of the child*. New York: Ronald Press.

Mahoney, G., Finger, I., & Powell, A. (1985). Relationship of maternal behavioral style to the development of organically impaired mentally retarded infants. *American Journal of Mental Deficiency, 90,* 296–302.

McCall, R. B. (1977). Challenges to a science of developmental psychology. *Child Development, 48,* 333–334.

McCall, R. B., & Appelbaum, M. I. (1973). Bias in the analysis of repeated-measures designs: Some alternative approaches. *Child Development, 44,* 401–415.

Nesselroade, J. R., & Baltes, P. B. (Eds.). (1979). *Longitudinal research in the study of behavior and development*. New York: Academic Press.

Nunnally, J. C. (1967). *Psychometric theory*. New York: McGraw-Hill.

Olson, D. H., & Schaefer, M. T. (1981). Assessing intimacy: The PAIR inventory. *Journal of Marital and Family Therapy, January,* 47–60.

Orden, S., & Bradburn, N. M. (1968). Dimensions of marriage happiness. *American Journal of Sociology, 73,* 715–731.

Piaget, J. (1983). Piaget's theory. In P. Mussen (Ed.), *Handbook of child psychology* (4th ed, pp. 103–128). New York: Wiley.

Rae-Grant, N., Thomas, B. H., Offord, D. R., & Boyle, M. H. (1989). Risk, protective factors, and the prevalence of behavioral and emotional disorders in children and adolescents. *Journal of the American Academy of Child and Adolescent Psychiatry, 28,* 262–268.

Rappaport, J. (1981). In praise of paradox: A social policy of empowerment over prevention. *American Journal of Community Psychology, 9,* 7–25.

Raudenbush, S. (1988). Educational applications of hierarchical linear models: A review. *Journal of Educational Statistics, 13,* 85–116.

Reich, J., & Zautra, A. (1983). Demands and desires in daily life: Some influences on well-being. *American Journal of Community Psychology, 11,* 41–59.

Robinson, N. M., & Robinson, H. B. (1976). *The mentally retarded child* (2nd ed.). New York: McGraw-Hill.

Roosa, M. W., Beals, J., Sandler, I. N., & Pillow, D. R. (1990). The role of risk and protective factors in predicting symptomatology in adolescent self-identified children of alcoholic parents. *American Journal of Community Psychology, 18,* 725–741.

Rutter, M. (1985). Resilience in the face of adversity: Protective factors and resistance to psychiatric disorder. *British Journal of Psychiatry, 147,* 598–611.

Rutter, M. (1987). Psychosocial resilience and protective mechanisms. *American Journal of Orthopsychiatry, 57,* 316–331.

Sameroff, A. J., Seifer, R., Barocas, R., Zax, M., & Greenspan, A. (1987). Intelligence quotient scores of 4-year-old children: Social-environment risk factors. *Pediatrics, 79,* 343–350.

Seeman, J. (1989). Toward a model of positive health. *American Psychologist, 44,* 1099–1109.

Stanley, M. A., & Maddux, J. E. (1986). Cognitive processes in health enhancement: Investigation of a combined protection motivation and self-efficacy model. *Basic and Applied Social Psychology, 7,* 101–113.

Surgeon General. (1979). *Healthy people: The Surgeon General's report on health promotion and disease prevention.* Washington, DC: U.S. Department of Health, Education, and Welfare.

Trivette, C. M., Dunst, C. J., Hamer, A. W., & Jodry, W. L. (1988a). *Personal Well-Being Rating Scale.* Unpublished scale, Center for Family Studies, Western Carolina Center, Morganton, NC.

Trivette, C. M., Dunst, C. J., Morrow, J. B., Jodry, W. L., & Hamer, A. W. (1988b). *Personal Assessment of Life Events Scales.* Unpublished scale, Center for Family Studies, Western Carolina Center, Morganton, NC.

Turner, R. R., & Reese, H. W. (Eds.). (1980). *Life-span development psychology.* New York: Academic Press.

Warr, P., Barter, J., & Brownbridge, G. (1983). On the independence of positive and negative affect. *Journal of Personality and Social Psychology, 44,* 644–651.

Werner, E. E. (1985). Stress and protective factors in children's lives. In A. R. Nicol (Ed.), *Longitudinal studies in child psychology and psychiatry* (pp. 335–355). New York: Wiley.

Wohlwill, J. F. (1973). *The study of behavioral development.* New York: Academic Press.

Zautra, A., & Sandler, I. (1983). Life events needs assessment: Two models for measuring preventable mental health problems. In A. Zautra, K. Bachrach, & R. Hess (Eds.), *Strategies for needs assessment in prevention* (pp. 35–58). New York: Haworth Press.

Modeling Duration and the Timing of Events

Using Survival Analysis in Long-term Follow-up Studies[1]

Judith D. Singer
John B. Willett

INTRODUCTION

Developmental psychologists conducting long-term follow-up studies describe the ways in which children grow and change over time. Researchers ask, for example, How do children's cognitive and motor skills develop over time? Does the rate of change differ from child to child? Does it differ for boys and girls? For ill and healthy children? These questions focus on individual change and on differences in individual change across children. From

[1] Prepared for the Workshop on Long-term Follow-up Strategies, National Institutes of Child Health and Human Development, Bethesda, Maryland, June 1989. We presented an earlier version of this paper at the Society for Research in Child Development, Biennial Meeting, Kansas City, April 1989. Please direct comments to either author at Harvard University, Graduate School of Education, Appian Way, Cambridge, MA 02138. The order of the authors was determined by randomization.

a statistical perspective, these questions treat time as an independent variable, as a predictor of individual children's skills and behavior.

Some researchers also frame another, considerably different type of research question, in which time is a dependent variable, an *outcome* in its own right (Singer & Willett, 1991). In addition to asking how much or how fast children change over time, these researchers ask how much time elapses before a specific event occurs or a particular milestone is reached. These questions focus on duration and on differences in duration across children: How long do mothers breastfeed their children? How long do children stay in day care? How long do children's friendships last? How much time does it take for a child to master a task? Do these times differ by the child's gender, health, or participation in an early-intervention program? In our view, in fact, the ability to ask and answer research questions about time represents a fundamental advantage of long-term follow-up studies over cross-sectional research.

Yet, the ability to address such research questions comes with its own difficulties, particularly with regard to statistical analysis. In this chapter, we outline the major analytic issues that researchers analyzing time as an outcome face and we present a conceptual introduction to specially derived statistical techniques—the methods of survival analysis—designed to address these issues. We begin by illustrating the many types of research questions about time as an outcome that might arise in long-term follow-up studies. We then describe methods for answering such questions, show how to interpret their results, and identify relevant published sources containing further information.

RESEARCH QUESTIONS IN WHICH TIME IS THE OUTCOME

Many areas of developmental psychology involve the study of time as an outcome (Singer & Willett, 1991, describe more than 100 such studies). Here, we present six research questions about duration—the first two deal with short-term duration, the last four focus on duration over the long-term.

- Mother's response times: How long does it take a mother to respond to her baby's cry? Do some mothers respond more quickly than others? Are they younger mothers or older mothers? First-time mothers or second-time mothers?
- Children's attention spans: How long are children's attention spans? Do children who were premature babies have shorter attention spans than children who were carried to full-term? Do boys have shorter attention spans than girls?
- Time to master a task: How long does it take to master a maze? Is the

length of time shorter for children who attended an innovative training program?

- Duration of breastfeeding: How long do mothers breastfeed their infants? Does duration of breastfeeding differ by maternal employment? By attendance at educational programs encouraging breastfeeding? By maternal attitudes toward breastfeeding?
- Time to pass a developmental milestone: How long does it take to reach the stage of formal operations? Does duration differ by gender? By the home environment? By the prenatal environment? By the application of an innovative treatment or training program?
- Recidivism: How much time passes before juvenile delinquents commit another crime, or drug-addicts return to addiction? Does this time differ by characteristics of their treatment? By the availability of family and social support?

Researchers can also learn much about long-term processes by reframing a research question traditionally stated using time as a predictor by using time as an outcome. Reformulation provides a different perspective on the phenomenon under study. Many questions about age differences that are usually phrased using time as a predictor, for example, can be profitably reframed as questions about duration, using time as the outcome. For example, rather than asking, Are there age differences in children's pattern of moral development? we can ask, How much time passes before children reach a particular stage of development?

Regardless of research domain, whenever time is treated as the outcome, two types of analytic questions can be posed. The first concerns the average length of time that passes before a specific event occurs, or a particular milestone is achieved: How many months does the average mother breastfeed her child? How many years does the average childhood friendship last? The second concerns the relationship between duration and other predictors. Most researchers want to know more than simply what happens on average; they want to know what factors contribute to variation around the average. Why do some mothers breastfeed for years, whereas others breastfeed for a few months? Why do some friendships last a lifetime, whereas others fizzle soon after beginning? These relational questions focus on variation in duration as a function of predictors—Does the time it takes for the event to occur differ by group membership, treatment, or environment?

HOW DO WE ANSWER RESEARCH QUESTIONS ABOUT DURATION?

Researchers studying duration typically collect data on a sample of children for a preselected time period (usually as long as the researcher can afford). The outcome variable is the amount of time that passes before the event of interest occurs. But how are such data to be analyzed?

One might guess that a good first step would be to estimate the mean length of time until the event occurs among members of the sample. Second stage analyses focusing on factors associated with duration could then be conducted using duration (or perhaps the natural logarithm of duration) as the outcome in a regression analysis or an analysis of variance.

Most researchers attempting to implement this approach will encounter an analytic dilemma. What duration value should they give to those children who do not experience the event of interest before the end of data collection? These children possess *censored* durations—we know only that the event did not occur within the period of observation. Data collection must end at some point, and as developmental researchers usually discover, data collection invariably ends before every child has experienced the event in question. With limited data collection resources, and limited time periods for follow-up, it is rare that by the time data collection is over, every child will have mastered the task, every child will have left day care, and every friendship will be over. Some perfectly ordinary children will be missing a value for duration simply because data collection has terminated.

We illustrate this dilemma in Figure 1, which depicts the number of months nine children waited before being placed in a foster home. The small explosion indicates placement. Daphne, Graciella, and Hua waited relatively short periods of time ($\leq$ 12 months); Brendan and Eddie waited longer ($\geq$ 24 months); Fred never was placed. What would our data set look like if data collection ended after 20 months? We would not know the waiting times for Brendan, Eddie, and Fred; all we would know is that they waited *at least* 20 months. If these children are to be included in statistical analyses, it seems as though a numeric value must be assigned to their unknown waiting-times. But what value could possibly be assigned?

One tempting, but unsatisfactory, solution is simply to eliminate the censored observations from the data set and study only those children placed within 20 months. This strategy distorts the distribution of waiting-times. If some children wait more than 20 months, the overall true length of time to placement is certainly longer than that found among children placed within 20 months. Data on children still waiting tell us a great deal, especially about the probability that children wait longer than the length of data collection. Accurate analysis of duration data must attend to the nonplaced children, even though their waiting-times are censored and unknown.

Yet another strategy, which is still flawed, but which at least includes the censored cases in the analysis, is to create a dichotomous outcome that indicates whether or not placement occurred within the data collection period. This new outcome could take on the value 0 for children placed before the end of data collection (those whose waiting-times were "short"—20 months or less), and the value for 1 for all others (those whose

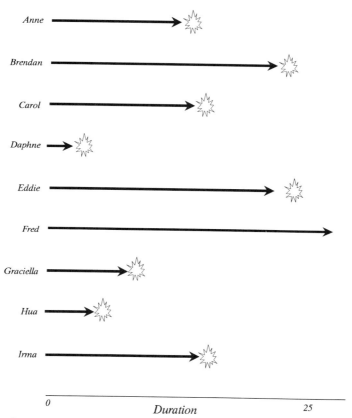

Figure 1   Hypothetical length of time to placement in foster care for nine children.

waiting-times were "long"—more than 20 months). Then logistic regression analysis, appropriate for a dichotomous outcome, could be used to investigate factors associated with "short" or "long" waiting-times.

Although dichotomization can be a helpful exploratory strategy, its routine application is unsatisfactory for two related reasons. First, analytic results are sensitive to the temporal cutoff point determining who waited a "long" time and who waited a "short" time. Unless the length of data collection is substantively meaningful, and not a function of convenience or cost, this approach is very haphazard and arbitrary. Second, the strategy throws away much information. Known variation in duration on the early side of the dividing line is completely ignored. Use of a 20-month criterion time does not distinguish children who waited 19 months before those who waited only 1 month. Such senseless equating of children is substantively inappropriate, and will also reduce statistical power.

THE CONCEPT OF SURVIVAL ANALYSIS

Survival analysis is the preferred analytic alternative. The techniques of survival analysis permit incorporation of both censored and noncensored cases into a single analysis, and inclusion of all the variation in waiting-times occurring before the end of data collection. Originally developed by biostatisticians analyzing clinical lifetime data (Cox, 1972; Kalbfleisch & Prentice, 1980), sociologists and economists refer to the methods of survival analysis using the term *event-history analysis* (Allison, 1984; Blossfeld, Hamerle & Mayer, 1989; Tuma & Hannan, 1984).

Originally, survival analysis was used to answer research questions in medicine such as: How long do cancer patients survive after diagnosis? After treatment? After remission? After relapse? Because the event of interest was death, the language of survival analysis remains shrouded in dark and foreboding terms. For example, when conducting survival analyses, we do not examine duration directly, but alternative quantities that remain meaningful for data sets that include both censored and noncensored observations, the *survivor function* and the *hazard function*.

We illustrate the use of survival analysis with an example based on data collected as part of the National Day Care Home Study (NDCHS; Singer, Fosburg, Goodson, & Smith, 1978). Among the many research questions investigated in the NDCHS were (a) How long, on average, do children remain in individual family day care homes? and (b) What factors are associated with variation in the duration of family day care? Although our example describes how long children stay in family day care, we could just as easily be analyzing data describing how long friendships last, how long before juvenile delinquents commit another crime, or how long it takes to master a task.

The Survivor Function

Survival analysis begins with the survivor function—a plot of the probability of "survival" versus time. For the population of children in our example, the survivor function indicates how likely it is that a randomly selected child will remain in day care longer than each specified period of time—1 year, 2 years, and so on. At the beginning, when all children enter day care, 100% are "surviving," and the survival probability is 1.00. Over time, children leave day care and the survival probability drops steadily toward 0.00, the value of the function when all the children have left. Because data collection usually ends before everyone leaves, sample survivor functions rarely reach zero. Formal mathematical definitions of the survivor function are given in Allison (1984), Kalbfleisch and Prentice (1980), or Miller (1981).

In Figure 2, we present the sample survivor function for all children in the NDCHS. About 82% of children remain in (survive) day care more than 1 year, about 72% survive more than 2 years, and about 50% survive more than

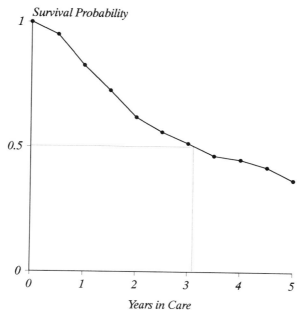

Figure 2   Sample survival function for all the children in the day-care study data set.

3.1 years. This last number is the estimated *median lifetime,* an intuitively appealing summary statistic that indicates the time by which half the sample has left day care. In summarizing the survivor function, the median lifetime incorporates information from both censored and uncensored cases and answers the descriptive question: How many years, "on average," does the typical family day care arrangement last? Transforming the information contained in survival probabilities into a median lifetime allows us to answer our research question in the metric in which it was originally posed—the metric of time.

The Hazard Function

If a large fraction of continuing children suddenly leave day care in a particular time period, the survivor function drops sharply (as happens in our example between .5 and 1 year, and between 1.5 and 2 years). Sudden drops in the slope of the survivor function indicate particularly "risky" periods—times when children are at higher risk of leaving day care.

One way to identify particularly risky time periods is to look for such changes in the slope of the survivor function. Alternatively, the researcher can examine the hazard function—a sensitive barometer designed for detecting changes in the slope of the survivor function. Mathematical definitions

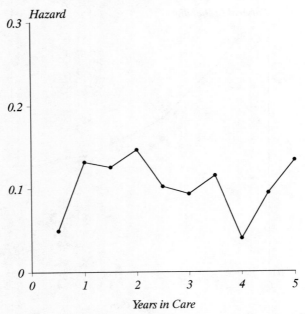

Figure 3   Sample hazard function for all the children in the day-care study data set.

of hazard are related to the probability that a child will leave day care *given that she or he has remained in care until the immediately prior instant*[2] (Allison, 1984; Kalbfleisch & Prentice, 1980; Miller, 1981). The hazard function is a plot of the risk of leaving care at each point in time, given that the child has remained in care up until that time. The magnitude of the hazard indicates the risk associated with each time period. Figure 3 presents the sample hazard function corresponding to the sample survivor function in Figure 2.

Inspecting a sample hazard function helps identify particularly "risky" time periods. Thus, we can determine whether the first 6 months of care are especially risky, for example, or whether the second 6 months are riskier than the first, and so on. If many children leave day care at a specific point in time, as might happen 5 years after entry among children placed as newborns, the hazard will be high at that time, indicating the increased likelihood that any randomly selected child will leave. If, at an earlier time,

[2] Explicit definitions of the hazard function distinguish between duration measured discretely and duration measured continuously. In the former case, hazard is a conditional probability, and in the latter case it is a rate (Kalbfleisch & Prentice, 1980). The duration data discussed in this chapter were obtained discretely and hence we have framed our discussion in terms of the conceptually appealing conditional probability.

say between 3.5 and 4 years after entry, relatively few children leave, the hazard will be low, indicating that this time period is not very risky at all. Singer and Willett (1991) presents plots of prototypical hazard functions and the kinds of information that can be retrieved from them.

IDENTIFYING PREDICTORS OF DURATION

Having examined duration in the sample as a whole, the next step in a survival analysis is to investigate factors associated with variation in duration. We might want to explore, for example, the relationship between the duration of family day care and characteristics of children (e.g., family background) and characteristics of the day care home (e.g., caregiver qualifications).

A good exploratory strategy for investigating the relationship between predictors and duration is to plot sample survivor or hazard functions for subgroups of children who share values of the predictors. We illustrate this strategy in Figure 4, which displays sample survivor functions for two groups of children—those in the care of a relative, and those in the care of a nonrelative. The two plots are distinct and clearly separated; the sample survivor function for children in relative care is consistently "higher" than the sample

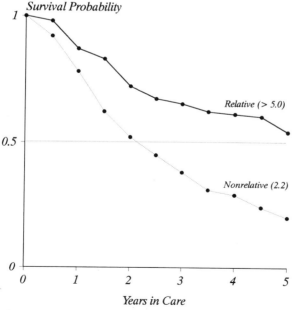

Figure 4   Sample survivor functions for two groups of children: those in the care of a relative and those in the care of a nonrelative (estimated median lifetimes are given in parentheses).

survivor function for children in nonrelative care, indicating children stay in relative care longer.

The corresponding median lifetimes given in Figure 4 summarize this differential. For children in relative care, the estimated median lifetime of a day care arrangement is more than 5 years; for children in nonrelative care, it is 2.2 years. We can conclude, therefore, that in this sample, care provided by a relative lasts at least 2.8 years longer, on average, than care provided by a nonrelative.

Although sample survivor plots nicely summarize differences in duration by levels of predictors, these plots are poor indicators of especially risky time periods. Yet researchers conducting long-term follow-up studies often want to know when the event of interest is most likely to occur. When are family day-care arrangements most likely to end? Are relative and non-relative arrangements equally likely to end soon after they begin, or does relative care typically last until the child enters school? To explore these questions about risk, we examine sample hazard functions, plotted separately for the two groups.

Figure 5 displays sample hazard functions corresponding to the sample survivor functions presented in Figure 4. The most obvious feature of these plots is that, for all time periods, the estimated hazard for nonrelative care

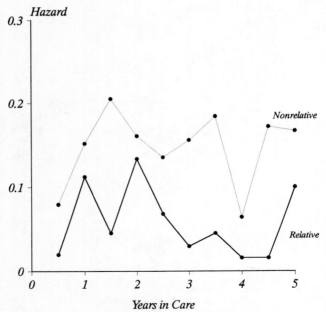

Figure 5   Sample hazard functions for children in the care of a relative and children in the care of a nonrelative.

is consistently larger than the hazard for relative care. Nonrelative care is always "riskier."

BUILDING STATISTICAL MODELS OF HAZARD

We have shown that plots of sample survivor and hazard functions readily depict relationships between duration and predictors. But just as we fit linear regression models to represent the relationship between an outcome and predictors, we need a methodology for representing the relationship between the outcome of interest in survival analysis and important predictors.

The preferred approach is to model the relationship between the entire population hazard function and predictors. To understand the concept behind these *hazard models,* let us reexamine the sample hazard functions in Figure 5. Think of "Type of Care" as a dummy predictor taking on two values (0 = relative care, 1 = nonrelative care). The effect of this predictor is to somehow displace the hazard functions vertically, relative to each other. When the predictor takes on the value 0 (relative care), the entire hazard function is lower relative to its location when the predictor takes on the value 1 (nonrelative care). In other words, the effect of the predictor is to move the hazard function up and down. We seek a statistical model that captures this "vertical" displacement.

We can represent this relationship by expressing the natural logarithm of hazard as a weighted linear combination of predictors, similar to the way that any continuous outcome can be expressed as a function of predictors in an ordinary regression model. (A logarithmic transformation of hazard is required because, by definition, hazard is strictly positive and therefore its range must be rendered unbounded before representation as a linear function of predictors.) A population hazard model that includes two predictors is

$$\log_e h(t) = \beta_0(t) + \beta_1 X_1 + \beta_2 X_2$$

where the X's are the two predictors, $\beta_0(t)$ is the "baseline" ($\log_e$) hazard function (the function when both X_1 and X_2 are zero), and β_1 and β_2 are unknown "slope" parameters summarizing the effects of the predictors. Using readily available computer software and a representative sample of duration data, we can easily estimate β_1 and β_2 and use the estimates, in conjunction with their standard errors, to decide whether the predictors have a statistically significant association with hazard.

It is perhaps easiest to understand the idea behind a hazard model by analogy with a corresponding linear regression model. Think of $\beta_0(t)$ as an "intercept" describing the shape of ($\log_e$) hazard when all the predictors have value zero. We write this baseline $\log_e$-hazard function as $\beta_0(t)$, a function of time, and not as β_0, an individual term unrelated to time, because the hazard function is itself a function of time. The baseline hazard function has a particular—but not necessarily uniform—profile over time.

The "slope" parameters β_1 and β_2 correspond to their cousins in a linear regression model; they quantify the magnitude of the vertical displacement in $\log_e$-hazard per unit difference in X_1 and X_2, respectively. They describe the vertical distance between the baseline $\log_e$-hazard function and the $\log_e$-hazard functions for each level of the predictors.

The most common strategy for fitting a hazard model to data is called the method of partial likelihood and, under certain additional assumptions, the whole process is often called Cox-regression (Cox, 1972). Although these estimation techniques are based on complex statistical theory, and most relevant technical papers assume mathematical sophistication, these models are now being used more frequently by empirical researchers because they can be estimated by popular statistical packages such as SAS and BMDP (see Allison, 1984; Blossfeld, Hamerle & Mayer, 1989). Without giving mathematical details, suffice it to say that the β's, their standard errors, and a chi-square goodness-of-fit statistic can be estimated, and having done so, inferences can be made to help evaluate the relationship between the predictors and survival (see Allison, 1984; Singer & Willett, 1993; Willett & Singer, 1991a).

SIX ADVANTAGES OF HAZARD MODELS

Analytically, the fitting of hazard models has several advantages. The first three advantages are similar to well-known advantages of multiple regression models, the next three are unique to hazard modeling. The unique advantages of fitting hazard models are explored in greater detail in Willett and Singer (1991b).

1. Several predictors can be included simultaneously in a single hazard model, so that several effects can be examined concurrently. When looking at individual plots of the hazard function as a function of different levels of each predictor, we often encounter small sample sizes in individual cells—relative care for children who entered care after age 2, for example. When estimating hazards models, we borrow strength across the full data set, rather than subdividing the sample into individual strata. We also can examine the effects of each predictor while controlling statistically for others.

2. Both continuous and categorical variables can be included as predictors in hazard models. We have illustrated how the effects of categorical variables on risks can be examined by including dummy variables as predictors in hazard models. Continuous variables can be treated similarly. In both cases, fitted survival and hazard plots can be constructed at substantively interesting values of those predictors shown to have a statistically significant effect.

3. Both main effects and interactions between predictors can be incorporated into a single hazard model. Not all predictors operate as main effects, sometimes the influence of one predictor is mediated by the effect of another. Hazard models are as flexible as their linear regression cousins—two-way, and higher-order, interactions between predictors can be examined by adding cross-product terms to main effects models. By including interaction effects in our models, we can determine, for example, whether the effect of relative care differs by the child's age at entry. Is the effect of relative care smaller among children who enter day care at or near birth?

4. Hazard models permit the values of a predictor to vary over time. The longitudinal nature of duration data creates unique problems for the data analyst. Many predictors themselves vary over time. The cost of day care, for example, changes with time and yet cost may maintain a constant per-dollar effect on duration. Such *time-varying covariates* are easily included as predictors in hazard models. This is an especially important feature for long-term follow-up studies. By incorporating time-varying covariates into hazard models, a researcher can examine relationships between developmental attributes.

5. Hazard models allow the influence of a predictor to vary over time. When we begin building hazard models, we usually assume that a predictor has the same effect in each time period—year 1, in year 2, in year 3, and so on. In terms of the sample hazard functions displayed in Figure 5, this is equivalent to assuming that a constant vertical separation between the two $\log_e$-hazard functions (i.e., by assuming that the corresponding hazard functions are proportional to each other). This is called the *proportionality assumption*. But if the effect of a predictor differs at different times, the proportionality assumption is violated and we can include in our models an interaction between the predictor and time to represent this effect (see Willett & Singer, 1993).

Although interactions between predictors and time may seem like an esoteric data-analytic luxury, a simple example illustrates just how common such behavior can be. Consider, for example, whether the effect of relative care will be constant each successive year of care, or whether it will differ from year to year. Is it not possible that the differential between the two types of care might be large in the beginning, when the nonrelative caregiver is truly a stranger, but that the differential might dissipate over time, as even a nonrelated caregiver becomes a pseudo-family member? In technical terms, we say that predictor (relative care) and time interact. This ability to model interactions between predictors and time allows researchers with long-term follow-up data to build more inflected models of children's development over time.

6. With hazard modeling, attrition from the sample can be investigated and cases lost to follow-up can be included in the analysis. Researchers collecting long-term follow-up data usually encounter attrition from the sam-

ple. Some families may move to other states; others may simply refuse to attend prearranged sessions with the researcher. More importantly, this depletion may be systematically related to characteristics of the children or to their background and treatment. When time is the outcome, sample attrition is simply another form of censoring. For instance, a child may remain in day care for 3 years, say, before disappearing from the sample through attrition. Nevertheless, this child can still be included in a survival analysis because she continues to contribute information on hazard up through the time she unforeseeably departs—her truncated career tells us much about the probability of remaining in day care for at least 3 years. In addition, if the researcher suspects that children lost to follow-up are qualitatively different from those who continue, an "attrition indicator" can be included as a predictor in any hazard model fitted, allowing the presence of systematic attrition to be evaluated.

DISPLAYING ANALYTIC RESULTS

Just as we summarize fitted multiple regression models by using plots of fitted regression lines, we summarize fitted hazard models with plots of fitted survivor and hazard functions. Figure 6 presents fitted survivor functions

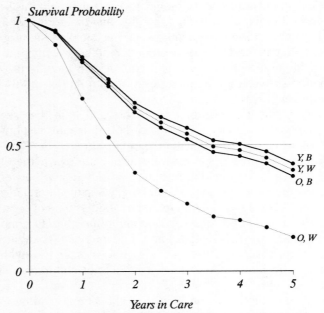

Figure 6 Fitted survivor functions obtained from a hazard model in which there were two predictors: (a) the age of the child on entry into day-care (Y = younger than 6 months, O = older than six months), (b) the ethnicity of the child (W = white; B = black).

from an estimated hazard model that represents the effects of two predictors: the child's ethnicity (White/Black) and the child's age at entry into care (under 6 months, over 6 months). These fitted survivor functions summarize two main effects and a two-way interaction: (a) children who enter day care earlier tend to stay longer; (b) black children stay longer than white children; and (c) the black–white differential is larger among children who enter day care at an older age.

We can also summarize our research findings by reexpressing our results in terms of duration, the metric in which our questions were originally asked. We do this by presenting estimated median lifetimes to summarize the fitted survivor plots (see Figure 6). For children who entered day care before 6 months of age, the fitted median lifetimes are 4.1 years and 3.5 years (for black and white children, respectively), whereas for children who entered after 6 months of age, the fitted median lifetimes are 3.2 years and 1.8 years. Examples of how the analytic results of survival analyses can be presented are given in Murnane, Singer, and Willett (1988, 1989) and Murnane, Singer, Willett, Kemple, and Olsen (1991).

SUMMARY

In this chapter we have argued that research questions about duration—questions that treat time as an outcome—are a rich area for inquiry in long-term follow-up studies. Such questions not only provide an arena for new investigation but also enable old questions to be asked in new ways, providing an alternative and potentially informative perspective.

Answering these questions by inspecting the sample survivor function circumvents negative biases associated with censoring. To increase sensitivity, the sample survivor function can be reexpressed as a sample hazard ("risk") function. To test hypotheses about the relationship between critical predictors and risk we can fit statistical models that represent hazard as a function of one or more predictors. Based on the fitted models, predicted survivor functions can be plotted at substantively interesting values of the predictors. Finally, any analytic findings can easily be translated back into the metric of interest—the metric of duration—using the median lifetime as a summary statistic. So, although we may take a somewhat circuitous analytic path, the data have been modeled appropriately and we have emerged able to make valid statements about time as an outcome.

REFERENCES

Allison, P. D. (1984). *Event history analysis: Regression for longitudinal event data.* Sage University Paper Series on Quantitative Applications in the Social Sciences (Series No. 07-046). Beverly Hills, CA: Sage.

Blossfeld, H. P., Hamerle, A., & Mayer, K. U. (1989). *Event history analysis: Statistical theory and application in the social sciences.* Hillsdale, NJ: Lawrence Erlbaum.

Cox, D. R. (1972). Regression models and life tables. *Journal of the Royal Statistical Society,* B, *34,* 187–202.

Kalbfleisch, J. D., & Prentice, R. L. (1980). *The statistical analysis of failure time data.* New York: Wiley.

Miller, R. G., Jr. (1981). *Survival analysis.* New York: Wiley.

Murnane, R. J., Singer, J. D., & Willett, J. B. (1988). The career paths of teachers: Implications for teacher supply and methodological lessons for research. *Educational Researcher,* *17*(6), 22–30.

Murnane, R. J., Singer, J. D., & Willett, J. B. (1989). The influences of salaries and "opportunity costs" on teachers' career choices: Evidence from North Carolina. *Harvard Educational Review, 59*(3), 325–346.

Murnane, R. J., Singer, J. D., Willett, J. B., Kemple, J. J., & Olsen, R. J. (1991). *Who will teach?: Policies that matter.* Cambridge, MA: Harvard University Press.

Singer, J. D., Fosburg, S., Goodson, B. D., & Smith, J. M. (1978). *National Day Care Home Study Research Report.* Final Report of the National Day Care Home Study (DHHS Publication No. 80-30283).

Singer, J. D., & Willett, J. B. (1991). Modeling the days of our lives: Using survival analysis when designing and analyzing longitudinal studies of duration and the timing of events. *Psychological Bulletin, 110,* 268–290.

Singer, J. D., & Willett, J. B. (1993). It's about time: Using discrete-time survival analysis to study duration and the timing of events. *Journal of Educational Statistics. 18*(2) 155–195.

Tuma, N. B., & Hannan, M. T. (1984). *Social dynamics: Models and methods.* New York: Academic Press.

Willett, J. B., & Singer, J. D. (1989). Two types of questions about time: Methodological issues in the analysis of teacher career path data. *International Journal of Educational Research, 13*(4), 421–437.

Willett, J. B., & Singer, J. D. (1991a). How long did it take . . . ?: Using survival analysis in educational and psychological research. In Linda M. Collins & John L. Horn (Eds.), *Best Methods for the analysis of change: Recent advances, unanswered questions, future directions* (pp. 310–327). Washington, DC: American Psychological Association.

Willett, J. B., & Singer, J. D. (1991b). From whether to when: New methods for studying student dropout and teacher attrition. *Review of Educational Research, 61*(4) 407–450.

Willett, J. B., & Singer, J. D. (1993). Investigating onset, cessation, relapse, and recovery: Why you should, and how you can, use discrete-time survival analysis to examine event occurrence. *Journal of Consulting and Clinical Psychology, 61*(6), 952–966.

Toward a Developmental Epidemiology

Stephen L. Buka
Lewis P. Lipsitt

INTRODUCTION

The health problems of children in the United States have shifted dramatically throughout this century. Since the early 1900s there has been a remarkable decline in the major infectious diseases of childhood, such as diphtheria, scarlet fever, tuberculosis, and smallpox. Paralleling this decline in infectious disease has been a relative rise in the prevalence of chronic diseases and disabilities, with major research efforts during the 1950s and 1960s directed toward the study of neurological and sensory disorders. Since 1970, there has been increasing concern for psychiatric, behavioral, educational, and social disorders of childhood and a call to study these "new" or psychosocial morbidities of childhood and adolescence (Haggerty, Roughmann, & Pless, 1975).

The discipline of epidemiology and the practice of public health have been central to our understanding and amelioration of the forms of childhood disorder that were prevalent during the first half of this century. Traditional

Developmental Follow-up

methods of *infectious disease epidemiology* (Hopkins, 1983) led to recommendations for improved sanitation, nutrition, and housing programs at the turn of the century, which, coupled with the widespread use of vaccines and antibiotics, have virtually eradicated many of these life-threatening diseases. Similarly, application of methods of *chronic disease epidemiology* has increased our understanding of the genetic, prenatal, and perinatal causes of many neurologic and sensory disorders of childhood. Modification of obstetrical practices and the use of genetic screening techniques, based largely on this wave of epidemiologic research, have reduced the incidence of these childhood conditions.

This successful history of translating scientific data into public health practice resulted from two major features of epidemiologic research: (a) the emphasis on disease or disorder classification, and (b) the identification of significant antecedent or risk factors for these disorders. These in turn lead to two practical products of epidemiologic research—prediction and prevention. Only by first accurately determining those who *have* a particular disorder will we be able to eventually predict those who *will* develop the disorder. Inaccurate disorder classification muddies the prediction process; accurate classification accelerates this process. The priority in epidemiologic research of determining what *groups* do and do not have a particular disorder derives from the interest in predicting, in other samples or populations, which *individuals* will develop the disorder (or their probability of doing so). "If epidemiology is to make any contribution to science, then generalizability and the reciprocal relation between individuals and group phenomena must hold" (Walker, 1991, p 25). The second practical application of epidemiologic research is prevention. Knowing the early conditions, experiences or "exposures" that precede and may cause the disorder of interest provides opportunities for preventive intervention, even before the causal processes or mechanisms are understood.

From past successes with infectious and chronic diseases, it is reasonable to expect that comparable applications of epidemiologic methods can lead to reductions in the forms of psychosocial disorders of childhood and adolescence of growing public concern over the past 20 years. However, although preestablished methods have been available for the study of both infectious and chronic diseases of childhood, it is not clear that methods truly appropriate or optimally suited for the epidemiologic study of psychosocial disorders of childhood yet exist. In psychiatry, for instance, techniques developed with adult populations have been applied to the study of childhood and adolescent disorders with some success, and information on the prevalence of many forms of childhood psychiatric disorders has been established (Costello, 1989). However, the utility of these basic descriptive data to inform our understanding of the etiology, prediction, and prevention of such conditions remains limited. Just as childhood psychopathology is not a "miniaturized" version of adult conditions, downward extensions of methods appropriate for the study of adult psychiatric disorders are largely inadequate for the epidemiologic investigation of the developing child.

Unlike infectious diseases or chronic physical conditions, the processes and manifestations of emotional, behavioral, and social disorders in children and adolescents are in many ways different from those of adults and, for the first time, the epidemiologic study of childhood conditions requires an approach distinct from that used for adults. Significant public health advances in the understanding, treatment, and prevention of these "new morbidities" of children and adolescents will require the formulation of a new set of epidemiologic concepts, principles, and methods, a "developmental epidemiology" that expands on existing methods and also reflects our current understanding of the unique qualities of the growing and developing child. In particular, a productive epidemiology of child and adolescent psychosocial conditions requires improved conceptualization, measurement, and classification of "disorders" as a first step toward improved prediction of individual risk and refined characterization of antecedent "risk factors" to facilitate preventive efforts. This chapter describes the general principles underlying a new form of "developmental epidemiology," with particular emphasis on the application and extension of the growing body of work described as "theoretical" or "modern" epidemiology.

MODERN EPIDEMIOLOGY—A GROWING BODY OF RESEARCH PRINCIPLES

The term *modern epidemiology* has been used to characterize a set of overarching conceptual and theoretical principles recently described in the epidemiologic literature: "the systematized body of epidemiologic principles by which to design and judge such studies [that have] begun to form only in the last two decades" (Rothman, 1986, p. 1). Epidemiology has outgrown prior definitions such as "the study of the distribution and determinants of disease," or "the study of disease in human populations," along with distinctions such as descriptive versus analytic epidemiology, observational versus experimental, or chronic versus acute disease epidemiology. The discipline of modern epidemiology now centers on a set of general scientific principles that guide the study of the *occurrence of disease and disability*, or, more generally, "event" occurrence (Miettinen, 1985).

The goal of epidemiologic research is neither description nor observation, but rather "to evaluate hypotheses about the causation of disorders and to relate these event occurrences to characteristics of people and their environment" (Rothman, 1986 p. 23). Although basic information on rates and proportions, the building blocks of epidemiologic research, may be useful for administrative and actuarial applications, this information alone is generally uninformative for advancing scientific knowledge about the etiology of disorder. The essence of modern epidemiology entails those research designs and analytic principles that guide the observation of event occurrence *for the purpose of formulating scientific statements* and the interpretation of those observations into inferential statements about etiology. This sequence of moving from observation to causal inference about the processes underlying event occurrence characterizes the modern epidemiologic method.

For example, a researcher may pose the question, what proportion of delinquent youth become criminal adults, follow a sample of delinquent arrestees into adulthood, and estimate this proportion. This observation or result, in and of itself, is of limited scientific value and falls far from the requirements of useful epidemiology. How does the rate of adult criminality among delinquent adolescents compare to the rate for nondelinquents? How typical or representative was the sample of delinquents on which the observation was based? If the rate of criminality among delinquents is indeed higher than among nondelinquents, and if this finding has some generalizability, then what can be inferred about the causal process or mechanism linking these two phenomena? Are both delinquency and adult criminality "caused" by some persistent underlying constitutional or environmental factor? Or is the delinquent behavior in its own right a causal factor for subsequent criminality? How? The technical and conceptual methods for addressing these questions lie at the heart of modern epidemiology and serve to move this branch of science from observation to causal inference.

Central to this orientation is the priority placed on empirical statements of event occurrence and the Popperian view that the empirical content of a hypothesis is measured by how falsifiable the hypothesis is (Popper, 1965). The fundamental task in epidemiologic research is to quantify the occurrence of disorder, to contrast differences in disorder occurrence between groups, and to generate estimates of the absolute and relative effects associated with certain characteristics. From these empirical estimates of the relative and absolute rates of occurrence associated with particular risk characteristics flows the process of causal inference.

A key element of this approach is the concept of observing the emergence of events or disorders within a common and well-specified subject population. This feature is demonstrated most clearly through prospective studies in which a cohort of initially disorder-free subjects is followed through time to observe the onset of disorder. In this design, depicted in Figure 1, subjects with and without certain antecedent features ("exposed" or "not exposed") are followed prospectively through time and observed for "event" occurrence. Smokers and nonsmokers are followed to observe events or cases of lung cancer; children from divorced versus intact families are followed to

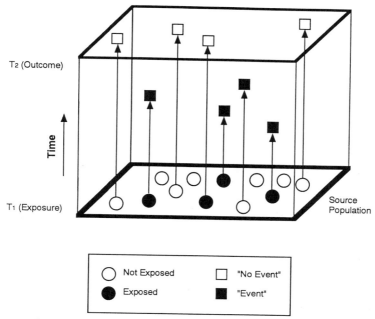

Figure 1   Schematic representation of prospective or cohort study.

observe cases of behavioral disorder. Either an entire population of interest may be studied, or the study may be limited to members sampled from within a population.

The methods of specifying the source population (to which the study results can be generalized) and sampling from within this population to select the study sample are critical to the study's potential for yielding data informative to the inductive process. This represents one of the major departures of epidemiology from the traditional approach in developmental psychology. The developmental literature is replete with prospective studies of samples of "convenience," ranging from Piaget's own children to volunteer undergraduates. These are expected to produce little epidemiologic or scientific yield for two major reasons. First, the "observations" derived from convenience samples cannot be readily generalized to any larger source or representative population. Second, convenience samples are typically "inefficient" in a statistical sense; that is, they do not provide the optimal distribution of "exposed" and "nonexposed" subjects (and those with and without key confounding factors that the investigator would like to examine). Principles for subject selection in cohort studies have been well described in the epidemiologic literature (Rothman, 1986; Walker, 1991). For instance, in Figure 1, all of the exposed subjects in the source population are selected for follow-up, as well as an equal number of randomly selected nonexposed subjects.

From this design, estimates of the proportion of subjects experiencing the event at a given point in time (prevalence) or throughout the period of follow-up (cumulative incidence) are derived, or the actual rate of event occurrence (incidence rate) may be the focus of attention. Absolute and relative differences in these rates and proportions between exposed and not exposed subjects are calculated and used to generate scientific inferences. The central question posed through this design is, in a particular population, is the rate (or proportion) of events among subjects with a specific antecedent characteristic different from those not having this characteristic? Does this event occur more often among certain types of individuals in this study population?

The time and expense required for prospective cohort studies has led to increased attention in recent years to the design and conduct of case-control studies (Schlesselman, 1982). Although the design is different, the questions addressed remain the same: what are the rates of a particular disorder for subjects with and without a certain antecedent condition? With the modern paradigm, this design is no longer a simple comparison of subjects with and without disorder ("diseased" vs. "nondiseased"; Miettinen, 1985). Instead, the "control" group is regarded not as a sample of subjects without disorder but rather as a referent sample, which, together with the "case" group, yields information on the *exposure/antecedent characteristics of the population* from which the disordered group arose. This view is markedly distinct from earlier approaches, which regarded the case and control groups as essentially two distinct samples, yielding information on those with and without the event of interest.

For example, suppose we are interested in examining the relationship between reported sexual abuse in childhood and subsequent adolescent suicide. We hypothesize that sexually abused children have higher rates of adolescent suicide than nonabused children (using official reports as our measure of sexual abuse). A prospective cohort study to examine this relationship would be impractical on several grounds: (a) it would be difficult to identify and enroll a sexually abused sample, (b) adolescent suicide is such a relatively rare phenomenon that very large numbers of exposed and nonexposed (abused vs. nonabused) subjects would be required, and (c) the length and cost of a prospective study would be considerable. Instead we elect to conduct a case-control study. Using traditional methods we would (a) identify all cases of adolescent suicide in our target population (say, occurring in California during a 5-year interval), (b) select an appropriate number of controls (nonsuicides), and (c) compare the rates of reported sexual abuse between the cases and controls. However, this would not necessarily answer the question we began with, namely, is the rate of adolescent suicide higher among subjects who have and have not been abused? In epidemiologic terms, we know the numerators for these two rates, that is, the number of adolescent suicides who were and were not abused as children. What we need is an estimate of the denominators—the numbers of abused and nonabused children in the source population from which the suicides arose.

As shown in Figure 2, the case-control or case-referent design can be viewed as a means of estimating this unknown denominator. Looking backward through time for all of the cases of adolescent suicide (black squares), we have one estimate of the number of abused and nonabused children (black circles and white circles, respectively) in our source population. This is obviously a biased and inadequate sample for estimating the proportion of children who were abused (unless there is truly no relationship between suicide and sexual abuse). We know the distribution of exposures for all of the cases; we need to estimate this for the noncases as well. Because in many instances it is impractical to determine the exposure history of *all* noncases (white squares), a representative sample of noncases is selected—the control or referent sample (white squares with dashed lines). Following these subjects backward through time we can estimate the distribution of abused and nonabused children among the noncases. Combining this estimate with the proportion of abused and nonabused subjects in the

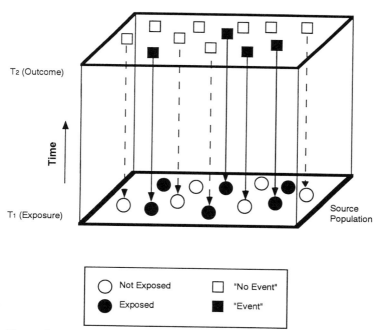

Figure 2   Schematic representation of case-control or case-"referent" study.

case sample provides us with the missing denominator, that is, the total number of abused and nonabused children from which our cases of suicide developed. Through this radically different design we can approximate the same rates and proportions that we hoped to, yet were unable to, derive from a prospective cohort design.

Another advance in modern epidemiologic writing concerns efforts to distinguish causal and noncausal antecedents of the event under study—true risk "factors" versus mere risk "indicators" (Miettinen, 1985). The "cause" of a disorder can be defined as any event, condition, or characteristic that plays an essential role in producing an occurrence of the disorder (Rothman, 1986). Epidemiologic research seeks to determine which antecedent conditions are essential characteristics of the disorder occurrence (i.e., true risk factors) as opposed to mere risk indicators or confounding variables. Current epidemiologic reasoning argues against single models of causation, and asserts that the cause of any effect must consist of a constellation of components that act in concert (Rothman, 1976).

Rothman (1976) describes "sufficient causes" as the set of minimal conditions and events that inevitably produce a disorder. These, in turn, result from a constellation of components, termed *component causes*. These components do play an essential role in the causation of a disorder, and therefore qualify to be classified as "causes," yet, on their own, they are not sufficient to result in disorder (disorder arises only when the entire critical constellation of component causes, comprising the sufficient cause, is present). These components may be regarded as necessary but not sufficient elements in the causal process. Any disorder may result from several different sufficient causes which, in turn, represent the combination of multiple component causes. This general model has dramatic implications for the understanding of interaction (all component causes "interact" in constituting a sufficient cause), and for understanding the strength of causality and the proportion of disease attributable to a specific cause. It also provides a means for conceptualizing and implementing research designs and analytic strategies that reflect the multifactorial etiology of most disorders, in particular, those in the behavioral, emotional, and social realms.

This approach is schematized in Figure 3, where the single exposures of Figure 1 are now depicted as a set of component causes which, when present in concert, lead to disorder occurrence. For instance, prenatal trauma and family poverty may act as component causes that contribute to, but do not in and of themselves result in, the development of conduct disorder. Possibly, only when accompanied by school failure and lack of parental guidance is the total set of component causes completed that result in a sufficient cause for the occurrence of conduct disorders. Other component causes (such as peer rejection or lack of recreational facilities) may combine with these and separate risk factors to generate other constellations of sufficient causes for conduct disorder. Complicating the prediction problem further is the

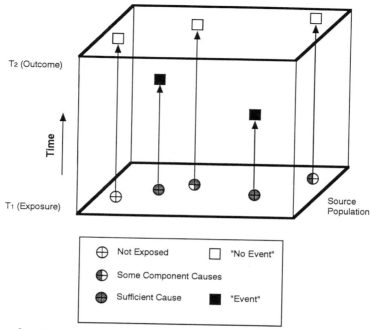

Figure 3   Schematic representation of prospective study with four component causes.

likelihood that at least some of the component causes will be continuous rather than dichotomous factors, with the likelihood of an outcome or disorder (event occurrence) being determined by variations in the strength or saliency of this component.

DEVELOPMENTAL EPIDEMIOLOGY—A MULTIDISCIPLINARY HYBRID

Although these principles of modern epidemiology have significantly advanced the field, we propose that contributions from the developmental sciences are needed to apply these techniques most effectively to the study of childhood psychosocial disorders. As illustrated in Figure 4, we conceptualize a new form of developmental epidemiology as a hybrid discipline, drawing on the theories, principles, and methods of (a) modern epidemiology, (b) developmental psychology, and (c) a variety of specific content domains, including education, special education, psychiatry, and clinical psychology. The relative contribution of these applied disciplines will vary with the condition under investigation, be it school absenteeism, drug use, or depression.

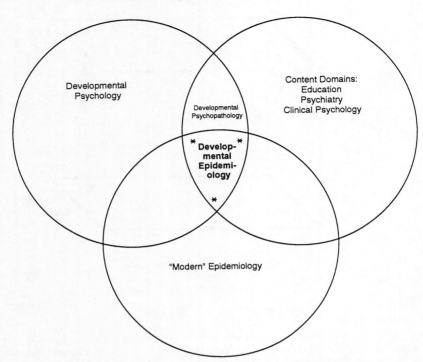

Figure 4   Developmental epidemiology: a multidisciplinary hybrid.

The utility of this orientation is demonstrated by the similarities between epidemiologic and, for instance, developmental approaches to the study of childhood psychopathology. The central concern in epidemiology of observing populations over time (either prospectively or retrospectively) to contrast the histories of normal and disordered members, currently lies at the heart of the field of developmental psychopathology. "Research on normal and atypical populations must proceed hand in hand in order to formulate a truly integrative theory of development that can account for normal and deviant forms of ontogenesis" (Cicchetti, 1990 p. 330).

Developmental psychopathology has been described as the "hierarchical integration" of two separate subdisciplines, developmental psychology and psychopathology (Cicchetti, 1984). The overlap of this branch of science with the content and principles of modern epidemiology suggests, at the same time, the potential for a newly integrated discipline of developmental epidemiology with related, yet distinct, features. Commonalities include (a) an interest in the emergence of disorder from within a population base, (b) the process of disorder causation, (c) multicomponent and multitemporal causes, (d) a person orientation, and (e) a concern with accurate measurement and classification. Differences between these orientations, however, indicate the new capacities that can be anticipated with this integrated approach. Simply stated, two anticipated results of this new discipline are, on the one hand, an enrichment of the design and analytic methods used in the study of psychopathology and other forms of "new morbidity" and, on the other, evolution from static to more dynamic theories of disorder causation in traditional epidemiologic investigations.

As developmental psychopathology lies at the intersection of developmental science and the study of psychopathology, we propose a form of developmental epidemiology that further emanates from the integration of a modern epidemiologic approach with the study of psychopathology. Similar approaches could be used to study other psychosocial conditions of childhood and adolescence. In the following section, we briefly describe some of the features each of these contributing disciplines bring to the proposed hybrid of developmental epidemiology.

Contributions from Developmental Psychology

Epidemiology seeks to observe the emergence of events or disorders within certain classes of members in a specified population. In this respect, epidemiology has much in common with traditional methods of the field of child development, particularly the longitudinal approach to understanding the onset and appearance of developmental milestones. Whereas epidemiology typically seeks and documents the onset of developmental aberrations or anomalies, the longitudinal approach to the study of normal child development, refined through developmental psychology, targets outcome variables that are essentially normal and expected, such as the age of onset of walking, talking in three-word sentences, pulling oneself to standing, and becoming toilet trained.

Whereas epidemiology targets the onset and progression of disorders, developmental psychology seeks to follow the unfolding of essential constancies or universalities of growth and behavior. This is not to say that developmental psychology eschews abnormal processes. On the contrary, during the last several decades developmental psychology research has been much concerned with the precursors of adverse developmental pathways. Thus, researchers now study bullying behavior in adolescents with a view toward understanding the precursors of such behavior in earlier manifestations of hostility and aggression (Olweus, 1984). Similarly, much research has been done in recent decades on the developmental antecedents of cerebral palsy, mental retardation, and other psychological and neurological disorders (Broman, Nichols, & Kennedy, 1975). The methods of traditional child development have been successfully transported into the fields of abnormal behavior or developmental psychopathology to the point that it has become, in many instances, impossible to distinguish studies carried out by child developmentalists from those done by epidemiologists (Cicchetti, 1984; Rutter, 1983; Sameroff, 1983; Werner & Smith, 1992).

The study of the sequencing of salient life events, then, is the principal concern of both developmental psychology and epidemiology. Both fields, too, have gone far beyond the mere chronicling of event occurrences. Contemporary work in both fields emphasizes eventual assessments of causation, although this objective is first approached through studies of correlative occurrences.

Contributions from Developmental Psychopathology

Stroufe and Rutter (1984 p. 18) define developmental psychopathology as "the study of the origins and course of individual patterns of behavioral maladaptation, whatever the age of onset, whatever the causes, whatever the transformations in behavioral manifestation, and however complex the course of the developmental pattern may be." Garmezy (1991) describes some of the central elements of this field of study: (a) longitudinal inquiry, (b) an orientation toward individual persons rather than variables, (c) rigorous investigation of life histories, (d) consideration of multiple causes, and (e) an adaptational or organizational perspective toward the grouping of behaviors. Cicchetti (1990) and others have highlighted the importance of contrasting the development of both normal and pathological functioning. Although major advances have been made in all of these areas, much work remains to transform these broad and conceptual goals into clearly operationalized research methods. As we will discuss, critical tasks include (a) constructing classification systems that are developmentally sensitive, (b) generating analytic and design methods that assess the impact of multidimensional causes and reflect multiple pathways to a common disorder, and (c) developing improved measurement techniques (Garber, 1984).

An Example

The need to consider multiple causal influences that accumulate over the life course rather than single and static risk factors in the etiology of childhood psychosocial disorders has been well documented. The role of prenatal trauma in the etiology of behavior disorder provides a telling example (Buka, Lipsitt, & Tsuang, 1988). Initial reports suggested that adverse events during pregnancy and delivery could result in a "continuum of reproductive casualty extending from death . . . and perhaps even to behavior disorder" (Pasamanick, Rogers, & Lilienfeld, 1956 p. 613). The search for the reproductive "causes" of later emotional and behavioral disorder continues to this day (Ward, 1991). Although certain neurological and psychiatric disorders, such as cerebral palsy, mental retardation, and schizophrenia, appear to be directly related to reproductive and perinatal hazards, less severe forms of behavioral and emotional disorders are not (Buka, Tsuang, & Lipsitt, 1993; Werner, 1989). Only when combined with preexisting familial factors (Kandel & Mednick, 1991) or subsequent difficulties in the caretaking environment (Sameroff & Chandler, 1975) do the component causes of pre- and perinatal trauma join in an interactive fashion and constitute a sufficient cause that may result in the development of a psychosocial disorder.

The fact that many childhood disorders result from a series of component causes that accumulate over time and thus result in a sufficient cause for the disorder, event, or condition of interest is depicted in Figure 5. Following the previous example, certain subjects (subject 1 in the figure) may have a

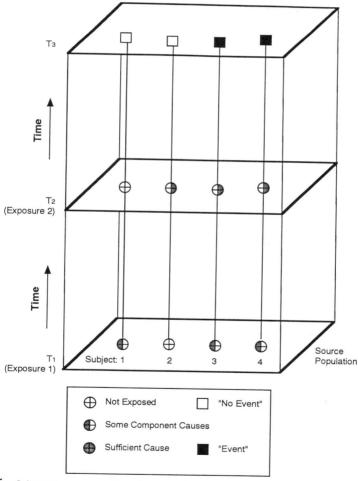

Figure 5   Schematic representation of prospective study with time-varying component causes.

particular exposure or component cause at an early stage (T1), such as prenatal trauma, but in the absence of additional component causes or risk factors at subsequent ages (T2) will not develop behavioral problems. Similarly, subject 2 is not "exposed" to the early risk factor of prenatal trauma, but does experience family disruption at a later age (T2) and also avoids behavioral problems. It is only those subjects who experience the entire set of component causes (prenatal trauma at T1 and family disruption at T2) who go on to develop behavior disorders.

The final step in approaching a developmental epidemiology, and possibly the most difficult conceptually and operationally, concerns the characterization of the behavioral, emotional, or psychosocial events or outcomes of interest and scientific relevance. Rather than counting discrete states that are evaluated at a single time and place, a developmental approach uses an adaptational or organizational perspective to group behaviors that takes into consideration the expression of disorder over multiple contexts and times. The goal is to measure phases or strands, rather than mere points, along the life-course trajectory: sequences of behavior that are expressed over time and setting (see Figure 6).

By attempting to describe and characterize behavior from an adaptational and organizational perspective there are often no clear rules as to how the target outcomes or dependent variables should be measured and defined. Developmental conditions or events that may be regarded in one culture as of special relevance or importance may be of little or no concern in another culture. If, for example, we were interested in studying the causes of late weaning from breastfeeding, our classification approach would differ dramatically by culture. Weaning after 1 year of age would be considered "late" in the United States, but on-time for many developing countries (Whiting & Child, 1975). If we were interested, instead, in studying "overly enmeshed mothering," with time of weaning as one component of a condition that is manifested throughout the early years, the "event" classification process becomes even more difficult. Similarly, behaviors that are appropriate in certain contexts may be maladaptive in others, and thus of special epidemiological interest. For instance, aggression and physical contact are valued on the football field but not in the classroom. Absolute criteria for event classification will be relatively uninformative in studies of developmental epidemiology; measurement and classification approaches that consider the cultural and situational context of the behavior are required.

Developmental approaches to the classification of behavioral events must also consider the relative stability of the behaviors of interest over time. The nature of human development is such that dispositions to behave in a particular way vary with age. The expression of hostility and aggression, or dependency, in a preschool-aged child has quite a different appearance from aggression in a teenager, and still different from that in a middle-aged person. To study the continuities and discontinuities, as well as the

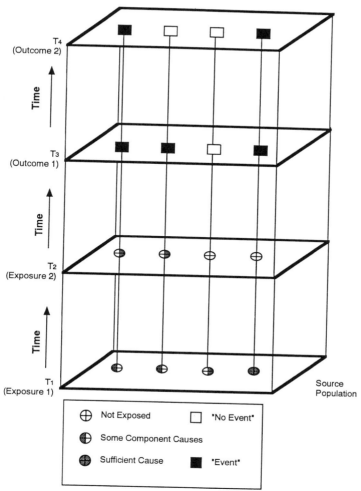

Figure 6 Schematic representation of prospective study with time-varying component causes and developmental classification of disorder.

transformations of behavioral dispositions across the life span, requires the devising of observational or psychometric tools that will honor the changing overt behavioral repertoire of the aging human. Although there are some domains of behavior, such as shyness (Kagan, 1989), that are fairly consistently manifested in comparable ways over age, other domains of behavior, such as dishonesty, look quite different in the preschooler than in the adolescent. The challenge for the developmental epidemiologist is to tap into the assessment of the characteristic at different ages with age-appropriate tools while at the same time maintaining the trait's thread through the succession of developmental assessments. As it happens, Erikson's (1982) allusion to the "tapestry" of development provides an apt metaphor for the changes in style of an attribute over the life stages while the trait substrate continues to flow throughout the life span.

METHODS OF DATA ANALYSIS AND INTERPRETATION

The data analytic methods of developmental epidemiology draw on a variety of approaches recently described for the analysis of longitudinal observational data. Broadly, the analytic requirements are to (a) define, describe, and classify the outcome events or disorders of interest; (b) define, describe, and classify antecedent risk indicators of interest; (c) generate empirical statements regarding the relationship of these outcome and antecedent conditions; and (d) move from these empirical statements to statements of causal inference. Particular attention is given to the consideration of multivariate and multitemporal expressions of both outcome and antecedent conditions. Accordingly, under a developmental perspective, the methods used to classify disorders of interest (outcome conditions) will generally be appropriate for antecedent conditions as well; both presumably are multidimensional and appear over time. Of course, unidimensional static methods for classification may also be used to examine simpler models of causation.

Methods that have been described to handle the problem of multivariate classification at a single time point are all concerned with identifying naturally occurring clusters of individuals with similar characteristics. These include: factor analyses, loglinear analyses (Feinberg, 1981), and a variety of cluster analytic approaches including latent profile analysis (Magnusson, 1981), configural frequency analysis (Krauth & Lienert, 1982), and "prediction analysis" (Brown, 1988). This approach has been extended to consider constellations of individuals on multidimensions and multiple time points, including methods to identify dynamic typologies or "dynatypes" (Huizinga, 1979; Shih, 1970) and longitudinal cluster analysis (Bergman, 1991).

In instances of repeated measures of the same variable across time, methods developed for multivariate analysis of individual growth curves are of interest (Bryk & Raudenbush, 1987; Rogosa & Willet, 1985). These methods apply for the analysis of continuous measures. Recently developed methods for analysis of repeated categorical outcomes exist that permit the consideration of time-varying covariates and missing data (Liang & Seger, 1986). Issues of missing data can also be addressed by a number of regression-based imputation procedures, capitalizing on multiple assessment points, in which a missing subject's outcome status is imputed based on prior values.

CONCLUSION

The purpose of this chapter has been to describe some of the principles that underlie a truly developmental approach to the conduct of epidemiology and to begin to define the boundaries of a new scientific hybrid, developmental epidemiology. We have highlighted some of the recent conceptual and methodologic advances of the field of modern epidemiology and argued that, although critical elements, these techniques alone are insufficient to reveal the causes of most psychosocial disorders of children and youth. This form of epidemiology requires infusions from the theoretical advances of developmental psychology and the substantive advances made in the various content disciplines of clinical psychiatry, psychology, special education, and the like.

The term developmental epidemiology has been used increasingly in several theoretical papers of recent years (Costello & Angold, 1991; Kellam et al., 1991; Scott et al., this volume), although with various meanings and orientations. We take these early expressions as a healthy sign of a budding stage of scientific development that is ready to emerge as a hierarchical integration of the contributing subdisciplines that have undergone significant refinement and differentiation in recent years. In addition to these theoretical presentations, there are at least three major research groups that describe their work as developmental epidemiology. At Duke University, Angold and Costello have approached the measurement of childhood psychopathology for epidemiologic studies from a developmental perspective (Costello & Angold, 1991). The Child and Adolescent Psychiatric Assessment (CAPA) instrument represents an effort to assess psychiatric symptoms using an interviewer-based methodology that may be more sensitive to developmental variations than traditional respondent-based approaches (Angold, 1990). The landmark longitudinal studies of children in the Woodlawn area of Chicago (Kellam, Brown, Rubin, & Ensminger, 1983) have also been described as developmental epidemiology. The focus of this group, both in the Woodlawn studies and other research relating to the prevention of psychiatric disorders, substance use, and school difficulties, has been on the multiple components that accumulate in a developmental fashion and result in disorder occurrence (see Figure 5). Finally, with a focus on criminal and antisocial behavior across the life span, the Program on Human Development and Criminal Behavior (Tonry, Ohlin, & Farrington, 1990) is implementing the full model shown in Figure 6. The study and analytic design of this research project reflects the dual objectives of (a) examining the multiple causal factors that accumulate from different settings and stages of development and contribute to the etiology of antisocial behavior, and (b) characterizing subjects' antisocial behaviors based on expressions across settings, times, and informants.

The demand for serious public health responses to the new psychosocial morbidities of children and adolescents mounts daily. As with earlier epidemics, there is hope that science will generate improved techniques for both the early *prediction* of individual children at risk for the development of disorders and methods for wide-scale *prevention.* These are reasonable products of epidemiologic research, but traditional methods will need to be modified to address the unique developmental features of these psychosocial conditions. The simple exposure-disease model (Figure 1) needs to be expanded in both directions. Methods to classify disorders must become less static and consider behavior expressed over multiple contexts and times. Measurement and analyses of antecedent risk factors will need to consider multiple events that accumulate over the life span (Figure 6).

Perhaps, the preliminary principles and methods described here will help guide the conduct and analysis of future epidemiologic investigations of the current "epidemics" of behavioral and social disorders affecting large numbers of youth in society today. As in past work with infectious and chronic diseases of childhood, the joint efforts of epidemiologic investigation and public health practice will lead, one hopes, to the reduction of these "new" morbidities of children and youth.

REFERENCES

Angold, A. (1990, October). *Semi-structured psychiatric interviews for children and adolescents.* Verbal presentation at the American Public Health Association Annual Meeting, New York, NY.

Bergman, L. R. (1991, March). *Methods of longitudinal data analysis.* Paper presented at meetings of the European Science Foundation—Network for Longitudinal Studies, Budapest, Hungary.

Broman, S. H., Nichols, P. I., & Kennedy, W. A. (1975). *Preschool IQ: Prenatal and early developmental correlates.* New York: Halstead Press.

Brown, G. W. (1988). Causal paths, chains and strands. In R. Rutter (Ed.), *Studies of psychosocial risk: The power of longitudinal data.* Cambridge University Press.

Bryk, A. S., & Raudenbush, S. W. (1987). Application of hierarchical linear models to assessing change. *Psychological Bulletin, 101,* 147–158.

Buka, S. L., Lipsitt, L. P., & Tsuang, M. T. (1988). Birth complications and psychological deviancy: A twenty-five year prospective inquiry. *Acta Paediatrica Japonica, 30,* 537–546.

Buka, S. L., Tsuang, M. T., & Lipsitt, L. P. (1993). Pregnancy/delivery complications and psychiatric diagnosis: A prospective study. *Archives of General Psychiatry, 50,* 151–156.

Cicchetti, D. (1984). The emergence of developmental psychopathology. *Child Development, 55,* 1–7.

Cicchetti, D. (1990). Perspectives on the interface between normal and atypical development. *Development and Psychopathology, 2,* 329–333.

Costello, E. J. (1989). Developments in child psychiatric epidemiology. *Journal of the American Academy of Child and Adolescent Psychiatry, 28,* 836–841.

Costello, E. J., & Angold, A. (1991). Developing a developmental epidemiology. In D. Cicchetti & S. Toth (Eds.), *Rochester Symposium on Developmental Psychopathology* (Vol. 3). Hillsdale, NJ: Laurence Earlbaum.

Erikson, E. H. (1982). *The life cycle completed: A review.* New York: Norton.

Feinberg, S. E. (1981). *The analysis of cross-classified categorical data* (2nd ed.). New York: Wiley.

Garber, J. (1984). Classification of childhood psychopathology: A developmental perspective. *Child Development, 55,* 30–48.

Garmezy, N. (1991, March). *Developmental psychopathology.* Paper presented at meetings of the European Science Foundation—Network for Longitudinal Studies, Budapest, Hungary.

Haggerty, R. J., Roughmann, K. J., & Pless, I. B. (1975). *Child health and the community.* New York: Wiley.

Hopkins, D. R. (1983). *Princes and peasants: Smallpox in history.* Chicago: University of Chicago Press.

Huizinga, D. (1979, April). *Dynamic typologies: A means of exploring longitudinal multivariate data.* Paper presented at the Tenth Annual Meeting of the Classification Society, Gainesville, FL.

Kagan, J. (1989). Temperamental contributions to social behavior. *American Psychologist, 44,* 668–674.

Kandel, E., & Mednick, S. A. (1991). Perinatal complications predict violent offending. *Criminology, 29,* 519–529.

Kellam, S. G., Brown, C. H., Rubin, B. R., & Ensminger, M. E. (1983). Paths leading to teenage psychiatric symptoms and substance use: Developmental epidemiological studies in Woodlawn. In S. B. Guze, F. J. Earls, & J. E. Barnett (Eds.), *Childhood psychopathology and development.* New York: Raven Press.

Kellam, S. G., Werthamer-Larsson, L., Dolan, L. J., Brown, C. H., Mayer, L. S., Rebok, G. W., Anthony, J. C., Laudolff, J., & Edelsohn, G. (1991). Developmental epidemiologically based preventive trials: Baseline modeling of early target behaviors and depressive symptoms. *American Journal of Community Psychology, 19,* 563–584.

Krauth, J., & Lienert, G. A. (1982). Fundamentals and modifications of configural frequency analysis (CFA). *Interdisciplinaria, 3,* 1–14.

Liang, K. Y., & Seger, S. L. (1986). Longitudinal data analysis using generalized linear models. *Biometrika, 73,* 13–22.

Magnusson, D. (1981). Some methodology and strategy problems in longitudinal research. In F. Schulsinger, S. A. Mednick, & J. Knop (Eds.), *Longitudinal research: Methods and uses in behavioral science.* Boston: Nijhoff.

Miettinen, O. S. (1985). *Theoretical epidemiology: Principles of occurrence research in medicine.* New York: Wiley.

Olweus, D. (1984). Aggressors and their victims: Bullying at school. In H. Frude & H. Gault (Eds.), *Disruptive behaviors in schools.* New York: Wiley.

Pasamanick, B., Rogers, M. E., & Lilienfeld, A. M. (1956). Pregnancy experience and the development of behavior disorder in children. *American Journal of Psychiatry, 112,* 613–618.

Popper, K. R. (1965). *The logic of scientific discovery.* New York: Harper & Row.

Rogosa, D. R., & Willett, J. B. (1985). Understanding correlates of change by modeling individual differences in growth. *Psychometrika, 90,* 726–748.

Rothman, K. J. (1976). Causes. *American Journal of Epidemiology, 104,* 587–592.

Rothman, K. J. (1986). *Modern epidemiology.* Boston: Little, Brown.

Rutter, M. (1983). School effects on pupil progress: Research findings and policy implications. *Child Development, 54,* 1–29.

Sameroff, A. J. (1983). Developmental systems: Contexts and evolution. In W. Kessen (Ed.), *Handbook of child psychology: Vol. 1. History, theory, and methods* (4th ed.). New York: Wiley.

Sameroff, A. J., & Chandler, M. J. (1975). Reproductive risk and the continuum of caretaking casualty. In F. Horowitz (Ed.), *Review of child development research* (Vol. 4). Chicago: University of Chicago Press.

Schlesselman, J. J. (1982). *Case control studies: Design, conduct, analysis.* New York: Oxford University Press.

Scott, K. (In press). Developmental epidemiology. In S. L. Freidman & H. C. Haywood (Eds.), *Developmental follow-up: Concepts, domains and methods.* Academic Press.

Shih, F. (1970). *Dynatypes: A new tool for sequential analysis applied to urbanization processes.* Unpublished doctoral dissertation, University of Colorado, Boulder, CO.

Stroufe, L. A., & Rutter, M. (1984). The domain of developmental psychopathology. *Child Development, 55,* 17–29.

Tonry, M. Ohlin, L. E., & Farrington, D. P. (1990). *Human development and criminal behavior: New ways of advancing knowledge.* New York: Springer-Verlag.

Walker, A. (1991). *Observation and inference.* Boston: Epidemiologic Resources Institute.

Ward, A. J. (1991). Prenatal stress and childhood psychopathology. *Child Psychiatry and Human Development, 22,* 97–110.

Werner, E. E. (1989). High-risk children in young adulthood: A longitudinal study from birth to 32 years. *American Journal of Orthopsychiatry, 59,* 72–81.

Werner, E. E., & Smith, R. S. (1992). *Overcoming the odds: High risk children from birth to adulthood.* Ithaca, NY: Cornell University Press.

Whiting, J. W. M., & Child, I. R. (1975). *Child training and personality: A psychocultural analysis.* Cambridge, MA: Harvard University Press.

Developmental Epidemiology

Keith G. Scott
Kimberly H. Shaw
Jennifer C. Urbano

INTRODUCTION

This chapter concerns the application of epidemiological methodology to the study of developmental outcome. Epidemiology, in its most generic sense, is the study of the *occurrence of discrete events* (Miettinen, 1985). Most commonly, it has been applied to the study of factors that lead to the occurrence of medical diseases. Medical epidemiology has proceeded by studying "the distribution and determinants of disease frequency in human populations" (Hennekens & Buring, 1987). In this context, epidemiology has supplied the quantitative methodology for the development of public health programs for the prevention of disease. This has been done by monitoring occurrence and by identifying and eliminating the sources of risk and/or agents of transmission. There is a proud history in epidemiology of identifying sources of transmission *before* the underlying processes were known. For example, the transmission of cholera via polluted drinking water was established in 1854, 30 years before the bacterial transmission of disease (Snow, 1949) was understood. More recently, smoking has been linked to lung

Developmental Follow-up

351

cancer without an understanding of the carcinogenic mechanism (Doll & Hill, 1950).

The epidemiologic methods we will describe are deeply rooted in empirical procedures to guide inquiry. They have been developed over more than a hundred years in the study of the etiology of disease. However, until the middle of this century, the search for and the prevention of disease focused on infectious disorders such as cholera. In general, such diseases are caused by a single factor or agent, are of short latency from exposure to onset, and lead rapidly to death or recovery. Acute infectious diseases are quite unlike developmental disorders. Childhood behavioral and psychological disorders have multiple factors in their causation, onset varies across a wide age span, and in general they are neither fatal nor readily remediated. In other words, they are chronic and multifactorial in their etiology. Thus, the methods of infectious disease epidemiology are not of obvious use in the study of childhood behavioral outcomes. The methods of modern epidemiology (Hennekens & Buring, 1987) emerged in the study of disorders such as cancer and heart disease. Epidemiology, therefore, became concerned with chronic diseases caused by multiple risk factors with long onset latencies. These methods can now be applied to the study of outcomes that have origins in the perinatal period, in infancy, and in childhood.

Developmental epidemiology is the study of the distribution of behavioral outcomes in infancy and childhood and the indicators of their occurrence. An indicator, or factor, is any characteristic of a person, time, or place that influences outcome for good or bad. They include biological, sociological, and environmental factors, characteristics, exposures,[1] or experiences. The events of interest could include risk factors linked to behavioral disorders, or positive factors linked to enhanced development. The methodology is equally applicable to the study of mental retardation or giftedness. However, epidemiologic methodology has rarely been used to study positive outcomes and in most of this chapter we will use the term *risk factors* and be concerned with negative outcomes. A concern with "protective" or "enhancing factors" would be appropriate and important but has not been the focus of research to date.

A COMPARISON OF EPIDEMIOLOGICAL METHODS AND TRADITIONAL DEVELOPMENTAL PSYCHOLOGY METHODS

Traditional Developmental Psychology Methods

In treating individual differences, developmental psychology has based its methods on the psychometric tradition of tests and measures. The statistical

[1] The term *exposure* is used very broadly to cover any factor, good or bad, that is a characteristic of an individual or their experience. Thus, a subject may be "exposed" either to violence or to an intervention.

model chosen has the mean as the major measure of central tendency and linear variance estimates as the measures of the size of an effect. Based on these models, group differences are tested using the t test or an analysis of variance. The relationship among variables are described again using linear regression with an emphasis on correlation, partial correlation, and multiple regression. Recently, modeling using path analysis has exacerbated this excessive reliance on correlational methodology. For many applications in describing population differences, such as in general intelligence, these procedures may be highly appropriate. However, they are epidemiologically uninterpretable (Rothman, 1986). The outcomes of interest may be associated with only a small part of the range of the predictor variable. As part of the total distribution, we are concerned with *low* birthweight, *mal*nutrition, and *abuse* and *neglect* as parts of a continuum of child care. Strong predictors of the occurrence of discrete outcomes can appear to be weak in terms of correlations or mean differences when only a small part of the range is relevant.

The negative outcomes of interest to those studying children are relatively rare events. Table I shows the rate per thousand of disorders of childhood that require special services at 7 and 11 years of age, according to school records. They occur at such a low frequency that they can have only a small

Table I Distribution and Rate of Educational Handicaps for the 1991 Dade County Public School Population

	Age			
	7 years		11 years	
Educational classification	Rate/1,000	# of cases	Rate/1,000	# of cases
Learning disabled	20.3	500	78.7	1,735
Emotionally handicapped	4.2	104	9.1	201
Speech problems	30.1	742	15.7	347
Language problems	2.8	68	0.5	12
Educable mentally handicapped	4.0	99	7.8	173
Trainable mentally handicapped	2.3	57	2.7	59
Profoundly mentally handicapped	1.2	29	1.2	27
Physically impaired	2.3	57	1.1	24
Hard of hearing	0.6	15	0.5	11
Visually impaired	1.0	24	0.4	9
Deaf	0.5	13	0.6	13
Autistic	0.7	18	0.5	12
Severely emotionally disturbed	0.6	14	2.7	60
Gifted	24.1	594	55.0	1,212
Normal	910.0	22,356	820.0	18,145
Total	—	24,690	—	22,040
Grand Total		46,730		

effect on mean differences in psychometric scores for the total population of school children. It follows that the risk factors associated with these rare outcomes will account for only a very small portion of the total variance. Direct statements can not be made regarding frequency of outlying cases in the distribution from variance estimates, nor mean differences. The practical importance of this point can be illustrated with some analyses of the relations between Low Birthweight (LBW; ≤ 2500 g), intelligence (IQ), and mental retardation.

In an earlier chapter, Scott and Masi (1979), drawing on an existing data set (Wiener, 1968), compared the outcome of two samples at 7 years of age. One sample was LBW (≤ 2500 g) and the other Normal Birthweight (NBW; > 2500 g). Both groups were similar in ethnicity, social class, and maternal age. The main results are shown in Table II. As can be seen, a small mean difference between the LBW and NBW groups of 4.9 IQ points was associated with twice the rate of mild mental retardation and five times the rate of severe handicaps.

Epidemiological Indices of Risk

Regression models do not provide answers to questions about the changes that a child will be normal or handicapped (Greenland, Schlesselman, & Criqui, 1986) and are therefore of reduced practical value. Categorical analysis of the data allows us to calculate measures of outcome in terms of indices of risk which are directly useful in applied settings. As we shall see, such measures are of great utility. Table III summarizes some of the epidemiological indices of risk that can be derived from different research

Table II A Comparison of Mean IQ and the Relative Risk (RR) of Handicaps at Age 8–10

	Birthweight of group	
	≤ 2500 g	> 2500 g
Number of sample given IQ test	417	405
Mean WISC IQ	89.8	94.7
Percentage with IQ 50–79	26%	13%
	($N = 109$)	($N = 54$)
Percentage with IQ below 50 and/or severe sensory or gross motor disability	3.69%	0.74%
	($N = 16$)	($N = 3$)
Relative Risk (RR)	5.3	2.0

Note. In a study designed to assess the absolute value of the RR, a much larger sample would be required. Please see the text for a more detailed discussion.

Table III Summary of Epidemiological Indices of Risk Illustrated by the Outcome of Special Education as a Result of Low Birthweight

Exposure	Outcome		
Low birthweight	Special education (SE)		Total
	YES	NO	
YES	A	B	M_1
NO	C	D	M_2
Total	N_1	N_2	N

PROSPECTIVE STUDIES

In a PROSPECTIVE STUDY, samples are drawn on the basis of *exposure* (LBW/NBW).

* Relative Risk (RR), the ratio of bad outcomes in the exposed as compared with the nonexposed sample
* Prevalence of outcome in the exposed group, $p_1 = A/M_1$
* Prevalence of outcome in the unexposed group, $p_2 = C/M_2$

$$\text{Relative Risk} = p_1/p_2$$

CASE-CONTROL STUDY

In a CASE-CONTROL STUDY, groups are formed on the basis of *outcome* (SE/Normal).

* Exposure Odds Ratio (OR), the ratio of the odds of exposure (to LBW) in the group with the bad outcome compared with the group with the normal outcome
* Odds of exposure in the *cases* (SE group) = A/C
* Odds of exposure in the *controls* (Normals = B/D

$$\textit{Exposure Odds Ratio} = (A/C)/(B/D) = AD/BC$$

* Frequency of Exposure (E), the proportion of cases in the sample that have been exposed to the risk

$$\textit{Frequency of Exposure } E_{(A)} : M_1 \div N$$

* Attributable Fraction (AF), the proportion by which the incidence rate of the bad outcome in the entire population would be reduced if the exposure were eliminated

$$\text{Attributable Fraction} = \frac{\{E_{(A)} * [OR_{(A)} - 1]\}}{\{E_{(A)} * [OR_{(A)} - 1]\} + 1}$$

designs: Relative Risk (RR), exposure Odds Ratio (OR), and Attributable Fraction (AF).

The relative risk is the comparison of the relative rate of occurrence of a disorder in a group where a risk factor is present compared to one where it is not. Consider the example of a mother who has a premature delivery and thus a LBW infant. She wants to know what the chances are that her child will be handicapped or normal. The overall correlation of birthweight and IQ is approximately 0.2. That is, 4% of the variance is accounted for by birthweight. This information is of little use in assessing the outcome for an individual child. However, information about the RR is directly relevant. Depending on the particulars of the actual birthweight, she can be given an estimate, either in terms of the risk compared with a NBW infant, or what proportion of infants like hers will develop normally.

The ability to estimate the proportion of at-risk or exposed infants who will end up normal or impaired is also central to the needs of prevention planners. They must tell policy makers how many children will need what service and at what age. The senior author of this chapter was asked to address such a question some years ago. He was asked to estimate the potential impact on the occurrence of mental retardation of a state initiative to intervene with LBW infants. Despite a very large follow-up literature on LBW infants, the answer was not readily available. It required that the set of data previously described, and shown in Table II, be reanalyzed in terms of categorical childhood disorders, rather than population differences.

Mental retardation, learning disabilities, child abuse, and the psychopathological disorders of childhood are statistically rare events. Individually, they will account for small parts of the total variance on continuous measures of child outcome and will show up as small differences in means between high- and low-risk groups. Further, the disorders of childhood are often not homogeneous entities. Learning disabilities, as the name suggests, may be a collection of disorders that share some common symptoms. That is, they result from multiple biological, sociological, and environmental events that produce *low frequency,* but very serious, conditions in children. The research methods of epidemiology are most appropriate to the study of this type of problem.

The exposure odds ratio is the odds that an outcome is associated with a given exposure. It is important because in multifactorial disorders, only some of the outcomes may be due to a particular exposure. The attributable fraction provides another measure of the impact of an exposure on the number and rate of cases. The AF is the portion of all cases that are linked to a given exposure. Examples of their calculation are provided in Tables IV and V. In a later section we will consider the exposure OR and AF in greater detail (see Table III). Both are based on the analysis of retrospective data and will be described in the discussion of case-control studies.

Measurement of Interactions

The assessment of risk in epidemiology is based on the sufficient-component causal model.[2] In principle, there are necessary and sufficient

---

[2] For the present discussion, an event, experience, condition, or personal characteristic that plays an essential role in producing a developmental outcome is defined as a "cause."

Table IV Occurrence of Low Birthweight (LBW) in Cases (Special Education Students) and Controls (Regular Education Students)

	Cases		Controls	
	Special education		Regular education	
	%	N	%	N
Strata I				
(Born 1978–1979)				
VLBW + LBW	17.4	20	10.1	19
NBW	82.6	95	89.9	169
Total	100.0	115	100.0	188
		OR = 1.87		
		(0.9 < OR < 3.88)		
		95% Confidence		
Strata II				
(Born 1978–1979)				
VLBW + LBW	15.6	45	10.5	47
NBW	84.4	244	89.5	402
Total	100.0	289	100.0	449
		OR = 1.58		
		(0.99 < OR < 2.18)		
		95% Confidence		

Note. This table is based on placement in 1988, when the sample was drawn.

Table V Calculation of Attributable Fraction

Strata I

Frequency of Exposure $(E_{(A)}) = .13$

$$\text{Attributable Fraction (AF)} = \frac{.13 \times (1.87 - 1)}{\{.13 \times (1.87 - 1)\} + 1}$$

$$= \frac{.113}{1.113}$$

$$= 10\%$$

Strata II

Frequency of Exposure $(E_{(A)}) = .13$

$$\text{Attributable Fraction (AF)} = \frac{.13 \times (1.58 - 1)}{\{.13 \times (1.58 - 1)\} + 1}$$

$$= \frac{.075}{1.075}$$

$$= 7\%$$

Note. See Table III for a description of the AF.

causes for an outcome to occur. Some of these causes are known and can be specified, but others, at a given stage of knowledge, remain to be discovered. However, although they are not identified, the undiscovered causes are not considered random. The outcome, then, is the total combined result of the sufficient causes attenuated only by errors of measurement. The identified sufficient causes are typically a combination of more than one agent or factor. Components of one sufficient cause may also be components in one or more other sufficient causes. Nevertheless, each sufficient cause can be considered independent in the sense that it can occur alone. This postulated independence is critical to all analyses of interactions. If the causes are not independent, then the assessment of an interaction between them is not possible.

Multiple single agents may be individually sufficient causes of an outcome. Outcomes that occur as the result of more than one agent or factor in combination and over and above their action are said to be interacting. Thus a developmental disability could be due to a single sufficient cause such as low birthweight, or the single sufficient cause of poverty, or it could result from the interaction of these factors, which is in itself a sufficient cause. To the extent that we can determine that there is Relative Excess Risk (RER) associated with the combination of these factors, independent of their separate action, we have an interaction. Rothman (1986) has argued that this additive model of interaction is the simplest and most general case. Special statistical models such as a multiplicative or constant rate/ratio of exposure and outcome, as in a linear model, are special cases of the simple additive model.

It should be pointed out that, except for very contrived examples, the causes in the study of developmental outcome will almost always be combinations of agents, exposures, and personal characteristics that occur in life experience. It will almost always be possible to conceptualize the analysis of a cause into subagents at the same or at a different level of analysis. In this sense, interactions may always be present. For example, poverty, as a cause of poor child outcome, may be a combination of agents such as inadequate nutrition, lack of language stimulation, and neglect. However, the analysis of child outcome, in terms of very low income, can be useful for many purposes. Epidemiology proceeds at a level of analysis that is useful in planning treatments for populations or for individuals. Thus the level of analysis at a point in time is anchored to a given application but may be refined as knowledge progresses.

The relative risks shown in Table VI are intended for purposes of illustration only. In practice, they are simply derived from the rates of cases in each of the cells as we have previously illustrated. Using as a reference group those who are neither low Socioeconomic Status (SES) nor LBW, we can simply calculate the relative excess risk (Cole & MacMahon, 1971) as is shown in the table. The joint effects of SES and LBW are estimated by the RER in this example as 5.0. That is, RER quantifies the joint effect of the

Table VI   Arbitary Example to Illustrate
Estimation of Relative Excess Risk (RER)

Birthweight (BW)

		Normal	Low
SES	Normal	A 1.0	B 3.0
	Low	C 2.0	D 6.0

RER for BW
  B-A = 3.0-1.0 = 2.0
RER for SES
  C-A = 2.0-1.0 = 1.0
RER for SES in combination with BW
  D-A = 6.0-1.0 = 5.0

two factors independent of the relative increase in outcomes associated with each alone.

The simple additive model of interaction can be extended to other statistical models such as a multiplicative model. However, there are no obvious reasons to do this from the perspective of public health planning or clinical prediction. Reasons may be present from theoretical perspectives in developmental theory, but these are not strictly epidemiological. Even when such tests of theory are the focal point of interest, certain practical issues must be faced in the estimation of interactions.

The main issue that confronts the researchers who wishes to estimate the RER due to an interaction, is the size of the sample that may be required. Presumably, this problem pertains to any estimate of an interaction term, regardless of the model employed. In the example we have just presented there were two causes considered requiring estimates of the RER for the following:

1. SES
2. LBW
3. SES in combination with LBW

If we add a third cause to this set, say a measure of neonatal illness such as Length of Hospital stay (LH) at birth, RER estimates are now required for the following:

1. SES
2. LBW
3. LH

4. SES in combination with LBW
5. SES in combination with LH
6. LBW in combination with LH
7. LBW in combination with LH and SES

Now these seven estimates will each require some minimum number of cases before an estimate can be made. As we have seen, the base rate for most negative outcomes is already very low. Three causes and the respective interactions must be divided seven ways. The assessment of the interaction between multiple causes will require very large samples, as the number of possible interactions increases geometrically with the number of causes. A result of this analysis is that complex interactions may be impossible to estimate because of the required sample sizes.

Confidence Intervals for Estimating Risk

The main purpose of epidemiological enquiry is to estimate the distribution of the determinants and their relationship to the frequency of outcomes. The sample sizes required are therefore primarily chosen to achieve sufficient *precision* in making these estimates. That is, the issue of sample size is linked to *accuracy* of measurement. This approach contrasts with the aim in inferential statistics where the major goal is to have a sufficient *power* to achieve statistical significance so a *decision* can be made. A point estimate from epidemiological data would not be exactly the same each time because of errors of measurement. The confidence interval specifies the range of values that would encompass a given percentage of point estimates. Thus in Table VII we give the limits within which 95% of the point estimates of relative risk would lie. Confidence intervals, along with the point estimates, convey information simultaneously about the magnitude and the precision of the effect. It should also be noted that the intervals can be used to give confidence in the description of the finding that there is no effect. This is

Table VII   Relative Risk Estimates from a Historical Prospective Study

	VLBW	LBW	NBW
Total	139	221	207
Normal achieving	107	178	178
Exceptional	32	43	28
Prevalence	.23	.19	.13
Relative risk	1.70	1.44	1.0
95% confidence limits	1.08–2.69	.93–2.23	

Note. Cohorts I & II from Carran, et al. (1989) have been combined. The chi-square for the linear trend = 5.3, $p = .02$.

particularly important in ruling out the effect of some perceived, but actually nonexistent, hazard or risk.

In general, the larger the risk the smaller the sample size that will be required to achieve a given level of precision. When risks are high, epidemiologic analyses can establish the magnitude of risks with a very small sample size (Adams, Khoury, & James, 1989). However, some hazards that may be of low relative risk are of great public health concern; very large sample sizes may be required. This relationship has given rise to the misconception that all of epidemiological enquiry requires large sample sizes. The conditions that require large sample sizes are those where the increase in risk is small. They become important when they are also very prevalent. The obvious examples are toxins in the air and in water supplies where whole populations are exposed. In this instance a RR of 1.1 of exposed to unexposed samples for a birth defect or cancer would be very serious. The effects of lead exposure on child development is an example of such a concern. There are many other examples that are almost totally unresearched. For instance, we know very little about moderate levels of malnutrition during infancy on long-term child outcomes for mental retardation and other learning problems.

Sampling

In epidemiological research, Miettinen (1985) argues that the aim is not to obtain a sample to represent a general population in the sense proposed by Campbell and Stanley (1963); rather, it is to harvest a group of individuals who share some characteristic or experience so that an outcome among them may be generalized to *any abstract population* that is similar. In a clinical trial, the treatment is the experience that is harvested. In analytic studies, *drawing the sample* is often the most critical operation in carrying out the study. Researchers wish to obtain groups of exposed or disordered persons so that they can generalize the results to the abstract case of any exposed or disordered group. A comparison or control group should be as similar as possible to the exposed or disordered group in all respects *except* the presence of the exposure or disorder, as the case may be.

Bias may creep into the comparisons that lead to the estimates of risk if samples are not carefully obtained. There are many sources of bias. Self-referred or selected individuals are often more likely to have a disorder than those contacted randomly. Particular hospitals are usually associated with a reputation for treating particular diseases leading to what is known as Berkson's Bias. There are strong gender, social, economic, and ethnic correlates of outcomes and any systematic differences in these variables between groups can lead to biased estimates of risk. To investigators trained in traditional experimental methods, some of these sources of bias can be quite unintuitive. For example, in the sections that follow, we will consider case-control studies. Here, the operation of matching the subjects on *any* variable, positively or negatively correlated with the outcome, can lead to an underestimation of risk.

Given that risk estimates are sensitive to sampling bias, careful description of the samples and how they are obtained is an important requirement for a quality report in epidemiological research.

Categorization of Continuous Measures

In epidemiologic research it is often necessary to subdivide continuous measures into categories of both exposure and outcome to calculate indices of risk. The reasons for categorization are more than just statistical convenience. Consider the case of exposure. There are traces of lead in many products such as ceramic dishes and drinking water. In water, the range may be from almost none to perhaps 10+ parts per million. Through much of this range, from 0 to 3–4 parts per million, there may be no discernible link with outcome. The vast majority of water supplies would probably lie in this range. As a result, a correlation between lead level and child IQ, based on a population sample, would likely be very small and probably insignificant. However, if one harvested a sample of cases where there was exposure to lead content in the water in the range of 3–10 parts per million, and contrasted it with one where the lead level was negligible, then a different result would be obtained. Another example is provided by Eisen, 1992, who examined the link between neonatal illness, as measured by length of hospital stay, and being classified as educationally handicapped 10 years later. Overall, they found a significant ($r = .19, p > .01$) but trivial correlation (3.6% of the variance) between number of days of hospitalization and placement. When the data were categorized by number of hospital days and cross-tabulated by birthweight group, the result shown in Table VIII was obtained. To do this, they carefully examined scatter plots of hospital days against outcome within birthweight groups. They found that the sickest infants (> 50 days hospitalization) were all under 1500 g birthweight and it was within this group that the link between neonatal sickness and outcome lay.

Table VIII   Table of Relative Risks: Relative Risk of Special Education Placement

	Jackson	Memorial	Hospital	Subsample
	New	LBW	VLBW > 50days	VLBW > 50 days
Regular education	186	181	59	30
Special education	30	49	21	19
Relative risk	1.0	1.5	1.9	2.8
Confidence interval		1.0–2.3	1.3–3.1	1.7–4.5

Commonly, a continuous scale will need to be divided into high- and low-risk groups so that a discussion can be made about who should receive early intervention services, that is, to decide who should be served with a program of prevention.

Categorization of continuous measures of outcomes is also necessary to decide who should receive treatment or special services. Only by examining distributions of exposures and outcomes, often cross-tabulated by other variables, can one grasp where and how to categorize. If such a search of the distributions reveals a clear systematic pattern, the initial categorization will probably be quite robust except perhaps immediately at the category boundaries. However, one should always try to cross validate the categories on an independent sample to rule out the possibility of chance associations. For applied purposes, either in programs of prevention, intervention, or treatment, it is necessary to categorize continuous measures to make the assessments of risk interpretable.

CLASSIFICATION OF RESEARCH DESIGNS IN DEVELOPMENTAL EPIDEMIOLOGY

Developmental Epidemiology Study Types

Figure 1 shows the major study types proposed for developmental epidemiology. The cornerstone of the proposed methodology is *surveillance*, or descriptive epidemiology. Surveillance is the branch of the discipline that

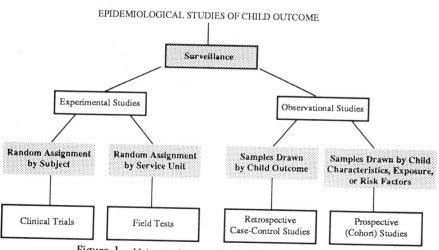

Figure 1   Major study types for developmental epidemiology.

monitors the frequency of cases in a population over time. The following are the major uses of epidemiological surveillance.

- Generation of etiological hypotheses
- Sample size estimation
- Monitoring trends in incidence or prevalence
- Rapid identification of onset of epidemics
- Estimation of service needs
- Assessment of effectiveness of applied interventions
- Public policy analysis

Traditionally there are two main surveillance measures. The number of new cases is the *incidence;* the *prevalence* is the total number of cases present at a given point in time. To most developmentalists, surveillance is the entire field of epidemiology. In fact, it is only the beginning point for inquiry. Major methods used in surveillance include survey research, analysis of birth and death certificates, and the study of health service records. A great deal of the power of surveillance comes from the ease with which trends and shifts in frequency can be monitored as part of a pattern of occurrence. For example, Doll and Hill (1950) noted a 15-fold increase in deaths from lung cancer in England over a number of years. They also observed that there was a parallel increase in the number of long-term smokers. In other countries, they found long-term smoking rates and lung cancer rates had similarly increased. Subsequent research focused on the issue of whether this *interindividual* effect from cross-sectional data would hold up when individual smoking and lung cancer records were linked in a longitudinal data set to provide *intraindividual* comparisons.

Effective surveillance of childhood behavioral disorders is presently limited to data from national survey research and is virtually nonexistent on a community basis. An example of the potential use of a surveillance system is to monitor, year to year, the number of children in a school system referred for behavior problems. This could be the starting point for an investigation that links the observed in behavior problems to substance abuse among pregnant women. Such an epidemic is widely believed to have occurred (Toufexis, 1991), but has not been rigorously documented by surveillance. Surveillance, as the term suggests, is concerned with monitoring changes in the frequency of outcomes over time. It is the descriptive process that helps in the creation of formal hypotheses about the connection between exposure and outcome. These hypotheses can then be tested by the use of more formal research designs. These designs will be discussed in the following section.

Developmental Epidemiology Research Designs

Major Issues   The major issues in the selection of the appropriate research design are summarized in the following list:

- Is the main purpose to estimate the magnitude of risk or to test a clear hypothesis?
- What sample size will be required to have a good chance of detecting a difference if it is present or of obtaining a satisfactory estimate of the magnitude of risk?
- Can the variable or factor of interest be manipulated experimentally?
- Is the study about a prospective or retrospective association; that is, (a) among those who are at risk, what is the frequency of the outcome? or (b) among those who have the outcome, what is the frequency of exposure to the risk factor?

First, if there is no clear question, surveillance data is absolutely essential before investing in any other study type. The reasons for this are apparent if one examines Table I. One (erroneous) interpretation of Table I, for making design decisions, is that the sample size is 46,730. On face value this is absurd. However, data from major longitudinal studies are frequently cited in terms of the total sample size rather than the outcome group who are of interest. The critical sample size in designing outcome research is the size of the group, for example, learning disabled or blind, who are being studied rather than the overall research group. Without some surveillance data the prevalence is unlikely to be known. We will return to discuss this at the end of the chapter as it applies to traditional longitudinal studies of child development.

Second, the very low prevalence of many childhood outcomes make *any* prospective design that will study a sample other than one that is *extremely* high risk, impractical. For example, consider Profound Mental Handicap as an outcome. It occurs at a rate of approximately 1/1000 (in Table I, 1.2/1000). To accumulate a sample of even 50 cases in a prospective design, sampling randomly from the population, a sample size of 50,000 would be necessary, without allowing attrition. Clearly, prospective studies are impractical for many outcomes.

The next issue concerns the risk factor of key interest. Does the hypothesis involve a risk factor that can ethically and practically be manipulated by the research team? Although the experimental method is scientifically the most rigorous, for many factors of interest the experimental method will not be possible. One cannot randomly assign children to birthweight groups nor manipulate many environmental conditions. Other manipulations would lie outside the socially and ethically acceptable range of child care practices. However, where experimental studies are not possible other nonexperimental research methods such as cohort and case-control studies can be used. These methods have been widely used in the study of chronic diseases. Basically, they are observational in the sense that different groups are being studied who have been exposed to different factors and have different outcomes. They are highly analytic in the methods and logic that governs the comparisons that are made.

The final major issue in selecting a research design depends on the form of the hypothesis. Hypotheses can be of two main types. In the first, one aims to look forward from cause to effect. Thus it could be hypothesized that the presence of a factor (e.g., LBW) in one group in the study population will result in a significant increase in the frequency of an outcome (e.g., special education placement) compared to the gorup where the factor is absent (e.g., NBW). Such hypotheses lead to prospective or cohort[3] studies where the samples are drawn as representative of the populations with and without risk status. The second type of hypothesis is in the form of looking backward from the outcome to see what may have been the cause. Such hypotheses lead to retrospective or case-control studies, where the samples are drawn on the basis of the outcome and retrospective data are searched to risk factor or agents.

Prospective or Cohort Studies   These studies draw samples that are representative of the populations with and without risk. They are followed longitudinally, either in real time, or from extant record.[4] Population estimates of relative risk, the ratio of bad outcomes in the exposed as compared to the nonexposed sample, are therefore available. As we have seen, longitudinal studies are usually impractical for very low incidence conditions because of sample size requirements.

A marked difference in our understanding of risk can *sometimes* be obtained from a prospective as compared to a retrospective study. Consider pregnancy as an outcome. Viewed prospectively, having intercourse could be identified as a risk factor for pregnancy. Sexual intercourse probably results in pregnancy from one in every several hundred couplings. That is, compared to abstinence, it involves a high level of risk. Viewed retrospectively, all pregnancies are associated with having had sexual intercourse. That is, the odds that pregnancy was preceded by sexual intercourse is 1, save for the occasional case of artificial insemination.

A study of the educational outcome of Very Low Birthweight (VLBW; ≤ 1500 g) and LBW (1501–2500 g) as compared to NBW (>2500 g) infants (Carran, Scott, Shaw, & Beydouin, 1989) illustrated a prospective study. In a historical design, two birth cohorts, born in 1974–1975 and 1978–1979, were identified in hospital logs. The outcome assessed was the educational placement in 1988. Table VII summarizes the results. As can be seen, there is a trend for the RR to increase as birthweight decreases. However, the

---

[3] In epidemiology, the term *cohort* has been used to denote a group in a prospective study which are often called cohort studies. Life span developmentalists borrowed the term and have used cohort with a broader meaning. We suggest avoiding the term, where possible, to avoid confusion.

[4] Both prospective and retrospective case-control studies can be based on existing clinical or health files that are referred to as extant records; such studies are called "historical," as in a "historical prospective study" or a "historical case-control study."

absolute size of the RR was not as large as many may have expected from clinical impressions.

Retrospective or Case-Control Studies Retrospective or case-control[5] studies draw samples on the basis of the outcome, and retrospective data are searched for risk factors or agents. The sample is buttressed by a comparison group from the same population without the outcome. This is the most economical and effective design for low incidence conditions. The case-control study is the most important innovation in research methodology to come from modern epidemiology (Schlesselman, 1982).

Retrospective methods have generally been held in low regard because they are seen as relying on subject recall and therefore very prone to bias. This can be a serious problem, but methods of checking the data have often been found. Some case-control studies rely on extant records and are totally free of the recall bias problem. Also, the methodology of case-control studies differs markedly from prospective or experimental studies and may seem unintuitive to those familiar with these more traditional approaches. For instance, matching the case and control groups on a variable related to the outcome, unless taken into account in the analysis of the data, will produce serious bias. This bias is almost always in the direction of underestimating population risk (Rothman, 1986; Schlessman, 1982). Among the major advantages of case-control studies are that they are relatively few subjects and are suitable for the study of low prevalence outcomes and where the developmental outcome takes some time to appear.[6] They are also relatively quick, inexpensive, and, if appropriately designed and analyzed, can be used to study multiple factors simultaneously.

The use of case-control methodology in studying developmental outcome is illustrated by a study by Shaw (1989). She asked, what is the prevalence of low birthweight among children in special education, as compared to regular education? Referring to Table IV, this becomes the ratio of the odds of exposure among the cases as compared with the rate of exposure among the controls; that is, the exposure odds ratio or OR. As can be seen, this increase in the odds that a child in special education as compared with one in regular education was of suboptimal birth is quite modest, from 1.5 to 1.8 times as likely from these preliminary estimates.

To more directly estimate the impact of birthweight on the need for special education services, one can calculate the proportion of children who are in special education that may have their placement attributed to LBW. The attributable fraction (AF) is the increase in the rate of occurrence of LBW

---

[5] The term "case-control" has sometimes been applied to prospective studies. In this chapter, we follow the more recent practice of restricting the term "case-control" to retrospective designs.

[6] The time between exposure and outcome is the "latency" of the outcome. Case-control studies are useful for the study of long latency outcomes.

among the cases as compared with the controls. In theory, if LBW was prevented, this is the decrease one could expect in the need for special educational services. It thus serves as a basis for estimating the impact of programs of prevention on the need for services and is one of the major epidemiological indices of effect size (Adams et al., 1989). The AF may be easily calculated from the data collected in the execution of a case-control study as shown in Table V. It can also be calculated using the RR obtained from a prospective study, if, *in addition,* the prevalence of the exposure in the population is known.

Epidemiological indices of risk, confidence intervals, and a variety of other related analyses can be calculated using a number of software packages designed for the purpose. They will run on most personal computers. The public domain EPI INFO (Dean, Dean, Burton, Dicker, 1990) was produced through a collaboration of the Centers for Disease Control and the World Health Organization. This easy-to-use package includes a simple word processor and a program to create questionnaires as well as calculate epidemiological indices. It is an outstanding tool for field research as it will run on many laptop computers. A more advanced commerical package, TRUE EPI (Gustafson, 1991), includes a large number of programs for categorical data analysis as well as the standard statistical programs found elsewhere.

Case-control studies are often conducted before making the major investment that a clinical trial requires because of their reduced cost in terms of time, effort, and resources. That is, surveillance data may be cross-validated by case-control studies before performing expensive clinical trials. However, even with the additional data from the case-control studies, the data are still observational. For important issues, particularly surrounding expensive treatments, the cost and strong inference provided by a random experiment may be desirable.

Clinical Trials   Clinical trials are a refined version of the randomized experimental designs familiar to developmental psychologists. Their great advantage is that they result in very strong inferences about causal links and, thus, the validity of interventions. Because of their importance, they have received extensive attention from epidemiologists. The methodology is considered in great detail elsewhere (Shapiro & Louis, 1983), and is the topic of a major journal, *Controlled Clinical Trials.*[7]

Some essential facts about clinical trials need to be considered. First, they are very expensive and probably are a once-in-a-lifetime event for a given intervention. They should only be done when an outcome of major importance is at issue. Second, they need to be conducted with such care that questions about experimental bias are completely ruled out. Even the

---

[7] Available from Elsevier Science Publishing Co., Inc., 52 Vanderbilt Ave., New York, New York 10017.

perception of possible bias is a serious matter in such costly and important studies. Third, the statistical aspects of the design must receive attention to ensure that the design has sufficient statistical power to have a reasonable chance of achieving a conclusive result (Kraemer & Thieman, 1987). The issue of statistical power will make interventions to prevent low prevalence outcomes unfeasible because of the very large sample sizes that would be required. Finally, a clinical trial is often not possible. Reasons for this include: the hypotheses are about inherent characteristics of individuals that cannot be varied, the manipulation would be unethical, human subjects would be placed at unacceptable levels of risk or embarrassment, and the exposure or risk experience is hypothesized to be of too long a duration to be studied.

A clinical trial provides data on the difference in the rate of favorable and unfavorable outcomes as a function of the intervention. In addition, it allows the calculation of an OR; that is, the odds that those who did not receive the intervention will be classified as abnormal compared with those who did.

The outstanding example of a behavioral clinical trial on child outcome is the Infant Health and Development Program (IHDP; IHDP, 1990). This was an eight-site randomized clinical trial designed to test the efficacy of an early developmental intervention in reducing the developmental and health problems of LBW ($\leq$ 2500 g) premature infants ($\leq$ 37 weeks). All the children, including the Comparison/Follow-up Group, received basic pediatric health care and social services. In addition, the Intervention Group received an intervention focused on child development and family support. The Follow-up and Intervention Groups were further stratified, at randomization, to heavier and lighter groups (2001–2500 g or $\leq$ 2000 g) and by site. The major outcome point was at 36 months of corrected age. Mean IQ differences in favor of the Intervention Group were 13.2 for the heavier infants and 6.6 for the lighter. This translated into an OR of 2.7. That is, the odds that the Follow-up Group would have scores in the mentally retarded range (<70) was 2.7 times greater than for those who received the intervention. The advantages and disadvantages of the various designs are summarized in Table IX.

TRADITIONAL CROSS-SECTIONAL AND LONGITUDINAL DESIGNS IN CHILD DEVELOPMENT

The traditional cross-sectional and longitudinal designs used in child development research are of limited use for epidemiological research. The cross-sectional design can lead to useful data about the prevalence of a factor or outcome at a single point in time. However, one cannot tell how the prevalence is changing, that is, if the rate of occurrence is due to a stable characteristic of individuals or is the result of an exposure. An example

Table IX   Summary of Advantages and Disadvantages of Various Designs Used in Outcome Research

---

Advantages and disadvantages of prospective (cohort) designs
Advantages
1. Allow for the complete history of exposure to be documented *within* each subject. That is, the data and comparisons are intraindividual.
2. Useful in the study of rare exposures.
3. Allow for the establishment of rates of disease in both exposed and unexposed populations.
4. Allow for quality control of the data collection procedures and measurements.
5. Make possible the collection of a wide range of measures that would not all be available in any extant or clinical record.
6. Make it possible to eliminate or control selection bias.
Disadvantages
1. Prevalence of the exposure in the population cannot be estimated from the data.
2. Large numbers of subjects will be required to study low prevalence outcomes.
3. Takes a long time to conduct.
4. Choice of measures made at a given time may be inadequate in the face of advancing knowledge and the development of new methods of measurement.
5. Maintaining high follow-up rates is difficult. Differential dropout can lead to systematic bias.
6. Typically are very expensive.

Advantages and disadvantages of cross-sectional studies
Advantages
1. Are easy to implement at low cost.
2. If repeated at a fixed interval (say, annually) give a good estimate of changes of frequency of exposures and outcomes in a population. In this case they are called surveillance studies.
3. Allow for quality control of data collection and measurement procedures.
Disadvantages
1. Are very open to bias in the selection of the subjects.
2. The comparisons are across subjects. That is, they are interindividual. The comparisons and correlations are thus ecological rather than individual.
3. Ecological correlations are liable to misinterpretation.

Advantages and disadvantages of case-control studies
Advantages
1. Are useful in the study of rare outcomes because adequate samples can be obtained. For this reason, for very rare outcomes, this may be the only practical design.
2. Are useful in the study of conditions that have a long latency between exposure and outcome.
3. Rely on relatively small sample sizes.
4. Can be carried out quickly at modest cost.
5. Are particularly valuable early in the study of an outcome to rapidly confirm observations from surveillance data.
6. Can be used to study multiple potential causes of an outcome.
Disadvantages
1. Rely on recall or existing records to document exposure.
2. Checks on data quality are often not possible.
3. Selection of an appropriate comparison (control) group can be a problem. Great care must be exercised to avoid bias.
4. Rates of occurrence of an outcome in the exposed and unexposed individuals cannot be determined.

(continues)

Table IX *(continued)*

5. Design and analytic considerations are different from those in experimental studies and are not well known in the research or clinical community.

Advantages and disadvantages of a clinical trial

Advantages

1. Direct control over the exposure or treatment of interest.
2. Strong inferences can be made about the causal connection between the manipulation and the outcome.
3. Excellent pretreatment equivalence of the compared groups is achieved through random assignment.
4. Most apparent sources of bias can be controlled through blinding and carefully monitored measurement.

Disadvantages

1. The major variable of interest may not be accessible to experimental manipulation. For example, persons cannot be randomly assigned to groups due to personal characteristics such as size, weight, and so on, to hazardous conditions such as smoking and nonsmoking, or where the study might involve withholding treatment. Thus, many questions cannot be addressed with this design.
2. Clinical trials are usually very expensive to conduct.
3. Sufficient sample size is required to ensure that there is enough power and precision to reach a clear conclusion. This may be impossible for study of the treatment of rare conditions.
4. Dropout from a trial is difficult to control and can severely impair the validity of the conclusions.

---

is provided by Table I which gives the rate of various educational exceptionalities at two ages. In Table I, the prevalence of children classified as learning disabled *increases* from age 7 to 11. However, the prevalence of speech problems *decreases* over the same span. One cannot tell from the cross-sectional data if these are due to different cases or due to children being reclassified. For this reason, the cross-sectional design, when used in outcome studies, is a surveillance tool rather than an analytic design.

The longitudinal study used in child development to study growth and development is not the best design for outcome research. Unless it is designed with *preplanned* comparison groups, it becomes an uncontrolled prospective study. In analyzing such a study, one can attempt post hoc to find a comparison group from within the sample. For example, if behavior problems are found in part of the prospective study sample, one could look at the other subjects to see post hoc how they differed in exposure. However, the process lacks rigor and power. The lack of rigor is because post hoc hypotheses and group formation are inferentially weaker than when the process is planned. The lack of power is because there are likely to be too few cases in the sample with either the outcome or exposure of interest. As we have seen in Table I, many outcomes are low prevalence and, thus, only a very large longitudinal study would have sufficient subjects. Further, despite attempts to be all encompassing, the study may also fail to collect the critical data on either exposure or outcome, or both. Concerns change from the time of inception of a study that may last years, to the time of outcome. Large scale longitudinal studies that are descriptive efforts to achieve major insights about developmental outcomes are simply too expensive, both in cost and professional effort, to be justified. Our position is that longitudinal studies on outcome should not be implemented without strong hypotheses and sufficient information about prevalence of outcomes to ensure that there is a reasonable chance of discovering and estimating the level or absence of risk.

SUMMARY AND DISCUSSION

In this chapter, we have attempted to give a very brief introduction to epidemiology as it is applied to the study of developmental outcome. We have coined the term *developmental epidemiology* to describe this branch of the discipline. Epidemiology is an empirical method of data collection and analysis, therefore, we have provided examples of research on child outcome that has utilized the method. In doing this, we have only summarized many issues that have been considered at great length in the epidemological literature and are relevant to the study of child outcome. There is much more that could be said about both the design and analysis of each of the design types we have considered, in particular case-control studies that are considered in detail elsewhere (Schlesselman, 1982).

The emphasis on data and research design is not unintentional. At present, we do not have good estimates of the prevalence of childhood behavioral disorders, nor about their etiology. A major reason, we believe, is that there has been an excessive reliance on correlational methods when most of the interest is in diagnostic classification as a precursor to the design and testing of prescriptive interventions. Services are delivered to those children who fall under categorical labels, such as those used in special education or by clinicians (DSM-III-R, 1987). Tests need to categorize rather than describe performance relative to the mean and variance (Scott & Hogan, 1982). The construction of future tests must be carried out so that components that detect outliers are identified and included. An example of this approach has recently been reported by M. S. Scott and Perou (1994).

The role of epidemiology in the construction and validation of theories of child development deserves further comment. Epidemiology does not deal with the mechanisms of transmission or theories about them. Thus, developmental epidemiology should be seen as quite catholic with respect to theories of development or what they predict about the causes of child outcome. Data collected using the methods of developmental epidemiology will certainly be of use in evaluating theory and testing theoretical hypotheses, but are not part of any theory in particular. In this respect epidemiological models are like regression methods. However, quantitative predictions can be made, based on epidemiological data, about the frequency of outcomes in another study or setting. These predictions can, in turn, be tested either in further analytic studies or in clinical or field trials. However, these are not theoretical in the sense that they are about mechanisms or processes of outcome formation.

A consequence of categorizing data is a loss of statistical power (Kraemer & Thiemann, 1987). If this is a major concern, inferential tests of continuous data can be carried out *before* categorization. However, testing hypotheses is secondary to the major purpose of epidemiological enquiry. The *main objective in developmental epidemiology* is to estimate the magnitude of risk due to antecedent factors on the occurrence of discrete child outcomes to thus arrive at an understanding to guide prevention efforts. This is also one of the major goals for many researchers in child development.

ACKNOWLEDGMENTS

The preparation of this chapter was partially supported by FDLRS/Mailman, a specialized university center of Florida Diagnostic and Learning Resource System, funded through State General Revenue Appropriations to provide multidisciplinary evaluation services to exceptional student education and by the Florida Interagency Office of Disability Prevention (Centers for Disease Control Grant# U59-CCU403363-04). Dr. Eleanor Levine of FDLRS/South is thanked for her long-term support and help in accessing the prevalence data presented here.

REFERENCES

Adams, M. J., Jr., Khoury, M. J., & James, L. M. (1989). The use of attributable fraction in the design and interpretation of epidemiologic studies. *Journal of Clinical Epidemiology, 2*(7), 659–662.

American Psychiatric Association. (1987). *Diagnostic and statistical manual of mental disorders (DSM)* (3rd ed., rev.). Washington, DC: American Psychiatric Association.

Campbell, D. T., & Stanley, J. C. (1963). *Experimental and quasi-experimental designs for research.* Chicago: Rand-McNally.

Carran, D. T., Scott, K. G., Shaw, K. G., & Beydouin, S. (1989). The relative risk of educational handicaps in two birth cohorts of normal and low birthweight disadvantaged children. *Topics in Early Childhood Special Education, 9*(1), 14–31.

Cole, P., & MacMahon, B. (1971). Attributable risk percent in case-control studies. *British Journal of Preventative and Social Medicine, 25,* 242–244.

Dean, A. D., and Dean, J. A., Burton, A. H., & Dicker, R. C. (1990). *Epi Info, Version 5: A word processing, database, and statistics program for epidemiology on microcomputers.* USD, Incorporated, Stone Mountain, GA.

Doll, R., & Hill, B. (1950, September 30). Smoking and carcinoma of the lung: Preliminary report. *British Medical Journal,* 739–748.

Eisen, L., 1992 *Length of neonatal hospitalization as a predictor of long-term psychoeducational placement.* Unpublished doctoral dissertation, University of Miami.

Greenland, S., Schlesseman, J. J., & Criqui, M. H. (1986). The fallacy of employing standardized regression and correlations as measures of effect. *American Journal of Epidemiology, 123*, 203–208.

Gustafson, T. L. (1991). *True Epistat 4.0.* Epistat Services, 2011 Cap Rock Circle, Richardson, TX 75080.

Hennekens, C. H., & Buring, J. E. (1987). *Epidemiology in medicine.* Boston: Little, Brown.

Infant Health and Development Program (IHDP). (1990). Enhancing the outcomes of low-birth-weight, premature infants: A multisite, randomized trial. *The Journal of the American Medical Association, 263*(22), 3035–3042.

Kraemer, H. C., & Thiemann, S. (1987). *How many subjects? Statistical power analysis in research.* Newburg Park, CA: Sage.

Miettinen, O. S. (1985). *Theoretical epidemiology: Principles of occurrence research in medicine.* New York: Wiley.

Rothman, K. J. (1986). *Modern epidemiology.* Boston: Little, Brown.

Schlesselman, J. J. (1982). *Case-control studies: Design, conduct, analysis.* New York: Oxford.

Scott, K. G., & Hogan, A. E. (1982). Methods for identifying high-risk and handicapped infants. In C. Ramey & P. Trohanis (Eds.), *Finding and educating the high risk and handicapped infant* (pp. 69–82). Baltimore: University Park Press.

Scott, K. G., & Masi, W. (1979). The outcome from and utility or registers of risk. In T. M. Field, A. M. Sostek, S. Goldberg, & H. H. Shuman (Eds.), *Infants born at risk: Behavior and development* (pp. 485–496). New York: Spectrum.

Scott, M. S., & Perou, R. (1994). A screening test built of cognitive bricks: Identification of young LD children. In S. Vaughn & C. Bos (Eds.) *Research issues in learning disabilities: Theory, methodology, assessment, and ethics* (pp. 83–105). New York: Springer-Verlag.

Shapiro, S. H., & Louis, T. A. (Eds.). (1983). *Statistics: Textbooks and monographs: Vol. 46. Clinical trials.* New York: Marcel Dekker.

Shaw, K. H. (1989). *The contribution of low birthweight and other medical complications to educational handicaps.* Unpublished doctoral dissertation, University of Miami, Coral Gables, FL.

Snow, J. (1949). *Snow on cholera.* Cambridge: Harvard University Press.

Toufexis, A. (1991, May 19). Innocent victims. *Time,* pp. 56–60.

Wiener, G. (1968). *Long-term study of prematures: Summary of published findings* (Report No. PS003651). Washington, DC: Office of Education, Department of HEW. (ERIC Document Reproduction Service No. ED043389).

RESEARCH
AT
THE
CUTTING
EDGE

Child Care and Child Development: The NICHD Study of Early Child Care

The NICHD Early Child Care Network[1]

[1] The study is directed by a Steering Committee and supported by the NICHD through a cooperative agreement (U10), that calls for a scientific collaboration between the grantees and the NICHD staff. The authors of this paper are investigators who designed the study and/or subcomponents of it. They are affiliated with NICHD and with the 10 grantee institutions or their subcontractors. The participating institutions and the investigators are as follows: 1. The National Institute of Child Health and Human Development: Sarah L. Friedman, Kaye H. Fendt, Mark I. Appelbaum (from Vanderbilt University), Henry N. Ricciuti (from Cornell University), and Peter C. Scheidt; 2. University of Arkansas: Robert H. Bradley and Bettye M. Caldwell; 3. University of California at Irvine: K. Alison Clarke-Stewart; 4. University of Kansas: Aletha C. Huston and Marion O'Brien; 5. University of New Hampshire and Wellesley College: Kathleen McCartney and Nancy L. Marshall; 6. Pennsylvania State University and University of Pittsburgh: Jay Belsky, Celia A. Brownell, Susan B. Campbell, and Jeff F. Cohn; 7. Temple University: Marsha Weinraub and Kathryn A. Hirsh-Pasek; 8. University of Virginia: Deborah A. Phillips; 9. The University of Washington: Cathryn L. Booth and Susan J. Spieker; 10. The University of Wisconsin and Timberlawn Research Foundation: Deborah L. Vandell and Margaret T. Owen; and 11. University of North Carolina: Martha J. Cox.

The Steering Committee. Chairpersons: Henry N. Ricciuti (May 1989–April 1991), Bettye M. Caldwell (April 1991–June 1993), and Lewis P. Lipsitt (October 1993–present). Members: Mark I. Appelbaum, Jay Belsky, Cathryn L. Booth, Robert H. Bradley, K. Alison Clarke-Stewart, Martha J. Cox, Kaye H. Fendt (August 1990–August 1992), Sarah L. Friedman, Aletha C. Huston, Bonnie Knoke (September 1992–present), Kathleen McCartney, Deborah A. Phillips, Deborah L. Vandell, Marsha Weinraub, and Sumner J. Yaffe.

Primary responsibility for preparing the chapter was taken by Bettye M. Caldwell and Robert H. Bradley. (Reprint requests should be addressed to the Office of Research Reporting, NICHD, Building 31, Room 2A 32, 9000 Rockville Pike, Bethesda, Maryland 20892.)

INTRODUCTION

Around the beginning of the last decade of the twentieth century, a watershed event occurred in America. For the first time in history, the majority of infants living in the United States were receiving a significant amount of their care from someone other than their mothers (U.S. Dept. of Commerce, 1992). This shift came as no surprise to those who have followed trends in family demographics over the past three decades. In effect, the change in typical care for young children reflects many other aspects of family and community life, in particular, changes in maternal employment. Over the last 30 years participation of mothers in the work force has dramatically increased (Hayes, Palmer, & Zaslow, 1990; Hoffman, 1989; Scarr, Phillips, & McCartney, 1990). During this same period the average age of children whose mothers began to work away from home and to rely on alternate child care decreased substantially (Fox & Fein, 1990). Changes in patterns of child care have also arisen in the context of changes in community institutions, changes in patterns of interaction within families and neighborhoods, and changes in the general economic circumstances within the society (U.S. Dept. of Commerce, 1992).

In spite of these family and societal changes, sequentially documented by demographers in easy-to-comprehend form, the realization that millions of infants were spending significant amounts of time in the care of someone other than their mothers seemed to catch many people by surprise. That realization escalated to concern for some, reflecting their anxiety about the broad pattern of changes in family and community life that have surfaced during the last several decades. For others, the concern was related less to the societal changes than to their conviction that children's development is tightly bound to the relationships formed with a very small number of primary caregivers (particularly their mothers) very early in life, relationships that may be disrupted when such care is not constantly available. Well-entrenched cultural beliefs, psychological theory (Bowlby, 1969; Jaeger & Weinraub, 1990), and research findings (Ainsworth, Blehar, Waters, & Wall, 1978; Clarke-Stewart, 1973) have emphasized the important role of mothers in the development of infants and young children. For still others, the concern derives from the observation that a high-quality system of alternative care has not yet fully evolved in this country (Caldwell, 1986; Phillips, McCartney, Scarr, & Howes, 1987). Whatever "system" exists arose largely to meet the demands of the market, and the market has not always been attuned to quality. The fact is, as we near the end of the twentieth century, many families find themselves in conflict, trying to effect a balance between ideals about family life and childrearing on the one hand and emerging realities of maternal employment, changing family lifestyles, and the available options of early child care on the other.

Whatever particular issue gives rise to the concern about possible effects associated with early alternative care, all such concerns are united by the common belief that to do well in life children must experience good care during their early years. In this context, it is noteworthy that the first wave of research on infant day care was conducted to demonstrate that high quality programs could be beneficial to children living in home environments offering insufficient stimulation and support (see Caldwell & Richmond, 1968). As the service began to be used by more and more families, and as quality was known to vary widely, questions began to emerge as to whether children from families with fewer problems and more economic and psychological resources could expect such benefits or whether such an experience might represent a net experiential loss to unselected children in the population at large. To investigate that possibility, researchers have been busy over the last three decades studying the effects of various patterns of care on children, each study focusing on those aspects and outcomes of care that strike the researcher or funding agency as important.

Despite the large research effort during the past decade (see reviews by Belsky, 1988, 1990; Chase-Lansdale & Owen, 1987; Clarke-Stewart, 1989; Hayes et al., 1990; Friedman, Brooks-Gunn, Vandell, & Weinraub, in press; Lamb, Sternberg, & Prodromidis, 1992; Phillips et al., 1987; Silverstein, 1991), our understanding of the effects of child care on child development is incomplete. Scientists who represent different theoretical orientations make different predictions about these effects: Some suggest that early and extensive alternate care increases the risk of poor socioemotional development, whereas others believe that adaptive competence in children is more a function of the quality of care received, the fit between a child's characteristics and experiences, and the overall pattern of supports available to child and family. This state of affairs derives from the fact that issues pertaining to child care and its effects are numerous (Friedman et al., in press; Hayes et al., 1990) and conceptually interdependent. Most of the time, studies of child care have been too small in scope to deal with more than isolated issues. Small studies cannot provide a comprehensive understanding of the interplay between the environments of home and child care, of the interplay between these environments and characteristics of the children, or of the cumulative effects that these interactions are hypothesized to have on the development of children. To overcome some of the limitations of small studies, investigators have formally reviewed the literature and/or conducted cross-study analyses of findings from diverse studies with common research questions and measures (Belsky, 1990; Clarke-Stewart, 1989; Lamb et al., 1992; Phillips et al., 1987). But such reviews and analyses are constrained by the information available in existing studies. Consequently, much about the complex relationships surrounding early child care remains poorly understood.

In sum, at about that point in U.S. history when the proportion of infants receiving a significant amount of their care from someone other than their mothers first reached 50%, we had a body of empirical work (partly driven by theories of human development) that gave rise to an array of provocative questions and that set the stage for a new generation of studies about early child care. The question is, What should be the character of the next generation of studies on early child care? Emerging theories of human development suggest that, to be productive, the new generation of studies should ask anew two basic questions: (a) What does it *mean* to do well? and (b) What does it *take* to do well? The studies from previous generations of early child care research, as good as some of them were, operated from assumptions about what it means to do well (e.g., manifest a certain type of behavior vis-à-vis one's mother or one's peers). They also operated on assumptions about what it takes to do well, most often by ignoring all contexts save the alternate caregiving context and failing to consider key individual differences in children and families.

A HOLISTIC VIEW OF EARLY CHILD CARE: INVESTIGATING THE CONTEXT AND DYNAMICS OF DEVELOPMENT

Recently promulgated theories of human development suggest that *studies of early child care should be more holistic in orientation:* Development in any particular domain is part of a tapestry of developments in many different domains within the organism and in those systems of which it is a part (Ford & Lerner, 1992). New theories also suggest that *studies be more concerned with context.* Studies of development even at the cellular level make clear that the process of development is context dependent (Gottlieb, 1991; Sameroff, this volume). Child care, whatever the source, occurs in the context of a certain pattern of family circumstances and events and in the context of an overall pattern of care (Greenberger & Goldberg, 1989). Each part of the context affects the others and each can be understood best in relation to the others (Campbell, 1990). Finally, new theories suggest that studies of early child care use research designs, approaches to measurement, and strategies for data analysis that more accurately represent the dynamics of development (Appelbaum, Burchinal, & Terry, 1989; Burchinal & Appelbaum, 1991; Willett & Singer, 1991, Singer & Willett, this volume).

Many previous studies utilized an essentially linear, "main effects" approach to studying early child care (see Sameroff, this volume, for a discussion of nonlinear approaches). When studying the "effects" of certain patterns of care on some aspect of child development, researchers did not examine how other child factors, other contextual factors, or other caregiving factors served to moderate or mediate these "effects" (Baron & Kenny, 1986).

Rarely did they look at the sequence of changes within and among child, family, context, and patterns of caregiving across time. Thus, we have little understanding about how each of the factors within the system regulates the others, and how the importance of factors within the system changes across time with adjustments in other factors. We are left with making statements about "average effects"—and maybe even making erroneous statements about "no effects."

The new theories challenge us again to be mindful of when and how we observe whatever we study (Booth & Mitchell, 1988; Bradley, 1992). Just as a new generation of studies benefits from asking anew such basic questions as what do we mean by doing well, they also benefit from considering anew how we look at the phenomena under study. The rapidly changing culture in which children are developing should make us question whether we have the most useful view of development as indexed by our current measures. For studies of early child care, the issue of attachment is considered central. The critical question is, Are the standard methods of measuring attachment robust in the changing context of child care? (Jaeger & Weinraub, 1990). In a related sense, the rapidly evolving context of caregiving should make us question whether we have the most useful view of caregiving quality (Caldwell, 1986). When and how should we measure such key constructs? These questions mandate at least two courses of action: (a) use of theory to anchor findings in a broader network of ideas, and (b) use of multiple measurement processes as a hedge against error.

Role of Theory

In general, theory should play a greater role than in past studies in driving the designs of a new generation of studies on early child care (McCartney, 1990; see Horowitz, this volume). When this occurs, a model quite different from those that have guided most previous studies will be adopted. Earlier studies have been driven by eminently practical questions. Only rarely have they been designed to test particular theoretical propositions, except those related to attachment. As a result, it is not always easy to interpret findings from particular studies, and it is not always easy to integrate findings across studies. Significant gaps remain in the whole story of early child care. Use of theory to shape study designs will not guarantee a better research product, but it will help us to understand better and to evaluate the products of the research.

The use of theory should also help us develop testable hypotheses in advance of staging a study and analyzing the data from a study. This is important to the advancement of science. Too often, the previous generations of studies (both studies of early child care and longitudinal studies in general) have been conducted without prior hypothesis formulation. Analyses were therefore often exercises in pure empiricism—"We'll find what's there to find." We have seemingly been fortunate in advancing our understanding of children's development in early child care despite eschewing the more rigorous approach of establishing theoretically testable hypotheses before designing and conducting the research, but, clearly, there is a danger in continuing to depend on such fortuitous events as we examine in greater depth the complexities of caregiving and its context.

Multiple Measures

Because behavioral development is a complex function of organism–environment transactions, manifesting its character as a unique fusion of these exchanges, variables studied in holistic research ought to be measured in multiple ways. For example, the evaluation of child care quality could involve either structural or process variables, or both. Structural variables refer to easily measured aspects of the child care environment such as the ratio of care providers to number of children, the qualifications of the providers, and the number of children in the child care setting. Process variables reflect the quality of the care with more immediacy (e.g., responsiveness and sensitivity to the emotional and intellectual needs of children). Ideally, process variables must be based on live observations of the experiences children have with other children and adults in their care arrangements. A holistic research strategy would call for inclusion of both types of indices of quality of care.

Multiplicity should also be ensured in outcome measures—especially those dealing with the socioemotional domain of development. Techniques for measuring such behavior in young children that can boast of perfect reliability and validity simply do not exist. Accordingly, once areas of concern are identified—such as attachment security, compliance, or social competence with peers—multiple measures of the chosen constructs need to be either selected or designed. Although cognitive development is perhaps less vulnerable to measurement instability than is socioemotional development, in very young children even this domain needs to be sampled with more than one measure. Thus, in a study that aims to define clearly and comprehensively, multiple measures of variables can only strengthen the design.

The NICHD Study of Early Child Care represents an attempt to overcome many of the shortcomings of earlier research in a way that is more holistic, context-sensitive, and dynamic (see Sameroff, this volume). From its inception, the study was designed to be a benchmark in modern research strategy. The conditions that made this possible include adequate funding to allow the procurement of a large sample across multiple sites; time for previously independent researchers to meld their ideas into a cohesive unitary design and to choose variables, develop measures, and plan analytic strategies for the family, child care, and child domains; careful training of all data collectors across sites; and ensured support for a period long enough to allow documentation of the interplay of these contextual forces in helping to shape the development of the children and to influence total family functioning. What follows is a brief description of the study and a history of the decisions that framed it.

THE NICHD STUDY OF EARLY CHID CARE: HISTORY AND STRUCTURE

The study was initiated by the NICHD director and his staff. It was inspired by recommendations emanating from a meeting of leading child care researchers convened by the National Center for Clinical Infant Programs and based on a review of the literature by NICHD staff. The primary goal of the study is to examine variations in early child care for infants and toddlers from a variety of family backgrounds and to study the effects of these variations on children's development. More specifically, the study will

- describe the relationship between infants' child care arrangements and children's concurrent and long-term development (i.e., their social, emotional, language, cognitive, and physical development);
- determine how the social ecology of the home moderates the effects of child care;
- determine how individual differences among children moderate the effects of different patterns of infant care on child development;
- determine the consequences of maternal employment and child care choices on family relationships, parental mental health, family stress, and other key family variables;
- map the natural history of early child care in the 1990s to establish baseline data for the kind and amount of alternate care being used by families;
- identify child care attributes that are associated with child care quality; and
- identify demographic characteristics and parental characteristics associated with families' child care decisions.

To achieve the goals of the study, a multicenter research network was created. A request for applications (RFA) for cooperation in research with NICHD staff (U10 or "Cooperative Agreement") was announced in the NIH Guide for Grants and Contracts. Ten independent awards were made. All principal investigators know that approximately 75% of their time and effort had to be dedicated to a common protocol followed at all 10 sites. Each site was allowed to use approximately 25% of the resources allocated for data collection for site-specific research. Even so, all site-specific research plans were carefully reviewed to ensure that they did not in any way compromise the common protocol.

The first task for the investigators was to shape a common protocol for data collections at the 10 participating sites. This was accomplished through the efforts of a Steering Committee, consisting of a chairperson, the principal investigators from the 10 data collection sites, NICHD program staff, a methodologist, and staff of a Data Coordination Center established at NICHD to serve only this project (see Footnote 1). Contributions to the plan also came from co-principal investigators, study coordinators, and research staff at the 10 data collection sites.

Ongoing implementation of the study is directed by this Steering Committee and executed at the 10 data collection sites. Data management is handled jointly by the internal Data Coordination Center at NICHD and by an external data analysis unit established at Vanderbilt University where the methodologist is employed. All data are collected on computer-ready Scantron forms and forwarded to the central NICHD Data Coordination Center, where monitoring and quality control occur. Data analysis will be carried out primarily at the external site. Overall coordination is handled by NICHD, with progress monitored by an advisory board of independent behavioral science researchers and by NICHD staff.

RESEARCH MODEL

The model that has guided the shaping of the common protocol assumes that the effects of child care are best considered within an ecological/developmental framework that incorporates information about (a) the family and home, (b) the child care environment, and (c) individual differences among children. The conceptual framework for the study is portrayed in Figure 1. It is a generic framework that amalgamates key constructs from several ecological/developmental models (Bahg, 1990). The model both circumscribes the total set of ecological/developmental constructs to be considered in the study and provides sufficient detail for the caregiving aspects of the family setting. Most available models do not give such explicit attention to caregiving per se.

The model in Figure 1 portrays home environments, the child care environments, and the children's characteristics as interdependent; each influences outcomes for children, for parent–child relationships, and for families. Furthermore, the model indicates that family demographic characteristics are associated with features of alternate child care (quantity, quality, type, stability, and time of entry) and to aspects of the home environment, as well as to personal characteristics of family members. In sum, this model allows the study to move beyond the determination of possible developmental risks or benefits that may be presented by child care as an isolated influence. The aim of the study is much broader; namely, to determine how the effects of nonmaternal care vary as a function of child care quality, the extent of

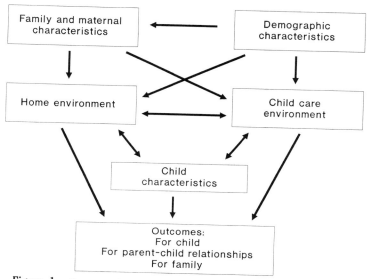

Figure 1 Conceptual Framework for NICHD Study of Early Child Care.

its use, and characteristics of the children and of their family and home. Our interest is in concurrent as well as in long-term and cumulative effects of environments on outcome. We view development as complex, with particular outcomes at one time setting the stage for the next developmental phases. In addition, we recognize that the same strengths or difficulties in children's development or in their relationships may be manifested in different ways at different points in the life course and by children living in differing circumstances.

The components of the model were further explicated as follows. Demographic characteristics to be studied include family income, parental education, race, type of family (single parent or two parent), family size, and shifts in family structure over time. Under family and maternal characteristics, we chose to study mother–partner relationships, maternal personality, stresses and supports, and parental attitudes, beliefs, and expectations. The home environment is defined by the quality and quantity of maternal care and by physical and organizational characteristics. The child care environment is defined in terms of the type of care (home, family, center, or multiple, i.e., different types of care arrangement each day or each week), the quality of care, stability of care arrangements, hours per week in care, duration of care, and age at entry. Child characteristics on which we chose to focus include age, gender, temperament, and health. Outcomes for the children are in the domains of cognition, language, social and emotional development, health, and physical growth. Outcomes in terms of mother–child relationships include attachment relationships and related constructs. Outcomes for the families are defined in terms of mother–partner relationships.

STUDY DESIGN

At each of the 10 data collection sites, a minimum of 120 infants and their parents were enrolled in the study (range = 123–150). Mothers were contacted in the hospital shortly after their infant's birth and were invited to participate. At that time, the mothers were given a brief description of the study, and, shortly after their return home, arrangements were made to conduct a home visit 1 month later for purposes of actual enrollment.

Sample Enrollment and Composition

Participants for the study were recruited from designated hospitals at the 10 data collection sites (see Footnote 1). Recruitment began in January of 1991 and was completed in November of that year. A total of 1364 families with full-term healthy newborns were enrolled. Potential participants were selected from among the 8986 mothers giving birth in the study hospitals during selected sampling periods. The sampling periods were established on a site-by-site basis by the Data Coordinating Center to ensure an unbiased and fully representative sample at each site. Participants were selected in accordance with a conditionally random sampling plan, which was designed to ensure that the recruited families (a) included mothers who planned to work or to go to school full time (60%) or part time (20%) in the child's first year, as well as some who planned to stay at home with the child (20%), and (b) reflected the demographic diversity (economic, educational, and ethnic) of the sites. Actual percentages pertaining to the three groups (full-time work or school, part-time work or school, stay at home) at the end of recruitment were 53%, 23%, and 24%, respectively. As Table I shows, the recruited families came from a wide range of socioeconomic and sociocultural backgrounds (19% minorities, 11% low education). Both two-parent families (86%) and single-parent families (14%) were included. This method of subject enrollment allowed the study to have a heterogeneous (though not nationally representative) sample. It was designed to afford access to a wide spectrum of child care arrangements, including in-home and family arrangements, family day care, and center care. In the process of selecting participants, the following exclusionary criteria were used: (a) mothers younger than 18 years of age at the time of the child's birth, (b) families who did not anticipate remaining in the catchment area of the study for at least 3 years, (c) children with obvious disabilities at birth or who remained in the hospital more than 7 days postpartum, (d) mothers with known or

Table I   Selected Demographic Characteristics of Sample

Characteristics	N	%
Educational level—mother		
<12th grade	152	11.1
High school/GED	328	24.8
Some college	389	28.5
BA level work	324	23.8
Postgraduate work	171	12.5
Ethnicity of mother		
White	1111	81.5
Black	179	13.0
Native American	4	0.3
Asian	32	2.3
Hispanic	31	2.3
Mixed	7	0.5
Partners at home		
No	194	14.2
Yes	1170	85.8
Mother's plans for hours/week at work or school during child's first year		
<10 hours	329	24.1
10–29 hours	307	22.5
30+ hours	727	53.3
Don't know	1	0.1

acknowledged medical problems including substance abuse, and (e) mothers not sufficiently conversant in English.

Schedule of Assessments

Beginning with the time of enrollment (the 1-month home visit), families were scheduled for extensive periodic data collections that terminate when the child is 3 years old. Over this 36-month period, research assistants from the sites visit each child at home, in child care (if used), and in a laboratory playroom. Assessments are made of the child, the parent(s), and of the social and physical characteristics of whatever caregiving environment the family uses. Table II displays the schedule of assessments.

As Table II shows, research assistants make home visits when the child is 1, 6, 15, 24, and 36 months old. The child is assessed in the laboratory setting at 15, 24, and 36 months, and, for children in alternate care at least 10 hours per week, the child care situation is observed when the child is 6, 15, 24, and 36 months old. Research assistants also telephone families every 3 months for ongoing status reports. These particular age points were

Table II   Data Collection Schedule

	Child's age (months)				
Visits	1	6	15	24	36
Home	X	X	X	X	X
Alternate care		X	X	X	X
Laboratory			X	X	X
Phone	X	XX	XXX	XXX	XXXX

selected to coincide with important periods in the development of the child and the family. They are based on developmental theory in such areas as attachment and language, as well as theory and research on family systems (Cox, Owen, Lewis, & Henderson, 1989). Assessments include natural and semistructured observations, interviews, questionnaires, and standardized measures of intellectual, linguistic, social, and emotional development.

A more complete and tangible understanding of the diversity and breadth of assessments obtains when the full array of measures used at each assessment point is examined. For illustrative purposes, we have chosen the 15-month assessment point. A complete list of all measures for the 15-month assessments is contained in Table III.

At the 15-month home visit, mothers respond to a lengthy, structured interview that deals with child and family health matters, major events in family life, maternal and paternal employment, the reasons for maternal employment, mothers' role satisfaction, and maternal attitudes regarding child care arrangements and separation. The mothers also complete a battery of standardized questionnaires, including ones dealing with family finances, depression, separation anxiety, work–family strains, interpersonal relationships, parenting experiences/stress, and job strains. The HOME Inventory, a measure of the quality and quantity of stimulation and support available to the child in the home environment, is administered as part of the home visit, and the mother and child are videotaped while involved in a structured play situation. From the children's medical records, as well as from the mothers' reports, we obtain information concerning the children's experiences with ear infections. Mothers also complete the MacArthur Communicative Inventory of Language Development.

At the 15-month child care assessment, consisting of two visits of approximately 3 hours each, there is an extensive structured interview with the caregiver that deals with the characteristics, qualifications, experience, and goals of the caregiver. If the child is in center-based care, the director completes a lengthy questionnaire that includes information about financial arrangements for the center, demographic characteristics of children served by the center, the director's background and her role as director. For home-

Table III Overview of Study Assessments at the 15-Month Visit

Home Visit
HOME Inventory (Caldwell & Bradley, 1984)
Mother–child interaction ("3 boxes"; adapted from Vandell, 1979)
Interview to update information (measure developed for project)
  Household composition
  Health of child, mother, and father
  Employment and School experience of mother and father
Questionnaires
  CES-Depression Scale (Radloff, 1977)
  Parental care (Separation Anxiety; Hock, Gnezda, & McBride, 1983)
  Availability of social support (Marshall & Barnett, 1993)
  Family finances (Belle, 1982)
  Parenting experiences (from Parenting Stress Index, Abidin, 1983)
  Combining work and family (employed mothers only; Marshall & Barnett, 1993)
  Job Role Quality Scale (Marshall & Barnett, in press)
  My child care (measure developed for project)
  MacArthur Communicative Inventory (Bates et al., 1989)

Lab Visit
Solitary play: levels of play (Belsky & Most, 1981), attention (Breznitz & Friedman, 1988)
Strange Situation (Ainsworth & Wittig, 1969)
Snack procedure (Morisset, 1988)
Bayley MDI (Bayley, 1969)
Growth measures (height, weight)

Child Care Visit
Director interview[a] (adapted from National Daycare Staffing Study; Whitebrook, Howes, & Phillips, 1990)
  Background and role
  Child demographics
  Financial arrangements

Profile (Abbott-Shinn & Sibley, 1987)
  Physical features
  Curriculum

HOME Inventory[b] (adapted from Caldwell & Bradley, 1984)

Caregiver Interview (adapted from National Daycare Staffing Study; Whitebrook, Howes, & Phillips, 1990)

Caregiver questionnaires
Caregiver stress (measure developed for project)
Child rearing attitudes (modernity; Schaefer & Edgerton, 1985)
CES-Depression Scale (Radloff, 1977)

Observations in Child Care Setting (ORCE)
(Measure developed for project)
Child Behavior
Caregiver Behavior

Caregiver Ratings of Drop-Off and Pick-up Behaviors
(McCartney & Beauregard, 1991)

[a] Center-based care.
[b] Home-based care (family day care and nanny care).

based arrangements, comparable information is obtained from the child care provider. Through a process of observation and interview, the child care visitor completes a center or home version of the Assessment Profile of Early Childhood Programs (Abbott-Shim & Sibley, 1987) and, for home-based arrangements, completes a child care version of the HOME Inventory (Caldwell & Bradley, 1984). The profile assesses health and safety provisions, the quality of the materials and curriculum, and, where relevant, the extent to which the care setting is individualized. The quality of the adult work environment is also assessed. The greatest amount of time during the child care visit is spent making detailed observations of interactions between the target child and the child's caregivers using a time sampling procedure developed for the study. These observations result in both discrete behavioral and qualitative ratings. The child's caregiver also completes a series of questionnaires addressing the behavior of parent and child during drop-off and pick-up, the caregiver's attitudes about caregiving, and feelings of depression.

The focus of the 15-month lab visit is the child. The child participates in the Strange Situation attachment procedure and is administered the Bayley Scales of Infant Development. The child is also videotaped during a snack and during solitary play to get measures of attention and levels of cognitive functioning. Finally, the child is weighed and height is measured.

STUDY HYPOTHESES

Because of the complexity of the model guiding the creation of the research design, hypotheses involving simple cause–effect relationships were not constructed. Two major sets, labeled Primary and Secondary, have been formulated. The primary hypotheses concern outcomes associated with varying amounts of nonmaternal care during the first 3 years of life, age of entry into nonmaternal care, and the type, stability, and quality of child care. Secondary hypotheses relate to covarying influences of the family environment on children, to demographic and family characteristics associated with different child care patterns, to the effects of nonmaternal care on family characteristics, and to quality indicators in child care arrangements. Because of space limitations, only illustrative examples will be given here.

Primary Hypotheses

All primary hypotheses deal in some way with relationships between infants' nonmaternal care arrangements and developmental outcomes. Predictions relating to interactions among various aspects of the family's ecological system, as these relate to outcomes associated with nonmaternal care, are also classified as primary hypotheses. Occasionally, both developmental theory and previous empirical research can suggest different or opposing hypotheses. In such cases, both are formulated and will be tested. In all hypotheses, extensive nonmaternal care is defined as more than 30 hours per week. The following are examples of the study hypotheses.

Quality   Quality of child care will be positively related to socioemotional, language, and cognitive development in the first 36 months of life. It will have more influence on these outcomes than quantity, timing of entry, stability, or type of care.

Quantity   Two conflicting hypotheses will be tested. (a) With quality, age of entry, type of care, and stability of care held constant, children in extensive nonmaternal care in the first year of life will have developmental outcomes that are not significantly different from children who are cared for primarily by their mothers. (b) Compared with children who experience full-time maternal care or part-time nonmaternal care, children who experience extensive nonmaternal care during the first year of life will be less likely to manifest secure attachment to their mothers at age 15 months, and, at ages 2 and 3, will show less competent social behavior with children and adults, manifested in higher levels of aggression and noncompliance.

Quality and Quantity   The effects of quality (positive and negative) are expected to increase with increases in the quantity of time the child spends in the nonmaternal care setting.

Quality of Maternal and Nonmaternal Care   If both maternal and nonmaternal care are of high quality, outcomes will be positive regardless of quantity, timing, stability, or type of child care.

Family Attributes and Child Outcomes   Better quality care will attenuate the negative impact on children of family risk factors such as poverty, stress, poor parental health, depression, and so on.

Child Attributes   Children who have frequent or chronic health problems will be more vulnerable to the negative effects of low quality care (maternal or nonmaternal) than those with infrequent or minor health problems.

Secondary Hypotheses

As already indicated, these are of major importance for developmental theory but are not directly linked to the effects of nonmaternal care. Again, only a few examples will be given.

Home Environment Influences   Quality of parenting by mother and quality of the home environment will be positively related to socioemotional, cognitive, and language outcomes for the child.

Demographic, Contextual, Marital, and Parental Characteristics   The quality, quantity, timing, type, and stability of child care will be associated with family characteristics and environmental events impinging on the family. Low income, financial and social stress, cost of child care, unavailability of child care, low social support, marital dissatisfaction, restrictive child rearing attitudes, and non-child-oriented reasons for selecting care (e.g., proximity, cost) will predict use of low quality care.

Relations among Regulatable Child Care Characteristics   Low quality adult–child interactions in care will be associated with unsafe and unhealthy physical conditions, low salaries, and rapid turnover of caregivers.

These examples should serve to communicate the range and precision of hypotheses that can be tested within the present research model.

MAPPING THE TERRAIN OF CHILD CARE

Near the end of the eighteenth century much attention was devoted to mapping the largely unexplored geography of America. There was a sense of inevitability about movement across the country; thus, there was a need for information that would make the move easier and more productive. At the end of the twentieth century, there is need for mapping a more intimate terrain, the terrain of family life styles and choices—largely for the same reasons. There is, again, a sense of inevitable movement into relatively uncharted new circumstances and a need for information that can help in the transition. This time the challenge is not to cartographers but to social scientists. The NICHD Study of Early Child Care is part of a new era of broadly focused studies propelled by a significant pattern of societal change in the postindustrial age.

The NICHD study focuses carefully on *processes,* particularly the process of caregiving. The issues of *what* caregiving processes contribute to continuity and discontinuity in behavioral development and *how* these processes contribute to behavioral development are central to the study. It is the pattern of caregiving inputs (processes) that are presumed to support potentially adequate development, and it is the pattern of caregiving that is undergoing such rapid change currently. There is, in fact, concern that the pattern of care now becoming more common may contribute to "lawful discontinuity" in behavioral development. This study will help determine whether such concern is justified.

In many respects, the model used to guide the NICHD Study of Early Child Care, with its attendant array of measures and plans for data analysis, conforms to Horowitz's (this volume) recommendations for the next generation of studies on human development. She eschews the idea that development can be usefully understood by applying simple models. She argues, "It is time to relinquish the simple models of prediction and adopt ones that attempt to approximate the complexity of human behavioral development (p. 39)." The study reflects Horowitz's notion that we can best understand continuities and discontinuities in development by tracking the course of development and its context and by analyzing the putative processes that support or disrupt those continuities. The study's periodic assessment of key organismic and environmental markers is also consistent with Sameroff's (this volume) contention that "developmental outcomes are not a product of the initial characteristics of the child or the context or even their combination. Outcomes are the result of the interplay between child and context across time, in which the state of one impacts on the next state of the other in a continuous dynamic process" (p. 53).

The broad aim of the NICHD Study of Early Child Care is to increase understanding about child care arrangements and their linkage to family life and children's development. The study is designed to provide empirical data that will be useful in the formulation of social policy regarding infant care. Much effort and many resources are being devoted to protecting the integrity of the study; to an extent rare in the annals of science. The strategies employed to do this include: (a) appointment of an independent scientific advisory group; (b) employment of a study methodologist; (c) involvement of both NICHD and independent investigators in directing the study; (d) the use of rigorous training, certification, and monitoring systems the aim of which is to achieve and maintain high quality data; (e) the use of significant incentives and family friendly assessment practices to minimize attrition; (f) the use of multiple types and sources of measures; (g) the adoption of an ecological/developmental framework to guide the study; (h) the formulation of hypotheses prior to study implementation; and (i) the participation of a large, diverse study sample.

That this approach to developmental follow-up research is not without disadvantages should be obvious. The study will be neither cheap nor quick; however, once the initial period of data collection and analysis is over, a rich lode of archival data (questionnaires, observations, videotapes) will be available to other scientists interested in developmental follow-up studies. We can anticipate that this broader usage of data from the project, merited at least in part by its scope and the care with which it is being conducted, will produce continuing scientific dividends and thereby reduce its apparent cost. Its design represents a marked improvement over previous studies dealing with the effects of alternate care. Thus the NICHD Study of Early Child Care should not only foster a new generation of studies on issues surrounding child care but also offer more definitive information to families and policy makers as the trends in child care and family life, so notable at the end of the twentieth century, continue to evolve into those of the twenty-first.

REFERENCES

Abbott-Shim, M. & Sibley, A. (1987). *Assessment profile for early childhood programs.* Available from: Quality Assist, Inc., 368 Moreland Avenue, N.E., Suite 210, Atlanta, GA 30307.

Abidin, R. R. (1983). *Parenting stress index manual.* Carlottesville, VA: Pediatric Psychology Press.

Ainsworth, M. D. S., Blehar, M., Waters, E., & Wall, S. (1978). *Patterns of attachment.* Hillsdale, NJ: Lawrence Erlbaum.

Ainsworth, M. D. S., & Wittig, D. (1969). Attachment and exploratory behavior of 1-year olds in a strange situation. In B. M. Foss (Ed.), *Determinants of infant behavior* (Vol. 4, pp. 113–136). London: Metheun.

Appelbaum, M. I., Burchinal, M. R., & Terry, R. A. (1989). Quantitative methods and the search for continuity. In M. H. Bornstein, & N. A. Krasnegor (Eds.), *Stability and continuity in mental development* (pp. 251–272). Hillsdale, NJ: Lawrence Erlbaum.

Bahg, C. (1990). Major systems theories throughout the world. *Behavioral Science, 35,* 79–107.

Baron, R., & Kenny, D. (1986). The moderator-mediator distinction in social psychological research: Conceptual, strategic, and statistical considerations. *Journal of Personality and Social Psychology, 51,* 1173–1182.

Bates, E., Beeghly, M., Bretherton, I., McNew, S., O'Connell, B., Reznick, J. S., Shore, S., Snyder, L., & Volterra, V. (1989). *The MacArthur Communicative Inventory: Infants.* Unpublished test available from: Dr. Larry Fenson, Developmental Psychology Laboratory, San Diego State University, San Diego, CA 92182.

Bayley, N. (1969). *Bayley Scales of Infant Development.* New York: Psychological Corporation.

Belle, D. (1982). *Lives in stress.* Beverly Hills, CA; Sage.

Belsky, J. (1988). The effects of day care reconsidered. *Early Childhood Research Quarterly, 3,* 235–272.

Belsky, J. (1990). Parental and nonparental child care and children's socioemotional development: A decade in review. *Journal of Marriage and the Family, 52,* 885–903.

Belsky, J., & Most, D. (1981). From exploration to play: A cross-sectional study of infant behavior. *Developmental Psychology, 17,* 630–639.

Booth, C. L., & Mitchell, S. K. (1988). Observational research methods. In N. Woods & M. Cantanzaro (Eds.), *Nursing research methods* (pp. 278–299). St. Louis, MO: Mosby.

Bowlby, J. (1969). *Attachment and loss: Vol. 1. Attachment.* New York: Basic Books.

Bradley, R. H. (1992). *Matters of scale, points of view, plotting the journey for children at risk: The cartographers art.* Presented at the 6th International Conference on Children at Risk. Sante Fe, NM, September.

Breznitz, Z., & Friedman, S. L. (1988). Toddlers' ability to concentrate: The influence of maternal depression. *Journal of Child Psychology and Psychiatry, 29,* 267–279.

Burchinal, M., & Appelbaum, M. I. (1991). Estimating individual developmental functions: Methods and their assumptions. *Child Development, 62,* 23–43.

Caldwell, B. M., & Richmond, J. B. (1968). The children's center—A micro-cosmic health, education, and welfare unit. In L. Dittman (Ed.), *Early child care: The new perspectives.* New York: Atherton Press.

Caldwell, B. M. (1986). Day care and early environmental adequacy. In W. Fowler (Ed.), *Early experience and the development of competence* (pp. 11–30). San Francisco: Jossey-Bass.

Caldwell, B. M., & Bradley, R. H. (1984). *Home Observation for Measurement of the Environment.* University of Arkansas at Little Rock, Little Rock, AR.

Campbell, S. B. (1990). *Behavior problems in preschool children.* New York: Guildford Press.

Chase-Lansdale, P. L., & Owen, M. T. (1987). Maternal employment in a family context: Effects of infant–mother and infant–father attachments. *Child Development, 58,* 1505–1512.

Clarke-Stewart, K. A. (1973). Interactions between mothers and their young children: Characteristics and consequences. *Monographs of the Society for Research in Child Development, 38* (6-7, Serial No. 153).

Clarke-Stewart, K. A. (1989). Day care: Maligned or malignant? *American Psychologist, 44,* 266–273.

Cox, M. J., Owen, M. T., Lewis, J. M., & Henderson, V. K. (1989). Marriage, adult adjustment, and early parenting. *Child Development, 60,* 1015–1024.

Ford, D. H., & Lerner, R. M. (1992). *Developmental systems theory.* Newbury Park, CA: Sage.

Fox, N., & Fein, G. G. (1990). *Infant day care: The current debate.* Norwood, NJ: Ablex.

Friedman, S., Brooks-Gunn, J., Vandell, D. L., & Weinraub, M. (In press). Effects of child care on psychological development: Issues and future directions for research. *Pediatrics.*

Gottlieb, G. (1991). The experiential canalization of behavioral development theory. *Developmental Psychology, 27,* 4–13.

Greenberger, E., & Goldberg, W. A. (1989). Work, parenting, and the socialization of children. *Developmental Psychology, 25,* 22–35.

Hayes, C. D., Palmer, J. L., & Zaslow, M. (1990). *Who cares for America's children. Child care policy for the 1990s.* Washington, DC: Academic Press.

Hock, E., Gnezda, M., & McBride, S. (1983). *The measurement of maternal separation anxiety.* Paper presented at the biennial meeting of the Society for Research in Child Development, Detroit, MI.

Hoffman, L. W. (1989). Effects of maternal employment in the two-parent family. *American Psychologist, 44,* 283–292.

Jaeger, E., & Weinraub, M. (1990). Early maternal care and infant attachment: In search of process. In K. McCartney (Ed.), *Child care and maternal employment: A social ecology approach* (pp. 71–90). San Francisco: Jossey-Bass.

Lamb, M. E., Sternberg, K. T., & Prodromidis, M. (1992). Nonmaternal care and the security of infant–mother attachment: A reanalysis of the data. *Infant Behavior and Development, 15,* 71–83.

McCartney, K. (1990). *Child care and maternal employment: A social ecology approach.* San Francisco: Jossey-Bass.

Marshall, N. L., & Barnett, R. C. (1993). Work–family strains and gains among two-earner couples. *Journal of Community Psychology, 21,* 64–78.

Marshall, N. L., & Barnett, R. C. (1993). Variations in job strain across health care and social service settings. *Journal of Community and Applied Social Psychology, 3,* 261–271.

McCartney, K., & Beuaregard, K. (1991). Child care separation/reunion scale. Durham, NH: University of New Hampshire. Unpublished measure.

Morisset, C. E. (1988). Mother–child language coding manual. University of Washington, Seattle, WA. Unpublished coding manual.

Phillips, D. A., McCartney, K., Scarr, S., & Howes, C. (1987). Selective review of infant day care research: A cause for concern. *Zero to Three, 7,* 18–21.

Radloff, L. (1977). The CES-D scale: A self-report depression scale for research in the general population. *Applied Psychological Measurement, 1,* 385–410.

Scarr, S., Phillips, D., & McCartney, K. (1990). Facts, fantasies and the future of child care in the United States. *Psychological Science, 1,* 26–35.

Schaefer, E., & Edgerton, M. (1985). Parental and child correlates of parental modernity. In I. E. Siegel (Ed.), *Parental belief systems: The psychological consequences for children* (pp. 287–318). Hillsdale, NJ: Lawrence Erlbaum.

Silverstein, L. B. (1991). Transforming the debate about child care and maternal employment. *American Psychologist, 46,* 1025–1032.

U.S. Department of Commerce, Bureau of the Census (1992). *How we're changing. Demographic state of the nation: 1992.* (Current Population Reports, Special Studies, Series P-23, No. 177). Washington, DC.

Vandell, D. L. (1979). The effects of playgroup experiences on mother–son and father–son interactions. *Developmental Psychology, 15,* 379–385.

Whitebrook, M., Howes, C., & Phillips, D. (1990). *The National Day Care Staffing Study: Who cares? Childcare teachers and the quality of care in America.* Available from: Child Care Employee Project. 6536 Telegraph Avenue, Oakland, CA 94609.

Willett, J. B., & Singer, J. D. (1991). How long did it take? Using survival analysis in educational and psychological research. In L. M. Collins & J. L. Horn (Eds.), *Best methods for the analysis of change: Recent advances, unanswered questions, future directions* (pp. 310–328). Washington, DC: American Psychological Association.

Index